Race, ethnicity and the media

Also in this series

Race as News, two general studies on attitude change by Otto Klineberg and Colette
Guillaumin, and a study of the British national press by Paul Hartmann, Charles
Husband and Jean Clark; Introduction by James D. Halloran

Ethnicity and the media

An analysis of media reporting
in the United Kingdom, Canada and Ireland

The designations employed and the presentation of the material in this publication
do not imply the expression of any opinion whatsoever on the part of the Unesco
Secretariat concerning the legal status of any country or territory, or of its authorities,
or concerning the delimitations of the frontiers of any country or territory.

Published in 1977 by the United Nations
Educational, Scientific and Cultural Organization
7 Place de Fontenoy, 75700 Paris
Printed by Imprimerie des Presses Universitaires de France, Vendôme

ISBN 92-3-101454-4 √

0108650

Preface

In December 1969, Unesco organized a Meeting of Experts on the Role of Mass Media in a Multi-racial Society. This meeting recommended that further research should be undertaken on the influence of the mass media on behavioural patterns and in changing attitudes, particularly in the areas of race and of ethnicity.

As a follow-up of this meeting Unesco published *Race as News* (1974). This book was divided into two sections. The first dealt with the state of research, the second was a case study of the British national press.

The present publication *Ethnicity and the Media* explores issues raised in *Race as News*—issues as to the relationship between the press and the society of which it is part.

The studies cover three different situations: race in the British provincial press, Punjabis in the Canadian press, and the conflict in Northern Ireland in the newspapers of Northern Ireland, Great Britain and the Republic of Ireland. All three studies, however, attempt to analyse the complex relationship between news, reporting, attitudes and society.

The book is introduced by James D. Halloran of the Centre for Mass Communication Research, University of Leicester.

Unesco hopes that the discussion started in *Race as News* and continued in *Ethnicity and the Media* will help in the reassessment of the use and functioning of the media in situations of conflict. However, the views expressed are those of the authors and not necessarily those of Unesco.

Contents

Introduction

James D. Halloran[1]

In this book we report and discuss the results of three studies. The first, 'Race in the Provincial Press', a case study of five newspapers in the West Midlands region of England, was conducted by staff from the Centre for Contemporary Cultural Studies at the University of Birmingham. The second, 'The Sikhs of Vancouver', a case study of the role of the media in ethnic relations, tackles the same general problems but in Western Canada, some 6,000 miles from the English Midlands. The Canadian work was carried out by Joseph Scanlon and his collaborators from Carleton University in Ottawa. The third research project reported in the book, the work of Philip Elliott from the Centre for Mass Communication Research at the University of Leicester, United Kingdom, has a somewhat different focus in that it is primarily concerned with reporting social conflict in Northern Ireland. Essentially it is a study of the news coverage of the Northern Ireland situation in Great Britain, Northern Ireland and the Republic of Ireland.

Although the focus of the Northern Ireland study is different in quite a number of aspects from the other two (we shall see that there are also considerable differences between the Canadian and Midlands studies), all three works do have something in common. This is largely because they were planned as a follow-up to, have been influenced by, or are related in some way or other to the work reported in the 1974 Unesco publication, *Race as News*.

The main research results reported in this earlier Unesco publication dealt with the manner in which the British national press handled the question of race in the period 1963–70. The research, mainly content analysis, was carried out by Paul Hartmann, Charles Husband and Jean Clark from the Leicester University Centre for Mass Communication Research. Not surprisingly the approach adopted by Philip Elliott, also from Leicester, in his analysis of the news coverage of Northern Ireland, is not entirely unrelated to the methods adopted by his colleagues in the race study. In some ways it may be seen as a development and extension

1. Centre for Mass Communication Research, University of Leicester.

of these methods. Moreover, in their Canadian work Joseph Scanlon and his helpers claim to have

followed the classification system prepared by researchers at Leicester—and attempted to identify all East Indian material in the two Vancouver daily newspapers according to these classifications.

The 'basic method' used in the West Midlands study was also inherited from the earlier Leicester project on race coverage in the national press. However, the Birmingham team had some reservations about what they refer to (mistakenly, I think, with regard to Hartmann's work, and particularly so with regard to that of Elliott) as 'straightforward content analysis'. As far as their own methods of analysis are concerned, they modify Hartmann's earlier approach and feel that in 'explicitly raising some broader theoretical questions' they have 'kept alive the essential problems of conceptualizing and analysing forms of ideological production in their structural and cultural environs'.

It is arguable that *Race as News* did just that, and Elliott's work, reported here, certainly does. However, this is not the place for a debate on conceptualization or methodology, particularly as the Birmingham team accept, in quoting from Hartmann's work, which in turn reflects the oft-stated Leicester approach to mass-communications research, that there is general agreement on the 'basic context'.

Elements of racial conflict in British society and the impingement of the mass media upon this process cannot be understood apart from the structure of the society as a whole and the major conflicts of interest that govern its course.

In this connection, with regard to the work reported in this book and to any recommendations for change that may stem from it, I can only repeat what I wrote in *Race as News* and have argued for many years, that is that it must be recognized that the media do not exist in isolation and must be studied in relation to other institutions within the wider social, economic and political settings. In brief, this means that we cannot adequately study the relationship between media and race, or media and conflict, as though they were entirely separate questions independent from other historical, sociological and economic questions. They are integral parts of a complex whole, and one of the major tasks of research is to challenge the oversimplified partial definitions and mythologies which exist in this area. One of the most important things that research can do for those working in the media is to make the implicit explicit and to make people aware of the nature and the implications of those basic assumptions which underlie their day-to-day activities. Such critical analysis is often the first step in producing constructive change.

There is no need to review or summarize the earlier work on the media and race in this introduction, but it is worth while first to draw attention to the continuity in the Unesco research programme and secondly to refer, albeit briefly, to those results and interpretations in *Race as News* which have some bearing on the research reported in these pages.

It was argued in *Race as News* that the structure of news reporting or 'news values' may mean that certain minority or non-élite groups within any given country may have to engage in 'negative' behaviour before they are noticed by the media, or before they are given the opportunity to put their point of view. Some groups are left out in the cold. Others, by hook or by crook, get invited inside—even though not everyone welcomes them on their arrival.

Referring to some other research by Elliott and one of his colleagues, Peter Golding, the point was made that news should not be seen as a more or less imperfect reflection of events in the world. Attention was also drawn to the regularities in the news process which lead to distortions and imperfections and to the characterizations of news coverage such as the sameness of presentation across the media, the lack of variety, the interpretations within set frameworks already established on other occasions, the heavy stress on events and on negative aspects, and the lack of background material and explanation.

It was also suggested that ethnocentrism, event orientation, human interest, story cycles and story perspectives were typical of British media treatment of foreign stories. Elliott and Golding have written that some of these perspectives may reflect direct interests, but others may be a consequence of the discontinuous flow of information, the need to simplify and the superficial fragmentation of reality which these entail. Furthermore, so it is held, all these perspectives have ideological consequences, in the same way as the other general regularities in news reporting mentioned earlier. For example, attention is concentrated on political leaders and political crises, limiting the range of explanations of social conflict and change which can be offered. In the same way, the range of possible means considered for resolving conflict in any society are limited. There is a tendency to define those outside established governments (even including illegal established governments such as that in Rhodesia) as deviant, ephemeral and inconsequential.

There is, then, a case for a thorough examination of the application and implications of 'news value' in the mass media. The 'taken-for-grantedness', the apparent inevitability, the legitimizations and justifications of the situations, and, at times, the making of virtue out of journalistic necessity should not be allowed to go unchallenged.

We might at least start thinking about new criteria, although it will be appreciated that the structures and values that we seek to change did not develop, nor are they at present maintained in a vacuum. They are an integral part of the prevailing system of mass media structure, organization, control and ownership. Awareness may be lacking, the process may not always be a conscious one, but the values are learned on the job.

It is important to remember that it is not just news and race in which we are interested, but the whole news process in our particular media system. The former issue, important though it is, can be adequately studied only within this wider framework.

Some other, more specific points made in the earlier work, and relevant to the studies reported here include the following: press coverage on the whole was such in quantity as to sustain public awareness of race as a major principle of classification; concerning overseas material, the emphasis was on conflict, oppression, injustice and violence; home news was more varied, but the main focus was on central political issues of the time such as the control of immigration and related legislation; intergroup hostility, discrimination and the activities of the politician Enoch Powell (the symbol of anti-immigrant feeling) figured prominently—in fact, once race had come to be seen as relating to Enoch Powell, his views tended to be brought into any discussion on the subject. In both cases, home and overseas, the general trends became more pronounced over time. Race-related material that could be handled within this framework was more likely to be covered than that which did not fit so neatly.

This pattern of results has been interpreted as indicating the existence of a structure of inferences about the significance of race in the United Kingdom that has led to a selective emphasis over the period. One effect of this emerging news framework has been that the perspective within which coloured people are presented as ordinary members of society has become increasingly overshadowed by a news perspective in which they are presented as a problem. The emerging framework is such that, as the number of coloured people and the social concern over race relations has increased, so attention has moved away from the relation of coloured people to the major social resources of housing, education and employment—which must be regarded as an important part of the underlying basis of interracial hostility in the country—towards the hostility itself and its manifestations, including the concern to keep coloured people out of the country and the concern to regulate hostility by the various laws and machinery set up to these ends. The press has reflected pressures that, on the one hand, have sought to exclude coloureds from British society, and, on the other, have aimed to reduce discrimination against them; but has not at the same time paid proportionate attention to those factors that must be regarded as part of the underlying cause of anti-immigrant feeling and discrimination. The British news media have clearly failed to deal adequately with the underlying basis of racial conflict and the 'conflict framework' they have used has facilitated the scapegoating of coloured immigrants.

But, most important, coloured people have not on the whole been portrayed as an integral part of British society. The United Kingdom is not recognized as a multi-racial society. Instead, the press has continued to project an image of the United Kingdom as a white society in which the coloured population is seen as some kind of aberration, a problem, or just an oddity, rather than as 'belonging' to the society. This is given more force, because there is such a remarkable similarity in news coverage right across the whole range of national papers, irrespective of their editorial position.

Other points that were made in *Race as News*, and worth repeating here because of their relevance to the studies covered in this book, include the reminder that the major news media are staffed by white personnel and serve a mainly white audience, and consequently the 'public' which dictates newsworthy events will be a white public. The day-to-day tensions and problems which are the crucial concerns of the coloured population are not primary concerns of the white public. Only the symptoms of these conditions, such as social disturbances, impinge upon whites and hence it is only such 'events' which become newsworthy. The condition of the coloured immigrant is not in itself a matter of high interest to the white majority. Their interest is focused on the situations which are perceived as threats or as problems.

From this, and from earlier comments, it will be seen that it is not necessary to invoke individual bias to explain the media handling of race-related issues. Although prejudiced journalists obviously work in our media institutions, they are not central to the main problem as we see and define it. The main problem has to do with the news selection and production processes as they currently operate in media institutions in our society. An important thing to recognize in this connection is that individual good intentions and positive attitudes, although clearly welcomed, may count for little with regard to fundamental changes in media coverage, granted the existing system.

Before introducing the three studies, one further point may be made. It has just been suggested that one of the main problems was that the media tended to operate from what was essentially a white standpoint. 'There is too much of white talking to white about black.' 'Black news is reported from a white man's point of view and the real story is missed.' At one level there have been some attempts to deal with this problem. Minority groups have been given access to the media and it is thought by some that the development of community radio and television could lead to fundamental changes in this connection. However, we need to be very cautious here and on the look-out for the spurious. It is possible that the new developments may serve the needs of the minority no better than the old system or the general media outlets.

Most of the research results and the interpretations of them mentioned in this introductory chapter come from studies of the national press and national broadcasting systems. Clearly the same questions that were asked nationally ought to be asked of local, regional or provincial media. Comparisons could then be made with the national media and similarities and differences identified and examined. This was one of the main aims of the Birmingham study.

In 'Race in the Provincial Press', five newspapers in the West Midlands region of England were analysed. Three of the papers were daily evening papers, and two were weeklies. As might be expected, since the work was initially conceived as a follow-up study to *Race as News*, the media coverage of race by the selected provincial papers is not presented in a vacuum. The authors, in introducing us to the background of race in the West Midlands, rightly argue that any background to a presentation of race in the region must take into account the arrival, distribution and settlement of the immigrant population and the particular local, economic and cultural factors which shaped the response of the indigenous population—and this they do. The press is regarded as having played a crucial role in establishing an arena for negotiation between the host and immigrant populations, and the way in which this role was interpreted is the main focus of the study.

The report also provides more essential introductory or background material in its account (mainly derived from Ian Jackson's *The Provincial Press and the Community*) of the structure of the provincial press in the United Kingdom. History, development, circulation, readership, ownership, advertising and finance are all covered both generally and more specifically for the five papers selected for the study.

The characteristics which differentiate the provincial from the national press are identified and these include: (a) a longer and more complex history of the local press in which the kind of audience addressed depends on social as well as geographical considerations; (b) a conservatism about content and a self-consciousness about responsibility to the community which militate against the adoption of more extreme forms of 'popular' news presentation; and (c) a hypersensitivity to some kinds of news which may affect local interests. Attention is also drawn to the emphasis in the provincial press on the 'reassurance function' and the support and reinforcement of actively held institutional values, the muted presentation of local conflict, the tendency to confirm social harmony in the community and the 'capacity to represent the average, the normal, the status quo as the humane, the good and the unchallengeably right'.

However, in their interesting comments on the provincial press as a cultural institution, clarifying their approach to the research, the authors of the Birmingham report warn us that despite the important differences between national and provincial press, and between different types of the provincial press (evenings and weeklies), these differences may not be as important as the common ground which the provincials share with the nationals.

It is argued that the provincial press is clearly involved in managing a view of the social world, that it is essentially a conservative medium, that it is an ideology with 'its beliefs and principles, a programme for society, an ideal of human relationships—but is all the more powerful for appearing as common-sense'.

We are warned that the recognition of the several differences, which undoubtedly do exist, should not lead us to deduce that, consequently, local newspapers are significantly different in their cultural role from other media. Provincial media are part of a complex media system geared, so it is argued, to producing consensus. Differences may only be in the kind and form of consensus produced. Fundamentally, the local or provincial tends to complement rather than counter the national. If this is true, the provincial press thus does not offer an alternative, but functions as a back-up and confirmation of established ways of life through its interpretation of the local scene.

In examining the results of the Birmingham study let us remember the points made earlier from the work on the coverage of race by the national media; where possible make the appropriate comparisons; and see in what ways and to what degree the provincials 'bring the message home' and confirm the accepted ways of doing things.

In the brief comments on the results, which follow in this introduction, many of the differences between the different types of media are ignored. Other interesting points are also omitted, but all of these can be read in the full report. The main purpose of this introduction is to draw attention to some of the findings from this research which relate in some way or other to the earlier work reported in *Race as News*.

Overseas news can be race-related in several ways but most of the race-related coverage by the provincials had to do with countries like Rhodesia where a majority-minority situation existed. Generally, there was a strong element of support for white minorities, particularly in Rhodesia. On the whole, overseas news was presented in a manner which was self-contained, superficial and devoid of historical perspective.

Race was often presented through routinized stories. In the evening papers over one-third of all race coverage took the form of crime, usually violent and serious, or human-interest stories—these latter sometimes involving negative stereotyping. Immigration was an important topic and was defined mainly as an issue of control and political significance. Cultural differences were presented in mainly negative terms, and black immigrants were also linked with such social problems as overcrowding in housing and schools. The problems and contribution of black people in the sphere of employment received little attention, and the relationship between black people and the police was presented as unproblematic and of no special significance.

The main reference themes used in the press (cultural differences, housing and education) were not the same as the topics (crime, immigration, white hostility). They tended to offer a negative and locally rooted set of inferences which operated as evidence for a debate about race conducted in terms of race relations, immigration and white hostility.

The overall picture as far as the weeklies are concerned is substantially the same as for the evenings, although the weeklies do give more attention to health issues, emphasizing the immigrant population as carrying infectious diseases and overstraining hospital services. Incidentally, it is mentioned early on in the Birmingham report that racialism has little to do with facts about the immigrant population. For example, many of Powell's statements are not facts but scenarios. According to the Birmingham report, they stand 'not as facts but as images'. The research also shows that the tendency apparent in the pattern of reference themes in the evening papers towards a greater concentration on negative images was also present in the weeklies. There was a strong association between cultural differences and crime, and there was also a heavy emphasis on language culture and West Indian parties.

The authors of this work conclude that although the particular forms of race presentation in the provincial press are in many ways different from those of the national press, the overall effect is very similar. Referring to Hartmann's earlier work, they repeat that 'the way race-related material is handled by the mass media serves both to perpetuate negative perceptions of blacks and to define the situation as one of inter-group conflict'.

In examining the news values which determine how race comes to be presented in this way, the distinctive local practices (the parochial reference points, a stress on harmony and order, a conception of conflict as invariably soluble, a confirmation of respectability and the institutional status quo) are identified and their relationship to general news values indicated and discussed. From this, it is clear—and this is one of the main conclusions—that race as news cannot be fully understood in the absence of an appreciation of the processes and operations of routine news independent of race.

With the provincial press, news values ('those opaque structures of meaning in modern society' which govern operational practices and are held to be possessed by all journalists despite their apparent unawareness of how they are influenced by them) are obviously of crucial importance. However, we are warned of the dangers of overgeneralizing about news values because of 'the particular inflections in the provincial press'. For example, the press treatment of black people in housing and education is derived in part from non-racial discussions of these topics. With these, as with other topics, the framework within which they are treated is not so much irrelevant as inadequate. The main causes of the problem are left unanalysed.

The Birmingham report, in discussing the political problems of race relations, immigration and white hostility, illustrates the domination of race news by political definition. We are reminded of the role of Enoch Powell as described in *Race as News* when we read in the report on race coverage in the West Midlands of 'the apparently automatic news-worthiness of statements on race by the already politically powerful'.

Although there may be some differences when compared with the national press, the discussion in the provincials as in the nationals is essentially in white terms. 'The "structure of access" (whose activities and opinions become defined as newsworthy) operates against black experience.' The press have nothing to say on what it is like to be black in the United Kingdom, for the principal issues are defined by white authority and the problem of being black is not one of them. 'Small wonder that black groups are largely suspicious of the local press.'

In the concluding passages in *Race as News*, it is argued that further research is required into the whole matter of news frameworks. Attention is drawn to the fact that some kinds of material—crime news about coloured people, for example—are not typically dealt with by the national press within the race framework, but would appear to be treated within the frame of reference employed for other crimes. The final paragraphs in the Birmingham report refer to the same problem:

Some [news values] appear to operate in all kinds of news and merely treat race as any other topic (violence, confrontation with the police). Others appear peculiar to race—the exploitation of cultural differences. . . . We have then two sets of news values often intertwined but conceptually distinct: those of the provincial press defining news in general, and those of the white media defining the race issue.

This conclusion forces the Birmingham team to ask if special news treatment is required for race issues and—not surprisingly from their conclusions—they answer both yes and no. The 'no' refers to those news values which apply to all news, and the 'yes' 'to those news values which appear particular to race and require a special effort of comprehension and remedial action'.

In the report on the Canadian study, 'The Sikhs of Vancouver', Joseph Scanlon concludes with a call for remedial action to change a situation in which 'the press has not done the sort of digging, interpretation and backgrounding that, in my opinion, was so obviously needed'. As a professor of journalism he sees the solution in 'increasing professional standards in journalism through professional education'. Earlier in his report, Scanlon had argued for improved media performance through specialized reporting, attempts to get the story behind the story, more interpretative and background work, and through the building up of an aware, sympathetic coterie of journalists.

I doubt, however, if this approach would be shared or at least given the same priority by his fellow authors in this book, or by Hartmann and Husband in *Race as News*. It is not that these writers would not welcome an increase in journalistic standards (however these may be defined) and the other proposals, but that they would probably argue that this was an inadequate approach, or that such an approach would depend on other changes coming first. In *Race as News* there are references to the 'cosmetic remedies' of good intentions, special efforts, social reform and so on. Again these are welcomed, not despised, but it is argued there—and the evidence supports this—that more fundamental changes will be necessary in organization, structure and the whole media system before we have the changes in professional values and practices and in the treatment of race-related material that we all desire.

In reporting his research, Scanlon recognizes the limitations of content analysis (whatever the variety) and, like the other writers, attempts to set the media treatment of race-related material within the appropriate historical and social contexts.

Only with such a detailed history—a history not available elsewhere—can a proper evaluation of media performance be made. Only in the light of such material is it clear whether the media have, in fact, reported an accurate and total picture of reality.

Whether the media can ever provide 'an accurate and total picture of reality' is a debatable question that takes us beyond the terms of reference of this work. However, in a sense it is the type of thinking illustrated by this phrase, probably more characteristic of schools of journalism than research centres with a sociological or cultural bias, that at least in one way differentiates the Canadian work from the other two studies. The difference in approach is also illustrated in the following passage:

It is hard for a professional journalist to avoid the conclusion that the East Indians in Vancouver have been newsmakers during the past year. There is clear evidence of racial clashes. There is clear evidence of family feuds or vendettas. There is clear evidence of violent conflict within the community. Such stories, by any professional judgment, are newsworthy stories: it is not surprising they have got considerable play.

This may be true, but I doubt if it is the sort of approach or emphasis that one would expect to come from Birmingham or Leicester. Perhaps it should be mentioned here that these are not intended as critical comments of the good/bad, right/wrong variety. The intention is to illustrate the differences in approach.

These differences do not mean, of course, that all three studies do not share common ground—at least at certain levels of analysis. The reasons for this, associated with a common starting point, have already been given.

In his historical treatment of the East India and Sikh question, Professor Scanlon identifies five dominant themes, but he finds that only two of these have been adequately dealt with by the media. He states that the real problem is that, in general, the media have concentrated 'not surprisingly' on newsworthy stories (feuds, vendettas, clashes, community conflict, etc.), but that they have not included the explanatory material that might have made these problems understandable.

For example, with regard to one of the aforementioned themes, crime, 'the clashes were reported—often in headline form—the underlying problems have not been'. Moreover with regard to the other themes he concludes that coverage

rarely takes the form of an insight into cultural differences—the story of the changing nature of the community has not been well told if told at all—there is virtually no attempt to describe either the many pressures that exist when Sikhs adjust to Canadian society or the fact that many of them have made a successful adjustment.

Discussing his findings, Scanlon feels that they provide very strong support for the ideas advanced by Paul Hartmann and Charles Husband in their article, 'The Mass Media and Racial Conflict', for they conclude media coverage of racial relations takes place 'in a way that causes people to see the situation primarily as one of actual or potential conflict'. Furthermore, they argue that the media do not provide the background necessary for understanding that conflict:

While the media seem to play a major role in establishing in people's minds the association of color with conflict, their role of providing any kind of background information that would help make the race relations situation, including its conflict elements, more understandable, is relatively small.

The lack of background, explanatory, interpretative material receives particular emphasis from Scanlon. His discussion on the media emphasis on conflict without any explanation of underlying causes, leads him to support the argument developed in *Race as News*, namely, that news reporting is person-centred and that negative events are preferred to positive events:

The sameness of presentation across the media, the lack of variety, the interpretation within set frameworks . . . the heavy stress on events and on nevative aspects, and the lack of background material, emerge as the main findings. . . . The media makes us see all members of the labelled group as more alike than they really are.

The above quotation is taken from *Race as News* and is used by Scanlon in his concluding remarks, when he states that they also aptly describe the Vancouver situation. 'What is happening in Vancouver is largely what is happening in the United Kingdom.'

The main theme of the studies which have been mentioned so far in this introduction is the media in a multi-ethnic society. It is arguable, however, that Philip Elliott's work, 'Reporting Northern Ireland: A Study of News in Great Britain, Northern Ireland and the Republic of Ireland' does not easily fall under this heading, for essentially it addresses itself to the question of reporting social conflict. This is true, and we need not spend time here spelling out the differences between the situation covered in Northern Ireland and those covered in Vancouver and the West Midlands. As we shall see, the link between the three studies mainly centres on news values. We might also remind ourselves of a finding common to all the studies discussed so far, namely, that the media perpetuate negative perception and tend to define situations in terms of intergroup conflict. Perhaps a more appropriate title for all the works would be 'Reporting Social or Intergroup Conflict'.

In making a few brief introductory comments on Elliott's comprehensive and detailed study, I shall concentrate on some but by no means all those of his findings and interpretations which I feel may be related to what has already been discussed. This means that much research material of great interest will receive no attention. This should not be seen as any indication of its importance, but only as an indication of its perceived relevance to what has gone before.

The comprehensive and detailed nature of the study has already been mentioned. It should also be noted that the work is further characterized by a developed sociological approach to the study of the media, and to the study of news in particular. In discussing his research, Elliott reminds us that the two periods covered in his study of Northern Ireland 'were two moments in a continuing historical process' and, needless to say, he sets his work in the appropriate historical and sociological contexts. Elliott's work might also be seen, although perhaps on a different time scale, as a stage in a continuing process. This process has to do with the consistent application of a developing, particular sociological perspective to the study of the media and news. The advantages that stem from this and from continuity in research generally will, I think, be obvious to the reader.

In his analysis of what he calls 'violence and law enforcement news', Elliott concludes that in so far as a general image[1] of the conflict emerges in the British media, three factors would seem to be mainly responsible for it. Two of these are features of the way news is presented in the British media in such a way as to be both simple and of immediate human interest. Both these features are most characteristic of the popular press, but they extend into the quality press and the broadcast media. Simplicity involves both a lack of explanation and a lack of historical

1. Several examples are given which are not entirely consistent with the general case presented.

perspective; human interest, a concentration on the particular detail of incidents and the personal characteristics of those involved. The result is a continual procession of unique, inexplicable events.

According to Elliott, the third factor behind the production of a common image is the reliance on official sources to provide accounts of incidents, to identify victims and attribute violence. These sources and the way they are used by the media seem to be ambivalent as to whether the conflict in the north should be laid at the door of the Irish Republican Army (IRA), so as to emphasize its similarities with a conventional way, or whether it should be left as a meaningless series of incidents in which people are killed and injured, homes and businesses destroyed almost at random. Official sources also made the most of opportunities to show the violence as indiscriminate by emphasizing the innocence of the victims or the lucky escapes of bystanders, particularly children. Politicians condemning particular outrages were inclined to take the line that violence was meaningless and senseless.

It is important to note that the research shows that these factors were all less important in the Irish media. RTE apparently exercised considerable caution in making any explicit links between the IRA and violence. But generally the Irish papers were much more open about the information available to them, the relative value they put on it and so the account of events which seemed to them most plausible. In Great Britain scepticism of the official account was rarely shown. The reader was left to take it or leave it. The Irish papers, however, accepted the responsibility of pointing the reader in the right direction. Moreover the Irish media were less inclined to concentrate on simplicity and human interest in their presentation of the news. Partly this was because they were less preoccupied with the single story of violence in the north and more concerned about political developments and the political future of the province.

The research also established that in Belfast itself the non-sectional media were broadly comparable to the British media, in the sense that they tended to select events according to similar criteria and present them in a similar way. There was a sharp difference, however, between the apparent social function performed by the British media when faced with a case of terrorism on the British mainland. Following the Guildford bombs, the British media orchestrated a process of social cauterization for which there was no parallel in Ulster. There, the staccato repetition of particular incidents continued. Elliott argues that while in Great Britain the process of translating conflict into political, parliamentary debate is one of conflict resolution, in Northern Ireland political comment on violence tends to become a source of tension in itself, with arguments developing over who was prepared to condemn what sort of violence.

The chapter on violence and law enforcement is followed by one on political news about Northern Ireland, and again we have some interesting parallels with the other work. From the research it would appear that the coverage of political news in the British media reflected the same journalistic style of simplification and human interest as was apparent in the reporting of violence. In the two periods studied this took the form of an obsessive concentration on Enoch Powell in the first and the routine reporting of the formal details of the Convention in the second. The British media, in contrast to the Irish, were little interested in the immediate political issues raised by the Convention election except in so far as the Conservatives showed signs of breaking away from the bipartisan policy. The Irish on the other hand were concerned about the future role of the SDLP in the north.

Elliott found that the Irish media, particularly the *Irish Times,* were also interested in any sign of political activity on the question of Northern Ireland on the British mainland. This extended beyond the activities of politicians of the main political parties to include various fringe groups and activities which in Great Britain went largely unnoticed except in the pages of the *Morning Star.* He argues that the difference between the media coverage in the two countries reflects a difference in the way the story of Northern Ireland was defined, which in turn was dependent on the way the problem was regarded in the political culture of the two societies. In Great Britain, in spite of the fact that the Convention was the latest government initiative, the presence of British troops in the province, the low profile adopted by leading politicians and the placing of the conflict outside the arena of party politics, conspired to make both the problem and the news story appear to be mainly one of violence. In Ireland, however, there was much more concern about the political and constitutional future of the province and the relationship between the majority and minority there. In Northern Ireland itself there was the additional local issue of reacquiring some measure of regional political autonomy.

Additionally, in its treatment of 'other news' (not political, violence or law enforcement) the British media again concentrated on aspects of general human interest and treated all stories from the north as variations on the single story—'the troubles'. This was not the case, at least not to the same degree, for the Irish media.

Elliott, emphasizing the unusual aspects of the Northern Ireland situation, spells out in some detail, as the other writers have done in different circumstances, the dangers of over-generalizing about news values in different national contexts. He draws attention to similarities and differences.

The notion of importance in news values is one key to the way in which the news media in different countries come to reflect the ideology of their particular nation. There were particular differences of journalistic style between the Irish and British media, as there were also between the various press and broadcasting outlets in each country, but the main difference between them was one of national ideology, based on the different involvement of the two nation States in the Northern Ireland conflict. There was also a fundamental similarity between them. Both sets of media operate within similar liberal western democracies. They share similar assumptions about the sanctity of human life and the nature and scope of legitimate political activity.

The Northern Ireland work also provides other information which is relevant to the general theme of this book, much of it confirming or reinforcing the results of the other research reported earlier in this chapter.

Baldly stated—there is no space for elaboration—these include the observation that competition amongst the media tends to produce similarities rather than differences and that 'in the immediate situation the journalist is likely simply to follow working practices as the quickest route to a publishable story'. In particular, the research suggests that the reporter from a popular paper ('the sub-editor's paper') has little incentive to provide anything but routine coverage, and in Northern Ireland he usually has to do this without any credible alternative to set against the official sources.

Commenting on this situation, Elliott accepts that ultimately the question of who to believe must be a matter of judgement, but he detects a tendency in contemporary journalism, particularly marked in news broadcasting, to abdicate the responsibility for making such judgements. 'The source of an item or an interpretation may become a more important criterion than its truth or falsity.' Drawing attention to the possible consequences of this abdication of judgement, Elliott goes on to say:

Faced with a bald account of the facts, or rival versions of the facts laid side by side, with no elaboration of the meaning and significance of the incident, how else can the viewing public be expected to judge than by its preconceptions?

The research shows that there are many cases where the meaning and significance of incidents were not elaborated even in the most elementary ways. 'For most of the media, reporting Northern Ireland was mainly a process of recording the violence, building on this basic minimum of who, what, where.' However, as Elliott points out, this allegedly value-free reporting, with its simplicity and concentration on the facts, nevertheless contains a fundamental categorization of the troubles in Northern Ireland. It ensures that the conflict is seen in a particular light, and makes violence less rather than more explicable. This, argues Elliott, is more important than deliberate bias or distortion.

It taps a core value in Western liberal democracies, the sanctity of human life; a value which in itself is thoroughly laudable but which when incorporated into a dominant national ideology expressed implicitly and explicitly in news reporting is not without political consequences. The most important of these is to set those who resort to violence outside society.

This is a characteristic way

of isolating the present phenomenon from the past and exposing it to obloquy—to be found in the reporting of other types of deviance and other deviant groups. It is also a common feature of war reporting that the other side comes to be portrayed as sub-human barbarians simply because they are the 'other side'.

Elliott also makes the interesting point that:

Audience interest always ensures that death or injury to a national of the State is given more prominence than equivalent or greater sufferings endured by foreigners. It is common in war to find racial overtones in the conflict. Little value is placed on the lives of those on the 'other side', including civilians and non-combatants.

Northern Ireland may not be a war situation, race relations may not represent a conflict situation, but it is worth noting with Elliott 'that comparable processes are involved in reporting conflict situations with comparable consequences for the version of events carried in news output'.

There is much more in this interesting research that deserves comment, but space will not permit further treatment. Perhaps much of it was summarized by Elliott when he wrote:

Ostensibly the codes and practices of journalism are geared towards the specific ends of those organizations. In practice they also incorporate the goals and values of the state in which they operate. This is not done under its direction but in pursuit of the subordinate goals of the news organizations themselves, to collect and disseminate 'news' and to attract an audience for it. The same goals underpin such standard journalistic practices as paying attention to descriptive accuracy and looking for the human interest in any story. The consequence is the same. The values implicit in these styles of journalism ensure that the reports support the national ideology.

It was mentioned earlier that in several areas the research turned up data which did not appear to fit the general case being argued. That there are differences, both between media and journalist, is clear; what is more these differences cannot easily be dismissed—they are often of considerable importance. However, as Elliott reminds us,

there is little scope in modern news organizations for personal bias—to manifest itself in news coverage—to a large extent commercial considerations have ironed out partisan bias among the national news organizations.

He goes on to argue that ideally the free press is characterized by the fact that over time it should be possible for it to work out the 'internal inconsistencies that develop in the ideology it produces and the gaps which appear between the ideological account and the reality it is reporting'.

The problem is how to work this out. Those of us who have studied the media, and who have worked with journalists for many years, know how difficult it is going to be to get the news media in general, and individual journalists (no matter how well-disposed they are to research and inquiries) to recognize the true nature of the problem. They will not readily accept that there are such profound inconsistencies and discrepancies between their accounts and reality, be it in Northern Ireland, the West Midlands or Vancouver. They do not think that way, and as part of their professionalization they have developed formidable defences against the approaches of those who do.

We have seen that Scanlon wants professional education and higher standards but this, although obviously desirable on some grounds, may beg the main question. Professional education may produce more hardened professionals. Elliott calls not so much for increased competence in skills and crafts, but for 'a reflective, critical analysis of routine practices and their consequences through time'. Fine; but we are still left with the problem of how to produce this increased awareness. Let us hope that the research reported in this book is a step in the right direction. Unfortunately, journalistic reactions to earlier similar work do little to encourage our confidence.

Part I

Race in the provincial press

A case study of five West Midlands newspapers

Chas. Critcher
Margaret Parker
Ranjit Sondhi

Centre for Contemporary Cultural Studies,
University of Birmingham

This report was prepared over eighteen months from March 1974 to November 1975. Conducted for the most part in provincial libraries, it has nevertheless been influenced by ongoing work at the Centre for Contemporary Cultural Studies, many of whose members have helped in ways they only half know. Stuart Hall provided the necessary encouragement and constructive criticism.

Part of our concern has been to analyse the kinds of linguistic terms which West Midlands newspapers have applied to race. Such is the power of the dominant terminology that we have had to struggle to rid ourselves of its influence, but have not always succeeded. Thus the word 'coloured' appears in our coding categories though we subsequently decided to abandon it in favour of 'black'. This term has been criticized on the grounds that it is itself a distinction on the basis of race and reproduces the classifications of racism, as well as obscuring the importance of racial groups outside the black-white dichotomy, such as Cypriots and Chinese. In the absence of any alternative, however, we have used the word 'black' instead of 'coloured' if only because the image of 'blackness' is a central component of black people's attempts to reassert their history, culture and political formations. We have also tried to maintain a distinction between 'racism' as a theory or assumption of inherent white superiority and 'racialism' as descriptive of discriminatory behaviour and attitudes. Again, we may have lapsed occasionally.

Chapter 1

Race in the West Midlands: statistical background

The nature of the evidence

With the death of Empire, and the growth of an international movement of labour, concern over black-white relations has accordingly shifted from remote ex-colonial territories to the emergence of black minorities on the very doorstep of the mother country. Steady immigration throughout the last decade from the new Commonwealth has established that, by and large, black people have come to the United Kingdom to stay. And because they have come primarily to work, it is in the 'labour-hungry', industrialized heart of England—the seven large conurbations—that the conflict between host and immigrant communities is located and where race relations has been raised as dominant social, cultural and political issues in local affairs. Excluding the London area, the West Midlands has the largest immigrant population of any of the conurbations. It must be emphasized here that the area under discussion is only a part—if numerically the larger part—of the West Midlands.

It is arguable whether numbers are of the essence. Undeniably, gross statistics for large areas become meaningless in the local context. But at the very least, a statistical analysis can help to define the extent, if not the nature, of the race 'problem' even at a regional level. For the purpose of our study, we have relied heavily on census data. Produced dicennially, the census provides perhaps the most reliable and exhaustive information about general aspects of British society. The consistency in its structure, and the definitions it applies, permit comparisons among regions and over time. It can yield, for very small areas, data that are unobtainable elsewhere. Besides, the 1961 Census, the 1966 Sample Census, and the 1971 Census of Great Britain neatly span the period of our study, and this convenience offsets the sometimes dilatory nature of some of the data on Commonwealth immigrants with which we had to contend.

We begin by expressing general reservations about the reliability of census information. Quite apart from providing statistics about the black population only indirectly, the census itself has its own characteristic defects that lower accuracy. A serious error is that of under-enumeration

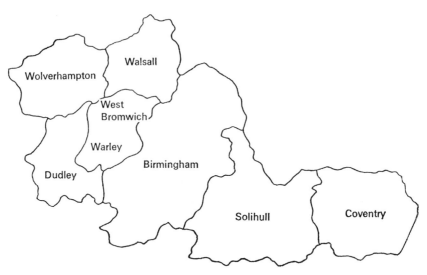

Fig. 1. West Midlands County Boroughs, 1974.

of the major black immigrant groups. Even though censuses have become progressively more accurate over the decade, it has been estimated that in 1971, for instance, the under-enumeration of the Pakistani-born population was nearly 29 per cent. Such errors would distort other statistics relating to housing conditions and socio-economic status, etc. Another consideration in the 1966 Sample Census is the random error inherent in any sampling process. Furthermore, a census based on the sampling frame of the one previous to it is likely to incorporate its drawbacks and inaccuracies. Finally, errors arising from incomplete coverage, inaccurate response and faulty processing can never be eliminated, only minimized. A consideration of all these errors, together with their possible cumulative effect, and the inevitable but undetectable real variations, would render us liable to gross misrepresentation if we proceed without caution in the interpretation of any census-based data on immigration, particularly at a subconurbational level.

Next, we define black people specifically to mean all those ethnically, and therefore culturally, and sometimes economically and politically, associated with four main regions of the new Commonwealth, i.e. Africa, the Caribbean, India and Pakistan/Bangladesh. Since these four groups form an overwhelming majority of the total black population of this country, we have excluded, though not on a point of principle, people from Sri Lanka, Hong Kong, Singapore, Malaya and other countries in Asia and Oceania. It is of especial significance to include wherever possible, the East African component (Kenyans, Ugandans and Tanzanians) with the Central and West African figures (Ghanaians, Nigerians, Gambians, Zambians, etc.) particularly since the former's proportion rose rapidly following the Asian exodus from East Africa during the late 1960s. For our purpose, therefore, ethnicity has taken precedence over birthplace.

Our definition, however, creates problems of precise enumeration of the black population of the United Kingdom and its regions. Census questions about birthplace and nationality are not designed to elicit information on race and colour. Even the introduction of a question on the birthplace of the respondent's parents in the 1971 Census has been criticized as causing future inconsistencies and becoming an unacceptable form of data substitution. We, therefore, have to rely on outside references to sharpen the accuracy of census data and to construct a more relevant picture of race in the West Midlands.

Our procedure is as follows: (a) we extract the black component of immigration to the conurbation from the old and new Commonwealth figures; (b) make deductions for 'white Asians' (a number of Indian- and Pakistani-born people of English descent—relics of the colonial past); and (c) make allowances for the children of black immigrants born in this country and therefore regarded as English for purposes of census enumeration, i.e. the 'black British'. More detailed studies might require further minor adjustments for whites recorded as Rhodesian or Asians regarded as African, but for our purpose, these details do not significantly affect the number or the characteristics of the black population at a local level. The extent to which corrections are necessary for white Asians and black British is gauged from the following.[1] Change in ratio of white Asians to black immigrants from 1961 to 1971 (West Midlands conurbation)—1 : 12 (1961); 1 : 30 (1971).

The economic activity, social class, housing and occupational patterns of the white Asian group resemble closely, and not unexpectedly, those of the host community in general. Their inclusion into immigrant statistics would create an erroneous impression of their position in social and economic terms. But we note that, since 1961, the relative proportions of white Asians have shrunk considerably, and in any case, do not significantly affect the numbers or characteristics of immigrants throughout the decade. (See also Table 1.)

We do not have information available about the distribution at regional and conurbation level for children born in this country to new Commonwealth immigrants. However, we feel it necessary to draw attention to the high proportion in the Midlands. For example, we note from some indicators of social deprivation reproduced in Holmans' *Socially Deprived Families in Britain*, that in 1966 the Soho ward had 20.7 per cent of its total population under 14 years of age, while the total population itself had 21.3 per cent born in the new Commonwealth. By 1971, even the national statistics showed an overrepresentation of black children under 5 years of age.

The proportion of the black population, born in the United Kingdom, has naturally risen as new children have been born into immigrant families. The almost total legislative restriction of immigration except for wives and dependants has further emphasized the statistical importance

---

1. G. B. G. Lomas, *Preliminary Report, Census 1971, The Coloured Population of Great Britain*, The Runnymede Trust; E. J. B. Rose *et al.*, *Colour and Citizenship, A Report on British Race Relations*.

of young 'black British' as a part of the non-white population. This has put a new complexion on race relations in the United Kingdom, as this group clearly has a claim to equal citizenship by right of birthplace. There does not seem, however, to have been much recognition of this change. The host society presistently fails to regard the black presence as part of itself. Even statisticians and social scientists have been guilty of treating the black British as an alien group by classifying them as 'second-generation immigrants'.

TABLE 1. Estimates of the British-born
black population—United Kingdom

Year	Black born abroad	Black born in United Kingdom	Percentage born in United Kingdom
1961	293,000	61,000	20
1966	710,900	213,300	23
1971	830,200	554,400	40

Source: Lomas, op. cit.; Rose et al., op. cit.; P. N. Jones, The Segregation of Immigrant Communities in the City of Birmingham, University of Hull, 1961.

However, as mentioned earlier, census figures do not of themselves yield accurate data about children of immigrants. Only in the 1971 Census was the question of birthplace of the respondents parents initially asked. The 1961 and 1966 figures for the black British are crude assumptions derived largely from outside information. Because of this uncertainty, this group has been left out of the statistics quoted in the following sections, with the knowledge that the table produced earlier may be used to provide only the roughest estimates for the number of black British in the West Midlands wherever necessary. We therefore refer throughout not to the black population of this country but only to those born overseas. Corrections for white Asians are included only where explicitly stated.

Numbers

Outside the London area, the West Midlands region has been the most important area of immigrant settlement: by 1971, 3 per cent (148,000 persons) of the total population in the area were recorded as being born in one of the four main regions of black immigration, representing 58 per cent of the total immigrant population from the old and new Commonwealth to the West Midlands. Numerically, therefore, the blacks have been the dominant immigrant group. West Midlands towns have never held the same metropolitan appeal as London has generated for black students, lawyers and doctors, so that black immigration here has been fairly recent, mainly in the 1960s, and largely of working-class origin. The conurbation, while supporting 15 per cent of the total British-born conurbational population of the United Kingdom, itself accounts for 20 per cent of the urban immigrant population (see Table 2).

TABLE 2. Black population as a percentage of populations
for the United Kingdom—all six conurbations
and West Midlands conurbation

Population	1961	1966	1971
Percentage black in United Kingdom	0.5	1.6	2.1
Percentage black in six conurbations	1.3	2.3	3.3
Percentage black in West Midlands conurbation	1.8	3.7	4.8

Source: Rose *et al.*, op. cit.; Lomas, op. cit.; 1966 Sample Census, 'Commonwealth Immigrant Tables', HMSO.

This shows the relatively high concentration of black immigrants in the West Midlands conurbation. In fact, one-sixth of all Caribbean immigrants to the United Kingdom have come to the conurbation and one-quarter of those from India and Pakistan.

Table 3 gives the ethnic distribution over the decade, showing how numbers of all groups have increased over time, but with relatively small changes in the proportion of immigrants to the West Midlands from the four areas.

TABLE 3. Ethnic distribution
of major black groups—West Midlands conurbation

Group	1961	1966	1971
African	n.a.	1,670	6,810
Caribbean	24,800	35,940	38,725
Indian	9,000	26,910	42,865
Pakistani	6,000	14,110	23,260
TOTAL BLACK	39,800	78,630	111,660

Source: Rose *et al.*, op. cit.; Lomas, op. cit.; 1966 Sample Census, op. cit.

The areal distribution of West Midlands immigrants is given in Table 4, produced in 1966/67 by the Institute of Race Relations (IRR) survey.

In terms of numbers, the immigrant population is by no means evenly distributed over the West Midlands region. In the first instance, as has already been stressed, it is centred in the conurbation—in 1971 80 per cent of black immigrants lived in such areas, compared with 45 per cent of the British-born population. Secondly, even within the conurbation, black groups are localized within clearly demarcated 'zones'. In the City of Birmingham in 1961, the percentage distribution of West Indians and Asians within the inner, middle and outer zones show a heavy over-representation of West Indians, and to a lesser extent,

TABLE 4. Racial composition of West Midlands towns

	Total population	Black Common-wealth	
Birmingham	1,106,040	70,000	Two-thirds Caribbean, rest Indian and Pakistani
Coventry	315,670	6,500	Two-thirds Indian with equal number of Caribbean and Pakistani
Dudley	63,890	5,250	Mostly Caribbean, with a few Pakistani and fewer Indian
Wolverhampton	150,200	7,500	Nearly equal number of Caribbean and Indian, few Pakistani
Smethwick (Warley)	67,750	4,500	Equal number of Caribbean and Indian with a few Pakistani
West Bromwich	97,600	5,700	Equal number of Caribbean and Indian, with a few Pakistani
Walsall	119,910	3,600	Over half Caribbean, rest Indian and Pakistani
England and Wales	47,135,510	829,750[1]	

1. 1966 *de facto* population of England and Wales.
Source: S. Patterson, *Immigration and Race Relations in Great Britain*, Oxford University Press/Institute of Race Relations, 1969.

Asians in the middle ring (see Table 5). Such evidence lends convincing weight to the theory that, in the process of suburbanization, the middle ring becomes a zone of transition in which the deserted homes of the aspiring classes become a sanctuary for the city's ethnic rejects as they seek to build up defensive communal institutions within a sort of colony structure. Finally, there is evidence that even within the high concentration zones, there is a distinct tendency towards clustering. In 1966, Soho ward in the City of Birmingham had 21 per cent of its resident population born in the new Commonwealth countries—a total of 5,910 black people (excluding their children) out of a total of 27,690. There may be further segregation of the type which gives rise to popular fears about whole areas being 'dominated' by black people, but such unevenness in density is only rarely experienced.

In general, West Midlands towns are popular with Asian and Caribbean immigrants alike, and, in this sense, have a more cosmopolitan nature

TABLE 5. Percentage immigrant settlement—City of Birmingham, 1961

Area	West Indian	Asian	Total population
Inner ring	6.8	17.6	8.6
Middle ring	80.4	64.9	30.4
Outer ring	12.8	17.5	61.0

Source: Jones, op. cit.

than towns like Bradford, where the black immigrant population is nearly all Pakistani-born, and Bristol where it is nearly all Caribbean. There is some evidence, however, of clustering by ethnic origin within the conurbation towns. For example, Handsworth and Aston districts in Birmingham in 1961 had a Caribbean component of 80 per cent in its total immigrant population, whereas in Newtown/Aston (and adjacent district), the dominant group was Asian with a proportional representation of 86 per cent. But no cluster has been overwhelmingly black and strictly segregated from the white population. In a terminological sense, the term 'ghetto' is not applicable to this situation, although the arrival of children in the few years before the 1962 Commonwealth Immigrants Act, and the continuous arrival of dependants since, together with the growing number of children born to black immigrants in the United Kingdom, have made black clusters more 'visible'. But there is still no racial polarization of the type that characterizes American cities. Even by 1971, Birmingham was the only city, apart from Bradford, whose black population made up (just) over 10 per cent of the total.

Demography

We see little reason to believe that demographic characteristics of separate ethnic groups in the West Midlands conurbation should be significantly different from that of any other provincial one. The relative youth of immigrants and the imbalance in the sex-structure of their community are well-known characteristics. Comparisons of age structures over the decade, however, reflect the normalization of this imbalance through the change in proportion of 'true' immigrants to those born in this country. Table 6 shows the demographic changes that have taken place during the last decade in the black population of the United Kingdom.

TABLE 6. Percentage age structure of immigrants—United Kingdom

Age (years)	1961		1966		1971	
	All black groups	Total popu-lation	All black groups	Total popu-lation	All black groups	Total popu-lation
Under 15	29	23	34	23	39	24
15–24	16	14	13	14	18	15
25–44	45	26	42	25	31	24
Over 45	10	37	11	38	12	37

Source: Lomas, op. cit.

Restrictive legislation has resulted in the decrease of the 25–44 working age group; the growing number of black British accounts for the increasing overrepresentation of the under-15 group. The normal sex-structure of this group has caused an evening out of the male/female ratios. However, the following shows how male dominance among the immigrant population of the West Midlands conurbation was particularly acute around 1966 (figures given are the number of males per 100 females):[1]

United Kingdom: 95 (1971).
Caribbean: 117 (1966); 109 (1971).
Indian: 164 (1966); 132 (1971).
Pakistani: 945 (1966); 346 (1971).

Rose *et al.* conclude that the West Midlands conurbation had had higher sex ratios than the country as a whole, indicating the special role that this area plays in the economic structure of the whole country.

An economy based primarily on metal trades and heavy manufacturing offers opportunities for unskilled and semi-skilled males [particularly so for Indians and Pakistanis]. Women may be employed in transport or in catering, but there is little here to attract the higher status immigrant with a non-working wife.[2]

The marital status of immigrants is difficult to assess as it raises the issue of cultural values as well as demanding a consideration of unbalanced sex-structure, i.e. the need to understand both the propensity for Caribbean people to have common-law unions and the fact that, in 1966, only 15 per cent of Pakistani men could possibly have had a wife in this country. However, the degree of marriage among all immigrant groups was notably higher in the Birmingham area than in London in 1966. There were more wives and fewer non-dependent females in Birmingham because the area does not support, like London, a large transient black student and professional population with its own separate class- and value-structures.

Fertility among immigrants is again closely related to their own culture and religion, and demographic character. Fertility among all immigrant groups is higher than that of the English population, but significantly lower than the rate in their home countries. Evidence from the Public Health Department of Birmingham shows a decline of West Indian births in each year between 1963 to 1967, when the number was 25 per cent lower than the peak figure in 1963. Fall in fertility could suggest that for this particular ethnic group, the family-building period was over. Fertility among Asians is assumed to show a similar decline as their marriage building and reunion comes to an end.

Economic activity and social status

At the heart of the United Kingdom's industrial activity, the West Midlands has consistently held great employment potential. The conurbation straddles the 'Black Country' of south Staffordshire and north Worcestershire—a name derived from the region's historical (and atmospheric!) association with mineral mining, smelting and metal manufacture. It has always needed labour. At first migrants came from Ireland, Wales

1. Lomas, op. cit.
2. Rose *et al.*, op. cit., p. 105–6.

and Shropshire, but the potential numbers of such migrants were limited and they also became less willing to perpetually do the heaviest and most arduous tasks. The expansion of the British economy in the late 1950s and early 1960s left the sector of industry of which the Black Country is a pivot crucially short of labour. The joint policy of government and industry was to seek to attract immigrant labour to just such areas.

The Black Country as a whole, in common with many industrial areas outside south-east England, has a relatively small proportion of its work force involved in distributive and service trades. The West Midlands conurbation is an overwhelmingly working-class area, and in this sense is typical of all provincial conurbations in England. In 1966, 69 per cent of the regions economically active males were factory workers (including foremen), 15 per cent were in the junior white-collar group and under 13 per cent in the top professional and managerial jobs.

Black immigrants were thus drawn to areas whose indigenous populations were everwhelmingly working class in their employment and life styles. These characteristics were to contribute crucially to the manner in which immigrants were received.

The demands of British industry led immigrant labour to the most menial tasks. Their employment was in typical Black Country settings as Table 7 may illustrate:

TABLE 7. Percentage major immigrant
occupations—West Midlands conurbation, 1966

Occupation	Indian	Pakistani	Caribbean	Total population
Number economically active	12,630	11,470	16,910	777,490
Furnace, forge, foundry and rolling mill workers	15.9	—[1]	7.8	4.3
Engineering and allied trades workers	19.2	22.3	25.7	28.3
Labourers	26.6	53.1	22.5	7.8
(Labourers in engineering and allied trades)	(9.9)	(37.4)	(11.9)	(3.6)
Transport and communications	—	—	10.3	6.3

1. — means that less than 7.5 per cent were enumerated.
Source: Rose *et al.*, op. cit.

It is to be emphasized that the black immigrant to the West Midlands has had little choice in employment. Immigrant skills have either proved irrelevant to advanced industrialism (e.g. fine West Indian carpentry) or been classed as inferior (e.g. Indian teaching qualifications). When immigrant employment patterns are examined in terms of class it becomes clear that the vast majority of immigrants have been consigned to the working class whether they like it or not (see Table 8).

There are differences however in employment patterns within the immigrant community in the West Midlands. Outside Birmingham only the Indians show any representation in the managerial/professional

TABLE 8. Percentage of immigrant groups
in types of occupation—West Midlands conurbation, 1966

Type of occupation	Indian	Pakistani	Caribbean	Total population
Managers, foremen, supervisors	2.2	0.7	0.4	12.3
Self-employed	2.9	1.7	0.9	4.5
Apprentices, articled clerks	2.9	0.3	2.2	4.8
Professional employees	2.6	0.3	0.2	3.0
General manual	89.4	97.0	96.3	75.4
TOTAL (per cent)	100	100	100	100
TOTAL NUMBERS	12,450	11,170	16,340	763,610

Source: Rose et al., op. cit.

category. Both the Pakistani and Caribbean immigrant in Dudley, Walsall, Warley, Wolverhampton and West Bromwich is strictly tied to manual labour. In the manual category itself, Pakistanis show a disproportionately higher percentage of workers as unskilled while the Indian and West Indian worker is equally represented in skilled and unskilled work. It is of great significance to note that in 1966 there were only 170 black foremen (of which 100 were in Birmingham alone) out of a total of 36,420 black workers.

So statistics regarding socio-economic positions of absolute or relative power and responsibility possessed by black workers in relation to the host population reveal how black people have not achieved positions of control. Well over 90 per cent of economically active black males in the West Midlands conurbation remained in the 'other' category (see Table 8) as compared to 75 per cent of the total population. The Political and Economic Planning report, Racial Discrimination, emphasized 'substantial discrimination in Britain against coloured immigrants in employment', and suggested that 'as immigrants became more accustomed to English ways of life, as they acquire higher expectations and higher qualifications, so they experience more personal direct discrimination'. The Birmingham area has had a very poor record, and despite national representatives of large employers and unions stressing the existence of equal opportunity, the report concludes that

people at local level raised many examples of discrimination and stressed the problems of employing immigrants. In addition to resistance to initial recruitment, there were demands for such things as separate canteen and toilet facilities, and rejection by a majority of employers of the possibility of promotion for coloured workers, because of the resentment they expected from their white staff.

Immigrant unemployment figures yield only that the patterns are very similar to those for the total population. There appears to be a tendency for black workers to be hardest hit during recessions, but the difficulties in estimating the working population amongst immigrants render detailed comparison between black and white unemployment rates extremely hazardous.

Housing

Particularly in the urban context, housing becomes one of the major social parameters in determining the quality of life of the city dweller. The urban immigrant may unwillingly drift into, or consciously select, but more typically is forced by circumstances, into the same area as his fellow immigrants. Statistics from the 1961 and 1966 Census data produce a convincing analysis of how immigrants are disadvantaged, with respect to the host population, in the field of housing as defined in terms of density (overcrowding), sharing households, household facilities and housing tenure. In producing such information for the West Midlands, we have recourse to a very useful study commissioned by the Institute of Race Relations (IRR), part of which concerns itself with the construction of special tabulations of those resident in particular immigrant households in 1966 within (a) the whole of the West Midlands conurbation and (b) within selected central wards of Birmingham, West Bromwich, Walsall, Wolverhampton, and the former borough of Smethwick. This area contained, in 1966, out of a total population of 650,000, almost 60,000 black people. The findings of this study are summarized below.

All immigrant groups live at a density of over one person per room in comparison with 0.6 person per room in the host population, and this single fact serves as an important diagnostic of the deprived housing conditions of black people. In the selected wards these immigrant densities are even higher.

Households are larger in immigrant communities than those in the host population, especially within the selected wards. Reasons are demographic, economic and cultural. West Midlands immigrant households are 57 per cent larger than English households. There is evidence from the comparison between inner selected wards and the outer tracts in the conurbation that 'the normal pattern of suburbanization among immigrant households with young children is being frustrated'.

In an area where the general level of sharing is lower than 5 per cent, 40 per cent of West Midlands immigrants are sharing accommodation. Such sharing would evidently have been higher, as, for example, in London, had the nature of available housing allowed this to be so. Nevertheless, the typically small terraced houses in the inner zones of big cities, which form the base of immigrant settlement, are intensively shared.

In so far as overcrowding is a measure of social and economic deprivation, figures again show immigrants to be worse off than the host community everywhere in the conurbation (see Table 9).

Sharing small terraced houses that do not lend themselves easily to conversion can intensify hardship due to lack of household facilities. For instance, only one-quarter of all immigrant sharers in the West Midlands had their own kitchen. Table 10 gives information about some of the more important facilities available or shared.

The IRR study concludes that though 'the small Birmingham terraced house has provided an acceptable niche for those immigrants who are fortunate enough to afford unshared accommodation', it creates 'lack of

TABLE 9. Percentage overcrowding indices—West Midlands conurbation, 1966

| | All blacks | | British | |
	>1 person per room	>1.5 person per room	>1 person per room	>1.5 person per room
West Midlands conurbation	57.4	30.0	12.3	2.9
Selected wards	59.3	31.4	14.3	4.4

Source: Rose et al., op. cit.

TABLE 10. Household facilities—West Midlands conurbation, 1966

| | Percentage households sharing bath | | Percentage households without bath | | Percentage households sharing W.C. | |
	All black	British	All black	British	All black	British
West Midlands conurbation	26.0	3.1	31.4	14.1	39.4	5.6
Selected wards	27.3	4.3	34.1	38.5	42.3	12.6

Source: Rose et al., op. cit.

space', 'high housing densities', and 'a high proportion of sharing households without kitchen facilities'.

It is in the very nature of private enterprise and a free market economy that the major proportion of the housing stock is out of the hands of local authorities. This, coupled with the fact that demand has always been in excess of supply, leads to the usual problems of scarcity, homelessness and inadequate housing—particularly so among disadvantaged groups such as immigrants residing in urban areas. Because of the pressure on local housing departments, highly selective procedures have been instituted and these, by and large, accentuate the problems of immigrant groups. Both Wolverhampton and Birmingham use a residential qualification that automatically rejects all newly arrived immigrants from council housing. With little chance of becoming council tenants, and tired of being at the mercy of private landlords, immigrants have to try to buy their own property and are subsequently trapped under the financial strain of meeting mortgage repayments and taking lodgers (often from their own community) or paying guests.

While over 60 per cent of all immigrant households in the West Midlands were owner-occupied, only 42 per cent of the British owned their own property (see Table 11). Outside the central wards, the differential was even greater. Only just over 8 per cent of immigrants rent from local authorities and over 31 per cent from private landlords, whereas 39 per cent of British households live in council accommodation and only 16 per cent in private. Of particular interest is the large proportion of black households in furnished accommodation where security of tenure has traditionally been more at risk than in other rented categories.

TABLE 11. Percentage housing tenure—West Midlands conurbation, 1966

	Owner occupiers		Rent from local authority		Rent unfurnished		Rent furnished	
	All black	British	All black	British	All black	British	All black	British
West Midlands conurbation	60.1	42.3	8.2	39.1	10.0	14.6	21.4	1.3
Selected wards	55.7	29.9	8.1	35.9	10.3	26.5	22.9	4.0
Rent	73.9	45.4	6.2	40.0	6.8	11.5	16.7	0.6

Source: Rose et al., op. cit.

There has been no move to suburbia by the working black population. The only move has been from one inner city zone of transition to another with much the same sort of housing situation. The fact that black people become trapped in certain inner city areas because of the housing market means they become prey to a cycle of deprivation which will further decrease their life-chances. This situation has been aptly summed up by Bob Holman:[1]

The deprived often suffer in more than one direction. One reason is the causal relationship between forms of deprivation. For instance, bad housing is not only likely to create conditions which inhibits a child's educational progress, it may also adversely affect his health, which, in turn, will lower his capacity as a wage earner, which will reduce his chance of ever obtaining adequate housing.

Comparison with 1961 statistics indicate only a very gradual process of diffusion into the preferred sectors of the housing market with little support from the municipal sector. West Indians have made the greatest improvements, Pakistani housing conditions may well have deteriorated. Indians still continue to be relatively the best-housed group within the black immigrant community and West Indians the worst. Changes that have taken place have been totally inadequate in improving the quality or quantity of the housing stock or in achieving a more even distribution of resources along racial lines.

Information on education, social welfare, health and law and order cannot be gleaned from census data. It comes instead from commissioned studies and local government departments. Such statistical preparations are often uncorrelated and their mode of presentation depends largely on the political attitude towards race prevailing at any particular point in time. We shall see, however, that despite the need for great care in their interpretation, these are the figures that are often misused and quoted out of context by press and politicians alike. Brief mention is made in the following sections about how the controversy surrounding the socialization of immigrants has been kept alive in the West Midlands towns.

1. Robert Holman, Socially Deprived Families in Britain, p. 143–4, Bedford Square Press, 1970.

Education

By 1966, the Department of Education had declared that the total of immigrant children represented just over 2 per cent of the total school population of Great Britain. The following year, the *Guardian* (11 February 1967) produced images of 'immigrants overcrowding schools' through its reports from an infant school in the district of Handsworth (Birmingham) where out of 390 children, 36 were English, 3 Pakistanis, about 100 Indian and the rest West Indian. In the *Birmingham Post* (7 February 1966) the city statistician was reported as estimating that, in two years time, 10 primary schools at the centre of the city would be attended wholly by black children, that 47 of the total of 77 schools in the area would have at least 30 per cent, and that only 4 would have no immigrant children at all. Such a tendency towards 'ghetto' schools was hardly understood in the light of the city's dogged policy of non-dispersal, the fact that most of these 'all black' schools were in the inner deprived areas, and that black people were not generally eligible for places, on grounds of religions, in 'voluntary' Church of England and Roman Catholic primary schools which formed nearly one-third of all local authority institutions. There were attempts to explain that immigrant children were not keeping white children out of schools by pointing out that the crisis in the inner ring areas was really due to a shortage of primary teachers. In any case, the percentage of immigrant pupils maintained in private and secondary schools had only risen from 9 per cent in 1968 to 9.5 per cent in 1970 in Birmingham, and in Wolverhampton from 11.8 per cent to 13.1 per cent over the same period. Immigrant representation in the 'blackest' parts of the West Midlands was still tame in comparison to some London districts (Brent 24.8 per cent and Haringey 26.7 per cent).

It seems to be clear that in education, as in housing, the presence of black immigrants has made visible serious deficiencies in the public provision of resources. Often, it has been alleged that the presence of black people has caused these problems. The available evidence suggests the problems were there before the arrival of immigrants and would still be there if they 'went home', voluntarily or otherwise.

Health and social welfare

Immigrant groups have been associated with contagious diseases (e.g. tuberculosis and smallpox), unsanitary living conditions, and over-straining of the National Health Service—in particular the maternity services—all of which have been used in anti-immigration campaigns. Immigrant health demands have always been represented with more emotion than realism. The 1963 report of the Wolverhampton Medical Officer of Health contained the following statement: 'Immigrants from the Commonwealth colonies who, according to the 1961 Census, were 3.9 per cent of the population, produced 22.7 per cent of all births.' In 1965, Dr John Lamb, Secretary of the South Warwickshire British

Medical Association, was reported as saying that it was 'virtually impossible' for English women to have their first babies in hospital because the beds were full of immigrants who had been living in unsanitary conditions. Only later were the immigrant birth rates put into perspective with reports from *The Times* (25 June 1965) that pointed out a large proportion of the demand for maternity beds coming from the Irish, and debate over the need to consider the age structure of immigrants that fell overwhelmingly into the child-bearing age when compared with settled populations.

In terms of social welfare, a 1967 study conducted by the National Institute of Economic and Social Research concluded that immigrants were less dependent on child welfare, unemployment benefits, and old-age pensions than the average British, and contributed more to national insurance than the host population. In 1966, £62 per head was being spent on the British population for all these rights—and only £52 per head on the immigrant population.

Since as we have explained earlier black people are concentrated geographically, they will appear to predominate as the clientele in social service agencies in their particular locality. Thus some social security offices (just like some doctors surgeries and some schools) will be used mainly by black people. One of the characteristics of racialist propaganda is to infer such situations are 'unnatural', and ignore their geographical logicality. And of course the 'unnaturalness' of totally white populations in some parts of a statistically multi-racial community is never suggested.

Law and order

With reference to law and order, again, the statistics are controversial. However, in 1966 Mr David Ennals, Under-Secretary for Home Affairs, refuting the charge that 'blacks cause crime', said that

a recent study in the area of Birmingham concludes that crime among immigrants tended to be *below* average. Fewer than 5 per cent of arrests made in a significantly coloured neighbourhood were, in fact, of coloured people.

More recently, the police and the press have been successful in generating a concern over the 'rising' numbers of black youth involved particularly in crimes of violence. However, just as some sections of the white population (male, young deprived working-class youth) are overrepresented in criminal statistics, so some sections of the immigrant population (young black British of West Indian parentage, often homeless and jobless) may come to be similarly overrepresented. And in any case, any rise in crime rates amongst blacks may be interpreted as more an effect, than a cause, of the way they have been treated by white society.

The status of 'facts'

We have represented a statistical background to race in the West Midlands. It is drawn from the concerns of government departments, the

Institute of Race Relations, and academic social science. They have been concerned with the relationship between the settlement and behaviour of immigrant communities and the long-established social problems of employment, housing, education, social services and crime. At the same time, they have undoubtedly believed that they have been counteracting the assertions of those who would characterize immigrants as responsible for decaying housing, overcrowded schools, underresourced social services and rising crime rates.

As we shall see, however, it may be a mistake to believe that racialism stands or falls to any significant degree on 'facts' about the immigrant population. The case of Enoch Powell's speeches is instructive here. His statistical arguments about immigrant birth rates may be discredited amongst social scientists and statisticians, but his real success has been to give the semblance of fact to a powerful image of immigrants—that 'they breed like rabbits'. All his most magnetic statements are not facts at all, but scenarios—of old ladies confronted by mess, classrooms without a white face. These stand or fall, not as the press thought, by whether these individual incidents could be proved or disproved to have happened, but by their focusing of generalized conceptions of black people into representative incidents. They stood, not as facts, but as images.

Thus any consideration of race in the West Midlands must take into account communally available self-images which preceded the arrival of black immigrants. Despite its long history of local immigration from Wales, Shropshire and further north; despite the relatively recent transformation of towns such as Birmingham into large cities occurring as it did only in the last quarter of the nineteenth century; despite the established presence of white immigrant populations, especially the Irish, but also smaller groupings such as Polish exiles; despite all this there is a deep-rooted parochialism in the West Midlands, especially in the Black Country area. One writer has simply said:[1]

The Black Country is built up, almost end to end; yet in some strange way it is still 'country' not 'town', a group of villages of various sizes. In each of these everyone knows everyone else, but beyond these borders you're a foreigner.

Here then is one lead into the distinctive characteristics of the local culture in which the reaction to black immigrants is rooted. It helps to explain why the history of race relations, even from a national perspective, is symbolized by events in Black Country towns.

The tabulations below reveal where the West Midlands have contributed significantly to race-related events in the United Kingdom.

National events

1958	Race riots in Notting Hill, London
1961–62	'Beat-the-ban' immigration from New Commonwealth
1962	Commonwealth Immigrants Act—severely curbing immigration

1. E. Chiman, *The Black Country*, Longman, 1972.

1964	Alien Restrictions Act
1965	White Paper on Immigration—restricting work vouchers
	Campaign Against Racial Discrimination (CARD) formed
	Race Relations Bill
1966	Central aid to local authorities with high immigrant populations
1967	Kenyan Asian crisis
	PEP survey revealing extensive discrimination in employment, etc.
1968	Race Relations Bill—extending powers of 1965 Bill
1969	Immigrants Appeal Act
	Leeds race riots
1971	Commonwealth Immigrants Bill—introduction of patriality

Local events of national import

1960–61	Formation of British Immigration Control Association (BICA) in West Midlands
1961	Dudley race riot
1964	Smethwick victory for Tory, Peter Griffiths on openly racist ticket
	Help provided by BICA in election campaigns at Perry Barr
1965	Potential race-riot in Wolverhampton, quelled by police
1967–68	Turban dispute in Wolverhampton
1968	Powell's Walsall speech (February) on how to control 'evil' of immigration. Powell's Birmingham Speech *v.* Race Relations Bill
1969	'Paki-bashing' in Midlands towns

In 1962, Dudley produced a serious race riot; in 1964, in Smethwick, an election campaign fought and won by a Conservative candidate on an openly racialist ticket; in 1968, a Wolverhampton M.P., Enoch Powell, became the first prominent politician to breach the liberalism (of word, if not of deed) of the Establishment, making his first major speech on the subject in Walsall. In Walsall itself, displaced racialism was evident in the long and bitter resistance of the town councils to the provision of a travellers' site within their boundaries.

Birmingham reflected racial tension in at least one council and one parliamentary election (Sandwell and Perry Barr), gave birth to the notorious British Immigrant Control Association, and was the scene of more than one Enoch Powell speech. Yet, perhaps because of its cultural heterogeneity—not to say anonymity—it never quite provided the flashpoints evident in the Black Country. It did, however, achieve a reputation for 'immigrant social problems areas'—in the early and middle 1960s the most publicized area was Sparkbrook; in the late 1960s, the focus shifted to Handsworth.

We have argued then that any background to a consideration of the presentation of race in the West Midlands must take into account the arrival, distribution and settlement of the immigrant population and the particular local economic and cultural factors which shaped the response of the indigeneous population. The press clearly had a crucial role to play in establishing an arena for negotiation between the host and immigrant populations. How they interpreted that role will become clear from our empirical study. But first, to aid us in these interpretations, there is a need to consider the general functions of the local press of different kinds in the United Kingdom today.

Chapter 2

The provincial press in the West Midlands

Structure of the provincial press in the United Kingdom

Historical survey

In this historical survey we shall look at the different types of newspaper, their genesis and expansion and how the provincial papers developed. The newspaper was established in the eighteenth century as a financially independent institution serving the commercial middle class with news relevant to the conduct of business. Between 1695 and 1730 a public press of three kinds was established—the daily newspaper (London-based), the provincial weekly newspaper and the periodical. Expansion was so rapid that by 1758 Dr Johnson could write: 'now . . . almost every large town has its weekly historian who regularly circulates his periodical intelligence.' The daily press, led by *The Times*, had a strong position and wide middle-class distribution, assisted by the new mechanical (steam) power.

Between 1770 and 1830, but particularly in the last twenty years of this period, repeated attempts were made to establish a radical press with a different social basis among the newly organized working class. These attempts were beaten down by successive repressive governments, but a popular press, in the form of the Sunday newspaper, was established in the 1820s. It had a wholly different character and function from the daily press. It was politically radical but its main emphasis was not political and included a miscellany of material—especially crime reports. By 1840 the most widely selling English newspaper was not *The Times* but one or other of these cheap (penny) Sunday papers.

In 1855 with the removal of the last of the taxes on newspapers, the daily press was transformed. A cheap metropolitan press, led by the *Telegraph*, quickly took over leadership from *The Times* and gained readers in an expanding lower middle class. At the same time a provincial daily press was firmly established. In 1855 alone, seventeen provincial dailies were set up (the *Birmingham Post* was established 1857). Many had

London offices so just distributed London-based news, but the development of news agencies increasingly freed them from dependence on London. The most successful reached circulations of up to 40,000 and, although small, the circulation was a significant expansion of the newspaper public. The provincial dailies were not in competition for different levels of public as in London. They sought to serve all readers in their area, so tended to follow a very general policy.

During the 1880s and 1890s the national press began to expand rapidly through the development of railway distribution which increased circulation. In the 1870s and 1880s a new kind of evening paper, taking much of its journalistic method from the Sunday press, was successfuly launched (*Manchester Evening News*, 1868; *Birmingham Evening Mail*, 1870; Wolverhampton *Express and Star*, 1874). The evening papers began a new stage of cheap press based in towns throughout the country. With the rise of interest in sport, particularly football, evening papers had a new function and a new class of readers. The form was radical—showing features of the new journalism, e.g. the interview, the cross-heading, American style headlines, etc. From this development, newspapers began to be read by more working men although a mass readership was not reached until well into the twentieth century.

In the 1890s cheaper daily papers such as the *Daily Mail* were developed for the lower middle classes. The basis of this change was economic. The new revenue for maintaining newspapers was based on new 'mass advertising'. With the growth of factory-made products, came a growth in this type of advertising—away from the dependence on commercial and business advertisements.

It can be seen then that the oldest form of newspaper in the provinces was the political weekly paper, followed 100 years later by the morning provincial paper (a development at first from London) for the middle-class business sector, with the provincial evening paper established shortly afterwards for the potential working-class audience. Initially, mainly news of national and international importance, particularly war, was published, but the growing provision of local news identified the early local newspaper with one particular community or region.

Type of newspaper

In the United Kingdom, there are still three main types of newspaper circulating in the provinces. The morning daily papers (of which there were only seventeen at the end of 1970) have the least significance in reporting community-based news. They are generally in competition with the morning national press—attempting to provide coverage of the national, international and local scenes all in one paper. Many are in acute financial difficulties, only able to survive through dependence on their offshoot evening papers which are generally independent and the nuclei of small groups themselves.

Of greatest importance to local communities are the daily evening newspaper and the weekly newspaper and it is on these two types that we shall concentrate in our study of the provincial press. Weekly and evening papers provide a very different focus of interest for their readers. The weekly paper tends to circulate in a very small geographical area providing news for a smallish audience who expect information about local residents, local issues and local neighbourhood organizations. The evening paper tends to be exclusively urban-based, but covers a fairly wide geographical area around the large conurbations, often overlapping weekly newspapers. They specialize in very 'hot' news (the main news of the day probably having been read in the morning) with a specialized local interest.

Circulation and readership

A look at circulation figures and numbers of newspapers will show the significance of the evening and weekly provincial press in the United Kingdom and the weakness of the provincial morning paper.

As indicated in Table 12, circulation of local weeklies and bi-weeklies is almost as great as that of the national morning papers. When provincial evenings are added, the local paper achieves even greater significance. This means that readers of provincial newspapers are more often in contact with local news and national news through a local filter than they are with national news direct.

TABLE 12. Circulation of classes of newspaper in the United Kingdom

	1937	1966	1969
Provincial evening	4,400,000	6,824,000	6,889,000
Weeklies and bi-weeklies	8,572,000	13,825,000	13,423,000
Provincial morning	1,600,000	1,954,000	1,973,000
National morning	9,980,000	15,954,000	14,804,000

Source: Cox and Morgan, 'Press Council Annual Reports', City Politics and The Press, p. 5.

The actual numbers of papers are subject to constant fluctuation but, as can be seen from Table 13, it is the provincial morning newspaper which has lost the greatest ground in the period 1921–69. Although six big city evening newspapers closed in the 1960s, leaving only two cities (London and Glasgow) with a choice of evening paper, other new papers opened leaving about the same number of papers in circulation. The

TABLE 13. Number of provincial newspapers

	1921	1947	1969
Provincial evening	89	75	81
Weeklies	1,485	1,162	1,163 (including metropolitan weeklies)
Provincial morning	41	25	22

Source: Ian Jackson, The Provincial Press and the Community, p. 17.

weekly papers have maintained roughly the same number although amongst them, too, some have closed and new ones have opened.

A study of readership produces even more interesting evidence of the importance of provincial newspapers. A survey, carried out by the Maud Committee on the Management of Local Government published in 1967, revealed that 79 per cent of the electorate claim to be regular readers of local newspapers, with another 10 per cent reading them irregularly. In the county boroughs, the 'regular' total was as high as 84 per cent. The Skeffington Committee on Public Participation in Planning, whose report was published in 1969, estimated that 'something approaching 90 per cent of the adult population are likely to read at least one local newspaper. . . .'[1]

The big city evening newspapers are characterized by a very high percentage coverage of households in the central urban areas. In 1969 the ten largest (including Birmingham, Coventry and Wolverhampton) averaged 82.8 per cent of households and total numbers of copies sold in the ten areas amounted to half the national daily sales of the *Daily Mirror*.[2] Evening newspapers tend to be taken by all sections of the community in their area of distribution, but are marginally more popular with the working classes and the margin increases moving from the south to the north of England.

Weekly newspaper statistics show that these are particularly favoured by middle-class readers and by the inhabitants of towns with a population under 100,000 and rural areas. There is a general trend of a higher percentage of households taking a weekly moving from the north to the south.

Ownership

Unlike the national newspapers which have long been under the control of large corporations, the provincial press has been largely dominated historically, by family and individual ownership. There is an increasing trend towards control of the provincial press by London-based chain groups, but about 45 per cent of evening papers and 75 per cent of weeklies are still owned by regional groups or individual proprietors. However, many of the regional groups are growing, with large-scale investment in other forms of media business, very similar to the corporations although not on such a vast scale. The 1947 Royal Commission on the Press was largely inspired by anxiety about increasing monopoly ownership. The chain organizations, therefore, came under special scrutiny, but the Royal Commission concluded in 1949 that the current level of chain ownership did not call for any remedial action but thought that any future increases would be undesirable.

Nevertheless, groups have been slowly adding to their numbers and the pace of expansion accelerated during the 1960s. By 1969, 55 per cent of English and Welsh provincial newspapers were owned by five London-

1. Paragraph 104–14.
2. Jackson, op. cit., p. 34, from Evening Newspaper Advertising Bureau statistics.

based groups:[1] (a) News of the World Organization Ltd (2 evening papers, 23 weeklies); (b) Associated Newspapers, Northcliffe group (12 evening papers, 29 weeklies); (c) United Newspapers (5 evening, 35 weeklies); (d) The Thomson Organization (9 evening, 22 weeklies); and (e) Westminster Press Group (9 evening, 83 weeklies). In 1964 a maximum of 18 per cent of the weekly press was owned by the major groups, but by 1969 this had grown to 25 per cent (200 papers).

The development of chain ownership may have serious implications for the provincial press. As long as it is in local hands there is at work an established tradition of responsibility to the community. However conservative and patronizing such responsibility may be, it does curb the worst excesses of profit maximization. Though in business to make a profit, local newspapers have a peculiar sense of their role in the community, as is shown by one typical piece of evidence to the 1947 Royal Commission:[2]

I believe in local newspapers being in the hands of local people who have at heart the welfare of the district in which they work, and have their recreation and interests in the district in which they spend their lives.

National combines have their own version of this in, for example, their concept of themselves as watchdogs of the people. But, as developments in the national press have shown, such considerations do not weigh as much in policy-making as the need to sell. The audience may itself ensure, through its purchasing power, that the local newspaper continues to reflect local news and interests, but the ultimate exercise of financial, and thus editorial, power from London, may have unknown effects on the extent and kind of news coverage in the provincial press.

Finance

A crucial aspect for the continuance of any newspaper is finance. Whatever motive there might be behind the setting up or running of a newspaper, it is undoubtedly true that a newspaper is a business which must make a profit. The national daily newspapers have reached the extreme position where they must sell at least 1 million newspapers to survive. The provincial press is obviously not at that level, but concentration on the profit-motive does affect the structure of the local newspaper.

The major source of revenue for any newspaper is advertising which is of far greater significance than sales. Table 14, using statistics calculated by the 1962 Royal Commission on the Press, shows that for every type of newspaper, except the popular Sunday, advertising produces more than half the necessary revenue.

It is interesting to note that the 'qualities' are more dependent than the 'populars' on advertising, because of the differences in circulation figures, but can still command advertising by having a prestigious readership. The provincial evening figures come midway between the 'quality'

1. ibid., p. 24–5.
2. Holmesdale Press Ltd, quoted in Jackson, op. cit., p. 27.

TABLE 14. Comparison between sales and advertising, 1960

Type of paper	Percentage sales	Percentage advertising
National morning		
'Qualities'	25	75
'Populars'	45	55
Sundays		
'Qualities'	21	79
'Populars'	51	49
Provincial evening	38	62
Provincial weeklies	21	79

Source: Denys Thompson (ed.), Discrimination and Popular Culture, p. 82.

and 'popular' national morning papers; and the weekly papers are the same as the 'quality' Sunday papers in their almost total dependence on advertising revenue.

The size of circulation also affects the type of advertising used by various newspapers. Those with over 100,000 (national papers and larger evening papers) will sell display space of various sizes, whereas the smaller newspapers and weeklies will derive more revenue from classified advertising which is always local in origin.

Rates of advertising which can be charged are also affected by the size of circulation (and, more significantly, readership). For example in 1964, the *Birmingham Evening Mail* with a circulation of 408,539 charged the following rates for a display advertisement: page, £1,300; 24 column inches, £132; 8 column inches, £44. The Bolton *Evening News*, which in the same year had a circulation of 88,107, charged £250, £36 and £12 respectively.[1] In the smaller newspapers more profit will be made from one column inch of classified advertisements than from one column inch of display. Local classified advertising is seen as the most important form, partly because of the local flavour imparted and partly because it is more profitable. Cars or houses for sale, situations vacant, personal announcements are the major categories.

In the papers published daily the proportion of advertising grows larger as the weekend (when most spending is done) approaches and it is not just coincidence that most of the weekly papers are published at the end of the week—on Thursday or Friday.

Advertising is so competitive and crucial to the financing of local papers that local 'give away' advertising papers (such as the *ABC Weekly Advertiser* in Birmingham) are bought up by the local newspaper proprietor not only to boost his own income but also to prevent competition for advertising revenue.

The question of whether advertisers influence policy of newspaper editors is discussed by Jackson in his assessment of evidence to the 1947 Royal Commission. He suggests that there is no direct influence, but

1. Jackson, op. cit., p. 203.

points out that editorial policy seems to be geared to not upsetting advertisers. Thus there is generally no critical analysis of consumer interests.

Summary

We have shown that the major characteristics differentiating the provincial from the national press are as follows:

A longer and more complex history in which the kind of audience addressed depends not only on geographical but social considerations.

A higher overall sale than daily nationals and a high percentage of household readership.

Ownership still in regional rather than national hands.

A consequent conservatism about content and a self consciousness about responsibility to the community which militate against the adoption of more extreme forms of 'popular' news presentation.

A similar dependence to the nationals on advertising revenue, but which is different in kind and source.

A hypersensitivity to some kinds of news which may affect local interests, e.g. consumer advice.

These characteristics become clearer if we examine them in more detail for the provincial press of the West Midlands.

Structure of the provincial press in the West Midlands

For the West Midlands study, we have taken the area of the fairly recently formed West Midlands Metropolitan County which covers both large cities, small towns and some rural areas. (For boundary lines, see Fig. 1, page 28.)

Within the area there is one daily morning paper (the *Birmingham Post*), one Sunday weekly paper (the *Sunday Mercury*), three daily evening papers (the *Birmingham Evening Mail*, the Wolverhampton *Express and Star* and the *Coventry Evening Telegraph*) all based in the large urban conurbations, and about thirty weekly papers throughout the region.

Ownership

The pattern of ownership has been radically changed by mergers and takeovers in the last twenty years. The dominant form, once that of the family business, is now that of the limited company, issuing shares, owning groups of newspapers, and often involved in all types of mass-media presentation. Interlocking directorships and a virtual monopoly situation in their own areas ensures a spirit of peaceful coexistence amongst businesses which are rarely in direct competition.

The present characteristic of ownership is that it is all regionally based and all rival papers have been taken over so that there is a monopoly situation in each district. In 1947 the Westminster Press Group (based in London and one of the biggest owners of the provincial press) did have a strong hold on the Midlands. It owned the now-extinct *Birmingham Gazette*, which was a rival morning paper to the *Birmingham Post*, and the *Evening Despatch* which competed with the *Birmingham Mail* and was merged with the *Mail* in the early part of 1963. (The paper was called the *Birmingham Evening Mail and Despatch* for a time until 'Despatch' was dropped to produce the *Birmingham Evening Mail*.) The Westminster Press Group also owned the *Sunday Mercury*.

Many of the weekly local papers struggled to remain independent, but are now all incorporated into locally owned groups which have merged those which covered similar areas, e.g. the *Smethwick Telephone* was merged with the *Warley and Oldbury News* to produce the *Warley News Telephone* in 1966.

The pattern of ownership of the provincial press is quite different from that of the national press, where a few large monopolies are in competition for the same audience. The large regional evening papers, for instance, have their own distinct circulation areas which hardly ever overlap.

Of the three main ownership groups, the Express and Star (Wolverhampton) Ltd is the smallest. It has as its subsidiary the Midlands News Association Ltd which publishes the Wolverhampton *Express and Star*, the *Sporting Star* and *Wolverhampton Chronicle* (weekly). The *Shropshire Star* and *Shropshire Journal* are owned by other subsidiary companies. The Express and Star Group is fairly tight-knit with only a few outside interests.

Coventry Newpapers Ltd owns the *Coventry Evening Telegraph* and (outside the West Midlands Area) the *Cambridge Evening News*. The company is a subsidiary of the Yattendon Investment Trust which appears to be the holding company of the Iliffe family's interests. The *Coventry Evening Telegraph* was established in 1891 by Lord Iliffe's father and has been a family possession over since. The Yattendon Trust also has investments in Coventry broadcasting.

The Birmingham Post and Mail Group Ltd is the largest owning company in the West Midlands. There are two main subsidiary groups, Birmingham Post and Mail Ltd, which publishes the *Birmingham Post*, *Birmingham Evening Mail* and *Sunday Mercury*, and West Midlands Press Ltd, which publishes a series of weekly papers in and around Birmingham (Warley, Walsall, West Bromwich, Brewood, Rugeley, Cannock, Dudley, Tipton, Wednesbury, Hednesford, Solihull, Sutton Coldfield, Erdington and Castle Bromwich).

The group also owns ABC Weekly Advertiser Ltd (a give-away advertising paper), T. Dillon & Co. (a chain of over seventy newsagents shops), Midland Air Tour Operators and four sound-radio companies. There are also links between the Coventry and Birmingham owning groups. Lord Iliffe, chairman of the Coventry group, is also vice-chairman of the Birmingham Post and Mail Group. R. P. R. Iliffe, his son, who is a director of Coventry, is also a director of Birmingham and chairman of the *ABC Weekly Advertiser*. J. L. Brown is a director of both companies.

However, not only are there these relationships between regional groups but also formal links with other media and finance groups. The Chairman of the Post and Mail Group, Sir Eric Clayson, is also a director of Associated Television (ATV), Lloyds Bank (Midlands) and Sun Alliance Assurance. The Duke of Atholl and W. B. Morrell are directors of both the Birmingham Post and Mail Group and the Westminster Press Group—the largest London-based group, owning over 100 provincial newspapers throughout the country. The Westminster Press Group is a subsidiary of Pearson Longman which owns the *Financial Times* and Penguins as well as numerous radio companies and small publications. W. B. Morrell is also chairman of Turret Press (Holdings) Ltd, a group which publishes almost fifty trade and commercial papers. The Duke of Atholl is also chairman of other companies.

Thus, apparently independent groups have interests which are closely aligned and serve to act as safeguards against to 'poaching' on each other's territory. The Midlands News Association Ltd (Wolverhampton) is the most close-knit group with few tendrils spreading elsewhere. They do have some connections with broadcasting and travel.

Choice of newspapers for study

In order to study race in the provincial press in the West Midlands, we had to choose a selection of newspapers which could provide comparative data and which also covered different types of area. We decided on the three evening newspapers (the Wolverhampton *Express and Star*, *Birmingham Evening Mail* and *Coventry Evening Telegraph*), each of which circulates in distinct regions.

There are also a great many weekly newspapers published in the West Midlands. Although their readership is fairly small, we felt that we should give some consideration to weekly papers as they would reflect local issues very clearly. We wanted a spread through the region and to also reflect different areas of immigration. One difficulty was that a great many newspapers were owned and published by one company so that layout, format and, in many cases, news covered were very similar. The major paper within this group and one which was of great interest because of its involvement in race relations in the 1960s is the *Warley News Telephone* (previously the *Smethwick Telephone*). We decided on this paper and looked for two others in order to have three weeklies and three dailies to study.

To obtain some idea of the style of the different newspapers and also to enable us to consider the use of Leicester's topics and subtopics, we carried out a pilot survey of a sample of current local papers over a period of three and a half weeks. Table 15 shows briefly the results of that pilot survey.

We had already chosen the *Warley News Telephone* and decided on the *Dudley Herald* because of the unusual combination of a low number of items and a high percentage of immigrants. This left a choice between the *Walsall Observer* and the *West Bromwich Midland Chronicle*. In the end we decided on the *Walsall Observer* because of its distinctive 'Black

TABLE 15. Results of the pilot survey

Paper[1]	Number of copies	Number of items on race	Average per day	Percentage immig. 1967
DAILY EVENING				
Wolverhampton *Express and Star*	13	66	5.7	4.7
Birmingham Evening Mail	14	60	4.3	6.4
Coventry Evening Telegraph	13	39	3.0	2.0
WEEKLY				
Warley News Telephone	3	17	5.6	7.1
Dudley Herald	4	6	1.5	7.7
Walsall Observer	4	21	5.25	2.5
West Bromwich Midland Chronicle	4	15	3.75	5.0

1. All papers except *West Bromwich Midland Chronicle* were finally chosen for study.

Country' flavour, because of the importance of gypsies in the area (an interest for a study in depth) and because West Bromwich is well covered by the *Birmingham Evening Mail*.

We were very disappointed, however, in not being able to complete our study of the *Dudley Herald*. Although we began with the few back copies which were available at the *Dudley Herald* office, it was impossible to continue as most of the papers had been destroyed once they had been placed on micro-film by Dudley Library.

We decided against looking at the *Birmingham Post* because it is a morning daily paper, much more closely related to the national press, and against the *Sunday Mercury* which is a unique paper and could have afforded little comparative data.

Circulation and readership

A brief look at each paper will give some idea of its size, circulation and readership. Table 16 shows the circulation figures for each newspaper in 1963 and 1970. Figures for national press and London evening papers are added for comparative purposes. Although these figures cannot be taken as completely reliable records, they do show certain trends and differences between the national and local press. In terms of overall circulation, the marked decline in the sales of national 'popular' papers is not matched by the provincial newspapers. Only the *Birmingham Evening Mail* appears to have suffered a marked decline in this period, but this is not so great as the decline in the two London evening papers. (By 1973, in fact, both Coventry and Wolverhampton show an increase in circulation although the *Birmingham Evening Mail* shows a further slight decline.)

Readership figures for 1963 for the three evening papers shown in Table 17 are simply based on estimates and subjective data but do help to show that these papers penetrate a significant percentage of houses and that there is very little overlap of readership. Thus, expansion for these newspapers is not an increase in size of distribution area but a

TABLE 16. Average daily circulations of British daily papers
London evening papers, provincial evening papers and weeklies

	1963	1970
BRITISH DAILY PAPERS		
Daily Express	4,224,148	3,518,664
Daily Mail	2,479,466	1,814,331
Daily Mirror	4,630,964	4,443,584
Sun	—	1,721,533
Daily Telegraph	1,290,012	1,415,656
Guardian	266,243	304,102
The Times	254,754	375,055
LONDON EVENING PAPERS		
London *Evening News*	1,387,623	1,016,478
London *Evening Standard*	729,241	530,040
PROVINCIAL EVENING PAPERS		
Birmingham Evening Mail	404,169	375,693
Wolverhampton *Express and Star*	235,347	233,425
Coventry Evening Telegraph	109,863	127,958
WEEKLIES		
Walsall Observer	48,443	44,726
Smethwick Telephone	18,264	28,475
(*Warley News Telephone*, from 1966)		

Source: Audit Bureau of Circulations Ltd.

TABLE 17. Readership figures for West Midlands evening newspapers[1]

	Birmingham Evening Mail	Coventry Evening Telegraph	Wolverhampton Express and Star
Total readership			
Number	928,000	295,000	613,000
Percentage	57	67	54
Readership by occupational status (percentage)			
ABC_1	61	58	46
C_2DE	59	70	57
Readership by age (percentage)			
16–44	58	68	52
45 and over	61	65	56
Overlap readership (percentage)			
Birmingham Evening Mail	—	7	11
Coventry Evening Telegraph	2	—	—
Wolverhampton *Express and Star*	5	—	—

1. Figures for weeklies not available.
Source: Evening Newspaper Advertising Bureau Survey, 1963.

greater penetration into the chosen area. Although there are no figures available for the weekly press, Paul Foot estimates that 95 per cent of homes in the Warley area receive the *Warley News Telephone*.

The picture of readership presented in Table 17 does also seem to be

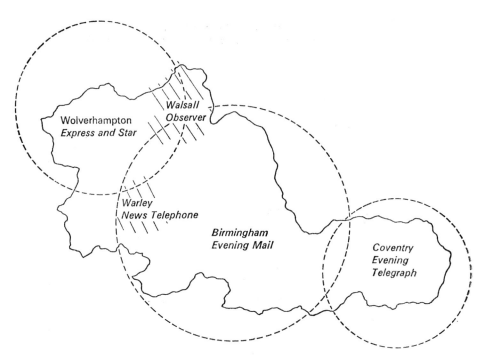

FIG. 2. Diagrammatic representation of circulation of five West Midlands newspapers: *Coventry Evening Telegraph*, *Birmingham Evening Mail*, *Walsall Observer*, *Warley News Telephone*, Wolverhampton *Express and Star*.

of an unstratified family audience. There is no significant difference in readership of social classes or age groups. Readership for national newspapers is very closely defined in terms of class: i.e. the so-called 'populars' are read more by classes C_2DE and the 'qualities' by ABC_1 although there is obviously some overlap.

Advertising and finance

More will be said later about the proportion of space in these papers taken up by different types of content. However, it is relevant to point out here that in all these provincial newspapers, advertising takes up about half the total space and is an important selling feature of the papers. Advertising, as in the press in general, is essential for the continuance of these papers. About two-thirds of the evening papers' revenue comes from advertising, whereas for the weekly papers it is as much as 80 per cent or more.

The provincial press in the West Midlands does show the characteristics typical of the provincial press in the United Kingdom. It can thus be justifiably used as an example of the provincial press in the United Kingdom in relation to the way in which it selects, develops and positions articles with a racial content.

The provincial press
as a cultural institution

The strength of the provincial newspaper lies in the service that it gives to its own region, a service which cannot be offered by newspapers published elsewhere. While a provincial must aim at being a 'complete' newspaper, it must provide its readers with news of their own local and district affairs, in short, become 'their newspaper'. It must mirror the region it serves and while aiming to command its readers' interest, must labour to deserve their trust.[1]

Little has been written on the British provincial press as a cultural institution—a reflection of both the relatively underdeveloped state of mass-media study, and its general concentration on national institutions. As we have pointed out, however, for many people at least half of the media news to which they are exposed is either local in origin or has been given a particular local perspective. The local flavour of much of what is thought of as news does not only apply to newspaper readership, where access to a national daily will be more than counterbalanced by an essentially local evening and a wholly local weekly. Much news output on television is also locally focused. Thus, the six o'clock national television news bulletin on both BBC and ITV is followed by longer regionally based programmes which offer local 'human interest' stories which are rarely, if ever, included in the national bulletin. The growth of local radio has further expanded the availability of news bulletins and programmes in which local events are given as much—if not more—prominence than those occurring at a national level.

Local newspapers are concerned to portray local as opposed to national events in the context of parochial or provincial rather than national identity. The issues they define as important, debate about which appears in editorials and letters, are generally confined to the town or city, though more general issues may be touched upon if they have implications for the locality or for the core values to which the locality adheres. Such examples might be crime, comprehensive education, or 'permissiveness'. They are differentiated from daily national newspapers less by their functions than by their perspectives. The layout of local newspapers is again similar to the nationals. It has tended to become more so in the period under review, with the two local weeklies in our sample reducing the size of their pages to approximate to a more tabloid form. It is however more moderate than that of the 'popular' dailies with less strident headlines and a more conservative use of photographs. All the newspapers in our sample, except the *Birmingham Evening Mail*, had one page on which the editorial, some sort of feature, and readers' letters appeared. This formalization of a debating forum is a common characteristic of British newspapers. Local papers, like dailies, carry regular news on sport, discursive articles on entertainment, and a specialized women's column or page. One important difference from the nationals is a much less clear-cut distinction between news and features. There is still some distinction in the evenings, but in the weeklies the heavy stress on human

1. *Birmingham Post* (Centenary Edition), 7 December 1957.

interest and local personalities as part of the news tends to leave only religious, gossip and gardening columns clearly distinguishable from ordinary news.

There are, further, differences between the two main kinds of local newspapers we have chosen to study—the evenings and the weeklies. They operate different kinds of local 'filters' on the news and pass different kinds of material through these filters. The evenings in particular are continuously faced with problems of selection, especially in choosing to emphasize local or non-local events. The choice of lead story is a case in point: local it generally is, but a dramatic national event not covered by the morning dailies will take prominence if felt to be important enough. For the weekly, such problematic choices do not have to be made. The lead story is the most 'newsworthy' event to have happened in the town during the past week. There is still of course an act of selection, but it is from a limited amount of material. National and international political crises, wars, famines, crashes and crimes, all of which must be scrutinized by evening newspaper staff, do not exist as news for the local weekly. Neither are there problems of identifying to the readership new characters in the drama of news.

Most weeklies are aimed at a small, sharply defined circulation area; the local institutions and community leaders will be relatively familiar to the readership. The editor's task is largely one of finding room for all the local news and cramming so many local names into the paper that he includes some known—in either a private or a public capacity—to every reader.[1]

Another difference between the two kinds of local newspapers in selecting the news is the balance between 'normal' and 'abnormal' news, or as Jackson usefully puts it, between 'order' and 'disorder' news. The evenings, closer to daily papers' definition of news as dramatic and sensational, are more likely to give special prominence to 'abnormal' or 'disorder' news, though it is as well to bear in mind Jackson's qualification that their presentation of such events is more like 'quality' than 'popular' daily newspapers. The weeklies do not subscribe to the established media maxim that 'the normal is not news'. They are precisely the place where the normal is news, and the principal rationale for the reading and writing of the local newspaper is to present the normal as newsworthy and thus as significant.

Jackson documents several kinds of news story, distinctive of the weekly local press, which serve to expose and confirm the normal. The local hero, for example, has overcome personal handicap, led the local community against bureaucratic threat, or demonstrated bravery in an accident. Jackson suggests:

News of them affords the reader solid grounds for reassurance about the patterns of local life, and suggests that not all young people are vandals, nor older ones crooks. Furthermore, it enhances the image of the community by revealing that amongst its citizens are people who can be admired for something more substantial than synthetic well-knownness.

1. Jackson, op. cit., p. 54.

Certain kinds of human-interest stories are selected by the local press for their ultratypicality, whereas the national press would use the criterion of atypicality. Long service with a firm, a golden wedding anniversary, a scholarship to Oxford—these appear in the local press as confirmation of the significance of ordinary local people's achievements and of the life styles and values which lie behind them.

There are then some differences between evening and weekly local papers in what they consider to be news—the process of selection. However, when it comes to interpreting events—what is called the process of signification; the provincial newspapers as a whole share the same assumptions some of which appear to be different from those made by daily newspapers:

If the popular daily, in seeking to entertain its readers, tends to stress aspects of deviation from institutional norms, the local press for the most part reports news which exemplifies institutional values and shows them to be actively held.[1]

Thus, even when conflict is presented as in local government, it appears in muted and superficial terms as a study of the Liverpool local press suggested.[2]

Of particular significance was the papers' attitude to conflict and controversy. They appeared to believe in a world in which the answers to a problem, if not self-evident, were susceptible of yielding to the scrutiny of 'reasonable' men. They either seemed unaware of the existence of inherent conflicts of interests between groups in the town or they chose to report politics as if these did not exist. Conflicts were dutifully reported; but the stress was almost always on the effects, rarely the causes. It was rare for the paper to take sides openly. Usually an appeal to reason, to 'the good of the town', a plea against immoderate language, was made. This provided in many cases a convenient way of appearing to make a constructive contribution without having to offend anyone by actually offering a lead to public opinion.

The provincial press appears to have taken upon itself the role of presenting the local community as basically a harmonious one—an image which as will be seen later has important implications for its interpretation of race. The potential anxiety about 'bad' news is overcome not by moral crusading in editorials or by the diversions of cartoons and jokes, pin-ups and sport—as so often seems the case in popular dailies—but by giving prominence to 'good' news.

Crimes, accidents and disasters may multiply and cause anxiety but the animal kingdom and the human life-cycle—especially birth, long marriage, and working service, and survival to a ripe old age—continue to afford an important staple of news balance for the local press.[3]

This kind of confirmation has a powerfull pull—one which other mass media, especially television, seem unable to exercise effectively in news

1. Jackson, op. cit., p. 116.
2. H. Cox and D. Morgan, *City Politics and the Press*, p. 133, Cambridge University Press, 1973.
3. Jackson, op. cit., p. 107.

form, though the success of such series as *Coronation Street* and *Crossroads* seem to work on the same principle as that noted by Jackson:

such reports assume a reader curiosity about the relationships of others, and meet any need for reassurance that the basic human values and institutions (e.g. the loyalties and security of marriage) are being carried on.

The provincial press is here clearly involved in managing a view of the social world. They may of course believe that they are merely presenting what their readers want, which in turn may have real roots, as in traditional working-class culture:

Working-class people are only rarely interested in theories or movements. They do not usually think of their lives as leading to an improvement in status or some financial goal. They are enormously interested in people. They have the novelist's fascination with individual behaviour—though not so as to put them into a pattern, but for their own sake . . . they are exercising their strong traditional urge to make life intensely human, to humanize it in spite of everything and so make it, not simply bearable, but positively interesting.[1]

The evidence of letters to the provincial press suggests the homely conservatism of such papers is widely shared by the readers:

The positive values held within the conventional wording and tone of protest include justice, humanity, civility, and social awareness. It is felt to be imperative that people should be able to call their homes their own, have sufficient money to live in warmth and comfort, and enjoy adequate basic services.[2]

Here is one key to the secret of the provincial press's almost unique appeal across class barriers. At the top the successful appeal is made to civic pride and the interests of the town, in the middle, to loosely defined principles of citizenship and at the bottom, to the rightness of everyday living.

Yet it may be questioned whether the provincial press can adequately define its role in terms of its readers' expectations. For the provincial press to reflect and confirm conventional ideas about the world and to ignore or attack deviations from them, is to add a special kind of ideological weight to the process of cultural conflict and change. It involves support not only for conventional values, but for institutions which allegedly express them. There is thus portrayed a culturally defined community of interest which allows evasion of conflict in the arenas of economic and political power. Not surprisingly, the family is the cornerstone of this culturally constructed conservatism. Provincial newspaper editors seem unanimous that their 'family readership' is an important determinant of what they print. And what they then print is often a continuous eulogy of the family. The argument is circular, and involves the crucial evasion of the family as itself an area of cultural conflict:

the family readership is seen as working against the inclusion of detailed reports that might be construed as salacious or distasteful; as a result, the

1. R. Hoggart, *Uses of Literacy*, p. 105, Penguin, 1965.
2. Jackson, op. cit., p. 152.

image that a community is given of itself is enhanced. In the long term particular readerships may conclude—that their communities at least are 'respectable'—even if the rest of the country seems to be degenerating.[1]

It is precisely this capacity to represent the average, the normal, the status quo as the humane, the good, the unchallengeably right, which constitutes one of the most powerful cultural thrusts in British life. It is an ideology—it has its beliefs and principles, a programme for society, an ideal of human relationships—but is all the more powerful for appearing as common sense.

Thus, the conservative influence of the provincial press is not primarily to do with party allegiance, although that is powerful enough. It is much more its ideological construction of the world through news which is most profoundly conservative. That substantially is Ian Jackson's conclusion to his detailed study:

This study of the provincial press has revealed that it is essentially a conservative medium. It strongly upholds family and institutional life; it typically demands discipline in regard to penology and education; it values conventions and traditions. Broadly speaking it endorses capitalistic assumptions and the Protestant Ethic.[2]

It is not being denied here that the provincial press does pay more than lip service to a notion of its own responsibility to the local community. There is certainly a more intimate relationship between producers and audience than almost anywhere else in the mass media, as Raymond Williams has pointed out:

There is a comparatively simple and visible social structure [in] the local paper: under some pressure, certainly, and with several contradictory features of chain ownership and monopoly, but still normally expressing a common experience which is there quite apart from the newspaper itself: of living in a particular place, sharing certain local needs and interests, facing certain local problems. The style of local newspapers—in journalistic terms often 'old-fashioned'—expresses at least this minimum level of known identity and relationship. It quite often abuses this sense of community, for political reasons, but as a structure it is still of the general kind I am offering to distinguish. The paper is to an important extent written *with* people if not *by* them; and in the sense that it is written *for* them this can be defined, quite reasonably, in terms of an interest larger than the paper itself: the interest of the local community.[3]

The subculture of local journalists certainly experiences forms of common interest. Reporters are not only likely to get face-to-face feedback from those they write about, but also live and have often been brought up in the community whose interest the local newspaper purports to represent. This is clearly a different content of newspaper production from that of the daily whose public remains undifferentiated and anonymous. There remains, however, a question of what this 'interest of the local community'

1. Jackson, op. cit., p. 41.
2. ibid., p. 278.
3. R. Williams, 'Radical and/or Respectable in Boston, *The Press we Deserve*, Routledge & Kegan Paul, 1970.

is and how it came to be formed historically. The local paper does not simply reflect this interest; it is a, if not in many cases the, crucial agency in forming and articulating this interest. If, as we have seen, conflict, disorder and dissent do not compose part of this interest, is not a falsely harmonious image of the community's interest being projected? And if it is not in the newspaper's commercial interest to criticize local business even at the level of consumer affairs does this make such criticism not in the interests of the community as a whole?

While Williams is correct to assert the qualitatively different nature of producer–public relations in the local press as compared with the national press, this should not lead us to deduce that such differences make local newspapers significantly different in their cultural role from other media. As a cultural institution, the provincial press appears to be different from the national press—in criteria of newsworthiness, in editorial appeals; in human interest stories, in layout, there are practices distinctive of the local press alone. Yet it would be a mistake to assume that the provincial press is therefore performing a cultural role which is independent of that of the mass media as a whole. The local press does not make sense unless it is understood, as it is read, as part of a complex of news media. The essential question then is what specialist role the local newspaper has within a range of news forms which may be available. To take papers alone, it is not impossible to imagine one working-class or lower middle-class family which could have delivered a popular daily, a local evening, several Sunday newspapers and a local weekly all within the space of a few days. Superficially the world of such Sundays as *The People* and the *News of the World*—sex, sensation and soccer—are poles apart from the decent routine news of 'the local'. The contradiction, however, may not be as sharp as it at first appears. If, as has been argued, all newspapers are in the business of producing consensus, the differences between them may only be in the kind and form of consensus produced. The style and tone of news and editorials may differ between 'quality' and 'popular' daily newspapers, but their conclusions may be similar. The same may be true of the differences between national and provincial newspapers. The local press may thus complement rather than contradict the national press, confirming that there is a good life to be led, despite the bizarre and the ugly; that people are still people despite politicians and permissiveness; that the town is still a meaningful community despite the spread of conurbations and the reorganization of local government. The cultural role of provincial newspapers may thus be to provide continuity and moral confirmation for established ways of living through its interpretation of local affairs. In so doing, it is not an alternative, but a back-up, to other news media which offer a consensual interpretation of the world at a national and international level. It brings the message home.

Chapter 3

Race in the West Midlands press: overseas news

There are three ways in which overseas news can be seen as related to race. The most immediately obvious relationship is when news from abroad is about relations between races overseas. While there are many countries where majority-minority racial situations exist, such news is likely, for a variety of reasons discussed below, to come from South Africa and Rhodesia, and the United States of America. A second sort of overseas news which can be related to race in this country is that which provides information about the home countries of immigrants to the United Kingdom. This may be especially important in forming ideas of how stable and 'civilized' such countries are. For this reason we included in our sample, whether about race or not, all news from the Indian sub-continent and from the West Indies. Thirdly, there is news from abroad which forms a composite image of what happens when black people are freed from the white man's influence, especially if such black people are seen as racially similar to immigrants to the United Kingdom. This consideration led us to include news from Black Africa as a likely component of a composite image of the negro in an international context.

Two kinds of news perspectives are brought to bear on these three sorts of overseas news. In one, the news is represented as coming directly from overseas and as being without any immediate implications for the British race situation. In the other, news from overseas is portrayed as having such implications and takes the form of speeches, organized activity, and expressions of public opinion in this country, often implying some action, voluntary or governmental, by the British people themselves. This distinction between 'direct-overseas' and 'home-overseas' news was more important to the news coverage than the country from which the news originated, and we shall discuss overseas news on the basis of this distinction.

Our pilot study had led us to believe that overseas news of all kinds would not constitute more than at maximum a quarter of all race-related material appearing in our sample of the West Midlands press. We, therefore, decided not to code the items under the same topics and subtopics as those used for coding home news. (We did however use these as reference themes.) South Africa, Rhodesia and the United States had subtopics designed for their particular race-relations situations (see Appendix 1). West Indian, Indian and Black African news was at first coded under the general subtopics provided by the Leicester study: politics, economic situation, public disorder and birth control. These subtopics prove unsatisfactory especially as that of birth control produced no items at all, and our extension of overseas news to Black Africa left 'public disorder' too vague. We therefore recoded at the end all news from India, Black Africa and the West Indies under subtopics we considered would help us to pinpoint the images conveyed by such news, those of (a) politics; (b) 'underdevelopment' (both economic and cultural); (c) riots and civil disorder within the country; (d) war involving two existent or potential nations; (e) natural disaster including accidents and famines; and (f) others.

Thus, though our approach was broadly comparable to that adopted by the Leicester study, there are some significant differences in the definition of which overseas news was race-related, and how some of it should be coded. In the discussion which follows, we shall consider evening and weekly newspapers as two separate groups, as we shall also do in relation to British material. Evening and weekly newspapers differ in frequency in format and in the criteria of newsworthiness they employ. The different samples would also make the addition of evening column-inch measurements to those of the weeklies of little value. We have thus divided our findings into the following sections: (a) the amount and distribution of overseas material in the evenings; (b) direct overseas material in the evenings as an aggregate; (c) home overseas material in the evenings as an aggregate; (d) differences between evening papers in their presentation of overseas news; and (e) home overseas material in the weeklies.

Overseas news in the evening papers

Our expectation, based on our pilot study, that all race-related overseas news in the evening papers would amount to less than a quarter of race-related home material was fulfilled, as Table 18 may indicate.

TABLE 18. Race-related news in the evening papers, 1963–70 (measurements in column inches)

British material	'Home-overseas'	'Direct-overseas	Total
14,022 (78 per cent)	1,565 (9 per cent)	2,309 (13 per cent)	17,896 (100 per cent)

Overseas news as a whole thus constitutes an average of 22 per cent of all race-related material, though there are already evident differences between papers we shall discuss later. Unlike British material which increases dramatically throughout the 1963–70 periods, overseas race-related material decreases. Dividing the eight years into two halves illustrates this (see Table 19).

TABLE 19. Overseas race-related news, 1963–70 (in column inches)

Type of overseas news	1963–66	1967–70	1963–70
Direct	1,418	891	2,309
Home	907	658	1,565
TOTAL	2,325	1,549	3,874

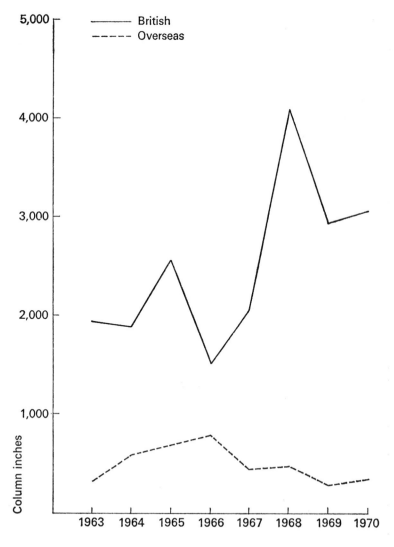

FIG. 3. British and overseas race-related material.

The contrast with British material is illustrated in Figure 3. We must note here an inverse relationship, apparently especially in the period 1965–68, between British and overseas race-related material. We suspect this is more than accidental, but examining the extent and significance of such a relationship is beyond the scope of this study.

A more general impression of the chronological distribution of 'direct' and 'home' overseas news may be gained from the bar graph (Fig. 4). Events in South Africa, Rhodesia and Black Africa are seen as having more implications for British people than those in the United States, West Indies or the Indian subcontinent. This demonstrates that past and present colonial responsibilities have more newsworthiness than the background of black immigrants to this country. Yet even the focus on Africa is a narrow one as Table 20 may show.

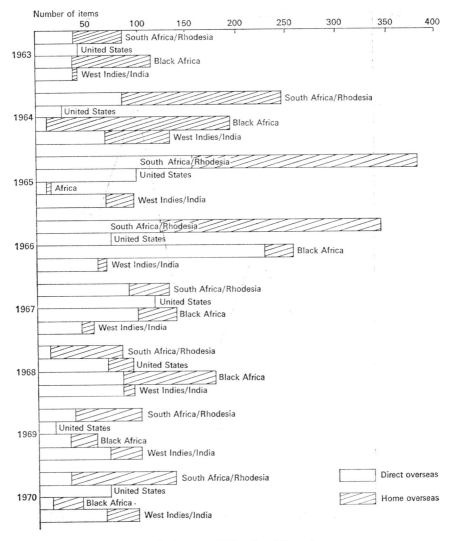

FIG. 4. A chronological distribution of 'direct' and 'home' overseas news.

TABLE 20. Forms of race-related material in evening papers
by number of items

	News items	Cartoons	Editorials	Features	Letters	Photos	Total
South Africa	39		1	2	5		47
Rhodesia	76		5	5	8		94
United States	58		1	3	1		63
West Indies	13			4	1		18
India	56		2	4	3	3	68
Black Africa	60	1	2	10	1	3	77
Other	10			2		1	13
TOTAL	312	1	11	30	19	7	380

Features are rare: only one in every twenty editions. Even less frequent are letters and editorials.

Our basic data demonstrates that overseas race-related material as a whole in the evening papers constitutes less than one-fifth of all race-related material. It declines over the period as a whole apparently in an inverse relationship to the rise in British race-related material. There are variations in the declared implications of news from different countries, and these generally derived from third parties (politicians, clergy, relief organizations, etc.), the papers themselves restricting background detail and comment. Doubtless it would be argued by editors that the superficiality of their presentation of race-related overseas material is an inevitable result of the priority given to local affairs, and is balanced by the daily papers' more detailed and lengthy treatment. Whatever the reasons, the effect is that race overseas appears in the provincial evening press only as dramatic conflict without history or logic.

Direct-overseas news in the evening papers

The distribution between countries of race-related overseas news in the three evening papers is shown in Table 21.

TABLE 21

Country of origin	Column inches	Percentage
South Africa	136	4
Rhodesia	472	21
United States	477	21
West Indies	94	4
India	378	17
Black Africa	647	28
Other	105	5
TOTAL	2,309	100

These differences were reflected in the average length of item —14 column inches for Black Africa, 12 inches for Rhodesia, 8–9 inches for India, West Indies and the United States, and 6 inches for South Africa.

It must be noted that news from the United States was in these papers as important a 'direct-overseas' reference point as that from South Africa and Rhodesia. If our argument about the racial significance of news from Black Africa is correct, it provided a dramatic portrait of instability in countries where the black man was self-governing. India more temperately provided another example. News from the West Indies was consistently low and would have been even less had not Anguilla been included in this category. We now propose to look at what kind of material news from each country provided.

South African news is concentrated in 1963 and 1964 which together provide twice as much direct overseas material as the subsequent six years. Of twenty-two items, two each come under pro- and anti-apartheid comments, two more are about political trials, six cover more general aspects of black and white conflict and ten are unclassifiable.

Rhodesia dominates overseas news from 1965 to 1967 and is basically concerned with the Unilateral Declaration of Independence (UDI), accounting for fifteen out of forty items. Overseas comment on UDI is equally divided between supporters and opponents of the régime. Such comments account for a further nine items. Of the remaining sixteen stories, nine come under 'other', six describe black-and-white conflict and one is an account of a political trial.

United States news also reaches its peak during 1965–67, and is overwhelmingly concerned with the civil-rights movement though, later, the emphasis is on reports of violent demonstrations and race riots. Together these account for 33 out of 54 items. Of the remainder, five are about black organizations and 16 of a more general kind. There are no items under the subtopic of 'efforts to calm the situation'.

A pattern emerges in the distribution of news from these three countries which may be seen as related to later discussion about race in the United Kingdom. There is less news from such countries after 1968, but from 1965 to 1967, the incubation period for the epidemic of anti-black immigrant feeling which breaks out in 1968, news from abroad is portraying black and white people as locked in conflict, and such conflict as an established crisis in South Africa, Rhodesia and the United States.

At the same time there is an increase, though less concentrated, in the amount of news emanating from those countries—Black Africa and India—where black people have insisted on and gained independence from European countries. The bulk of this news is concerned with dramatic and extreme events. Accidents and famine—as 'natural' disasters—are only one part of the drama, which is more predominantly civil and international wars.

News from the Indian subcontinent is mainly about India and not Pakistan, and totals fifty items. One-third are about political developments, notably the death of Nehru in 1964, the build-up to the Indo-Pakistan war in the same year and the electoral triumph of Mrs Gandhi in 1967. Natural disasters provide twelve items, especially a tidal wave in 1963 and a cyclone in 1970. The war between India and Pakistan dominates news from the subcontinent in 1965 and 1966 (nine items). An equal number of items cover riots and disorders which take especially dramatic forms. A few headlines may illustrate.

Forces Open Fire in Assam Riot—*Birmingham Evening Mail*, 10 August 1966.
Thirty Killed in Bengal Riots—Wolverhampton *Express and Star*, 11 March 1966.
Shots Fired by Calcutta Police—*Coventry Evening Telegraph*, 23 November 1967.

Such events have no background, least of all that of the general economic and cultural situations which we classified as the subtopic 'underdevelopment'. No items of direct-overseas news were recorded under that heading for the Indian subcontinent.

The portrait of Black Africa is similarly drawn with little reference to underdevelopment—only one 3-inch comment on the Tanzanian harvest prospects, out of a total of forty-five items. Black African items tend to be longer than those from India, partly because they are more dramatic. Thus, though politics accounts for nearly half (twenty) of the items, they are hardly routine:

Zanzibar Takeover—*Coventry Evening Telegraph*, 13 January 1964.
Nkrumah Overthrown—Wolverhampton *Express and Star*, 24 February 1966.
Clampdown in Uganda After President Shot—*Birmingham Evening Mail*, 20 December 1969.

The line between politics and riots and civil disorder (eleven items) is hard to draw, and the first is often presented in terms of the second.

At Least 62 Die in Tribal Fighting—Wolverhampton *Express and Star*, 10 April 1963.
Congo Mob Captures Embassy Staff—*Birmingham Evening Mail*, 24 October 1966.

Early in the period such images abound, and are reinforced by images of war in the Congo (eight items). A couple of articles on famine as a general problem and three unclassified stories complete the portrait of Black Africa.

The Indian subcontinent and Black Africa are sources of information about self-governing black countries which we have suggested are used as indications of how civilized—in politics culture and economy—the black man is when left to his own devices. The structure of direct-overseas news from these countries in the West Midlands evening press is such that it confirms the findings of Galtung and Ruge about news from nations which are 'culturally distant' and 'low in international rank'. They conclude that:[1]

From such countries, news will have to refer to people, preferably top elite, and be preferably negative and unexpected but nevertheless according to a pattern

1. J. Galtung and M. H. Ruge, 'The Structure of Foreign News', in J. Tunstall (ed.), *Media Sociology*, p. 271, London, Constable, 1970.

that is consonant with the mental pre-image. It will have to be simple and it should, if possible, provide the reader with some kind of identification—it should refer to him or his group of nations. This will in turn, facilitate an image of these countries as dangerous, as ruled by capricious elites, as unchanging in their basic characteristics as existing for the benefit of the top-dog nations and in terms of their links to those nations. Events occur, they are sudden, like flashes of lightning, with no build up and no letdown after their occurrence—they just occur and more often than not as a part of the machinations of the ruling or opposing elites.

Dilip Hiro has come to the same conclusion in his discussion of the 'stream of random images' which constitute British newspapers coverage of events in Africa and Asia:[1]

Like all news, these images are centred around conflicts, tensions, political upheavals, wars and famines. Violent anarchy in the Congo, the raping of white nuns by African soldiers, civil war in Nigeria, a coup d'état in Ghana, near revolution in Pakistan, starvation in Biafra and India—the list is endless, and will continue to be so for the simple statistical fact that Asia and Africa account for two-thirds of the world's population.
   The few sophisticated liberals and radicals may view these convulsions as an essential part of the social and economic development of these continents recently freed from the yoke of European imperialism. But for the many, these images provide continuing evidence that peoples of coloured races are indeed inherently anarchic, violent and quite incapable of self-help and self-rule.

It may be argued that the very local nature of the provincial press precludes it from covering any but the most dramatic of overseas news. We doubt this and our examination of differences between papers in their overseas coverage will show that such news does not select itself. Yet even if it were granted that a local newspaper is bound to carry only a relatively small amount of overseas news, there remains the question of presentation, of how far the news-worthy dramatic event is given any coherence or rationale. The failure of our attempt to apply reference themes to direct-overseas items is illuminating in this respect.
   It was not simply that reference themes derived from the home context of race relations were irrelevant to overseas situations. The issues of housing and education, for example, could be present in the portrayal of race relations abroad, at least in South Africa, Rhodesia and the United States, and they are not irrelevant to the development of the Indian subcontinent, West Indies and Black Africa. We found hardly any such references—two to education in Rhodesia, none at all to housing in any country. Most reference themes were incestuous—one dramatic aspect of the Rhodesian situation was referred to another in the same country, or to immediate reaction in Black Africa. If we exclude references within or between countries, we find hardly any reference themes at all for the 229 direct-overseas stories. South Africa and Rhodesia between them provided nine references each to white hostility and sport and enter- tainment. References to discrimination were few (eight) and occurred mainly in the United States context. That country provided the most

1. D. Hiro, *Black British, White British*, p. 295, London, Pelican, 1973.

powerful association of all, occurring twelve times, between black people and crime. This indicates—in slight form—a relationship which reappears massively in home news in the local press.

The evidence from reference themes tends to confirm that the presentation of direct-overseas news in the West Midlands evening press is relatively self-contained, superficial, and not contextualized. This is true of all three kinds of race-related material. That from multi-racial societies stresses intermittent violent conflict without historical cause or future solution. That from immigrants' home countries give little information about ordinary everyday life but stresses the dramatic and violent. That which contributes to an image of black self-government stresses the primitive and disorderly nature of politics and culture in such countries. It is hard not to conclude that such overseas material involves crude racial stereotyping which cannot but be injurious to British race relations.

It remains to see whether such stereotyping is in any way avoided in the discussion and action around the implications of direct-overseas news for British people, in what we have called 'home-overseas news'.

Home-overseas material
in the evening papers

The function of home-overseas material is to make explicit the significance of race-related events overseas for British people. This may be done through the agency of British people with particular interest in such events—a government spokesman, the head of a charitable organization, or a church leader. Equally, however, such implications may be drawn by the newspaper itself through editorials and features, or by the paper's readers writing letters on the subject. This may become clearer if we look at a table comparing the different news forms taken by direct-overseas and home-overseas news (Tables 22 and 23).

Though both predominantly take the form of 'hard' news stories, home-overseas produces slightly more features, and substantially more editorials and letters. Such differences are mainly accounted for by Rhodesia but there are also more home-overseas editorials features and letters on South Africa, the Indian subcontinent and Black Africa. This indicates that events in such countries are seen more in terms of British responsibilities and interests than in their own terms.

By and large, home-overseas news feeds off direct-overseas news. A graph of its chronological development (Fig. 5) follows closely that of direct-overseas news. There are however differences in the amount of British reaction dependent on the country from which the news originates (Table 23). South Africa and Rhodesia produce 27 per cent of news directly from overseas but account for 52 per cent of home-overseas news. Conversely news from the United States and the Indian subcontinent is seen as having minimal implications for the British people. Black Africa is the only region to have a fairly constant relationship between direct news and reaction in the United Kingdom. The average length of home-overseas story is very similar to that of direct-overseas story—Rhodesia

TABLE 22. Home-overseas and direct-overseas items by form

Country	News	Cartoons	Editorials	Features	Letters	Photos	Total items
Home-overseas							
South Africa	18		1	1	5		25
Rhodesia	41		5	3	5		54
United States	7		1		1		9
West Indies	4			3	1		8
India	12		1	2	3		18
Black Africa	21	1	1	6	1	2	32
Other	5						5
TOTAL FORM	108	1	9	15	16	2	151
Percentage of items	72		6	10	11	1	100
Direct-overseas							
South Africa	21			1			22
Rhodesia	35			2	3		40
United States	51			3			54
West Indies	9			1			10
India	44		1	2		3	50
Black Africa	39		1	4		1	45
Other	5			2		1	8
TOTAL FORM	204		2	15	3	5	229
Percentage of items	89		1	7	1	2	100

TABLE 23. Overseas news by country of origin

Country	Home-overseas		Direct-overseas	
	Column inches	Percentage of whole	Column inches	Percentage of whole
South Africa	178	11	136	6
Rhodesia	727	47	472	20
United States	64	4	477	21
India	134	9	378	16
West Indies	83	5	94	4
Black Africa	336	21	647	28
Other	43	3	105	5
TOTAL	1,565	100	2,309	100

and Black Africa the longest (10–11 column inches), South Africa, the Indian subcontinent and the United States the shortest (7 inches).

To summarize, home-overseas news depends chronologically on direct-overseas news but takes more discursive forms. It concentrates more on South Africa, Rhodesia and Black Africa than on other countries. Hence, home-overseas news differs from direct-overseas news in form and focus. There are also some differences in content.

News from South Africa is often given a specific local perspective and does not always fit our subtopic classification. A story headed 'Coventry

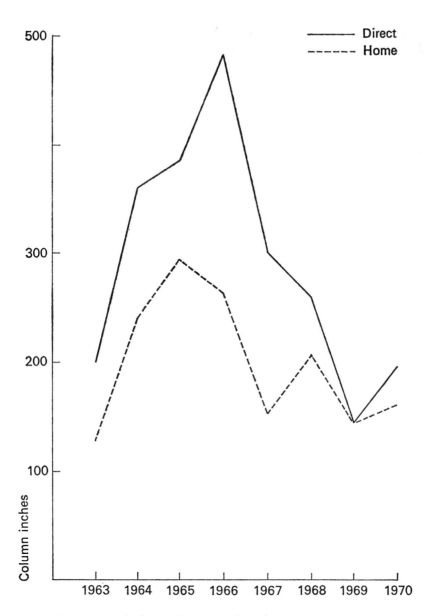

FIG. 5. Overseas news in the evening papers: chronology.

to Send Civil Flag to South Africa',[1] for example, had to be classified as 'other'. The rest of South African home-overseas news reports British protests against the South African régime especially over arms sales and sports teams in 1963 and 1970. There is only one editorial on the subject[2] approving unreservedly of a local Catholic priest's appeal for all Catholics to oppose apartheid.

1. *Coventry Evening Telegraph*, 4 February 1970.
2. Wolverhampton *Express and Star*, 22 February 1963.

Rhodesian home-overseas news is concerned overwhelmingly with the details of negotiations in and around UDI. There is some feature discussion of the effect of the Rhodesian issue on domestic politics. Editorials[1] take what they believe to be a moderate line, arguing continually for yet further negotiations with the Smith régime. Five letters all show a clearly pro-Smith line and evoke quite straightforward ideas of Rhodesian blacks as uneducated and incapable of self-government. Local opinion on the issue as represented in the evening papers is heavily in favour of the white minority.

Home-overseas coverage of race in the United States consists mainly of British reaction to the death of Martin Luther King, some of which takes the form of using the United States as a warning of what must not be allowed to happen here.

Concern with the West Indies is very small and would be even less but for the Anguilla furore. The remainder consists of celebrities and tourist attractions.

It is in British concern with events in India and Black Africa that home-overseas news introduces an element conspicuously absent from direct-overseas news. This is the theme of 'underdevelopment' as represented in the efforts of British religious and charitable organizations to finance small projects in India and Africa. This represents however only a partial modification of the dramatic image of such countries, which remains strong. Political *coups*, war and natural disaster still provide more home comment than more permanent characteristics. Black Africa also has a high number of unclassifiable items often with a 'human interest' focus.

Home-overseas news basically interprets direct-overseas news through a British perspective. Since direct-overseas news only includes the extreme and dramatic, such interpretation consists mainly of instant opinion on immediate events. Since the events are presented superficially, the reactions have some of the same characteristics. This is true even of the underdevelopment stories where long-term consideration of the economic and cultural situation of Third World countries is ignored in favour of short-term charitable gifts. The pose of the white man as benefactor comes out most clearly in coverage of Rhodesia where black people are perceived as too 'backward' to assume the responsibilities of democratic government. The understanding of race-related overseas events which appears in West Midlands evening papers is narrowly based, and tends to interpret them in racial if not racist terms.

Differences between evening papers

If local papers can only represent a small amount of overseas news, and that of the most dramatic kind, we would expect roughly the same amount and kind of race-related overseas news to appear in each evening

---

1. *Coventry Evening Telegraph*, four; Wolverhampton *Express and Star*, one.

paper. This is demonstrably not so. The papers differ in how much overseas news they report, the forms such news takes, and which countries the news comes from.

A statistical basis for comparison is not easily composed. One paper may have more overseas news proportional to British material because the latter is low, rather than because the former is high. Another may have only 10 per cent of its overseas material from Black Africa compared with a figure of 20 per cent for a different paper, but the absolute number of column inches and items may be the same. We have therefore presented three tables which aim to enable proportionate and absolute comparisons between papers, on the basis of: (a) the amount of home-overseas, direct-overseas, and British race-related material; (b) the forms taken by home-overseas and direct-overseas news according to country of origin; (c) the total amount of coverage given to news from different countries.

The proportions of home-overseas, direct-overseas and British race-related material

The papers differ in the ratio of race-related overseas material to British material and in the distribution of overseas news between the 'home' and 'direct' categories (see Table 24). Thus, the *Coventry Evening Telegraph* provides the most extensive coverage of race-related overseas material (over two-thirds of the British amount) which is divided equally between the 'home' and 'direct' categories; the Wolverhampton *Express and Star* publishes only one-quarter as much overseas material as it does British material, 'direct' news being twice as frequent as home overseas news; the *Birmingham Evening Mail* has proportionately the least overseas material, only one-sixth of the British amount, which takes the form of twice as much 'direct' as 'home' material.

These differences in distribution may affect the way particular events are handled, especially how much 'direct' background is given to an overseas issue presented mainly in the 'home' category. Rhodesia is a

TABLE 24. The proportions of home-overseas, direct-overseas and British race-related material (in column inches). The figures in parentheses are percentages

	Home-overseas	Direct-overseas	Total overseas	British	Total race-related
Birmingham Evening Mail	355	577	932	5,670	6,602
	(5)	(9)	(14)	(86)	(100)
Coventry Evening Telegraph	640	617	1,257	2,101	3,358
	(19)	(18)	(37)	(63)	(100)
Wolverhampton Express and Star	570	1,115	1,685	6,251	7,936
	(7)	(14)	(21)	(79)	(100)
All others	1,565	2,309	3,874	14,022	17,896
	(9)	(13)	(22)	(78)	(100)

case in point. For the *Coventry Evening Telegraph*, Rhodesia is primarily an issue about British policies, with little coverage of background news from Rhodesia itself. Thus, overall coverage of Rhodesia is in the ratio of 4 : 1 between 'home' and 'direct' overseas news. The Wolverhampton *Express and Star* in contrast, contextualizes the 'home' debate in black-and-white conflict in Rhodesia itself. The result is that 'home' and 'direct' coverage of Rhodesia are equal in a 1 : 1 ratio. The two papers thus differ in the extent and kind of news coverage of Rhodesia.

The forms of overseas news

The appearance of an event or issue in features editorials and letters can be taken as an indication of how important the newspapers take the topic to be. Again, there are differences between the papers, as Table 25 shows. Using this criterion the Wolverhampton *Express and Star* appears to give most importance to race-related overseas material, but when allowance is made for differences in the total number of stories, the *Coventry Evening Telegraph* is equally prepared to give detailed consideration to overseas affairs. The Wolverhampton *Express and Star* is particularly strong on Rhodesia and South Africa while the Coventry paper shows more concern with the Indian subcontinent and Black Africa. This last region is the main source of features in the *Birmingham Evening Mail*. Otherwise this paper not only shows the least interest in race-related overseas material generally, but is also the least prepared to cover overseas affairs in anything but news form. It is well to note, however, that for all three papers, more than 80 per cent of overseas items take the form of straightforward news stories.

Overseas news by country of origin

The papers appear to have different rank orders of importance for overseas news according to its country of origin. South Africa is the only country which receives similar proportionate coverage in all three papers (see Table 26). For the rest, each paper differs. The Wolverhampton *Express and Star* is the most idiosyncratic, giving proportionately more coverage than the other papers to Rhodesia, the United States and the Indian subcontinent, but its coverage of Black Africa amounts only to one-third of that present in the other two papers. The *Birmingham Evening Mail* and the *Coventry Evening Telegraph* give similar proportionate attention to South Africa, Rhodesia, and Black Africa, but differ in their coverage of the United States and India, the Birmingham paper favouring the former, and the Coventry paper the latter.

Thus, the three papers differ significantly in the amount of race-related overseas material they print, the form such coverage takes and the countries chosen to be most important. As a result, each paper offers a different portrait of the international background against which the British race-relations situation may be illicitly or explicitly placed. We may briefly indicate the different international perspective on race held by each newspaper.

TABLE 25. Forms of overseas news

	Birmingham Evening Mail						Coventry Evening Telegraph						Wolverhampton Express and Star					
	News	Cartoons	Editorials	Features	Letters	Photos	News	Cartoons	Editorials	Features	Letters	Photos	News	Cartoons	Editorials	Features	Letters	Photos
Home-overseas news																		
South Africa	4						9			1	2		5		1		3	
Rhodesia	11						13		4	1	2		17		1	2	3	
United States	0												7		1		1	
West Indies	0			1			5		1	2	1		4			2	1	
India	4	1	1	4			15			2	1		3				2	
Black Africa	5						3						1					
Other	0											2	2					
TOTAL	24	1	1	5			45		5	6	6	2	39		3	4	10	
(Total number of items)	31						64						56					
Direct-overseas news																		
South Africa	8						6						7			1		
Rhodesia	13				1		8			1			14			2	2	
United States	15			1			14						22			1		
West Indies	3						2						4			1		
India	12						13			1			19			1		1
Black Africa	12		1	1			19		1	2			8			1		3
Other							1						4			2		1
TOTAL	63		1	2	1		63		1	4			78			9	2	5
(Total number of items)	67						68						94					
All overseas combined																		
South Africa	12						15			1	2		12		1	1	3	
Rhodesia	24				1		21		4	2	2		31		1	4	5	
United States	15			1			14						29		1	1	1	
West Indies	3			1			7		1	2	1		8			3	1	
India	16	1	1	4			28			3	1		22			1	2	1
Black Africa	17		1	1			22		1	2			9			1		3
Other	0						1					2	6			2		1
TOTAL	87	1	2	7	1		108		6	10	6	2	117		3	13	12	5
(Total number of items)	98						132						150					

TABLE 26. Overseas news by country of origin (figures in parentheses are percentages)

Country of origin	Direct-overseas				Home-overseas				All-overseas			
	Birmingham Evening Mail	Coventry Evening Telegraph	Wolverhampton Express and Star	Total	Birmingham Evening Mail	Coventry Evening Telegraph	Wolverhampton Express and Star	Total	Birmingham Evening Mail	Coventry Evening Telegraph	Wolverhampton Express and Star	Total
South Africa	52 (9)	38 (6)	46 (4)	136 (6)	30 (8)	75 (12)	73 (13)	178 (11)	82 (9)	113 (9)	119 (7)	314 (8)
Rhodesia	95 (16)	67 (11)	310 (28)	472 (20)	167 (47)	268 (42)	292 (51)	727 (47)	262 (28)	335 (27)	602 (35)	1,199 (31)
United States	140 (24)	116 (19)	221 (20)	477 (21)	—	—	64 (11)	64 (4)	140 (15)	116 (9)	285 (17)	541 (14)
West Indies	27 (5)	12 (2)	55 (5)	94 (4)	7 (2)	—	76 (13)	83 (5)	34 (4)	12 (1)	131 (8)	177 (5)
India	68 (12)	115 (19)	195 (17)	378 (16)	34 (10)	56 (9)	44 (8)	134 (9)	102 (11)	171 (14)	239 (14)	512 (13)
Black Africa	195 (34)	265 (42)	187 (17)	647 (28)	117 (33)	208 (32)	11 (2)	336 (21)	312 (33)	473 (37)	198 (12)	983 (25)
Other	—	4 (1)	101 (9)	105 (5)	—	33 (5)	10 (2)	43 (3)	—	37 (3)	111 (7)	148 (4)
TOTAL	577 (100)	617 (100)	1,115 (100)	2,309 (100)	355 (100)	640 (100)	570 (100)	1,565 (100)	932 (100)	1,257 (100)	1,685 (100)	3,874 (100)

The *Birmingham Evening Mail* appears to treat all race-related overseas news as relatively less significant than the other two papers. In particular its coverage of news from the homelands of immigrants to the United Kingdom is sparse. This paper alone carries no overseas items related to race from any country not on our list. It may be said on balance to be the most parochial of the three papers as far as race is concerned, offering the narrowest and least-detailed international perspective on race relations.

The *Coventry Evening Telegraph* has proportionately more overseas news than the other two papers especially of the 'home-overseas' type. It is particularly interested in local opinion and action related to events in White and Black Africa, and seeks to encourage debate and involvement. It may thus be said to be the most 'internationalist' of the three papers.

The Wolverhampton *Express and Star* consistently differs from the other two in its approach to race-related overseas news. It attempts to give a background of news from Rhodesia against which 'home' debate should take place. It tends to play down the black image provided by news from Black Africa, concerned instead to cover race relations in the United States. The use of United States news as comparison and warning is the most distinctive attribute of its coverage, and helps to construct an international perspective rather different from that in the other two papers.

The differences we have outlined here are only those of the most crude and obvious type. They do not take account of some of the refinements of the content analysis method such as subtopics reference themes or headlines, much less of nuances in tone and image present in news coverage. We have chosen to give a brief indication of the differences to demonstrate the clear and significant process of news selection which provincial papers apply to race-related overseas news.

Home-overseas news in the weeklies

Direct-overseas news never appeared in either of the two weekly papers in our sample. However dramatic race-related overseas events may be, they are not seen as penetrating to the local community, which is presented in its local newspaper as politically and geographically self-contained. The weekly papers did, however, contain some home-overseas news, amounting to 3 per cent of all race-related material appearing in the *Warley News Telephone*, and 7 per cent in the *Walsall Observer*. There is already indicated here a kind of difference in approach we have already examined in the evening papers. The small number of items involved, however, would make detailed comparison of dubious significance and value. We shall, therefore, treat the news in the two papers as an aggregate, with the reservation that the *Walsall Observer* carried a greater proportion of such news. As we shall see later there could be a variety of reasons for this, including the Walsall paper's obsession with 'travellers' as well as the single-mindedness of the paper serving Smethwick.

We may begin then by asking where such news came from and what form it took. Both are represented in Table 27.

TABLE 27. Home-overseas news in the weeklies
(*Warley News Telephone* and *Walsall Observer*)

Country	News stories	Editorials	Features	Cartoons	Photos	Letters	Total items	Total column inches	Column inches (%)
South Africa	3					1	4	37	14
Rhodesia	2		2			6	10	95	35
United States						2	2	8	3
India	5			1			6	31	12
West Indies	1						1	2	1
Black Africa	7		1	1			9	71	26
Other	2						2	25	9
TOTAL	20	0	3	2	0	9	34	269	100

Home-overseas news in the weeklies is dominated by South Africa and Rhodesia which together constitute 49 per cent of the total. Black Africa is the other main source of news (26 per cent) with some from the Indian subcontinent (12 per cent). Since it is difficult to distinguish between news and features in weekly papers, the difference between the appearance of the forms must be ignored. The lack of editorials and photographs is not unexpected; the two cartoons are rather exceptional. Letters do represent a different form of news and demonstrate that race-related home-overseas news appears in the weekly press in different forms depending on the country of origin. South Africa, Rhodesia and the United States appear as matters of local opinion; Black Africa and India through the activities of local groups.

South African and Rhodesian race relations do not appear in news features or editorials but in letters. It is a peculiar function of the letter columns in weekly papers that they may concern themselves with issues which the paper itself does not cover. The column is seen as giving local people an opportunity to 'sound off' about the general state of the world. Some of the letters then can simply assume that an opinion about Rhodesia can stand by itself, without any special reference to local affairs. The debate is stronger, however, if there is such a local reference, and the majority of letters about Rhodesia are provoked by the suggestion put forward by Smethwick's Labour Member of Parliament in 1967 that the British government should use force to suppress the Smith régime. Over half the Rhodesian items, however, are not concerned with suppressing the Smith régime, but with praising it. They do not adopt the 'moderate' line that Smith has to be negotiated with because he is in power, but justify his white supremacist policy as correct, for quite explicitly racial reasons. A writer to the *Walsall Observer* on 6 November 1966 sounds a characteristic note: 'White Rhodesians have done a magnificent job and have made Rhodesia into a wonderful country—white Rhodesians should have our greatest sympathy and support.' On other occasions, emigrants to white-dominated countries openly seek to justify their new homelands, as when a Smethwick couple bound for South Africa in March 1963 suggest that 'the lot of the coloured population in South Africa is not as bad as it is painted in the press'. More subtly, some items, especially reports of business activities, discuss Rhodesia and South Africa without any reference to race. Such items did not appear in our sample, but were often read.

The weekly newspapers' presentation of White Africa either suppresses the race problem or gives voice to support for white supremacy. Such support is often quite openly racist, arguing that the black African is inferior to the white European, who is endeavouring to bring civilization to savage and ungrateful primitives.

News from the Indian subcontinent and Black Africa is more opaque in its presentation of a black image. It does not take the form of local opinion as expressed in letters, but the experience and opinion of local people who have recently visited these countries. The possible sources of such information are limited, since not everyone travels to and from Africa or the Indian subcontinent, and of those who do only some will be able or willing to give public speeches or talks. News from such countries is thus generally provided by those who have visited them in some charitable role offering friendship skills or gifts to overseas populations. Such people generally go under the auspices of a religious or voluntary organization, and it is, as it were, part of their contract that on returning to recount their experiences to those who made it possible for them to go.

Most home-overseas news appearing in these weekly papers which contributes to an image of black people in their natural habitat come through such 'local institutional filters'. Discounting two cartoons, all other items about Africa and the Indian subcontinent (thirteen in all) had such a 'local institutional filter': rotary clubs, 3; voluntary service organizations, 3; trade unions, 2; churches, 2; charity, 1; university, 1; immigrant organization, 1.

All these local institutions imply particular kinds of relationships to the 'black' countries. The local rotary clubs have regular talks and film shows of a general kind about Africa, and are committed to raising funds for specific projects, such as payment for treatment of a 10-year-old East African boy suffering from leprosy. Churches perform a similar role, contributing to a fund for an ambulance to be sent to Pakistan, though they seem intent on sending a missionary also. Three people are going to and from teaching posts in Africa. Freedom From Hunger Campaigners are collecting for famine victims in India; a university group is also to visit India, hoping to help alleviate starvation. Trade union activity includes a reciprocal visit from Kenya railwaymen and a collection for the Pakistan cyclone disaster. The Smethwick Sikh Temple's tribute to President Shastri stands alone in its concern with politics, and its identity as a local immigrant organization.

Such 'local institutional filters' of home-overseas news imply a clear post-colonial relationship with such countries. The individuals involved may have completely altruistic motives; that is not the point. Such news implies uncritical admiration for tokenism and evades more central political questions about the relationship between British citizens and overseas populations. Rare indeed is the Smethwick clergyman who in

November 1970 wrote a letter to his local newspaper advocating a substantial increase in British government overseas aid, and suggesting
opposition to such a move had racialist roots. More often individual acts
of charity are seen as sufficient contribution to the development of backward countries. Such development is always seen as totally unproblematic:
it is simply seen as the attempt to bring 'backward' nations up to British
'standards' and ignores the particular cultural economic and political
traditions of such countries.

Further, there is evidence of racial stereotyping. A story from the
Walsall Observer of 10 September 1963 may serve as illustration. Aldridge
Round Table was about to send a representative to a conference of
business organizations in Southern Rhodesia. It was due to be held at
the University of Southern Rhodesia where 'the Round Table has been
instrumental in establishing a Chair for the study of race relations'. A
send-off party was held:

Members of Aldridge Round Table wore African pith helmets in recognition of a
colleague, then removed them in his honour during celebrations . . .
Grinning war masks, war shields and a cannibal's cooking pot greeted
guests . . .
Mr. Ditchfield was dressed in khaki drill shorts . . . receiving adulations
from the vantage of a native litter . . .
I shall be spending much of my time on return in visiting Tables with a film
and talking about my experience and answering questions [said Mr Ditchfield].
One of our aims is the furthering of better relations between peoples.

The good humour of the occasion, and Mr Ditchfield's undoubted
integrity, do not compensate for the stereotyping of African culture, nor
for the colonialist conceptions of the white man's role in black countries.
Nineteenth-century ideas of Black Africa seem the only reference point
for an organization committed to bettering race relations.

The editorial staff of the *Walsall Observer* and the *Smethwick Telephone*
doubtless feel that in their selection of race-related letters and news
items, they are only seeking to reflect local opinion and activity. That
may be true, but it seems unfortunate that there has to be such a clear
condoning of such images. In the weekly press, race-relations overseas
news assumes either the form of advocating white racist supremacy,
or the reporting of white charity of the most token kind. The arrival
of black- and brown-skinned people to take up residence in local
communities reliant on such racial images is likely to be interpreted as an
affront to the prevalent assumptions of white superiority. The weekly
papers under consideration have done little to question and much to
confirm stereotypes of non-white people derived from an overseas context
but deeply rooted at home.

Summary and conclusion

We may summarize our findings on race-related overseas news in our
sample of the West Midlands press, as follows:
Overseas news can be seen as race-related in three ways representing

information from countries where majority-minority racial groupings exist (South Africa, Rhodesia, United States), countries from which immigrants to the United Kingdom originate (West Indies, Indian subcontinent), and countries where black self-government is a recent occurrence (Black Africa).

In the evening papers, all overseas material accounted for 22 per cent of all race-related material. There was a marked decline in the amount of such news in the second half of the period. It is possible that an inverse relationship exists between the chronological development of overseas and home race-related material.

As judged by the lack of reference themes and news forms other than 'hard' stories, direct-overseas news is relatively self-contained, superficial and lacking in historical perspective.

In 'home-overseas' news, the emphasis is on South Africa and Rhodesia. Editorial opinion on the latter favours compromise with the Smith régime. Reaction to Black Africa includes efforts to aid 'underdevelopment', presentation of which lacks economic or historical perspectives.

There are significant differences between the papers in their presentation of race-related overseas news: its amount, news form and country of origin. As well as indicating different perspectives among the papers, this demonstrates that such news is not self-evident, but subject to a process of news selection.

Home-overseas news in the weeklies tacitly or directly supports white dominant minorities overseas, especially in Rhodesia. A paternalist attitude towards self-governing black countries is evident, especially through the channels of 'local institutional filters'.

Our conclusion has to be that there is little in these papers' presentation of race-related overseas news to suggest that different racial groupings can peacefully coexist, or that there is anything to learn from race relations in overseas countries. When the issues of race relations and immigration emerged in the United Kingdom in dramatic form in 1968, they did so against a news background in which black self-government had been a violent failure (1963–66), white minority groups struggled to maintain their supremacy over black majorities in South Africa and Rhodesia (1965–67), and black minority groups in the United States asserted, first peacefully, then violently, their right to equal treatment (1967–68). As presented, the context is rife for prophets of doom.

It is not being argued here that newspapers should present only 'good' news from White and Black Africa or the United States. Certainly the maintenance of news values which report only 'trouble' about race relations gives an unbalanced portrait of overseas affairs. Yet, as important is the way dramatic events are contextualized; what possibilities of understanding are offered to the reader. The West Midlands papers under review offered little or no explanation for tribal conflict in Nigeria and the Congo, for black guerrilla movements in Southern Africa, for the emergence of the American Civil Rights Movement and its apparent escalation into violent confrontation. Without any explanatory framework, such events appear in newspapers as Hiro's 'stream of random images', unrelated to anything preceding or following. They are thus left open to crude interpretation: violence is the inevitable outcome of black self-government; Rhodesian and South African whites are struggling to avoid such a situation; the United Kingdom will become another United States. The easy solution to prevent racial conflict is to avoid any racial contact at all. Apartheid appears in its international form: immigration control.

We have found no evidence that any of these newspapers were fundamentally and substantially grappling with any interpretation whatsoever of race relations in an international context. It might be argued that local newspapers do not count it as their function to contextualize dramatic overseas stories. That is a task left to the dailies. But this is a circular argument. Just as the assertion that dramatic race-related overseas events must be published since they are newsworthy avoids the question of whether such a definition of newsworthiness should not be altered if its consequences are so damaging, so the argument that local newspapers cannot by definition cover overseas affairs effectively ignores the legitimacy of a provincialism which positively misrepresents race relations overseas. Consideration of race-related overseas news has brought us up against the definitions of news values and of local cultural responsibility operated by these newspapers. As we shall see, they operate as powerfully in the home context.

Chapter 4

Race in the West Midlands press: home news in the evening papers

Topics

Table 28 gives the total coverage of race in the United Kingdom as present in the three evening papers, divided into topics. In contrast to the Leicester study of national dailies where 37 per cent of race-related material was to be found on the topics of race relations and immigration, we found that the two major topic categories in the provincial evenings do

TABLE 28. Aggregate British race coverage by topic: evening papers

Topic	Percentage all column inches	Number column inches	Number items	Average item length (inches)
Crime	18	2,574	311	8.3
Human interest	16	2,260	208	10.9
Race relations	9	1,310	139	9.4
Immigration	8	1,158	116	10.2
Housing	6	797	62	12.9
White hostility	5	743	69	10.8
Cultural differences	5	721	57	12.7
Education	5	688	58	11.9
Discrimination	5	654	62	10.5
Sport and entertainment	4	598	48	12.5
Racial integration	4	565	42	13.5
Immigrant organizations	3	353	45	7.8
Employment	2	263	23	11.4
Health	1	182	24	7.6
Celebrities	1	174	17	10.2
Legislation	1	163	16	10.2
Numbers	1	152	18	8.4
Police	0.6	84	13	6.5
Discrimination by black	0.3	41	3	13.7
Black hostility	0.1	19	3	6.3
Other	5	662	49	12.7
TOTAL	100	14,121	1,383	10.2

not portray relationships between or within racial groups. Over one-third of race news here involves the presentation of individual black people in situations of crime or human interest. We shall argue later that the predominance of these kinds of news has important implications for general problems of method in newspaper analysis, as it raises the problem of the relationship between the presentation of individual black people and the image of black racial groups as a whole. Especially, it demands a means of analysing the mechanisms of typification and stereotyping, a task which seems beyond the scope of conventional content analysis. We can, however, give the general distribution of race news some depth by considering the relative frequency of subtopics, and the overall pattern of reference themes.

When black people appear as individuals in these evening papers, they do so primarily as persons suspected or convicted of crime. Over half such crimes are of a violent kind, as Table 29 shows.

TABLE 29. Crime subtopics

Subtopic	Column inches	Items
Violence	1,299	59
Sexual	18	5
Burglary	36	8
Robbery	142	12
Theft	59	11
Prostitution	40	6
Drugs	168	21
Immigration	123	17
Driving	74	12
Drink	37	5
Parties	75	7
Other crimes	374	39
Crime rate	79	3
Special punishment	4	1
General	46	5
TOTAL	2,574	311

The first subtopic (violence) is a loose category covering everything from common assault to murder. A more subtle classification should perhaps have been employed, but the general picture is clear. These West Midlands evening newspapers are clearly conveying a powerful image of black people as committing crimes of a sort likely to be perceived as especially serious (violence, 50 per cent; robbery, 6 per cent; drugs, 7 per cent; and illegal immigration, 5 per cent). The explanation of such a portrait may well in part lie in the general tendency of the press to define crime as a major category of newsworthy events. That does not alter the contrality of black crime to the portrait of race in the evening papers.

The potentially negative effect of the extensive coverage of crime on the image of black people is not balanced by their almost equally frequent appearance in human-interest stories. We rejected Leicester's label of 'normal', not only because normal news is a contradiction in terms even in the provincial press, but because it suggests that such news is flat and one-dimensional. Human-interest stories, especially when accompanied by a photograph, are replete with cultural meanings. When black people are featured, the situations are often racially charged: black people as victims of white crimes, domestic accidents especially from paraffin fires, runaway teenagers, black beauty queens—such stories may have implicit references to racial tension, overcrowded housing, familial instability, or sexual attitudes. We must thus dissent from Leicester's suggestion that: 'we can regard the . . . normal items as indicating the extent to which the press presents members of coloured minority groups as ordinary members of society not essentially different from other people.'[1] We cannot support our dissent as substantially as we would like, since we could only record explicit reference themes, which occurred 45 times in only 35 of the 208 stories. These were distributed amongst housing (9), cultural differences (6), employment, racial integration and crime (5 each), education (4), white hostility (3), Africa (2), health (2), Powell, immigration, race relations and racial tension (1 each).

We would thus emphasize the absolutely vital role of crime and human interest stories featuring black people as essential, routinized, but far from neutral, components of the presentation of race in these evening papers. We shall see when we examine the chronological pattern of topics that they have a complex relationship with other kinds of news; they are at least clearly not independent. Further examination of the subtleties in linguistic photographic and typographical construction of such stories is clearly needed to improve our understanding of these detailed personalized stories and their interaction with broader and more abstract racial issues.

Broad and abstract news appeared in the third highest topic of race relations (see Table 30).

TABLE 30

Race relations subtopics	Column inches	Items
Race Relations Board	67	9
Community relations organizations	239	28
General comments	350	33
Anti-immigrant speeches	46	4
Positive steps to improve	260	28
As an election issue	36	5
Anti-colour prejudice	270	29
Other	42	3
TOTAL	1,310	139

This must be considered as fundamentally a residual category—the largest number of items came under the subtopic 'General Comments'. More items and almost as many inches were devoted to the activities of the Race Relations Board and community relations organizations.

1. From the Leicester study of national dailies.

'Positive steps to improve the situation' were also present. Official race relations bodies are evidently able to command a good deal of publicity for their work. We also included under this topic heading 'anti-colour prejudice' statements which were not insubstantial though scarcely comparable with expressions of white hostility. The relative absence of race relations as an election issue indicates how exclusively race appeared in British politics as the issue of immigration.

The topic of immigration as a whole accounted for 8 per cent of all race-related column inches, well below the proportion of 20 per cent in the national papers as calculated by the Leicester study. The issue appeared as one primarily of control, and was an important presence in local politics (see Table 31).

TABLE 31

Immigration subtopics	Column inches	Items
Numbers entering/leaving Britain	52	8
Immigration control	339	35
Rights of entry	—	—
Cases of entry refused	34	6
Illegal entry (not crime)	99	12
Kenya Asians	98	8
As an election issue	388	33
Other/general	148	14
TOTAL	1,158	116

Immigration in these papers is defined even more tightly than in the nationals:

Immigration as portrayed by the press is not simply a matter of coloured people coming to settle in the country, it is more centrally a matter of keeping them out.

This definition appears through the advocacy of immigration control in and outside elections, and stories of illegal entry. There is little evidence of concern with statistics of net immigration, or any cases of refused entry by hostile authorities.

White hostility appears in almost exactly 5 per cent of all race-related inches and items. It took disparate forms as Table 32 shows.

TABLE 32

White hostility subtopics	Column inches	Items
Assault	152	13
Verbal	153	22
Demonstrations	238	14
Hostile Groups	138	12
Other	62	8
TOTAL	743	69

White hostility exists, and is reported extensively, especially when it takes the form of demonstrations. Further comment could only come from consideration of the way such hostility is presented, particularly the legitimating effect some kinds of publicity may have.

In discussing crime, human interest, race relations, immigration and white hostility, we have covered 56 per cent of all race-related inches and 61 per cent of all items. We now consider three areas of social life which might be expected to generate some racial tension in the local communities served by these papers: housing, education and cultural differences. These were indeed at different times quite central to press coverage of race in the West Midlands, yet overall they amount to only 16 per cent of all race-related inches and only 13 per cent of all items. Competition for resources and differences of life style are not even at this local level the primary terms in which race is defined by the press.

The topics of housing and education provide a generally negative assessment of the effect of black immigration, as Tables 33 and 34 show.

TABLE 33

Housing subtopics	Column inches	Items
Overcrowding, slums, multi-occupation	100	11
Causing housing shortage	27	2
Council housing	140	5
Causing whites to move out	43	5
Housing associations	—	—
Housing for whites only	—	—
No difficulties	10	1
Immigrants as landlords	199	15
Causing neighbourhood decay	179	7
Other, general	99	9
TOTAL	797	62

TABLE 34

Education subtopics	Column inches	Items
Overcrowding	269	17
Holding whites back	26	3
Dispersal	4	1
Good adjustment	9	1
Immigrants awaiting places	9	1
Special provision	158	15
Disadvantaged	7	1
Bad adjustment	—	—
Overseas students	56	3
Other, general	150	16
TOTAL	688	58

In housing, immigrants are associated with landlordism, slums and neighbourhood decay; the allocation of council houses to them is defined as problematic, and their arrival has on occasion motivated white people to move out.

In education, they are reported as overcrowding schools, and as the beneficiaries of special provision. The latter is often an ambiguous subtopic, which may be seen as a sensitive response to genuine need, or as privileged treatment depriving white children of resources.

Similar ambiguities of presentation and interpretation arise in the topic of cultural differences where the major subtopic is 'Special Cultural Provision', though the 'Description of Immigrant Cultures' is almost as prominent. These two together amount to just over two-thirds of all column inches (see Table 35).

TABLE 35

Cultural differences subtopics	Column inches	Items
Description of immigrant cultures	236	17
Language differences	35	5
Special provision	260	18
Differences in customs	72	4
West Indian parties	10	2
Negative evaluation of differences	23	4
Positive evaluation of differences	13	2
Other, general	72	5
TOTAL	721	57

Though there is little evidence of any interest in the evaluation of cultural differences, the treatment of racial integration would suggest that such differences must disappear. It is reported predominantly in terms of assimilation (see Table 36).

TABLE 36

Racial integration subtopics	Column inches	Items
Assimilation	338	24
Accommodation/adjustment	121	9
Pluralism	72	7
Minimal tolerance	27	1
Other	7	1
TOTAL	565	42

Integration then is presented as the successful efforts of immigrants to adapt to the British way of life. Some pluralism is evident and efforts to 'negotiate' with different races are apparent: but the overall assumption is that integration means assimilation.

The West Midlands evening newspapers presentation of discrimination is characterized by a heavy focus on individual cases, to the apparent exclusion of any discussion of discrimination as a pattern (Table 37).

TABLE 37

Discrimination	Column inches	Items
Acts of discrimination	477	47
Discrimination as a general topic	62	6
Cases referred to Race Board	72	6
Segregation of blacks	27	1
Discrimination, other	16	2
TOTAL	654	62

This concentration on individual cases and a disinterest in identifying patterns or systems may be seen as characteristic of all news rather than special to race news. Its effect on race news is especially damaging since it dodges the problem of the experience of black people as groups, and infers that accusations about a pattern of discrimination stands or falls by the proof of a few (six per year for all three papers) individual experiences.

Such accusations are often made by immigrant organizations (see Table 38). These receive relatively sparse coverage—only one-half the column inches given over to white hostility. Whether by chance or no, these items are consistently shorter than almost any other topic. Presentation of the activities of immigrant organizations stresses their involvement in politics and race relations generally, rather than the cultural and welfare services they offer their members.

TABLE 38

Immigrant organizations	Column inches	Items
Race relations	77	11
Welfare of immigrants	87	6
Cultural activities	21	6
Involvement in British politics	102	14
Other, general	66	8
TOTAL	353	45

This tends to suggest that immigrant organizations are not generally seen as newsworthy, when compared with official community relations organizations or expressions of white hostility. They appear most newsworthy when they impinge upon white society; their work within their own communities going virtually unnoticed. This can hardly be called an extensive or accurate portrait.

Of the remaining nine topics, eight may be considered as appearing at a level of frequency which is almost non-existent. This does not mean to say that they are insignificant. What the press do not cover may tell us as much about their perception of race as what they do focus upon. 'Reading for absences' can be a revealing exercise. But first we must note the peculiar role of sport and entertainment as a topic.

This topic would undoubtedly have provided many more items had we not excluded sports news and entertainment features from consideration. At a local level, the appearance of Asian teams playing hockey or football in local leagues, and West Indians playing cricket, represent an area of cultural negotiation of considerable importance. At a national level, the talent of black overseas players has transformed the state of English cricket; some non-white British heroes have appeared in other sports, notably John Conteh in boxing and many young athletes; and international sport of all kinds frequently involves black *v.* white situations. Had these pages been included sport and entertainment would quite possibly have emerged as prominently as crime and human interest, though again, we must stress that black sportsmen may be seen in as stereotyped terms as any other black people.

Sport and entertainment was only classified when it spilled out on to news pages, letters or editorials. The issue which emerged from such material was the controversy over the visit of South African sports teams (see Table 39).

TABLE 39

Sport and entertainment	Column inches	Items
'Keep politics out'	18	2
Against South African sports teams	67	7
Demonstrations over race and sport	173	11
South Africa and the Olympic games	—	—
South African cricket tour	170	14
Visits to South Africa and Rhodesia	25	2
Controversies over television and films	62	7
Other, general	83	5
TOTAL	598	48

We are left with eight topics which together amount to just 7 per cent of total coverage. Black people are not presented as racially discriminating or hostile, but neither are there many local celebrities with black skins. Health and numbers, two of the major planks of many an anti-immigrant platform, do not find any substantial expression in the press. Legislation as a national concern is not discussed in local terms.

The relative neglect of two topics—employment and the police—seems quite extraordinary. By the mid-1970s certainly these have come to be accepted as central race problems, especially for British-born black youth of West Indian parentage. These problems have a history, deeply rooted in the 1960s, which the press of the time in the West Midlands apparently knew nothing about.

Employment is after all what brought black people to the United Kingdom: the prospect of regular jobs and a resultant improved standard of living. To ignore that motivation, and the subsequent contribution made to the British economy made by black workers, is to seriously underrate a central dynamic of immigration and race relations. The reliance of British society on black people to staff its hospitals, run its bus services, sweat in its foundries, clean its offices and factories, goes unnoticed by the provincial press in the West Midlands. If it be argued that such work activities are not 'newsworthy', then it must be said that the criteria of newsworthiness are, not for the first time, helping to skew the press presentation of race.

Black people and the police rarely make news in these papers. Only in the *Birmingham Evening Mail* in 1970 was there any recognition of the problem, that one paper in one year carrying a third (4 out of 13) of the three papers aggregate number of items for the whole period—and then only because of an adverse Home Office report by a black community worker. Unless the problem of police-black relationships can be said to have exploded without reason or warning, then the evening press from 1963 to 1970, whether through ignorance or design, was failing to understand or publicize what was becoming a major source of racial tension in some areas of Midlands cities.

Reference themes

The analysis of reference themes reveals the extent and kind of relationships between different aspects of the race situation as presented in the press. With 1,029 reference themes for 1,381 topics such relationships are not infrequent. And if we exclude crime and human interest, 60 per cent of which items had no reference themes, the relationship is more evident: 954 reference themes for 862 topic items. Unfortunately, we were not able to exclude from our figures 'internal' references, e.g. from one aspect of housing to another, as the Leicester study did. Clearly some connections would be of a fairly straightforward kind.

It seems likely, however, that many references were to subjects altogether different from the main topic of the item. This may be illustrated by comparing the top ten topics on number of items with the top ten reference themes (Table 40).

TABLE 40

Topics	Items	Reference themes	Number
Crime	311	Cultural differences	125
Human interest	208	Housing	91
Race relations	139	Race relations	88
Immigration	116	Powell	79
White hostility	69	Education	74
Housing	62	White hostility	57
Discrimination	62	Immigration	54
Education	58	Racial integration	49
Cultural differences	57	Employment	48
Sport and entertainment	48	Immigrant organizations	48

Though six areas of concern appear in both groups—race relations, immigration, white hostility, housing, education and cultural differences—they are in different proportional relationships. And if we look at just the top five of each group we can see that, with the exception of the residual category of race relations, they are mutually exclusive. The four remaining major topics are crime, human interest, immigration and white hostility, accounting for 51 per cent of all news items. By contrast 36 per cent of all reference themes are provided by cultural differences, housing, education and Powell.

As a test of the kind of relationship which might exist between topics and reference themes, we noted the frequency with which cultural differences were used as a reference point in cases of crime. We found this relationship on thirty occasions. That is, almost a quarter of all references to cultural differences occurred in the context of crime. Eight of these references were to language, four each to description of immigrant cultures, differences in custom, West Indian parties and culture clash, one to special provision, and five were of a general kind. Cultural differences thus appeared as a negative reference point for the already negative topic of crime.

The emphasis on language as a cultural difference was evident in reference themes as a whole. Of the 125 references, 37 concerned language, compared with only 5 of the 57 topics. Other primarily negative presentations of cultural differences also increased in the reference themes—'differences of culture' and 'negative evaluation' which provided 14 per cent (7 items) of the subtopics composed 24 per cent (33 items) of the reference themes.

The increase in negative elements in reference themes as compared with subtopics was also evident in housing and education. In housing as a reference theme, there is a decrease in the amount of attention paid to council housing (from 12 out of 62 subtopics to 12 out of 91 reference themes) and immigrant landlords (from 15 out of 62 to 12 out of 91), but a huge increase from 18 per cent (11 out of 62) of subtopics to 34 per cent (31 out of 91) subreference themes in the 'association of immigrants with slums overcrowding or multioccupation.' In education as a reference theme there is less concern with overcrowding (17 out of 58 subtopics; 15 out of 74 subreferences), but 'whites held back' and dispersal jointly increase from 7 per cent (4 out of 58) subtopics to 20 per cent (19 out of 74) subreferences.

In two reference themes, there is some indication of an increase in more favourable subcategories. Under race relations, anti-colour prejudice provided 39 per cent (34 out of 88) of subreference themes, compared with 22 per cent (29 out of 139) of subtopics. And under racial integration the distribution of subtopics—assimilation 57 per cent, negotiation 21 per cent and pluralism 16 per cent—is more even in the reference themes—assimilation 35 per cent (17 out of 49), negotiation 31 per cent (15 out of 49), pluralism 18 per cent (9 out of 49). At this level, however, the number of reference themes is so small as to make comparison difficult. Employment and immigrant organizations are too infrequent as reference themes to make comparison worth while, and there is no difference from subtopics observable in white hostility and immigration.

Nevertheless, we think it remains accurate to say that overall reference themes tend to be significantly more concerned to stress negative aspects of immigration than the topics, which we have already noted to constitute a largely negative portrait. This is intensified by references to Enoch Powell, which occur in one-seventh of all topics (excluding crime and human interest) in the years 1968 to 1970. It may be—and we are being openly speculative here—that reference themes have an important role as assumptions on which arguments and speeches are based, rather than being the substance of the main argument. It is, for example, manifestly intolerant in an ethical sense to condemn black people simply for being culturally different, but such differences might bolster more 'respectable/rational' arguments about immigration, housing or education.

The suggestion that some areas of race may be used as foreground or core issues, while others exist as background or periphery, was tested in the Leicester study by the construction of a scale. The total topic items and reference themes for each heading are taken and the smaller figure divided into the larger one. A positive value is given when the topic figure is larger, a negative value when there are more reference themes. Our findings were as follows:

Mainly topics: crime, +9.42; sport and entertainment, +2.52; immigration, +2.11; discrimination, +1.72; race relations, +1.57; white hostility, +1.21; immigrant organizations, +1.06.

Mainly reference themes: racial integration, —1.16; education, —1.27; housing, —1.46; cultural differences, —2.19.

This tends to confirm our findings about foreground and background elements. The effect of reference themes on the overall portrait of race is shown in Table 41. The number of topic items for each heading is added to the total number of reference themes to give a figure of 'total

TABLE 41. Total mentions (percentages in parentheses)

	Topic items		Reference themes		Total mentions	
Crime	311	(23)	33	(3)	344	(14)
Human interest	208	(15)	—	(0)	208	(9)
Race relations	139	(10)	88	(8)	227	(9)
Cultural differences	57	(4)	125	(12)	182	(8)
Housing	62	(4)	91	(9)	153	(6)
Education	58	(4)	74	(7)	132	(5)
White hostility	69	(5)	57	(5)	126	(5)
Immigration	114	(8)	54	(5)	168	(7)
Discrimination	62	(4)	36	(3)	98	(4)
Immigrant organizations	45	(3)	48	(5)	93	(4)
Racial integration	42	(3)	49	(5)	91	(4)
Sport and entertainment	48	(3)	19	(2)	67	(3)
Employment	23	(2)	48	(5)	71	(3)
Powell	—	(0)	79	(8)	79	(3)
Health	24	(2)	23	(2)	47	(2)
Numbers	18	(1)	28	(3)	46	(2)
Legislation	16	(1)	40	(4)	56	(2)
Others	85	(8)	137	(14)	222	(10)
TOTAL	1,381	(100)	1,029	(100)	2,410	(100)

TABLE 42. Topic variations over time; evening papers aggregate

Topic	1963 A¹	1963 B²	1964 A	1964 B	1965 A	1965 B	1966 A	1966 B	1967 A	1967 B	1968 A	1968 B	1969 A	1969 B	1970 A	1970 B	Total (1963/70) A	Total (1963/70) B
Housing	90	6	54	6	164	16	82	5	189	12	78	5	84	7	56	5	797	62
Education	23	3	37	5	61	4	84	6	39	7	302	20	75	7	67	6	688	58
Health	—	—	6	1	32	5	13	2	—	—	32	5	40	5	59	6	182	24
Employment	27	4	—	—	18	2	40	4	21	2	74	3	73	6	10	2	263	23
White hostility	35	3	46	6	81	11	61	6	57	5	314	23	64	7	85	8	743	69
Crime	429	52	261	33	246	33	230	32	289	33	321	32	324	44	474	52	2,574	311
Celebrities	17	2	30	5	15	1	16	1	—	—	59	3	31	4	6	1	174	17
Immigration	69	4	239	18	190	23	13	2	65	9	372	30	59	11	151	19	1,158	116
Race relations	42	6	71	9	155	18	48	4	56	7	536	46	235	27	167	22	1,310	139
Immigrant organizations	12	1	27	6	41	5	6	1	4	1	88	11	60	9	115	11	353	45
Black hostility	—	—	—	—	—	—	—	—	13	1	—	—	—	—	6	2	19	3
Numbers	31	2	—	—	3	1	—	—	22	2	49	6	26	5	21	2	152	18
Discrimination	100	8	19	4	74	7	15	2	98	10	170	13	58	8	120	10	654	62
Discrimination by coloureds	—	—	29	1	—	—	—	—	—	—	—	—	6	1	6	1	41	3
Police	—	—	—	—	12	1	24	3	9	1	7	2	11	1	21	5	84	13
Racial integration	—	—	35	4	40	3	89	8	163	9	98	8	81	7	59	3	565	42
Cultural differences	36	5	15	3	130	8	71	4	76	6	176	12	109	10	108	9	721	57
Human interest	226	21	134	18	336	34	201	21	165	21	264	23	442	32	494	38	2,260	208
Legislation	5	1	8	2	13	2	—	—	—	—	118	8	13	2	6	1	163	16
Sport/entertainment	19	1	5	1	31	2	—	—	38	4	19	3	257	20	229	17	598	48
Other	33	4	9	2	94	7	101	5	20	3	213	15	91	9	61	4	622	49
TOTAL	1,192	123	1,025	124	1,736	183	1,094	106	1,324	133	3,290	268	2,139	222	2,321	224	14,121	1,383

1. A = Column inches.
2. B = Items.

TABLE 43. Reference themes variation over time: evening papers aggregated

Reference themes	1963	1964	1965	1966	1967	1968	1969	1970	Total
Housing	8	13	13	10	10	18	4	14	91
Education	2	10	7	3	3	25	17	7	74
Health	0	5	3	0	3	3	3	6	23
Employment	7	5	3	3	4	8	13	5	48
White hostility	2	7	11	6	4	7	10	10	57
Crime	12	2	2	4	1	2	3	7	33
Immigration	2	5	5	3	0	21	8	9	54
Race relations	2	5	7	4	10	19	23	18	88
Immigrant organizations	2	5	9	0	6	8	11	7	48
Black hostility	0	1	0	0	1	0	1	1	4
Numbers	1	6	5	1	4	5	4	3	28
Discrimination	0	4	9	1	1	10	8	3	36
Discrimination by coloureds	0	1	0	0	0	0	0	1	2
Police	1	1	1	0	0	4	2	9	18
Racial integration	3	6	9	5	4	13	5	4	49
Cultural differences	5	10	10	10	27	31	24	8	125
Legislation	0	5	5	0	2	16	10	2	40
Sport and entertainment	1	0	1	0	1	2	5	9	19
United States	0	0	0	1	1	2	0	1	5
India	1	0	2	0	1	3	0	2	9
West Indies	0	0	1	0	0	0	0	0	1
South Africa	0	1	0	1	0	1	3	0	6
Rhodesia	0	0	0	1	1	1	5	0	8
Black Africa	0	2	0	0	1	2	0	2	7
Commonwealth	0	0	2	0	0	0	0	1	3
Racial tension	0	3	1	2	0	8	1	0	15
Powell	0	0	0	0	1	47	18	13	79
British politics	0	3	4	0	0	6	3	3	19
Black power	0	0	0	0	1	2	0	5	8
Second-generation immigrants	0	0	0	0	0	0	1	0	1
Communism	0	0	0	0	0	0	0	1	1
Churches	2	2	2	2	0	7	5	10	30
TOTAL	51	102	112	57	88	271	187	161	1,029

mentions'. The inclusion of reference themes increases the proportionate share of total mentions covered by housing, education and cultural differences, mainly at the expense of crime and human interest, but there are also falls in the proportionate share of race relations and immigration.

Except in the case of cultural differences and housing, the addition of reference themes does not radically alter the pattern of news distribution. The more important effect of reference themes on news presentation is that they present a series of largely negative images of face-to-face issues—cultural differences, housing and education—against which more abstract problems of race (immigration, race relations, white hostility) are presented as discussed. What seems to be happening is that the race issue, even in evening papers serving cities with large immigrant populations, is primarily defined in terms which do not immediately derive from the characteristics of the local situation.

The definition of race used derives in part from long-established news

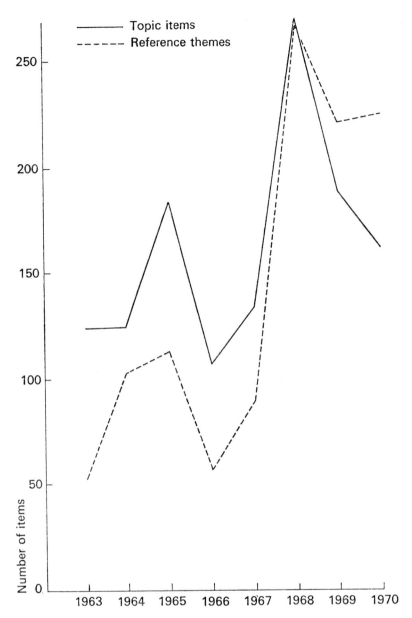

FIG. 6. Variation of news items and reference themes over time: evening papers aggregated.

values in the areas of crime and human interest, but these as we have argued are far from self-evident, and in a race relations context can provide very negative and/or stereotyped images of black people. The other main source of definition stems from concern with a partly diffuse, partly institutionalized area of race relations; the related problem of immigration, defined almost exclusively as a problem of control; and the increasing expressions of white hostility. It is for a debate defined in these terms that housing, education and cultural differences are summoned to give evidence. The main issues are not defined by any assessment of the race situation on the ground in any of the cities but by accepting the definition of the race problem adopted by potential political lobbies: i.e. anti-immigrant organizations and members of the Conservative Party. Their influence is even more apparent, if we examine their effect upon the chronological development of race news in these papers from 1963 to 1970.

Chronological pattern

The pattern which emerges from the following data on the chronological development of race news in the three evening papers, exhibits three major characteristics: (a) a continuous increase in the amount of all race news to the point where 54 per cent of all the race news for the whole period is concentrated in the last three years (1968, 1969 and 1970); (b) some shifts in the topics and reference themes which constitute the main definition of race news; (c) a pattern of quite extreme expansions (1965, 1968) and contractions (1966, 1969) of the amount of race news as a whole.

The absolute increase in the amount of race news may be illustrated by dividing the period into two halves. (See Tables 44 and 45.)

All the topics (except the insignificant category of discrimination by black people) increase in absolute terms. This means that all aspects of

TABLE 44. Comparison 1963–66 and 1967–70 evenings aggregated: topics

Topic	1963–66		1967–70		Total	
Housing	390	33	407	29	797	62
Education	205	18	483	40	688	58
Health	51	8	131	16	182	24
Employment	85	10	178	13	263	23
White hostility	223	26	520	43	743	69
Crime	1,166	150	1,408	161	2,574	311
Celebrities	78	9	96	8	174	17
Immigration	511	47	647	69	1,158	116
Race relations	316	37	994	102	1,310	139
Immigrant organizations	86	13	267	32	353	45
Black hostility	—	—	19	3	19	3
Numbers	34	3	118	15	152	18
Discrimination	208	21	446	41	654	62
Discrimination by coloureds	29	1	12	2	41	3
Police	36	4	48	9	84	13
Racial integration	164	15	401	27	565	42
Cultural differences	252	20	469	37	721	57
Human interest	895	94	1,365	114	2,260	208
Legislation	26	5	137	11	163	16
Sport and entertainment	55	4	543	44	598	48
Other	237	18	385	31	622	49
TOTAL	5,047	536	9,674	847	14,121	1,383

TABLE 45. Comparison 1963–66
and 1967–70 evenings aggregated: reference themes

Theme	1963–66	1967–70	Total
Housing	44	47	91
Education	22	52	74
Employment	18	30	48
White hostility	26	31	57
Crime	20	13	33
Immigration	16	38	54
Race relations	18	70	88
Immigrant organizations	16	32	48
Numbers	12	16	28
Discrimination	14	22	36
Racial integration	23	26	49
Cultural differences	35	90	125
Powell	0	79	79
Legislation	10	30	40
Churches	8	22	30
Others	40	109	149
TOTAL	322	707	1,029

race—even the supposedly independent categories of crime and human interest which increase in total column inches in the second half by 20 per cent and 53 per cent respectively—are receiving increasing newspaper attention. It is a matter of argument whether this simply represents an increase in the number of black people in the West Midlands. It seems to us more likely that it represents the increasing visibility and newsworthiness of the race situation which is pursued for the most part within pre-existent news categories.

This is not to say that the increase is constant across topics. With a mean absolute increase of 80 per cent neither crime nor human interest are expanding as fast as other types of news. Also increasing at a relatively slow rate are housing (26 per cent absolute increase between the two periods), immigrant organizations (68 per cent) and immigration (26 per cent).

Increases of 100–150 per cent, indicating the substantial core of the overall increase include white hostility (133 per cent), education (135 per cent), discrimination (114 per cent), racial integration (144 per cent) and employment (109 per cent). The largest absolute increases occur in sport and entertainment (887 per cent) and legislation (427 per cent).

These varying increases do not, however, have a particularly drastic effect on the proportional relationships of the different topics. The one important change is in the proportionate share of race news devoted to crime and human interest. Crime provides 23 per cent of news in the period 1963–66 but only 16 per cent in 1967–70.

Human interest declines from 18 to 15 per cent. These 'routinized' parts of race news are not, however, displaced by arguments about resources. Though the total amount of inches on the topic of education doubles, this represents a small proportional increase, from 4 to 5 per cent. With housing dropping off severely and employment constant, the proportion of race-related news devoted to these resource-oriented topics together actually falls from 12 to 11 per cent. The major increases are in sport and entertainment which increases from 2 to 4 per cent of news, and race relations increasing from 6 to 11 per cent. Sport and entertainment is essentially about British attitudes to race overseas and can be regarded along with Rhodesian news, as providing an international context for race relations. The expansion in race relations as a topic occurs particularly in the subtopics of community relations organizations and anti-colour prejudice statements. This represents a considerable recovery for the liberal lobby after its virtual absence in the first four years.

A roughly similar pattern is evident in the reference themes though the figures involved are small and proportional increases contain a large random element. There are, nevertheless, clear decreases in the proportional references to crime (the only reference theme to show an absolute decrease) which falls from 6 to 2 per cent and housing from 14 to 7 per cent. White hostility and racial integration decline from 8 to 4 per cent and 7 to 4 per cent respectively. As they increase slightly as topics, it is possible to interpret the changes as a shift from background to foreground concerns. The greatest increases in references are in race relations (6 to 10 per cent), cultural differences (11 to 13 per cent) and Powell (0 to 11 per cent). These three cover 34 per cent of all references in the second half of the period, whereas they were only 17 per cent of the first half's total.

There is no evidence of any particular closure or clustering of topics and themes over time. The shifts of emphasis are relatively small though the decrease in crime and human interest, the increase in race relations, and the penetration of white hostility and racial integration from reference themes to topics, indicate a sharpening of racial conflict and an expanded coverage of attempts to blunt it.

These two somewhat contradictory movements—towards greater conflict, and towards the elimination of prejudice and misunderstanding—are partly revealed by the different forms taken by the two peaks in absolute coverage in 1965 and 1968 and, especially, the 'troughs' of 1966 and 1969.

These peaks are not difficult to explain, as Leicester noted:

1965 saw the Government White Paper on Immigration and the first Race Relations Act, and in 1968 there was another Race Relations Act, another Commonwealth Immigrants Act and the emergence of Enoch Powell as an anti-immigrant symbol.

To that should be added for 1965 the effect of the Smethwick election result in late 1964. The troughs, however, are not so straightforward, since they involve a decrease in news not only in relation to the preceding years but also the succeeding years. It is as if the press, having overreacted by increasing the news, now compensates by overreacting in a decrease. In one year, race may be at its maximum newsworthiness; in

1. Leicester, op. cit., p. 44.

the next, it is at its minimum. It is difficult not to believe that quite conscious choices are being made in how much race news to present.

These points may become clearer if we look at the proportional distribution of race news (measured in column inches) in these peak and trough years (Table 46).

TABLE 46. Topics share percentage per year

	1965	1966	1968	1969
Human interest	20	18	8	21
Crime	14	21	10	15
Race relations	9	4	16	10
Immigration	11	1	11	3
White hostility	5	6	10	3
Housing	9	7	6	4
Education	4	8	9	4
Cultural differences	7	6	5	5
Racial integration	2	8	3	4
Discrimination	4	1	5	3
Percentage of news for whole period	12	8	23	15

In 1968, areas of conflict are more evident than in 1965. Housing and education increase from 13 to 15 per cent, white hostility from 5 to 10 per cent. But race relations—most of which is the 'liberal' lobby's activities—nearly doubles to become the most prominent news category of 1968. Racial integration and discrimination also slightly increase their share, neatly pointing both conflictual and apparently integrative mechanisms. This change in focus occurs because crime and human interest do not maintain their combined average proportions of news (34 per cent) as they do in 1965. In 1968 they cover only 18 per cent of news. The more disparate reference themes of 1965 are tightened in 1968 where Powell (18 per cent), cultural differences (11 per cent), education (9 per cent) and immigration (8 per cent) provide almost half of all references.

In both trough years crime and human interest confirm a return to normal news: 39 per cent in 1966 and 36 per cent in 1969. This represents a more dramatic change in the second year because of its relatively low presentation in 1968. In 1969, there appears a tendency not present in 1965 to play down housing, education and cultural differences and give more prominence to race relations. This no doubt does represent a real increase in community relations concern, and represents a different possibility of reporting more positive news.

The two-year periods 1965–66 and 1968–69 do have a different pattern of expansion and contraction. These have some effect on 1970 which looks more like a re-expanded version of 1969 than a return to 1963.

An overall comment on the chronology of race news would, however, have to stress its basic similarities of concern. It expands throughout the period, most dramatically in 1968, but this expansion occurs for the most part within the framework already accepted by these papers as appropriate to the portrayal of race. 1963 already shows a large coverage of immigration, housing, white hostility, cultural differences and education—21 per cent of all race news. 1965 gives further impetus to these topics and 1968 provides an explosion. In 1970, twice as much race news is recorded as in 1963, but its distribution is basically the same, with the exception that race relations doubles its share to 8 per cent. This similarity between 1970 and 1963 occurs not because 1965 and 1968 had only a temporary effect on the press portrayal of race, but because the press concept of race as a news issue was already in the terms of immigration, education, housing, cultural differences and white hostility. They could thus cover supposedly unprecedented moments of race conflict without basically altering but merely by expanding their conception of race. This may explain the papers' surprised reaction to the form rather than the content of Powell's speeches. They did not dissent from his basic concept of the immigrants' presence as detrimental to the welfare of the white population: their whole news coverage shares this concept. What they apparently could not stomach was his making manifest and open the racial hostility latent in such a concept. Powell did not have the effect of changing the parameters of the debate. He did not have to: the press, at least, was already in agreement with him.

Differences between evening papers

A consideration of the differences between the evening papers may help to reveal how far evening papers which are provincial in circulation and cultural perspective do actually draw on the situation in the immediate locality to portray race relations. We shall therefore compare the papers, initially according to the amount and distribution of topics and reference themes, and their variations over time.

An important first consideration is the proportion of news space devoted to race. In calculating this proportion of the paper which was race-related, we excluded advertisements, sports pages and entertainments and women's columns. We were then able to calculate what percentage of the remaining news space was related to race. We give the results in Table 47 and compare them with the percentage of each city's population which was immigrant according to the 1966 census.

TABLE 47

Newspaper	Overseas	Home-overseas	Home	Percentage immigrant population
Birmingham Evening Mail	0.4	0.2	3.7	6.4
Coventry Evening Telegraph	0.5	0.5	1.7	2.0
Wolverhampton *Express and Star*	0.9	0.4	4.8	4.7
All papers	0.6	0.4	3.7	n.a.

These figures do not tell us anything about the terms in which race was reported: merely its amount. While the other two papers give a coverage to race roughly proportionate to their populations, the *Birmingham Evening Mail* tends to under-represent news about immigrants.

TABLE 48. Comparison of evening papers: topics

Topic	Birmingham Evening Mail		Wolverhampton Express and Star		Coventry Evening Telegraph		All papers	
	Column inches	Themes	Column inches	Themes	Column inches	Themes	Column inches	Themes
Housing	515	34	268	24	14	4	797	62
Education	344	27	262	23	82	8	688	58
Health	99	14	83	10	—	—	182	24
Employment	139	11	105	9	19	3	263	23
White hostility	180	22	365	30	198	17	743	69
Crime	989	121	1,213	147	372	43	2,574	311
Celebrities	28	3	57	7	87	7	172	17
Immigration	562	51	522	54	74	11	1,158	16
Race relations	338	48	744	69	228	22	1,310	139
Immigrant organizations	85	13	186	20	82	12	353	45
Black hostility	6	2	—	—	13	1	19	3
Numbers	43	3	84	12	25	3	152	18
Discrimination	174	19	399	36	81	7	654	62
Discrimination by coloureds	35	2	6	1	—	—	41	3
Police	51	8	15	3	18	2	84	13
Racial integration	199	15	277	21	89	6	565	42
Cultural differences	324	25	241	21	156	11	721	57
Human interest	1,045	90	821	79	394	39	2,260	208
Legislation	60	6	91	8	12	2	163	16
Sport and entertainment	331	25	178	15	89	11	598	48
Other	123	8	431	36	68	5	622	49
TOTAL	5,670	547	6,350	625	2,101	211	14,121	1,383

More important, however, is a comparison of the forms of coverage. Our findings are presented in Tables 48–51. We have here a curious reversal of the situation we discovered in our consideration of overseas news. There, we found the same overseas events and issues given different emphasis; here, we have what are presumably in each city, according to its economic and social resources and the nature of its immigrant groups, rather different racial situations reported in substantially the same way.

TABLE 49. Topic percentage of column inches

Topic	Birmingham Evening Mail	Wolverhampton Express and Star	Coventry Evening Telegraph	Total (all papers)
Crime	17	19	18	18
Human interest	18	13	19	16
Race relations	6	12	11	9
Immigration	10	8	4	8
Housing	9	4	1	6
White hostility	3	6	9	5
Cultural differences	6	4	7	5
Education	6	4	4	5
Discrimination	3	6	4	5
Sport and entertainment	6	3	4	4
Racial integration	4	4	4	4
Immigrant organizations	1	3	4	3
Employment	2	2	1	2
Health	2	1	0	1
Others	7	11	10	9
TOTAL	100	100	100	100

All are agreed on the amount of space to be devoted to crime (between 17 and 19 per cent), cultural differences (4 to 7 per cent), education (4 to 7 per cent), discrimination (3 to 6 per cent) and racial integration (4 per cent). In reference themes, a similar pattern appears with the ranges being small in the major categories of cultural differences (11 to 14 per cent), housing (7 to 10 per cent), education (6 to 8 per cent) and white hostility and immigration (5 to 6 per cent).

Where there are differences, they mainly take the form of one paper deviating from a clear norm set by the other two. Thus the Wolverhampton *Express and Star* has a third less human interest than the other two papers, while the *Coventry Evening Telegraph* devotes only half as much of its news as the others to immigration. In reference themes the Wolverhampton *Express and Star* hardly unexpectedly concentrates relatively more on Powell. The *Coventry Evening Telegraph* shows more concern with churches and less with crime and numbers.

Other areas of substantial disagreement include housing: 9 per cent of the *Birmingham Evening Mail*'s total coverage, 4 per cent of that of

TABLE 50. Numbers of reference themes

Theme	Birmingham Evening Mail	Wolverhampton Express and Star	Coventry Evening Telegraph	Total
Housing	36	41	14	91
Education	23	40	11	74
Health	10	10	3	23
Employment	13	23	12	48
White hostility	20	27	10	57
Crime	15	15	3	33
Immigration	17	25	12	54
Race relations	21	50	17	88
Immigrant organizations	16	21	11	48
Black hostility	1	3	0	4
Numbers	12	14	2	28
Discrimination	12	18	6	36
Discrimination by coloureds	0	1	1	2
Police	10	4	4	18
Racial integration	19	23	7	49
Cultural differences	49	54	22	125
Legislation	14	18	8	40
Sport and entertainment	9	5	5	19
Commonwealth	0	0	3	3
Racial tension	7	5	3	15
Powell	21	48	10	79
British politics	5	11	3	19
Black power	3	4	1	8
Second generation	0	1	0	1
Communism	0	1	0	1
Churches	9	6	15	30
Overseas countries	12	14	10	36
TOTAL	354	482	193	1,029

the *Express and Star* and only 1 per cent in the *Coventry Evening Telegraph*. This relationship is reversed in the case of white hostility to which the *Coventry Evening Telegraph* gives the most attention (9 per cent), the *Express and Star* intermediate coverage (6 per cent) and the *Birmingham Evening Mail* least of all (3 per cent). These differences are less apparent in the reference themes, but the Coventry paper's minimal concern with housing is again reflected.

These are, however, small differences of emphasis within a common framework. For each paper crime and human interest provide a core of routinized news—35 per cent in Birmingham, 32 per cent in Wolverhampton and 37 per cent in Coventry. The main concept of race is in terms of key problems—cultural differences, housing, education, white hostility and immigration. These topics constitute 34 per cent of the *Birmingham Evening Mail*'s coverage, 26 per cent of the *Express and Star*'s and 25 per cent of the *Coventry Evening Telegraph*'s. In reference themes the same areas with the addition of Powell provide the main

TABLE 51. Reference theme percentages

Theme	Birmingham Evening Mail	Wolverhampton Express and Star	Coventry Evening Telegraph	All papers
Cultural differences	14	11	12	12
Housing	10	9	7	9
Race relations	6	10	9	8
Powell	6	10	5	8
Education	6	8	6	7
White hostility	6	6	5	5
Immigration	5	5	6	5
Racial integration	5	5	3	5
Employment	4	5	6	5
Immigrant organizations	5	4	6	5
Legislation	4	4	4	4
Discrimination	3	4	3	3
Crime	4	4	2	3
Churches	3	1	8	3
Numbers	3	3	1	3
Health	3	2	1	2
All others	13	9	16	13
TOTAL	100	100	100	100

framework of reference: 47 per cent of the *Birmingham Evening Mail*'s references, 49 per cent in the *Express and Star*, 41 per cent in the *Coventry Evening Telegraph*.

There are differences in most of the subtopic coverage of housing, education and white hostility. As one example, the *Coventry Evening Telegraph* devotes one half of its discussion of education to special provision, over one-third to overseas students, and only 5 per cent to overcrowding. The Wolverhampton *Express and Star* has nothing at all about overseas students, just 4 per cent on special provision and 43 per cent on overcrowding. The *Birmingham Evening Mail* records a similar figure for overcrowding but a third on special provision.

Such differences could be attributable to real differences in the local situation. Coventry may have better educational facilities, a greater willingness to make special provision for immigrant children and many more overseas students than the other two cities.

Broadly speaking, then, the newspapers share strikingly similar perspectives on race. Their definition of the issues is only marginally affected—by their choice of subtopic rather than the topic itself—by local conditions. Occasionally, however, these differences show through quite strongly, and indicate some pressure on news presentation to reflect the stance taken in editorials and features. This is especially so in their coverage of cultural differences and racial integration.

In cultural differences all the papers stress special cultural provision and description of cultural differences. There is much less unanimity, however, in reference themes where the most frequent mentions of cultural differences occur. The *Birmingham Evening Mail* stresses the negative effects of differences: of 49 references, 19 are to language and 10 to outright culture clash. In the Wolverhampton *Express and Star*, language and culture clash provide 12 and 8 respectively of the 54 references and are in part balanced by an emphasis on description of which there are 11 items. The *Coventry Evening Telegraph* on the other hand, while referring to language 6 times out of 22 references, and a further 4 times to differences in customs, also includes 3 to description and 2 to positive evaluation.

Similar considerations apply to racial integration both as a topic and a reference theme. This is illustrated in Table 52.

TABLE 52

	Birming-ham Evening Mail		Wolver-hampton Express and Star		Coventry Evening Tele-graph		Total (all papers)	
	A[1]	B[2]	A	B	A	B	A	B
Assimilation	10	8	12	8	2	1	24	17
Accommodation	1	5	5	7	3	3	9	15
Pluralism	3	2	3	5	1	2	7	9
Minimal tolerance	—	2	1	1	—	—	1	3
Other	1	2	—	2	—	1	1	5
TOTAL	15	19	21	23	6	7	42	49

1. A=Topic.
2. B=Reference theme.

Racial integration in the *Birmingham Evening Mail* is consistently presented as a task of assimilation, while the *Coventry Evening Telegraph* reports it as one of accommodation. The Wolverhampton *Express and Star* gives the most diffuse presentation: the attention given to assimilation is most prominent, but equalled by the combined totals of accommodation and pluralism.

Thus, though the basic framework for news presentation is common to all papers on some topics which have local features or involve very clear editorial choices, the papers appear to make patterned choices. The *Birmingham Evening Mail* chooses more conflictive aspects, the *Coventry Evening Telegraph* the least conflictive ones and the Wolverhampton *Express and Star* holds a position between the two.

The *Coventry Evening Telegraph* also appears to take a different line in the amount of race news it covers. It increases at a rate comparable to the other two papers, but is altogether more even, as the graph of annual column inches shows (Fig. 7). It is also the only one of the three papers to carry more column inches in 1969 and 1970 than in 1968.

It seemed to us that the similarity of news coverage did not reflect some substantial differences in the editorial attitudes adopted by the papers. We, therefore, extended our consideration of differences between the evening papers to examine the features and editorials.

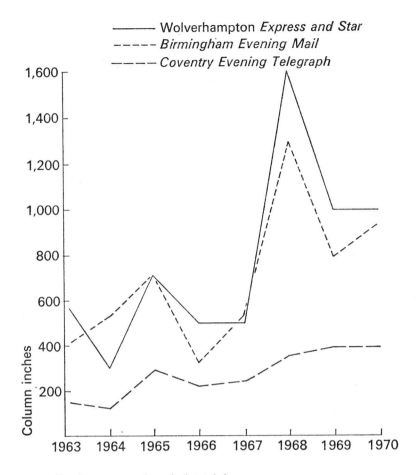

FIG. 7. Evening papers: column inch totals by year

Editorials and features in the evenings

The editorial and feature columns in these evening papers are the ascribed place for the presentation of opinion and explanation respectively. They thus provide an important acid test for the newspaper's definition of race, offering the possibility of expressing opinions or exploring backgrounds which dominant political definitions may not encompass. The first question to ask about the race editorials and features might thus be how far their topics and reference themes diverged from those of the news coverage. The answer is not at all as Table 53 shows. Race relations, immigration, housing, education and racial integration are the most prominent in both topics and reference themes though the most frequent area in the latter category is almost inevitably cultural differences. It should be noted here that the high number of reference themes per feature (2.75) is not matched in the editorials where there is an average of only one reference theme in each editorial. This indicates that the

TABLE 53. Evening papers: editorials and features

	Birmingham Evening Mail		Wolverhampton Express and Star		Coventry Evening Telegraph		Total	
	A[1]	B[2]	A	B	A	B	A	B
Topics								
Race relations	1	5	6	4	3	1	10	10
Immigration		6	5	1			5	7
Racial integration		1	3		1	1	4	2
Education	2	1	2	2	1		5	3
Cultural differences			2				2	
Immigrant organizations	1		1				2	
White hostility			1				1	
Employment		2	1				1	2
Discrimination			1				1	
Housing		3		1	1		1	4
Sport		1			1		1	1
Legislation		1	1				1	1
Human interest			1				1	
Other	1		2	2			3	2
TOTAL	5	20	26	10	7	2	38	32
Reference themes								
Housing		5	3	6		1	3	12
Education	2	4	5	3	1		8	7
Cultural differences		7	2	4		3	2	14
Race relations		5	5	1	1	2	6	8
White hostility		1		2		1		4
Immigrant organizations				2				2
Crime		3						3
Numbers		2	1	1		1	1	4
Legislation		4						4
Racial integration	1	2		1	2	1	3	4
Immigration	2	2				1	2	3
Discrimination		5	2				2	5
Employment				1	1	2	1	3
Churches						1		1
Racial tension						1		2
Powell	1	1	1	2	1		3	3
United States		1		1				2
Police		5		1				6
Black hostility	1	1					1	1
Other			2				2	
TOTAL	7	49	21	25	6	14	34	88

1. A = Editorial.
2. B = Feature.

features sought to relate different aspects of the race situation to each other, while the editorials sought to isolate the issues. This is a not uncommon contradiction in the press as a whole. When explanation is called for as in the features complex interrelationships are admitted in some form, but the expression of opinion in the editorials always resimplifies the issues. This is especially important in the first of the three papers to be discussed.

The Birmingham Evening Mail

The *Birmingham Evening Mail* carried only five editorials but a massive number of twenty features. This suggests that in contrast to both the other papers, features appear to be a more important perspective on race than editorials. While this means the discussion of race can be more wide-ranging, it also has the effect of giving features a perspective to follow—an editorial feature 'line'.

The features appear to cluster around two topics. In the earlier period 1963 to 1965, four out of six features are on immigration. By 1967 to 1970 this is still present in two features, but in four of the remaining seven a new problem has emerged in the shape of decayed immigrant areas: Sparkbrook and Handsworth.

Two of the early four immigration features are published in September and October 1964 and examine uncritically the Labour Party's conversion to immigration control, as evidenced by their latest political manifesto and an interview with Harold Wilson. A feature in the following year (10 February 1965), 'A Tougher Start for Immigrants', is an 'atmospheric' piece on the operation of the new immigration controls at London Airport. It accepts without protestation the difficulty that 'to an English Immigration Officer one bearded Sikh can look very much like another' and gives a sinister note to the overlap of sex and race, 'a blonde London girl waited with three Pakistani men'.

A reaction to Powell in May 1968, 'Immigration: The Way Ahead', tries to imbue the negative move towards tougher immigration control with positive elements, by examining the alleged success of the Dutch policies of tight control and compulsory dispersal. A weekly Christian column underneath manages to disapprove of unthinking white hostility, while agreeing on the necessity for the immigration policies advanced by such hostility.

An attempt to place the immigration debate in some sort of political perspective is made early on in October 1964 in an article headlined: 'Immigration: The Fire About Which Politicians Have Danced'. The lesson learnt, however, is that swift action must be taken to control the immigrant population in Birmingham estimated at 100,000, if a situation similar to that in Smethwick is not to emerge. Smethwick itself is the subject of a May 1965 feature 'Immigration Still The Issue at Smethwick', part of a larger feature on imminent local elections. Labour and Conservative manifestoes are reproduced without comment.

The theme of neighbourhood decay is present as early as January 1963 in a feature called 'The Problem Beneath The Surface In Balsall Heath':

This is a vivid portrait of a 'working-class suburb' in decay through the arrival of immigrants, 'drifters' and organized prostitution.

In 1967 the publication of a major sociological study of Sparkbrook results in parts of their findings being reproduced as 'The Anatomy of a Lodging House', and in the following year the Member of Parliament for Sparkbrook advocates some solutions to the area's problems: an increase in government and local authority spending, with special emphasis on the stimulation of voluntary organizations.

Comparisons are made with the Handsworth area in March 1967, asking if it has become a 'forgotten suburb'. A supplementary question, 'Are Immigrants Scaling the Barriers?', is answered in the affirmative. By 1970, however, the same area is portrayed as 'The Angry Suburb' following a Home Office commissioned report by a black community worker which emphasizes the alienation of black youth from white society, and their conflict with the police.

We cannot give the detailed attention to these articles which they merit, but it is clear that as far as the *Birmingham Evening Mail* is concerned the main problem is no longer just immigration, but the decaying areas of the city of Birmingham. Between them, these two subjects are the focus of thirteen of its total of twenty features.

Of the remaining seven articles, two feature local race-relations person-alities—a retiring headmaster (9 January 1967) and the new secretary of the West Midlands Conciliation Committee (24 November 1966). Another attacks a television comedy *Curry and Chips* (5 December 1969) as not conducive to race relations. In 1968, a short feature by the assistant editor explains the implications of the new Race Relations Act.

The remaining three articles look at particular problems. One is on education with a crude headline 'Coping With the No-English Children' (January 1966) which is matched by some crude descriptive caricatures of black children:

Subdued clothes of the English children, and brilliant colours and exotic costumes of Indian and Pakistani children, and frilly dresses and floppy bows of the West Indians. Boys who at a glance look like girls with shiny ebony topnots and plaits, and girls who look like boys in trousers and jackets.

A later article (March 1968) examines the problem of young immigrant school-leavers: 'Out of School: Now What?' A Youth Employment Officer admits that there is discrimination against them especially in white-collar jobs. Mrs Jill Knight, Member of Parliament, thinks differ-ently however. As a member of a Parliamentary Select Committee, she believes the problem of coloured school-leavers is wholly one of language as she reveals in a March 1969 article called 'A Plea To Give for Ever-more'. The language problem, she says was 'hammered home' by the 'scarcely comprehensible English' used by immigrant representatives when giving evidence.

Of the five *Evening Mail* editorials, two can be considered peripheral. One calls for care and moderation from the city council in deciding whether 'Black Power' organizations should be allowed to book school halls (21 April 1970). The other is a general editorial on the West Midlands economic, social and cultural diversity to which the arrival of immigrants has contributed (13 January 1964).

The other three editorials are directly about immigrants. In March 1970 the *Birmingham Evening Mail* declared itself behind a 'sane and realistic statement on race relations' made by Quintin Hogg which repudiated any policy of repatriation, but admitted the need for government aid to certain areas and a policy of immigration control. The editorial ends: 'He suggested that the key to good relations lay in providing adequate housing, education and employment. This is also the *Mail*'s view.'

However, at the height of the 'Powell peak' in 1968, the *Birmingham Evening Mail* carried two editorials—'No Room' (23 April 1968) and 'New Term' (6 October 1968) which inferred that the arrival of immigrants had caused rather than exacerbated the city's educational problems. The April editorial even went so far as to point out that the number of primary school-age children unable to find places (600) was the same as the number of immigrant children of that age who had arrived in Birmingham in the last six months. The October editorial linked the problem of white parents' reaction to almost wholly black schools with protests about a 'tinker' camp near a local school.

The *Birmingham Evening Mail* claimed in April 1968 that 'it did not wish to add fuel to the Powell controversy' but that the educational problem should be aired—'to ignore it would also be wrong'. However by emphasizing that problem in isolation, by inferring that it did not pre-exist the arrival of immigrants, by failing to balance the social needs of immigrants against their economic contribution, the *Birmingham Evening Mail* was accepting a definition of the race situation so close to that of Enoch Powell as to be distinguishable from his only by its tone. This is also true though in a more complicated way of its features which mainly hinge around immigration control and neighbourhood decay. The features give the illusion of depth and breadth when in fact their focus is a narrow definition of the problems of race relations.

The Wolverhampton Express and Star

This paper carried twenty-six editorials, more than twice as many as the other two papers, and its combined total of editorials and features were also more than the other two combined. The topics and reference themes have a wider range than the other papers, though there is a familiar clustering around the topic and reference themes of race relations, immigration, racial integration, education and cultural differences. It is worth noting that there are only three references to Powell, a measure of the *Express and Star*'s attempts to form an understanding of race which is independent of his outbursts.

The general approach of the Wolverhampton *Express and Star* can be gauged from a piece in July 1963—'Immigrants: Are they Necessary for Prosperity?' An outside writer—Richard Denman of *The Economist*—outlines an economic case for accepting the presence of black immigrants. He argues that they are willing to take up jobs white workers will no longer do, that they are more prepared to move about in search of employment than white workers, stick longer to their jobs, and draw less than their proportional share of unemployment benefit. There is, however, an economic argument for immigration control to avoid a surplus of labour. This kind of argument whilst unique amongst the papers can and does decline into a 'minimal tolerance' position where the host society is invited to tolerate immigrants even though it does not really like them, because they are necessary to its economic development.

More prepared to meet white hostility head on is the concluding article to a series of features in March 1966. 'Special writer' Ray Seaton analyses some of the racist ideas evident in letters to the newspaper provoked by the series, on the grounds that 'prejudices have to be studied, analysed and understood before they can be overcome'. Large chunks of the letters are reproduced with a commentary ranging from a patient explanation of the history of British colonialism to more sarcastic comments on more openly emotional racist comments. The article ends with an account of the work of Wolverhampton Council for Racial Harmony, allowing the conclusion that

Racial harmony is not being treated as an abstract ideal, but as an essential feature of life in a multiracial region, to be achieved only by practical and constructive efforts.

The same writer in an earlier (February 1965) article with a misleading headline—'Ghetto Menace on Housing Estates'—sought to dispel the myth (incorporated in that headline) that black immigrants create slums. An article in April of the same year recounted the work of Wolverhampton Council's Special Welfare Education Department, which had employed an Asian and West Indian welfare officer. The article does not deny the educational problems caused by the arrival of immigrant children, but neither does it contextualize them. The main stress is that such problems are soluble in the long run. Even here, however, the word coloured is persistently used, and the exploration of cultural differences is of a loose and decontextualized kind, e.g. 'In some ways the West Indian has no sense of time'.

Another attempt to normalize immigrant problems is apparent in a political feature of March 1966—'Can the Immigrants Decide the Fate of Harold Wilson?' An appeal by three immigrant organizations urging black people to abstain from voting is presented as a logical reaction to 'Labour's About Face on Immigration'. Yet even this article, with all its good intentions, cannot avoid stereotyping in its discussion of black immigrant's role as voters:

it must be recognized that a great many will not be on the voting register.

And there are a variety of reasons for this. In the first place, a good many can neither read nor write English. Again, many of the coloured immigrants entertain secret fears that if they return their voting forms, they will be laying themselves open to prosecution for overcrowding, to income-tax demands and other visitations from authority.

In somes cases, the filling-in of the electoral forms is left to the 'boss-man'—the landlord in the big old terraced houses where many families live together.

Like all stereotypes, this has some elements of truth in it; and like all stereotypes it exaggerates and generalizes particular characteristics into a negative image. West Indians receive similar treatment in the discussion of the organizational abilities of black immigrants:

While it might be possible to organize the Indians on some scale, the West Indians by and large and because of their ebullient nature, are probably incapable of being completely organized.

Of the remaining five feature articles, two show what can be done in education, and two do the same for race relations. One of the educational articles (November 1966) discusses the growth of nursery schools and their beneficial effects for immigrant children, while the other is an interview with the newly appointed headmaster of Grove Lane School, where 90 per cent of the pupils are black—'Patient and affable, the headmaster sees a challenge, not a dilemma' (September 1968). He emphasizes the possibility of solving outstanding problems through a process of integration, given time and dedication. On race relations, an article of June 1967—'So Little Time, So Much To Be Done'—follows in the wake of David Ennals, Under-Secretary for Immigrant Affairs. The clear objectives must be to achieve equality of opportunity. It suggests Ennals does not really understand the nature and extent of prejudice in Wolverhampton, and further criticizes him for spending too little time with immigrant leaders. Less pointedly, a feature of December 1968 tacitly approves the approach of Mrs Edith Ford, secretary for the West Bromwich Council for Community Relations, and her belief that: 'Personal relationships can overcome cultural and communication differences.' The final *Express and Star* feature is a very accurate reproduction of the argument of Paul Foot's book *The Rise of Enoch Powell* though the value of this is decreased by the extensive subsequent coverage given to the fact that Foot gave the wrong address for Powell's Wolverhampton home.

The Wolverhampton *Express and Star*'s editorial stance is not to deny the dominant definition of race, but to assert that existent problems are soluble in the long run. Thus, though an editorial of 14 January 1963 notes the concern of the National Union of Teachers about the problem of immigrant children, the local educational situation is assessed through realized or potential efforts to improve the situation: the opening of a new school in a mainly immigrant area (6 September 1968), a welcome for the advocacy of coloured school governors (23 November 1968) and an increase in immigrant teachers (5 October 1969).

The policies of Enoch Powell are adversely compared with those of Edward Heath whom it sees as having a qualitatively distinct and eminently more constructive approach (23 April and 21 September 1968), though again the *Express and Star* criticizes Powell more for the form than the content of his speeches. It also tends to reduce the problem of how to oppose Powell to one of law and order dismissing the 'anarchy' of both pro- and anti-Powell demonstrations: 'A Plague on Both Your Houses', 3 July 1968.

The Wolverhampton *Express and Star* is clearly opposed to discrimination of all kinds, though a little quick to praise minimally constructive moves made by the National Union of Labour Clubs (16 April 1963), a local working men's club (14 August 1963), or the Amalgamated Engineering Union (23 February 1967). It is heavily in favour of racial integration, applauding a housing committee suggestion for the establishment of multiracial clubs on housing estates (10 September 1965), opposing a segregationalist proposal of a city councillor (8 May 1968) and fully supporting the work of the local Council for Racial Harmony (7 June 1968). It can, however, suggest that integration can mean black conformity to white ways, as in its opposition to the idea of black parliamentary candidates to represent the special interests of black people (28 January 1964) or its scepticism whether the immigrant population is sophisticated enough to appreciate the 'delicate nuances' of British politics (27 August 1964).

The paper believes wholeheartedly in research by statutory or voluntary bodies. The Nuffield Foundation (28 September 1963), a Parliamentary Committee on Race (7 March 1969) and the Runnymede Trust (19 October 1970) all come in for fulsome praise. Government aid is also a necessity (23 July 1968 and 20 October 1969). Strongly disapproved of is any form of illegal immigration, and heavier penalties are proposed (24 August 1967 and 21 March 1970).

Overall the Wolverhampton *Express and Star* tests the boundaries of the dominant definition of the 'race problem', but only rarely moves beyond them. One such occasion is an editorial of January 1966 which underlines the need for immigrant labour to run the town's bus service which is seriously short of staff. More often the paper attempts to argue against intolerance but within the terms and problems such intolerance has defined. Thus, it is quick to positively evaluate cultural differences, as in this editorial description of the West Indian cricket team (30 July 1963):

To them cricket truly is a game to be played at all times in the best possible sporting spirit, and with as much gay abandon as the occasion permits.

It should be said, however, that the paper is clear about the nature of white hostility even if it is unsure how to combat it. An editorial of 25 September 1965 runs:

Jamaicans,
A 'Punch' cartoon shows a licensee telling cumstomers he cannot understand why India and Pakistan are not good neighbours, then turning a coloured man from his bar. The cartoon illuminates the racial ambivalence of many English people whose personal actions contradict their moral principles. It is what gives the English their international reputation for hypocrisy.

If Mr Norman Manley, leader of the Jamaican Opposition People's National Party, is right in saying that Jamaicans are tolerated here only on sufferance, we are in danger of becoming a nation of racial bigots. We subscribe to traditional Christianity and liberal precepts, accept political refugees, defend the underdog, oppose all forms of tyranny, listen appreciatively when others commend our tolerance—and then, according to Mr Manley, make coloured immigrants feel 'unwanted and alien'.

Relations will improve only when white and coloured people get to know one another better.

The last sentence is manifestly weak, but it is hard to imagine the rest of the editorial appearing in either of the other two papers. The editorial measures both the strength and the weakness of the *Express and Star*'s attempts to grapple with racial prejudice.

The Coventry Evening Telegraph

This paper carried seven editorials and only two substantial features. It was at once proud and complacent about what it perceived as Coventry's tradition of tolerance. An editorial of 29 October 1963—'Cosmopolitan Coventry'—conveyed a tone which was to dominate subsequent editorial discussion. An immigrant spokesman, Dr Dhani Prem, favourably compares the race relations record of Coventry with that of other Midlands towns and cities. The paper accepts and emphasizes this portrait, attributing the overall achievement to the positive attitudes adopted by the city council, local trade unions, and the cathedral. There is, however, no explanation of why other councils, unions and churches in other towns have believed differently. Instead, self-congratulation is expressed.

Coventry is not a place where race troubles are likely to occur. That is not to say antagonisms are never aroused.

Immigrants and residents do not always get along together easily from the start. Each has something to learn and there are some who will never learn. But the record of adaptability in Coventry is a good one.

We are entitled to look on the credit side occasionally to rejoice in some of the signs of basic goodness that motivates a community and makes for the good name of the city.

The first of the two features, provoked by the Institute of Race Relations national survey, is less self-confident and more anxious in its approach as the headline indicates: 'Britain Must Face The Challenge of Immigration' (27 August 1964). The report is interpreted as describing the process of absorbing immigrants as 'proceeding slowly though somewhat painfully'. The economic causes and benefits of black immigration are outlined before the social problems of housing and education are mentioned. Differences of language and culture are being slowly overcome partly because immigrants have shown themselves willing to participate in many parts of British life, especially by joining trade unions and various kinds of voluntary organizations. The discussion ends, however, on the ominous note with which it began; that unless we continue and improve our efforts we could undergo the same racial traumas as the United States. The main guarantee is our sense of tradition—'Our reputation as a generous tolerant nation is now at stake.'

The attempt to employ a broad perspective on race present in this feature is rarely so evident in the editorials. Problems are isolated, easy generalizations made and possible solutions left vague. Two examples are an editorial of 11 April 1966 on the responsibilities of the local Rent Office which specifically mentions the case of an immigrant landlord guilty of overcrowding, and an editorial welcome (6 February 1967) for the new immigrant language centres which blithely asks that the 'English way of life' should be taught as well as the English language.

The *Coventry Evening Telegraph* is quick to insist that moments of racial conflict are aberrant and quickly solved. Thus, a racialist attack on an Indian family's house in October 1967 is defused by the editorial insistence that the perpetrators were 'twisted creatures' and 'vandals'. Normality (tolerance) is represented in the action of white neighbours who help to remove daubings of paint. The conclusion is thus made too easy: 'Coloured people are now as much a part of Coventry as Irish, Welsh or Scots.'

On two of the major issues of race which involve questions of antagonism and opposition, those of Powell and the South African rugby tour, the *Coventry Evening Telegraph* diverts attention away from the main issues to that of law and order. It condemns anti-Powell demonstrators as 'Red Nazis' (8 May 1968), and deplores the open association of some Members of Parliament with plans for 'disorderly and potentially illegal demonstrations' against the tour (5 December 1969). The final editorial of March 1970 is also evasive, indulging in some cheap sarcasm at the expense of attempts to have some nursery rhymes referred to the Race Relations Board.

Once again it is in a feature (March 1969) that the calm sea of complacency is disturbed. 'Where Black Meets White and No one Notices' recounts the work of Coventry Overseas Students Association which through organized activities seeks to overcome intolerance of cultural differences and taboos on interracial sexual relationships. The overall tone is one of confirmation—here is another example of what good can be done. The reporter, however, adds an aside which touches on black feelings about white attitudes which suggests they neither experience nor believe in white tolerance:

I have spoken to many coloured people in Coventry about racial prejudice. A minority say they experience none, yet others say it is so intense they cannot wait to leave and go back home.

Such a comment is however a minor turbulence rather than a major storm. The *Coventry Evening Telegraph* gives a low profile to race and avoids defining the problem in terms of competition for resources or ineradicable differences of culture. However, while the definition of the situation proffered by white hostility is not accepted, neither is one derived from the immigrants own situation or experience evident. Instead of 'the immigrant problem', we do not have as the Wolverhampton *Express and Star* perceives a 'white hostility problem', but no problem at all to speak of, provided we preach and practice tolerance. This is a weak position to hold, and the weakness becomes more evident as the period moves on, the *Coventry Evening Telegraph* moving in its news coverage more and more towards the other two papers while maintaining its editorial line that the problems inherently defined in such coverage do not in fact exist.

The differences between the evening papers we have briefly examined here exist only within a common controlled pattern of newspaper coverage of race. There are some differences in editorial approach, use and type of feature, news topics and reference themes. There are also sometimes outright contradictions between the perspectives employed in editorials, features and news. Together with overseas coverage, these characteristics make possible the identification of slightly different patterns of approach in each paper. We shall consider the significance of the existence of these differences within a common framework in the conclusion. For the present, we need to consider the same problems in relation to the two weekly papers in our sample.

Chapter 5

Race in the West Midlands press: home news in the weekly papers

Topics and reference themes

The distribution of topics in the two weekly papers taken as an aggregate is substantially similar to that evident in the evening papers (see Table 54). The major difference is in the greater coverage of the race-relations topic. Some of the other differences tend to be attributable to the length of stories. Thus, the crime stories are even shorter than they were in the

TABLE 54. Topics in the weeklies combined

Topic	Average length of article (inches)	Number of items	Column inches	Per-centage all column inches	Percentage column inches (evenings)
Human interest	11.1	89	991	16	16
Crime	7.3	133	977	16	18
Race relations	10.3	95	973	16	9
Racil integration	21.9	23	504	8	4
Immigration	6.7	52	348	6	8
White hostility	10.9	31	338	6	5
Discrimination	13.8	22	303	5	5
Housing	11.0	25	275	5	6
Immigrant organizations	11.5	23	265	4	3
Cultural differences	8.1	31	250	4	5
Education	11.4	21	240	4	5
Health	9.1	17	155	3	1
Legislation	8.3	10	83	1	1
Employment	6.4	10	64	1	2
Sport and entertainment	9.6	5	48	1	4
Celebrities	13.0	2	26	1	1
Numbers	3.5	4	14	—	1
Police	—	Nil	Nil	0	0.6
Other	11.2	14	157	3	5.4
TOTAL	(9.9)[1]	607	6,011	100	100

1. Average length of all articles.

evenings, giving a column-inch total less than that of human interest. There are, however, exactly 50 per cent more crime than human-interest items. Immigration as a topic similarly appears in shorter items, often letters and has a greater share of items than it does of column inches. Conversely, racial integration items tend to be long, often pictures, and this accounts for the topic's greater prominence.

Overall, it is the similarity which is striking: the predominance of crime and human-interest stories, the essential conceptualization of the race problem in terms of race relations immigration and white hostility, the 'second order' status of local competition for resources and lifestyles in housing, education and cultural differences, the underreporting of employment and black–police relationships. The similarity is still there in the division of each topic into subtopics with evidence of if anything a narrower focusing of perspective than that of the evening papers.

The greater coverage of minor crimes in the weeklies tends to depress the proportion of violent crimes, but even so 32 per cent of all crimes reported in the weeklies are of this latter type. The coverage of race relations expands on all subtopics, but there is significantly less emphasis on 'positive steps'—15 per cent of the weekly race-relations subtopics compared with 20 per cent in the evenings, and an increase in race relations as an election issue from 3 per cent of the evenings to 13 per cent of the weeklies.

The clearest evidence of a narrowing focus is apparent in the subtopics of immigration and racial integration. The immigration issue is quite simply one of control (44 per cent) and of an election issue (55 per cent). No other considerations enter. As for racial integration, assimilation is even stronger than in the evenings, being the keynote of 7 per cent of all items.

The subtopics for white hostility and discrimination look like lightened versions of the evenings portrait, with more emphasis on hostile organizations and even less interest—only 4 per cent of all items—in discrimination as a general topic.

As for the key local issues—housing, education and cultural differences—their share of race coverage in the weeklies is slightly less than in the evenings—13 compared with 16 per cent—but this is compensated for by a greater concentration on health. In the housing and education subtopics, there is a negative emphasis similar to that in the evening papers, though its forms are slightly different. The association of immigrants with neighbourhood decay, slums and council house allocation is still very much apparent, but with a heavier emphasis on the housing shortage (8 per cent) and immigrants as landlords (30 per cent). In education lowering of standards is emphasized at the expense of overcrowding, but there is also a coverage of 'good adjustment of black children' of 20 per cent which was virtually non-existent in the evenings. The superficially educative subtopics in cultural differences—'descriptive of' and 'differences'—are only 16 per cent of the weeklies compared with 41 per cent in the evenings. There is, however, a greater coverage of 'positive evaluation', virtually non-existent in the evenings, but accounting for a quarter of the weeklies cultural differences items. Less ambiguous are the subtopics of the expanded health subject: over half are concerned with 'infectious diseases' and 'immigrants overstraining hospital services'.

This largely negative portrait is only partly balanced by the greater attention given to immigrant organizations, especially their involvement in cultural activities.

The controversies over the visits from South African teams which provide most of the sport and entertainment items in the evening papers do not impinge on the world of the weeklies, who divide what little news they do have in this category equally between television/film controversies and more general references to sport.

Reference themes

The 607 topic items in the two weekly papers produced 453 reference themes, an average of 0.74 per item, exactly the same as the evenings. In similar fashion again, the five major reference headings are not the same as the five major topics (see Table 55).

TABLE 55

Topics	Items	Reference themes	Number
Crime	133	Cultural differences	52
Race relations	95	Housing	48
Human interest	89	Education	31
Immigration	52	Employment	31
White hostility	31	Legislation	26
Cultural differences	31	Race relations	26
Housing	25	Immigration	24
Racial integration	23	Immigrant organizations	23
Immigrant organizations	23	Racial integration	22
Discrimination	22	Powell	20

Cultural differences as a reference theme appeared eleven times in the context of crime: only 9 per cent of the crimes but over 20 per cent of the total references to cultural differences of these eleven, seven referred to language.

Human-interest stories had more explicit reference themes in the weeklies than in the evenings. Only one-sixth of such stories in the evenings had reference themes (35 out of 208); in the weeklies nearly a third (26 out of 89). These 26 stories produced 30 reference themes of which 6 were to education, 5 to employment, 4 each to housing and white hostility, 3 to racial integration, 2 to cultural differences and the remaining 6 to a variety of themes. Here is evidence that the problem/news framework applied elsewhere to the press presentation of framework does penetrate the category of human interest as well as that of crime.

The general tendency noted in the evenings for subreference themes to be even more negative than subtopics is again apparent in the weeklies. In cultural differences, language is emphasized even more heavily and accounts for over a half of all such references. Housing, education and health follow the pattern of the evening subreference themes. One-fifth of the employment references are to black workers in the health services, but over a quarter to suggestions that black people take jobs from whites or to discussion of black unemployment rates. Legislation references are mostly of a general kind though there is considerable reference to the 1965 Act. In immigration and racial integration, the narrow focus of the subtopics is somewhat loosened: numbers and Kenyan Asians appear in the former, pluralism in the latter.

The numbers of reference themes being considered under each heading is really quite small and too much should not be read into variations. Nevertheless, the high random element in such small figures makes all the more remarkable the consistent reproduction of the same definitions already examined in the evening papers. The construction of a 'total mentions', Table 56 re-emphasizes the similarity of perspective as the distribution follows almost exactly that of the evenings.

TABLE 56. Total mentions in the weeklies (percentages in parentheses)

Heading	Topic items		Reference themes		Total mentions	
Crime	133	(22)	13	(3)	146	(14)
Human interest	89	(15)	—	(—)	89	(8)
Race relations	95	(15)	26	(6)	121	(11)
Cultural differences	31	(5)	52	(11)	83	(8)
Immigration	52	(9)	24	(5)	76	(7)
Housing	25	(4)	48	(11)	73	(7)
Education	21	(3)	31	(7)	52	(5)
White hostility	31	(5)	17	(4)	48	(5)
Immigrant organizations	23	(4)	23	(5)	46	(4)
Racial integration	23	(4)	22	(5)	45	(4)
Discrimination	22	(4)	20	(4)	42	(4)
Employment	10	(2)	31	(7)	41	(4)
Legislation	10	(2)	26	(6)	36	(3)
Health	17	(3)	14	(3)	31	(3)
Numbers	4	(0.7)	19	(4)	23	(2)
Powell	—	(—)	20	(4)	20	(2)
All others	21	(2.3)	67	(15)	88	(9)
TOTAL	607	(100)	453	(100)	1,060	(100)

The scale for measuring foregound and background is also substantially the same: crime, +10.23; race relations, +3.65; immigration, +2.16; white hostility, +1.82; discrimination, +1.10; racial integration, +1.04; immigrant organizations, 1.00; education, —1.47; cultural differences, —1.67; housing, —1.92; employment, —3.10.

Just as clearly as in the evenings, the major topics are not about local face-to-face interracial relationships or competition for resources. These—education, cultural differences, housing and employment—are more frequently used as a background to the essential questions: race relations, immigration and white hostility.

In general then the distribution of topics and reference themes, their further division into subtopics and subthemes, the relationships between them, and the total mentions of areas of concern, are substantially the same in the evenings and the weeklies. The chronology, however, looks rather different. The total volume of news expands earlier and does not show as dramatic an increase in 1968. Furthermore, there is only a marginal increase in the total amount of race news over the period as a whole: the last three years produce the same amount of news as the first three. Reference themes exceed items in 1968, as in the evenings, but this has already happened before, in 1963. Clearly the race problem defined as a number of (interconnected) issues has been established much earlier in the weeklies. Tables 57–59 summarize these trends.

Over the two periods, some topics decline in importance: housing, health, white hostility, discrimination, immigrant organizations, race relations and crime. Others come more into prominence: education, immigration, racial integration, cultural differences and human interest. The pattern is repeated in the reference themes with the additional decline of employment and legislation. It is possible to interpret these movements as a sharper form of the trend evident in the evenings: the maintenance and rejuvenation of conflict (education, immigration, cultural differences) yet a reassurance that day-to-day interracial living is devoid of tension (human interest, racial integration).

It would appear then that the Powell peak is less pronounced. His speeches did not have as dramatic an effect on the weeklies. The reason for this is the notorious anti-immigrant campaign of 1964–65 in Smethwick, which included an election battle between the two main

TABLE 57. Weeklies over time. Topics: 2 periods

Topic	1963–66		1967–70		1963–70	
	Inches	Items	Inches	Items	Inches	Items
Housing	189	18	86	7	275	25
Education	59	5	181	16	240	21
Health	109	11	46	6	155	17
Employment	29	5	35	5	64	10
White hostility	199	19	139	12	338	31
Crime	548	69	429	64	977	133
Celebrities	26	2	—	—	26	2
Immigration	153	23	195	29	348	52
Race relations	509	56	469	39	973	95
Immigrant organizations	170	15	95	8	265	23
Black hostility	—	—	—	—	—	—
Numbers	9	3	5	1	14	4
Discrimination	202	15	101	7	303	22
Discrimination by coloureds	—	—	—	—	—	—
Police	—	—	—	—	—	—
Racial integration	42	3	462	20	504	23
Cultural differences	82	13	168	18	250	31
Human interest	411	35	580	54	991	89
Legislation	69	8	14	2	83	10
Sport and entertainment	33	2	15	3	48	5
Other	44	4	113	10	157	14
TOTAL	2,878	306	3,133	301	6,011	607

TABLE 58. Weeklies. Reference themes: 2 periods

Theme	1963–66	1967–70	1963–70
Housing	36	12	48
Education	10	21	31
Health	8	6	14
Employment	17	14	31
Numbers	11	8	19
White hostility	11	6	17
Discrimination	11	9	20
Racial integration	13	9	22
Crime	7	6	13
Racial tension	7	8	15
Cultural differences	19	33	52
Immigration	9	15	24
Legislation	14	12	26
Race relations	10	16	26
Immigrant organizations	15	8	23
Powell	0	20	20
All others	32	20	52
TOTAL	230	223	453

TABLE 59. Weeklies. Topics and themes by year

Year	Topic		Reference themes
	Column inches	Items	
1963	744	83	84
1964	824	92	62
1965	860	85	53
1966	450	46	31
1967	692	73	30
1968	918	99	109
1969	779	66	50
1970	744	63	34
TOTAL	6,011	607	453

political parties on the issue of race. At this point, we become aware that the Smethwick paper has determined the chronological shape of the weeklies aggregate. We have in fact been dealing with two rather different chronologies. There would appear to be more difference between the two weeklies than between the weeklies and the evenings as groups.

Differences between the weeklies

The first major difference between the two weekly newspapers is that whereas the *Warley News Telephone* devotes a higher percentage of its total news space to race than any of the evening appers, the *Walsall Observer* produces the smallest proportion of race news. Table 60 illustrates this point.

TABLE 60. Percentage of news space to race

	Overseas	Home-overseas	Home	Immigrant population
Warley News Telephone	—	0.2	6.2	7.1
Walsall Observer	—	0.1	1.3	2.5
Weeklies, total	—	0.1	2.9	—
Evenings, total	0.6	0.4	3.7	—

The *Warley News Telephone* carries proportionally over two-thirds more news on race in the United Kingdom than the average for the evening papers, whereas the *Walsall Observer* coverage only just exceeds a third of the average. Furthermore, there are substantial differences between the papers in their coverage of topics and reference themes, and the distribution of race news over time (see Tables 61–64).

TABLE 61. Differences between the weeklies: *Warley News Telephone*, topics

Topic	1963–66		1967–70		1963–70		Percentage all column inches
	A[1]	B[2]	A	B	A	B	
Housing	183	17	3	1	186	18	4
Education	30	3	88	8	118	11	3
Health	86	9	0	0	86	9	2
Employment	17	2	24	3	41	5	1
White hostility	174	17	112	10	286	27	7
Crime	384	44	301	43	685	87	16
Celebrities	9	1	—	—	9	1	
Immigration	135	20	134	19	269	39	6
Race relations	462	49	311	26	773	75	18
Immigrant organizations	165	14	81	7	246	21	6
Black hostility	—	—	—	—	—	—	
Numbers	3	1	—	—	3	1	
Discrimination	161	11	60	5	221	16	5
Discrimination by coloureds	—	—	—	—	—	—	
Police	—	—	—	—	—	—	
Racial integration	11	1	384	16	395	17	9
Cultural differences	62	10	124	12	186	22	4
Human interest	231	19	329	25	560	44	13
Legislation	57	6	7	1	64	7	2
Sport and entertainment	19	1	15	3	34	4	1
Other	23	3	30	5	33	8	1
TOTAL	2,212	228	2,003	184	4,215	412	98

1. A=Column inches.
2. B=Items.

These differences only form a pattern if considered chronologically. Some of the topics which the *Warley News Telephone* covers extensively are concentrated in the earlier period. Race relations, white hostility, and immigrant organizations—on all of which the *Warley News Telephone* coverage exceeds that in the evenings—actually decrease as the period

TABLE 62. Differences between the weeklies: *Walsall Observer*, topics

Topic	1963–66		1967–70		1963–70		Percentage all column inches
	A[1]	B[2]	A	B	A	B	
Housing	6	1	83	6	89	7	5
Education	29	2	93	8	122	10	7
Health	23	2	46	6	69	8	4
Employment	12	3	11	2	23	5	1
White hostility	25	2	27	2	52	4	3
Crime	164	25	128	21	292	46	16
Celebrities	17	1	—	—	17	1	1
Immigration	18	3	61	10	79	13	4
Race relations	47	7	158	13	200	20	11
Immigrant organizations	5	1	14	1	19	2	1
Black hostility	—	—	—	—	—	—	
Numbers	6	2	5	1	11	3	
Discrimination	41	4	41	2	2	82	5
Discrimination by coloureds	—	—	—	—	—	—	
Police	—	—	—	—	—	—	
Racial integration	31	2	78	4	109	6	6
Cultural differences	20	3	44	6	64	9	4
Human interest	180	16	251	29	431	45	24
Legislation	12	2	7	1	19	3	1
Sport and entertainment	14	1	—	—	14	1	1
Other	21	1	83	5	104	6	6
TOTAL	666	78	1,130	117	1,796	195	100

1. A=Column inches.
2. B=Items.

wears on. Their predominance is, therefore, due largely to very extensive coverage in the early years. Conversely, some of the topics receive a relatively small proportion of the overall coverage because they are particularly absent in the early years, but tend to appear more frequently later on. The *Warley News Telephone*'s presentation of human interest stories in the second half of the period is proportionally quite close to the mean score for the evenings: 16 per cent as compared with 17 per cent. It is the very low proportion in the first half—only 10 per cent—which makes the overall figure the lowest of any newspaper. The amount of concern with education increases only slightly in the second half. The most dramatic increase is the racial integration topic: less than half of 1 per cent of all news in the first half, it accounts for one-fifth of race news in the second half.

Thus the *Warley News Telephone* does react to Powell, but does so primarily in terms of race-relations topics, not those of white hostility, education and immigration which do increase but not as dramatically as in the evenings. The total coverage for 1968 is not as high as that for 1963 and the 1968–70 total is well below that for 1963–65.

Not to be outdone in manifestations of independence, the *Walsall Observer* is the only paper actually to decrease its total coverage in 1968 (Fig. 8), mainly because crime and human interest decrease in numbers of

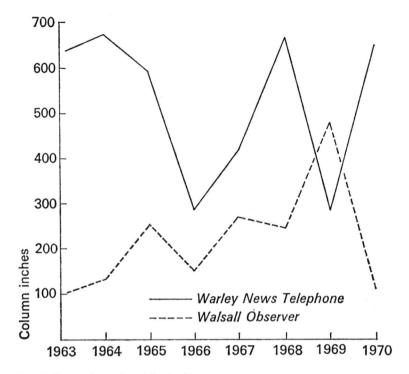

FIG. 8. Comparison of weeklies topic coverage.

stories and total column inches. It is their resurgence in the following year—there being more human interest inches in this year than any other—which determines the 'peak' coverage of 1969. Again uniquely, the *Walsall Observer* total coverage in 1970 is the lowest of all the eight years.

The topic distribution of the *Walsall Observer* is also deviant. By some quirk it seems to compensate for the *Warley News Telephone* as if they were diverging in opposite directions from the same norm. Where the Warley newspaper has the lowest human interest figure, the Walsall paper has the highest, at 24 per cent of all column inches. While the issues in Warley from 1963 to 1966 centre on race relations, immigration and white hostility totalling 35 per cent of all coverage, in Walsall they are less than half as important appearing in only 15 per cent of column inches. Indeed, during this early period the *Walsall Observer*, more than any other paper, has race appear through routinized news: crime (25 per cent) and human interest (27 per cent) covering more than half of all race-related news.

In the second half, race relations, immigration and education do increase their joint share of column inches from 16 to 27 per cent, but white hostility remains the same absolutely and decreases proportionally from 4 to 2 per cent, giving an overall coverage of white hostility lower than in any other paper. Human interest remains high at 22 per cent, and racial integration doubles absolutely, from 5 to 7 per cent.

TABLE 63. Differences between the weeklies:
Warley News Telephone, reference themes

Reference theme	1963–66	1967–70	1963–70	Percentage all reference themes
Housing	28	4	32	10
Education	8	12	20	6
Health	6	3	9	3
Employment	11	7	18	6
Numbers	11	4	15	5
White hostility	10	2	12	4
Black hostility	2	1	3	1
Discrimination	11	2	13	4
Discrimination by coloureds	—	—	—	
Police	—	1	1	
Racial integration	11	6	17	5
Crime	7	3	10	3
Racial tension	3	7	10	3
Cultural differences	12	23	35	11
Immigration	8	8	16	5
Legislation	12	7	19	6
Race relations	8	13	21	7
Immigrant organizations	15	8	23	7
Sport and entertainment	—	4	4	1
Powell	—	10	10	3
British politics	9	—	9	3
Black power	—	—	—	
Second generation	0	0	0	
Churches	5	4	9	3
Overseas countries	11	5	16	5
TOTAL	188	134	322	101

These differences are reproduced less dramatically in the reference themes. Some of the reference themes dominant in the Warley paper in the earlier period virtually disappear—housing, immigrant organizations and legislation are examples. Reference themes in the *Walsall Observer* increase along familiar lines: cultural differences, education, Powell.

It is our contention that these differences form patterns which merit explanation in terms of each paper's perception of the race situation in its immediate locality. The early years in the *Warley News Telephone* provide a sharp portrait of direct political conflict over race, involving an election and discussion of the very specific local issue of housing against a background of cultural differences and argument about legislation. During this period, human interest stories are very rare; and racial integration as topic and reference theme is to all intents and purposes extinct. Both these sorts of news increase dramatically in the second, while white hostility and race relations fall away. In 1968, there is a revival of interest in education, immigration and cultural differences, but this is largely confined to that year. The drop in overall coverage in 1969 is extreme. Meanwhile, the key issue of the earlier period—housing—provides only one item of 3 inches in the four years of the second half.

TABLE 64. Differences between the weeklies:
Walsall Observer, reference themes

Reference theme	1963–66	1967–70	1963–70	Percentage all reference themes
Housing	8	8	16	12
Education	2	9	11	8
Health	2	3	5	4
Employment	6	7	13	10
Numbers	—	4	4	3
White hostility	1	4	5	4
Black hostility	—	—	—	
Discrimination	0	7	7	5
Discrimination by coloureds	—	—	—	
Police	1	—	1	
Racial integration	2	3	5	4
Crime	4	1	5	4
Racial tension	4	1	5	4
Cultural differences	7	10	17	13
Immigration	1	7	8	6
Legislation	2	5	7	5
Race relations	2	3	5	4
Immigrant organizations	0	0	0	
Sport and entertainment	—	—	—	
Powell	0	10	10	8
British politics	—	—	—	
Black power	—	1	1	
Second generation	—	1	1	
Churches	3	1	4	3
Overseas countries	1	2	3	2
TOTAL	42	89	131	97

If the paper serving Smethwick provides most evidence of hostile conflict in the earlier yeras, that serving Walsall gives least indication that race is an important social and political issue, its news presentation being essentially of a routine kind. The *Walsall Observer* does react to 1968 by giving increased attention to housing, education, cultural differences and immigration, but white hostility receives little presentation, racial integration increases, and human interest remains high.

The reasons for these different patterns are quite distinct. In the Warley case, the paper appears to be making efforts to recover from and compensate for the very high level of conflict it encouraged in the early years. The intention to do this is strong enough for it to partially resist reopening the race issue in Enoch Powell's terms. It needs to be understood just what kind of role the paper played during the earlier period, and we propose briefly to analyse one very important edition as an illustration.

The issue of the *Smethwick Telephone* published on Friday, 9 October 1964 was the last before polling day, the following Thursday. Table 65 reproduces a list of the race-related items appearing in that issue, representing over one-third of its total news space. The analysis of topics and reference themes is given in Table 66.

... notices in the *Smethwick Telephone*: 9 October edition 1964

Page No.	Type of news[1]	Length (column inches)[2]	Headline	Topic[3]	Reference theme
1	N	4	Indian Assaulted Girl 18	Crime 1	
1	N	22	Tories Face Uproar	Race relations 6	
1	P	15	Prizewinning Nurses	Human interest	Employment d
1	N	5	Illegal Leaflets—Police Action	White hostility 3	
1	N	4	Griffiths Criticises Race Appeal	Other 2	
3	N	12	What Voting Tory Will Mean: Hugill	Race relations 6	Housing, Education j, Health g
3	N	5	Hit Former Landlord—£10 fine	Crime 1	
3	N	5	Shop Blast: Police Probe Goes On	Crime 1	
4	F+P	32	So Friends Won't Talk to Her	White hostility 2	
10	N	8	Regional Government Needed: Hugill	Race relations 7	
10	N	8	His Kick Flattened Lighter	Crime 1	
12	N	12	Sikhs Do Want to Integrate	Race relations 6	Racial integration e, Immigration organizations d
13	N	13	Town's Tories Isolated—Gordon Walker	Race relations 6	Employment d, Housing, Housing b, Education a, Employment
22	N	19	Candidate No. 4 Says: End Immigration	Immigration 7	South Africa f
23	L	4	Notorious Smethwick	Immigration 7	Black Africa
23	L	3	No Truth In This Tale	Race relations 6	Housing g
23	L	3	So We're All Racialists	Race relations 7	
23	L	2	Wrong Statement	Immigration 7	
23	L	2	Major Problems	Housing 10	
23	L	2	Bradford Supporter	Immigration 7	
23	L	4	What a New Voter Thinks	Immigration 7	
23	L	13	Why I Shall Vote Labour	Race relations 6	Housing b, Employment d
23	L	2	Hostels for Immigrants	Housing 10	
23	L	2	Three Questions	Race relations 7	
23	L	6	The Fourth Candidate	Immigration 7	
23	L	11	Sir Edward Didn't Refuse To Speak To Me—Griffiths	Race relations 6	Crime n, White hostility b
24	N	9	Students to Help Fight Tories	Race relations 6	
24	N	5	Why He Signed That Form	Immigrant organizations 4	

1. N = News; P = Photograph; L = Letter; F = Feature.
2. Total coverage, 237 inches.
3. A list of topics and subtopics are to be found in Appendix 1.

TABLE 66. Analysis of topics and reference themes

	Items	Inches
Topic		
Human interest	1	15
Crime (violent)	4	22
Race relations (anti-colour prejudice)	3	13
Race relations (as an election issue)	8	95
Immigration (as an election issue)	6	37
White hostility (all subtopics)	2	37
Housing (all subtopics)	2	4
Immigrant organizations	1	5
Other	2	9
TOTAL	29	237

Reference themes
5 Housing
4 Employment
2 Education
1 Health, racial integration, immigration organizations, white hostility, crime, Black Africa, South Africa

The routinized items—crime and human interest—have been swamped by the impending election news, though as we shall see, they bear some considerable relationship to it. Apart from this, however, the topics and reference themes are precisely those which form the basic framework for all the provincial press coverage of race. This fact has two implications. First, the *Smethwick Telephone* can represent and reinforce an openly racist political campaign without moving outside the news framework it shares with the other papers. This we suggest is because the framework itself implies a negative definition of black people and can be easily inhabited by openly hostile attitudes. Secondly, the difference between the *Smethwick Telephone* and the other papers is one of typography and language, which cannot be identified by content analysis.

A brief analysis of the front page of that issue may illustrate. Of nine substantial items, five have explicit race content. Sandwiched between these five are four other items: two on local strikes, one on the results of local cycling proficiency tests, and one inset picture of an 'eleventh hour' election candidate (who it transpires on the inside pages is standing on an anti-immigrant platform). These items grouped together in the middle of the page, cover just fourteen inches. The remaining fifty inches are all concerned with race. More precisely the lead story and the next two most prominently displayed, cover the imminent election; the other two, in significant juxtaposition with each other and the political items, are concerned with crime and human interest.

The anti-immigrant Conservative candidate Alderman Peter Griffiths appears in two of the three major stories—an extreme, not to say, indecent amount of exposure. In the first he accuses the Labour Party of deliberately organizing heckling at one of his election meetings; in the second he again attacks Labour for issuing leaflets aimed specifically at West

Indians. In another story, he is also being threatened with a writ by a Labour Party official for alleged defamation—a story without explicit race content: but this election had no other issues. The third explicitly race-related item reports a police investigation into 'anti-immigrant' posters which were found by 'an Indian' and reported by the local Labour Party to have no publisher's or printer's name.

Griffiths is clearly the dominant figure. The definition of race carried by his persona is not explicit, but no regular reader of the *Smethwick Telephone*, nor indeed any inhabitant of the town, would need it to be made so. Griffiths policy called for immigration control and repatriation on the basis that Smethwick had no resources, room or time for black immigrants. His definition of the race problem was only partly opposed by a Labour Party typically impaled on the twin horns of expediency and principle, seeing no contradiction in the advocacy of black immigration control and opposition to discrimination.

The power of that definition extends into 'routinized' race news. It is impossible to believe that the two non-political but race-related stories appearing on the front page did so by accident. In the crime item headed 'Indian Assaulted Girl 18', the themes of race and sex are intertwined, though the report is (as many stories of this kind in all the papers often were), extremely imprecise. The item records that the '40 year old Indian' assaulted a girl who replied by calling him a 'dirty hound', and that the girl's male companion grappled with the offender. It is, however, not clear whether the charge was indecent or common assault, nor how the incident began. Clearer is the fact that the Indian had been drinking, and was additionally charged with stealing a half-pint glass from a pub. The fine was £20, the costs £12 6s., but the nature of the defendant's plea is not recorded.

The characteristics of this article—its front-page prominence, the vagueness about charges, plea and details of the incident, the ethnic identification in the headline, the stress on the girl's age and the submerged sex theme—highlight it as the worst kind of reporting of black crime. It is very available for interpretation as a typical piece of immigrant behaviour.

To avoid total transparency, there is a qualification to such a possibility. A large (fifteen-inch) photograph of the prize-giving at a local hospital features three of the five most successful nurses as West Indian. For once, the human interest story does stand as a qualification to the crime story, and to the anti-immigrant obsession of the election. It stands in relation to the page, as does the large page 4 feature to the whole paper. That account of the extreme hostility of white friends and neighbours to a white couple who have adopted two West Indian children points up in an individual context the bigotry of white people as a real problem. It is a limited qualification, as the individual situation is not generalized to a point where white prejudice might be seen as the central component of the political context. Nevertheless, its presence—and that of the front page photograph—are important. They need to be understood as gestures towards a more 'balanced' position, and also show how at this point 'routinized' race news is being determined by political race news.

But in the end the political definition is totally supreme. What should be done about black immigrants is the argument: not what should be done about white hostility. This, it must be emphasized, was the first time that race appeared so openly in British politics. In his book *Immigration and Race in British Politics*[1] Paul Foot argued that the role of the *Smethwick Telephone* was crucial to Griffiths' success. He emphasizes the pre-1963 role of the paper under a domineering and racialist owner-editor.

Editorial leadership is clearly important as we have seen in the case of the Wolverhampton *Express and Star*. But while that paper was struggling against the tide of its own news values, the *Smethwick Telephone* simply swam with them. The news values of the West Midlands provincial press are in accord with a racist definition. When such a definition emerges in a political form, a paper may, as in the Wolverhampton situation, attempt to mobilize editorials and features against it, or it may simply see such a definition as logical and authentic. That is the stance of the *Smethwick Telephone* and, as a consequence, it became the mouthpiece of racialism.

Later the *Smethwick Telephone* partly withdrew from this position in both its news coverage and the editorials which appeared for the first time after its merger with the *Warley News*. It must be said that the retreat is only partial: the paper still felt justified in pre-dating Powell with a series of front-page stories on how immigrants had caused a crisis in local education.[2] Editorially, however, a more 'liberal' approach is adopted, at least in the seven editorials in our sample. The reaction to Powell is muted and deflected into strong support for the establishment of a Community Relations Council. An early editorial—'Apathy At Its Worst' (1 December 1966)—deplores public indifference to interracial social events organized as part of a 'People to People' week. Immediately after Powell's first speech, an editorial applauds David Ennal's suggestion that a Community Relations Council should be started, and supports the chairman of the Warley West Indian Association who has been working towards this end ('Race Relations', 15 June 1968). The frankly obstructive tactics of some Warley councillors at the inaugural meeting of the council four months later is deplored ('Stormy Launch', 30 June 1968), and the town council as a whole is later attacked for its persistent refusal to recognize the body ('Showing The Way', 29 October 1970). The *Smethwick Telephone* also takes a quite significant step of resurrecting some images of English colonialism in its arguments. Forestalling objectives to a proposal to issue an Asian phrasebook for English people, it says those who say Asians should learn English would do well to remember that ('Getting Through', 4 September 1969):

the classic Englishman abroad used to be the one who dressed for dinner in the jungle, had tea at four, NEVER learned the language, and communicated by bawling in English at the top of his voice . . .

1. Penguin, 1965.
2. See, for example, 'Education Crisis Looms' 22 February 1968.

Of the remaining two editorials, one is a critique of the Race Relations Act wording which prevents a local brewery from advertising for Asian landlords ('Inane Act', 6 August 1970). The other—significantly in 1969—is 'An Appeal to Reason'. Extremists on both sides of the race debate are asked to moderate their language—'let the arguments be frank, but let them go hand in hand with commonsense and an understanding of the other fellow's point of view'. Without being specific, the editorial writer indicates that the paper has set limits on what it will print, and censures 'those of our correspondents whose letters, because of their volatile nature, have helped fill our wastepaper basket rather than our columns.'

The *Smethwick Telephone* then does move away from its tacit support for anti-immigrant campaigns evident in the early 1960s. Yet this is only a slight change in news content, and the main 'definition of the situation' remains unaltered. The main new and scarcely radical concern is to support the institutionalization of conciliatory bodies with status but without power.

The *Walsall Observer* published five editorials on race, one, relatively isolated, in 1965, and two each in 1968 and 1969. Two were on educational topics, two on race relations generally and one on health. There were a large number of reference themes (fourteen) which were fairly disparate, except for three to housing and two to education. The *Walsall Observer* is a paper which shows an extreme editorial reaction to the activities of Enoch Powell, and is the only one to give him open and unqualified support.

Before Powell, race appeared rarely in editorials. The one which appeared in our example ('Schools and Racial Integration', 3 December 1965) recounts in glowing terms the achievements of a local secondary school in achieving the integration of its mainly Indian immigrant pupils. Yet even here there is an emphasis on the numbers—'grown every year'—of coloured children, and the problem—'internal teaching difficulties'—they bring. There is, too, a negative definition of success as the absence of problems—a 'complete lack of discrimination'— and the absence of tension—'white and coloured form one happy group'.

The effect of Powell's first speech on the paper's editorial opinion is dramatic. The town is suddenly under siege ('When Is A Problem Urgent?', 17 April 1968):

We may be in splendid isolation in so thinking, but we firmly believe that Walsall possesses an immigrant problem which is serious enough to rank alongside that of Birmingham and Wolverhampton . . .

As we have said times enough before, there are hundreds of houses in multi-occupation in Walsall alone. There are schools in which 60 per cent of the pupils are coloured. Yet there appears to be no sense of urgency . . .

There appears to be a widespread effort to smother the effect of Mr Enoch Powell's speech; to hide further reference to it from the public as if it had never been made. And one of the poses, apparently aimed at subduing any reaction, is to class any revelations about difficulties created by immigration as racialist. If facing facts is racialist, then we hope we are guilty.

This is one of the most transparent analyses we have encountered. There is an 'immigrant problem' not a white problem; multi-occupied houses and mainly black schools are a 'bad thing'; Mr Powell has tried to tell the truth and been gagged. The definition is arbitrary, unbalanced, and, on the last point, totally untrue, on our reading of the West Midlands provincial press.

Perhaps because it serves a relatively small locality compared with the evenings, the *Walsall Observer* gives quite specific local examples of more general arguments. A report of a group of Walsall headteachers later in 1968 is used to support the *Walsall Observer*'s case ('Immigrant Problem in Schools', 9 August 1968). The teachers' careful qualification that the main problem is not of colour but of language and dialect is accepted—carelessly since the editorial concludes help should be given to 'immigrant' children but not at the expense of 'white' children, thus neatly restoring the race paradigm.

Health is another problem—a 'Cause for Concern'— as an editorial of 21 February 1969 puts it:

If further evidence of the need for a stricter control on the influx of immigrants into this area were needed, it has been produced this week by Alderman Dr R. H. M. Baines, Chairman of Walsall's Town Council Health Committee. Representing the annual report of the Medical Officer of Health, Dr Baines stated that 75 per cent of cases of tuberculosis that had arisen in Walsall in 1967 had been discovered among the immigrant population.

The health authorities are no doubt tackling the question of housing and hygiene among the immigrants with energy.

The statement by Dr Baines indicates how vitally necessary it is to stamp out overcrowding and educate immigrants in dietary and other matters up to the standard accepted in this country.

Thus another ingredient has been added to the 'immigrant problem'—their lack of hygiene breeds diseases which white people have long eliminated. A fragment of reality has been woven into the fabric of an anti-immigrant tirade. Fragments which do not fit—such as the effect on the health of the locality of immigrant doctors and nurses—are conveniently ignored.

Despite its clear bias the *Walsall Observer* perceives itself as a champion of truth in its fifth editorial—(On Being 'Reported' On 'Race', 20 November 1969). The paper has been threatened with being reported to the Race Relations Board over two front-page stories: one on the deposit of excreta on the floors of the town's slipper baths which have an almost exclusively Asian clientele; the second criticizing the fact that Darlaston council had to be 'careful' in refusing a town-hall booking to an immigrant organization 'because they are coloured'. The *Walsall Observer* comments that the use of the Race Relations Act is threatening 'professional behaviour and comment' and declares its intention to stand firm:

If clear factual reporting on local affairs of public import concerning coloured immigrants is racial, then we are racialists. We are performing no more than our function in so doing, and would be doing less than our duty if we shirked it.

The whole of this report is an attempt to dispel the myth reproduced here—that the press reports 'the facts' about race as part of its 'duty'. It rests on the assumption that there are facts with an unproblematic status, that papers give equal access to all concerned, that the definition of a problem is simple and straightforward, that news selection is controlled by automatic processes, and that any criticism is a veiled call for censorship. We hope we have shown these assertions to be untenable.

If the editorial line of the *Walsall Observer* is clear, there remains the gap between it and the regular news coverage. If other papers like the Wolverhampton *Express and Star* are declaiming against racialism in its editorials, while reproducing an implicitly racialist definition of the situation in its news, the *Walsall Observer*, editorially the most hostile of the papers, consistently produces the least adverse distribution of race news. We are prepared to offer a simple explanation for this paradox. While other papers ran extensive news stories, editorials and features on the 'immigrant problem' especially in 1968 the *Walsall Observer* was concerned not to stay obsessed with the presence of another deviant group—travelling people. In the special study which follows we examine the *Walsall Observer*'s handling of this issue, and explain why we believe the paper's treatment of race needs to be understood as a result of a deflection of news coverage and local hostile activity on to the issue of travellers.

Chapter 6

Special study: 'Travellers' in the *Walsall Observer*

Our attention was drawn to the coverage of travelling people in the *Walsall Observer* by its high rate of incidence especially in the years 1968–70, and by some striking similarities between such coverage and the reporting of race in the other papers—especially the *Smethwick Telephone*. For various reasons, some of which will be suggested below, it seemed that certain constraints operating on the coverage of race did not apply in the case of travelling people. Thus a detailed examination of the reporting of travelling people might reveal the patterns and mechanisms of reporting hostility towards a minority group which were always partly disguised—with the possible exception again of the *Smethwick Telephone*—in the West Midlands press reporting of race.

We therefore looked in detail at the eighty-three items about travelling people which appeared in our original race sample. A proper account of such coverage ought to be chronological since significant and subtle shifts appear to take place in the *Walsall Observer*'s handling of the subject over the period. Our sample, however, would omit three-quarters of the traveller coverage which would distort such an account, but not that of a broader identification of themes and issues. We have therefore divided our examination into the following sections: (a) a comparison of race- and traveller-related material in the *Walsall Observer*; (b) an analysis of traveller-related material by themes and topics; (c) a note on 'positive' traveller-related news; (d) the 'labelling' process as revealed in headlines; (e) implicit and explicit analogies with race; (f) the editorial viewpoint; (g) a brief comparison with traveller-related material appearing in other West Midlands newspapers.

We begin then where we shall end, with the relationship in the *Walsall Observer*, between the coverage of race and that of travelling people.

Comparison of race-
and traveller-related material

It is important to recall the significant differences between the overall pattern of race coverage in the five papers as a whole, and that evident in the *Walsall Observer*. These may be briefly summarized as follows:

The *Walsall Observer* expanded its coverage (in both column inches and items) of race much earlier than the other papers, especially in 1967. Content was varied with no particular stress on white hostility or immigration.

It is the only newspaper to decrease its race coverage in 1968—again in both column inches and items. An increase was evident in the Powell-provoked categories of education, health and cultural differences, but the overall reaction to the events of 1968 was clearly much more muted than in other newspapers, especially in the total absence of white hostility items.

In 1969 the number of items decreases but column-inch coverage increases, especially in the more 'positive' categories of human interest and racial integration.

By 1970 race coverage has reverted to the size and shape of 1963.

The *Walsall Observer* is clearly much less affected in its coverage of race by Powell and related hostility, though editorially it is one of the more extreme advocates of a Powell line. We wish to suggest this difference is partly, if not wholly, accounted for by the *Walsall Observer*'s preoccupation with travelling people.

We present two graphs (Figs. 9 and 10) showing the amount and variation in coverage of traveller-related news compared with that related to race. Race coverage over the whole period is much greater, over 70 per cent more than that of travellers. The annual total of traveller-related items exceeds that of race only in 1970, and the column-inch total only in 1968—strangely but, as we hope to show, not paradoxically.

If we consider the period 1968–70 alone, however, a different picture emerges. Though there are more race-related items in this period (eighty-four as compared with sixty-nine), the coverage of travellers as measured in column inches is greater than that of race (944 inches compared with 882 inches). Put another way, during that three-year period, each weekly edition of the *Walsall Observer* was likely to carry two race-related and two traveller-related items, but whereas the average length of the former would be 10 inches that of the latter would be over 13 inches.

In addition, traveller-related material was more prominent in its position and type of news during the period. Of traveller-related items, 21 out of 69 (30 per cent) appeared on the front page, but only 6 race-related items out of 84 (7 per cent) did so. There were 8 editorials and 17 letters on travellers compared with 4 and 15 respectively on race.

Of course, the combined coverage of travellers and race still only accounted for a very small percentage of the total newspaper which could theoretically cover such items (between 3 and 4 per cent). Tinkers and immigrants were, however, a consistent and dramatic presence on the

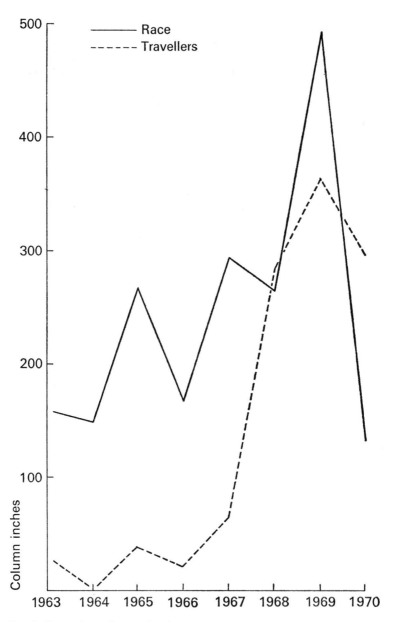

FIG. 9. Comparison of race-related and traveller-related news in the *Walsall Observer*, 1963–70 (column inches).

front pages and in editorials and letters. Indeed, the clear control being exerted—whether consciously or not—by the *Walsall Observer*'s editorial staff in this period may be interpreted as an attempt to protect the paper's massive commitment to presenting the 'routine as normal'. To have carried two lots of negative news of deviant groups, both tinkers and immigrants, might have threatened to spill over from front page news letters and editorials into the generally conflict-free inside pages,

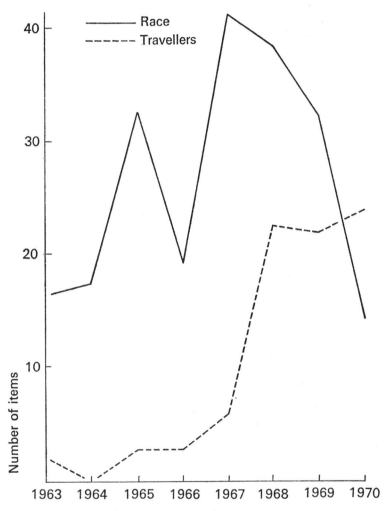

FIG. 10. Comparison of race-related and traveller-related news in the *Walsall Observer*, 1963–70 (number of items).

thus disrupting the news routine and appearing to place normality itself in jeopardy.

There is thus an inverse relationship in the comparative chronologies of race and traveller coverage in the *Walsall Observer*. At times, the total coverage of each is inverse. Thus by 1970 the initial proportionate news attention given to race and travellers in 1963 has been reversed, with nearly twice as much coverage of travellers as of race. Even when both receive extensive coverage together as in 1968 and 1969, there is an inverse relationship in the kind of news. The categories of race news which expand most are those of human interest and race relations, especially in 1969 when the presentation of hostility towards travellers is at the highest.

In our conclusion we shall attempt a theoretical explanation of how the *Walsall Observer*'s news values come to operate in this fashion. For the moment, we may note that race material in the paper appears to be conditioned by the amount and kind of traveller material at any one time.

Traveller-related material: themes and topics

Our initial reading of traveller-related material suggested it bore substantial comparison with race coverage. To test this hypothesis further, we slightly adapted the topic headings (though not the subtopics) we used on the race material and applied them to the *Walsall Observer*'s coverage of the travelling people.

Some slight emphases were changed—'white hostility' became 'local hostility'; 'immigrant organizations' as a heading was replaced by 'traveller organizations'. We also used these headings as reference themes. This gave us a method of content analysis extremely comparable with that used on the race material. We present the results in tabulated form in Tables 67 and 68.

Traveller-related stories were substantially longer than those race-related; and averaged 13½ inches compared with 9 inches. There were no significant differences between topics in the average length of story. The length of story, irrespective of topic, tended to increase over time from an average of 12 inches for the period 1963–67, to 14 inches in 1968–70. In 1969 the number of topics was roughly the same as in 1968 and 1970, but the volume of column inches increased by a quarter.

Bearing in mind these changes over time, the topic and column are broadly interchangeable. Both show just over 40 per cent of traveller-related stories as reports or expressions of white hostility. Of the coverage 16 per cent dealt with legislation though nearly all the comment was of a negative kind. Five reports presented travellers as convicted or suspected of crime, a low percentage (6) especially in view of its prominence in reference themes. The activities of traveller organizations and comments in their defence constituted another 8 per cent. Relatively minor topics were education (4 per cent), health (3 per cent), housing (3 per cent), while cultural differences and immigration were insignificant. Of stories, 16 per cent were not classifiable.

The most prominent reference themes were not those which scored high as topics. Health was the most frequent reference theme at 18 per cent, followed by crime at 15 per cent. Immigration was subdivided into 'local immigration', i.e. threats of immigration from neighbouring boroughs, and 'national immigration' generally with reference to Ireland. These two kinds of immigration reference constituted

TABLE 67. Traveller-related material by topic: number of items/column inches

Year	Local hostility		Legislation		Crime		Pro-traveller		Traveller organizations		Education		Health		Housing		Cultural differences		Immigration		Other		Yearly total	
	A[1]	B[2]	A	B	A	B	A	B	A	B	A	B	A	B	A	B	A	B	A	B	A	B	A	B
1963	2	35																					2	35
1964																							0	0
1965			2	24			1	16															3	40
1966	1	15					1	3													1	6	3	24
1967	2	22							1	3			2	6							1	35	6	66
1968	11	177	1	15	3	22			2	13	2	26			2	15			1	5	1	8	23	281
1969	12	193	5	82	2	48	1	...													2	44	22	367
1970	6	58	7	101			1	18			1	19					1	16			8	84	24	296
TOTAL	34	500	15	222	5	70	4	37	3	16	3	45	2	6	2	15	1	16	1	5	13	177	83	1,109

1. A = Items.
2. B = Column inches.

143

TABLE 68. Traveller-related material: number of reference themes

Year	Local hostility	Legislation	Crime	Pro-traveller	Traveller organizations	Education	Health	Housing	Cultural differences	Immigration Local	Immigration National	Tension	Police	Employment	Yearly total
1963							2								2
1964															
1965						1	2			1				2	6
1966															
1967			2		1	1	2					1	2		9
1968			4				2	1	2	1	2	1	1	1	15
1969	2	2	4	1			3		1		5	4	1		23
1970	2	2	1		2	2	3	2	3	1	1	1		1	21
TOTAL	4	4	11	1	3	4	14	3	6	3	8	7	4	4	76

15 per cent of the total. 'Tension', a variation of the race-related reference theme of 'racial tension' scored 9 per cent. Cultural differences rated only 8 per cent, but this was mainly because the significant area of cultural differences was portrayed as that of health and classified under that heading. White hostility and legislation, the two main topics, only scored 5 per cent each of the reference themes, as did education, employment and the police. Housing was the most infrequent reference theme except for traveller organizations and, rarest of all, 'pro-traveller', which scored only once.

The overall content of traveller-related material in the *Walsall Observer* was thus a blanket of white hostility, unruffled by any contrary opinions or organizations. Comment on legislation was also mostly hostile. The framework of reference most frequently employed was one which portrayed travellers as dirty, criminal, alien, etc., giving rise to communal tension. The *Walsall Observer* did not merely report but gave support to this image. Before examining the way this was done, a brief note is necessary on the small volume of reportage which ran contrary in some way to this image.

'Positive' traveller-related material

Since the overall tone of the traveller-related material was so negative, it was relatively easy to pick out those items with any element of positive comment. As we shall see this positive element was sometimes subsumed under more negative references, or was 'positive' in a rather particular way. Only sixteen items (under 20 per cent) of all tinker-related items managed to infer that there was another side to the question. Four were classified under the pro-traveller topic, three under that of traveller organizations. The only three traveller-related stories appearing as education and one of those on housing were by implication favourable as far as they implied (rather special) notions of integration. In the remaining five items 'pro-traveller' was a reference theme only, twice for a main topic of white hostility, three times for an unclassified topic.

The major pro-traveller item for the whole period occurs in November 1965 before the rapid expansion of traveller-related coverage. Headlined 'A Priest Who Champions A New Deal For Gipsies' it tells the story of a Roman Catholic priest who for twelve months has lived and travelled in a caravan to express his concern and support for gypsies. His attitudes are presented in some detail.

Father Griffiths said his aim was to change the attitude that local authorities and ordinary citizens had towards the country's gipsy population.

He said: 'People are always complaining that gipsies are dirty illiterate and too lazy to settle down in proper homes and find respectable jobs. But gipsies are certainly no dirtier than anybody else and they are only illiterate because the police and others never allow them to stay long enough in one place to give their children proper school educations. For the same reason, it is impossible for them to settle into a community and find work because people are always moving them on.

Father Griffiths said gipsies were doing the country a great service and saving the Government money by collecting scrap—their traditional method of earning an income.

Father Griffiths said mechanization and industrialization were the causes behind the rise to prominence of a gipsy problem.

He said: 'Once, gypsies could just fade into the countryside and find work on farms. Now, most farms can be operated by two men and a mass of machines, and there is no call for gipsy labour. All they are allowed to get on with is scrap collecting and, if the season is right, fruit harvesting.'

We have quoted this item at length because it is unique in our sample. It denies the validity of some elements of the popular stereotype of gypsies and explains others as the result and not the cause of prejudiced action. It suggests gypsies do make an economic contribution and outlines historical developments which have restricted their possibilities of earning a living. Not only would such comments not appear in the *Walsall Observer* in the later period, but they could not take such a wide-ranging form, since they would have to inhabit the problem as defined by the *Walsall Observer*. Thus in 1969 the Reverend J. Samuels does not challenge the stereotype, but pleads for humane treatment of travellers: 'I have been violently treated by the tinkers myself but I still feel they should be treated in the same way as other human beings' (13 June 1969).

Father Griffiths then is presented as news about a topic which is still relatively open. Part of the later power of the newspaper is to close the topic around a relatively few themes, of which the mechanization of farm labour is not one. Yet even at this early stage an ambiguous remark cannot be resisted—has Father Griffiths gone over to the other side?

'Father Griffiths has become so much of a gipsy that he has adopted their attitudes towards their common situations.'

Clearly on the other side is a letter of 30 December 1966 which gives a historical perspective on the growth of prejudice against travellers, suggesting no one objected to gypsies when he was a lad. The editor's reply, stressing that contemporary complaints are aimed at the tinkers not at the gypsies is a highly significant moment in the labelling of travellers which we shall examine in detail in the next section.

In 1967 no items are classifiable as 'pro-tinker' and in the avalanche of local hostility towards travellers in 1968 and 1969, one lone voice appears in our sample, a letter of 21 February 1969 which advocates properly supervised sites as the only way of minimizing friction and allaying the public's fears.

In January 1970 Walsall Debating Society narrowly favour the introduction of a travellers site. This is thus classifiable as 'pro-traveller' but the report itself gives equal prominence to the pro-traveller speech of Ivan Geffen and the hostile one of the local Member of Parliament, Sir Harry Goldsmidt.

That exhausts our list of specifically pro-traveller items: 4 out of 83. Three more small items—only 16 column inches between them—report the activities of traveller organizations over 1967–68. The West Midlands Gypsy Council organize a passive resistance to a council eviction in December 1967, and their secretary is reported as visiting Dublin in

May 1968 to protest about the harassment they have been receiving in the West Midlands. However, in view of the frequent cry of the local hostiles that travellers should 'go back to Ireland', and the six-month suspended sentence passed on Mr Connors reported elsewhere in the same edition, this report, to put it mildly, loses some of its impact. The third and longest report describes a submission by the International Gypsies Committee to Lord Kennet at the Ministry of Local Housing and Government that Walsall and the West Midlands are 'black spots of discrimination'.

Of the 'positive' items on education, one clearly meets the travellers on their own terms. Headed 'Learning the Dialects to Aid Teaching' (20 March 1970), it pictures members of the West Midlands Travellers Group listening to tape-recordings of travellers dialect to aid in their teaching programme. A spokesman is quoted as saying they wish to understand travellers' cultures, but not to infer they are in any way inferior. The other two education items are not so easy to interpret. They both occur in the same issue (23 February 1968) and concern involvement of Pheasey County Secondary Modern School in a caravan schoolroom at the new tinker site provided by Aldridge-Brownhills Council. In the first item the Council's clerk praises the experiment; in the second he is pictured making a presentation to a 'shy tinker girl' who was too nervous to attend the school speech day. In race-related material the reference them here would clearly be 'racial integration: absorption and assimilation'. Though still a tinker girl, she is becoming more like us, through education. The same implication is carried by a positive 'housing' item appearing in a later issue (14 June 1963). Norman Smith is a gypsy who has tired of being harassed as a tinker and is about to settle into an Aldridge council house. He hopes, as does the *Walsall Observer* headline writer, that 'Council Home is the turning point' and is even allowed to see his past life as part of a general human urge—'There's a bit of gypsy in everyone though. After all, people buy caravans to go roaming at weekends don't they?' This story takes on a special meaning, nestled as it is under a banner headline about Asians depositing excreta in Walsall slipper baths—a kind of juxtaposition which occurs more than once. Apart from this, the story can be positive because it is about someone ceasing to be a traveller, looking forward to enjoying that cornerstone of a normal life, a home of one's own.

Pro-traveller themes are present as references in five other stories. Two report debates, one at a West Bromwich college and the other in Aldridge Council, which give both sides of the issue, though both are relatively short. We have already quoted the pro-traveller presence of the Reverend Samuels in an item featuring Walsall's Action (anti-traveller) group which has issued an invitation to all traveller supporters to visit some tinker sites. The last two pro-traveller references occur in wholly negative contexts of attacks on a *Man Alive* television programme about travellers in Walsall which was held to be biased towards travellers.

Positive or partly positive news about travellers in the *Walsall Observer* is neither very extensive nor very penetrating. Two letters, a report on a debating society and an article on a priest are the total sum and form of pro-traveller attitudes outside the travellers themselves. One education topic is positive, two are integrationist, as is the one on housing. All the pro-tinker reference themes appear in neutral or negative contexts. As the tinker debate conducted in the *Walsall Observer* hardens, pro-tinker attitudes appear only and rarely in the letters column. Clearly local hostility is news in a way the activities of traveller organizations and their supporters are not. Editorial attitudes have come to define news values. The first step is to define the issue. This involves the crucial act of labelling.

Labelling travellers

It is an accepted tenet of modern deviancy theory that the relationship perceived by the representatives of normal society as existing between themselves and a deviant group or individual is revealed by the kind of label they attach to the outsiders. The label may be not merely descriptive but also prescriptive. To call juvenile delinquents 'thugs', 'hooligans', 'vandals' or more extremely 'animals', is to set them apart as not fully human, and further to suggest that any means necessary may be employed to bring them back into line.

Changes taking place in such labels may be of special significance. To the extent that people begin to use 'gay' as a label instead of 'queer', society may feel more tolerant of, and less threatened by, homosexuality. To trace the history of changes in the labelling of outgroups, then, is to reveal changes in the perceptions and attitudes of those responsible for such labelling.

In our society much of such labelling is carried out by the mass media. The provincial press has as always the particular local resonances to carry. In the period under review, all the West Midlands Press had to face up to the problems of labelling racial minorities. The *Walsall Observer* in addition was concerned to label travellers.

The label applied to racial minorities was substantially that of 'immigrants'. The word came to have very particular meanings. Implicit in the word was the assumption such people were coloured. Headlines including the word 'immigrant' were unlikely to be about the Irish. 'Immigrant' was also applied to children irrespective of their place of birth. It thus embraced, not only people of diverse ethnic origins and cultural groupings, but also their children. Hence, as we have noted, that illogical expression 'second-generation immigrants'.

In the case of race then the same word was given cumulatively shaped meanings which far modified the original definition of immigrant as a foreign-born person entering this country to stay. It came to mean all black people. The line it drew was one of colour.

This shift in meaning from a closely defined technical term to a label implying certain attitudes and judgements has been described as a move from a process of denotation to one of connotation. Stuart Hall has written[1]

---

1. S. Hall, 'The Determination of News Photographs', *Working Papers in Cultural Studies*, Vol. 3.

The term denotation derives from the Latin notare meaning 'to mark' but connotation (from connotare) means 'to mark along with', 'to mark one thing with another', or 'in addition to another'.

Whereas 'codes of denotation are precise, literal, unambiguous', connotative codes are

the configurations of meaning which permit a sign to signify, in addition to the denotive reference, other additional implied meanings. These configurations of meaning are forms of social knowledge, derived from the social practices, the knowledge of institutions, the beliefs and the legitimations which exist in a diffused form within a society and which order that society's apprehension of the world in terms of dominant meaning-patterns.

This is the interpretative framework which seems to us to best fit the changes in the labelling processes applied to both racial minorities and travellers in the West Midlands press. Whereas in the racial context, however, the process was to give an originally denotative word new cultural connotations, in the case of the travellers, connotation involved the use of different words altogether. The escalation of a campaign against travellers in the *Walsall Observer* can be gauged from the labels applied to them. We have in this study used the term 'travelling people' for its denotative rather than connotative meaning, and because it is all-embracing. For the *Walsall Observer*, however, such a term was insufficient. The first label, relatively denotative, was that of 'nomads', then more connotatively that of 'gypsies' and, finally, a label with very different connotations was used, that of 'tinkers'. This change can be represented diagrammatically, according to the number of times the different labels were used in the headlines of our sample (see Table 69).

TABLE 69. Headline labels in the *Walsall Observer* 1963–70

	Nomads	Itinerants	Gypsies	Tinkers	No use of group name	Total for year
1963	2					2
1964						0
1965	1		2			3
1966	2	1				3
1967		1		5		6
1968			1	18	4	23
1969				20	2	22
1970				13	11	24
TOTAL (1963–70)	5	2	3	56	17	83

The shift away from the connotatively neutral terms 'nomads' and 'itinerants' is clear. 'Gypsies' is used little, though not for long (the 1968 headline is a reference to the gypsies' council), for its connotations are ambiguous. Though 'gypsy' or more colloquially 'gippo' has a long history as a term of abuse, there are also more romantic connotations: traditional dress, camp fires, music. 'Tinker' has no such positive connotations only roughness, dirt and social malaise. This clearly fitted the *Walsall*

Observer's developing image of travellers more satisfactorily than the other terms. The shift from 'nomad' through 'gypsy' to 'tinker' is no simple terminological change. It is an index of rising hostility, not only or even necessarily amongst local people, but in the news values of the *Walsall Observer*.

The shift as represented in the headlines is particularly clear. At the level of news content, a more complicated attempt is being made to differentiate tinkers from other travellers, especially gypsies. Thus, prominence is given to an early remark (18 June 1965) by the Walsall Town Clerk. 'We are plagued by these people who travel through the area or settle for a while collecting scrap iron', said Mr Nicholls.

He explained these were not 'romantic' gypsies. 'They were people who made a filthy mess, leaving pieces of scrap iron everywhere.'

Here the *Walsall Observer* is representing an attempt to isolate 'tinkers' made by a town spokesman. The paper itself, however, strongly approves of the attempt, as the editorial response to a letter in December 1966 demonstrates.

The Problems of Itinerants

Sir,

When I was a boy gypsies were everywhere and nobody bothered. Ken Pearsall's letter is just another illustration of the intolerance which is so prevalent today, and the continued attacks on freedom. Whether I like gypsies or not, I admire them for the way they contrive to obtain a livelihood in face of such spite and bitter enmity.

L. Crump,
12 Albion Street,
Willenhall.

(The complaints are not levelled particularly against gypsies, but against itinerant caravan dwellers, many of whom, of course, are not gypsies—Ed. *Walsall Observer*.)

The tentative differentiation here is quickly settled in the following year, 1967, when 'tinker' appears and dominates as a label. Further differentiation occurs in a story of 26 January 1969 'New effort to prevent return of tinkers', where the Showmen's Guild are at pains to stress that 'there is a vast difference between showmen and tinkers'. The crucial distinction, however, between tinkers and gypsies is represented as being made by the latter themselves in a story of 11 July 1969. A reporter accompanies members of the (anti-tinker) Walsall Action Group visiting an established travellers' site in Bromsgrove. This story appears under the headline 'Occupants of Established Site Do Not Want Tinkers'. The reporter offers special legitimation to their gypsy host, since he is to be the source of implicit and explicit condemnation of the tinkers—'We were met at the site by a genial bare-chested man in his 30's who was unwilling to give his name'. In another context, to be sure, such an appearance would be portrayed as threatening, such anonymity as sinister. But then all the right things are said about tinkers by the gypsy.

We don't want them here. There's always trouble with them wherever they go. They can't keep themselves clean and they've got no respect for anybody.

A graphic account follows of a violent incident the previous October between the resident gypsies and arriving tinkers. A special complaint was the number of relatives the tinkers would invite to the site. The report, one-third of which describes the site, and two-thirds the gypsies condamnation of tinkers, ends:

If the reaction of the people on this site is to be believed, the combination of 'tinkers' and 'travellers' in one camp is like a mixture of oil and water.

The reporter is in some trouble here trying to make comparisons between non-comparable terms. 'Tinker' is connotative, but 'traveller' denotative—do not tinkers, then, travel? The criticism to be levelled is more substantial. It is not necessarily that no differentiation at all should be made. It is that such differentiation should be explicit and historically situated—the kind of examination, in fact, for which feature articles are designed. The *Walsall Observer* ought also to be consistent with its own differentiations at the level of policy. At that level, we found no evidence that the *Walsall Observer* favoured a gypsy site but not a tinkers' site. If such differentiation were substantially possible, as stories such as this try to indicate, the policy should be built around such differentiations. In fact the *Walsall Observer* opposes any site at all. It is thus open to the charge that it differentiates between different groups of travellers when it wishes to enlist the support of one group against the other; when it is endorsing prejudiced attitudes and policies, it lumps them together.

Nor is the *Walsall Observer* disturbed by the fact that neither the national nor the West Midlands Branch of the Gypsy Council accepts this distinction it makes, or that it is condemned by the International Gypsies Council. It does not even appear to be worried by the fact that blanket hostility towards 'tinkers' extends to 'gypsies', as was the experience of the man who moved into an Aldridge council house (14 June 1968). Coverage is given rather to the 'Mission to Gypsies' who 'oppose tinker tactics' (3 October 1969) and wish to join anti-tinker groups in making representations to the Prime Minister (2 October 1970).

The most disturbing aspect of all this is the way labelling infiltrates into news values. Events come to be reported in the terms defined by the connotative label. One report, for example—'Tinkers Threats Are Making a Nightmare Say Traders' (23 February 1968) is replete with images of violence which cannot but confirm already-stated assumptions about tinkers. Even the tinkers' hostility to the *Walsall Observer*'s reporters is seen as irrational. This formation of news reporting by labelling, and the kind of editorial legitimation we shall examine later, combine to give newsworthiness and credence to quite extreme forms of prejudice. In a report of a local Member of Parliament's meeting with residents living near a proposed tinker site, a man is pictured with the M.P. (13 June 1969). He is quoted underneath as saying 'If it was left to me I'd shoot them'.

The publishing of such a comment clearly marks the crossing of a boundary. The *Walsall Observer* is prepared to accept as legitimate the articulation of opinions which in other contexts it would brand as extreme or unrepresentative and would not cite. Thus the *Walsall Observer* along with other West Midlands papers, tended not to publish certain kinds of comments or letters about race because they were seen as abusive and not constructive. The question has to be asked—would such comment as that above, have been published in the context of an anti-immigration meeting or campaign? We suggest not. In the case of this minority group, however, it seems permissable. After all they are only tinkers. Such is the power of a label.

Travellers as immigrants

Many of the complaints levelled against travellers as reported in the *Walsall Observer* should be evident from what has gone before. They are seen as dirty and insanitary, criminal and violent, ignorant and illiterate, without proper sense of home life and civic responsibility. We shall deal shortly with the way in which editorials used these alleged characteristics as negative reference points by which to underwrite the virtues of normal life—home, family, work and citizenship. We wish to select elements of hostility towards travellers which emphasize their status as immigrants and which occasionally make explicit comparisons with black immigrants.

This is not a rare occurrence: twenty-four out of the eighty-three traveller-related items contained a substantial reference to the immigrant status of 'tinkers'. As we noted in our reference themes, part of this status is that of a local immigrant, i.e. from other parts of the country. Typical is a comment from an Aldridge councillor (29 January 1965):

It is not as if they are all our people, 90 per cent of them come in from Birmingham and out of the district. If we opened a site, people would come flocking in overnight from Birmingham again.

The interests of the town are often defined as being in conflict with those around it.

More significant for our purpose is the route through Ireland to general immigration policy. The letters are particularly strong on this point. One from January 1968 advocates sending the tinkers back to 'Liverpool or Eire'. Rhetorical questions are a useful device as a letter-writer in October 1969 discovers—'what have Irish tinkers ever done for the community or themselves?' In a letter in the same edition (3 October 1969), the United Kingdom is seen as the dumping ground for international outcasts: 'These people are subjects of Southern Ireland, and what help did they receive there? It is always the British who have to do it and consequently come in for a great deal of criticism.'

Such sentiments are not only those of untutored popular prejudice. They are heavily represented in the council chamber: 'Why must we allow every Tom, Dick and Harry into the country and inflict these problems on ourselves when they could be stopped at source?' (Tory leader, Staffs County Councillor, 1 November 1968). 'They should be deported whence they came. They should be sent somewhere and only allowed back when they are prepared to live by decent standards' (Mr H. Jones, Aldridge

Brownhills Council, 28 December 1968). 'These are not our people, they don't even live in this country' (Mr R. Arbell Walsall, 24 January 1969).

The organizations campaigning against 'tinkers' make the restriction of Irish immigration one of their demands, as the *Walsall Observer* reports of the ratepayers delegation to the council (18 April 1969): 'The trouble should be stopped at the root. Tinkers should be sent back to Ireland and no more should be allowed into the country.'

Such institutional opposition only just stops short of making direct links with black immigration. The explanation of the Walsall Action Group of their decision to write to Enoch Powell is significant: 'We feel he is the ideal man to represent us in view of his views on immigration and his recent excellent appraisal of the situation regarding Irish immigrants' (10 July 1970).

There is much patrolling of the boundary between the problems and language of race relations and that of justifying anti-tinker activity. One complex letter from two councillors in the *Walsall Observer* of 7 August 1970, is something of a classic in this respect. To provide a site would lay the council open to the charge of 'discriminating against our own people'. It is part of a wider majority-minority problem—'Do not let us be stupid as to bend so far back in order to please minorities that we cause affront to the orderly majority'. These people are foreigners; they have no right to 'walk into the country and demand the erection of pemanent sites'. Minorities only gain rights if they earn them.

If any person or persons can give us proof of need, we hope we will always feel the desire to help, within the limits of our physical capacity, irrespective of their colour, creed or calling, but we should expect that such people would in return, conform to the standards which form the bulwark of our existence; but to date the willingness of the itinerants to conform has been conspicuous by its absence and it is on this evidence that we take our stand.

The similarity between this and the language and assumptions of the race debate needs no stressing: 'discrimination against our own people', 'walk into the country', minorities asking for special rights, but refusing to integrate, etc. Change itinerant to immigrant and the letter might have appeared in the *Smethwick Telephone*. It is left to editorial comment, however, to draw direct analogies.

The comparison is made quite early on. In a 1968 editorial, 'The Tinkers Hold Their Positions' (19 April 1968) we come across the following passage decrying tinker intransigence:

Perhaps this is symptomatic of the age of vociferous minorities receiving attention more in ratio to the noise and nuisance they make than to their actual importance. For instance, Walsall has far more than its fair share of coloured immigrants, many of whom bring problems to the town. Yet although there must be a few hundred or more times the number of coloureds there is not a fraction of the trouble from them as there is from the belligerent tinkers.

The comparison is to the credit of black immigrants—offensively described as 'coloureds'—but there are still too many and they bring unwanted problems. A subsequent editorial, 'How Does the Town Feel On Tinkers?' (11 October 1968) makes clear what is partially disguised elsewhere, that tinkers and immigrants are fundamentally part of the same problem.

Birmingham has asked the Ministry for exemption from having to provide new sites for tinkers under the New Act. Are not Walsall's problems on immigration generally and its effects on housing, education and social services, sufficiently pressing to demand as much?

Editorials thus used the black immigrant group as a means of demonstrating just how badly behaved tinkers were; but this was, if significant, a relatively minor part of their overall argument against tinkers. That involved more wider-ranging themes and involved the legitimation of quite extreme anti-tinker tactics.

The editorial voice

Our sample threw up eight leading articles (one-tenth of the total number of items) all in the period from January 1968 to December 1970. Though there are variations over time as new developments become incorporated into the debate, there is an overall unity and repetition about the arguments used, sufficient for us to treat the editorials together as one corporate stance.

The way in which the argument is conducted is complex, for all its single-mindedness. The discussion twists and turns, away from the characteristics of the offending tinkers towards the activities of protest groups; the demand for action is focused first on Walsall Town Council then on national government at Whitehall: the technical problems of providing a site are juxtaposed with the inequity of Walsall's burden of the tinker problem; and within and between these elements run appeals to arguments outside the immediate context: to an ideal of citizenship incorporated in the image of the ordinary rate- and tax-payer; to the impotence of majority feeling in the face of noisy and influential minorities.

The effectiveness of the argument depends crucially on language: sentence construction, tone, image. We can only here offer a brief sketch of the total editorial stance of the *Walsall Observer* on the tinker issue, as represented in the following editorials:

'After All It Is A Free Country' (21 January 1968).
'When Authority Is Ignored' (23 February 1968).
'The Tinkers Hold Their Positions' (19 April 1968).
'How Does The Town Feel On Tinkers' (11 October 1968).
'Ratepayers Make Their Points Clear' (18 April 1969).
'Rates Are Now A Tinker Issue' (5 September 1969).
'Politics Opinion And People' (10 July 1970).
'Caravan Deadline Approaches' (7 August 1970).

Most of the editorials used the supposedly established characteristics of tinkers as their basis. Thus the provision of any site at all was seen as problematic, because there were bound to be arguments about access, and the fractious temperament of the tinkers would probably lead to violence. A more subtle objection to the tinkers way of life was voiced in the first of the editorials in our sample. Tinkers evade not only the law, but 'those burdens which so heavily affect the average household', for example rates, rents and motor taxation. They are thus able to acquire easily goods which others struggle to save for: 'the tinkers are not without personal possessions. They have private cars in many cases, as well as lorries for the collection of scrap and their caravans.' Of course, the argument runs, most of us are too civilized to emulate the tinkers, since there are (unspecified) dangers in the itinerant existence: 'the average worker is too conscious of responsibilities to expose his family to a wandering caravan existence.' The tinkers claim to rights has to be put in the perspective of their doubtful status as proper citizens: 'The tinkers say they are only claiming their rights. But what of the rights of the legitimate resident who is rated and taxed to the ears? It is certainly a free country. For some' (26 January 1968).

This kind of argument is constructed again and again in *Walsall Observer* editorials. That of 19 April 1968, for example, simply repeats the same arguments as 26 January 1968 but uses different words. It is also now beginning to mobilize the image of tinkers as inherently and invariably violent (11 October 1968):

Perhaps the most disquieting thing about the tinker problem is the violence that has already occurred or has been threatened concerning sites. At Aldridge guns have been fired. A Walsall councillor said on Monday that a tinker had threatened to stick a knife in his back and had also sworn 'on his brother's deathbed' to kill a councillor unless sites were arranged.

An early warning of potential violence had been given earlier in February 1968 when a *Walsall Observer* photographer was threatened with violence. As we saw with labelling, the editorial use of such images and definitions soon infiltrates news coverage. The lead story on 23 February 1969 is indicative of a developing editorial stance more than of developing news *per se*:

Tinkers Threats Are Making Life A Nightmare, Say Traders

Talk of violent recriminations by the Irish tinkers still encamped in George Street, Walsall, has caused alarm to occupiers of property in that street, where despairing traders fear to complain publicly in case threats against persons and property are carried out.

That occupants of the five or six tinker caravans, moved on to the roadway from the nearby car park by corporation workmen three weeks ago, seem to regard one side of the street as their own territory, was confirmed when two of them were hostile to two *Observer* editorial staffmen near the caravans on Wednesday afternoon.

Within easy earshot of two police officers on duty in the street one tinker youth blatantly warned 'Go away. There will be no photographs taken here or your camera will be smashed'. A man from the caravans reiterated this in belligerent tones and made further ominous threats.

This is a typical example of what the George Street residents and traders are faced with and it was summed up by one trader who said 'Now you can see what we are having to put up with. It's a nightmare.'

The report continues in much the same vein, including evidence of tinker threats from the impeccable source of the local branch of the Womens Royal Voluntary Service. The story is accompanied by a photograph of caravans obstructing the street.

What we are questioning here is not whether such incidents took place. It is rather the encoding of the news story. The use of words such as 'violent', 'threats', 'hostile', 'blatantly warned' to characterize the tinker attitudes allows no possibility for their anger being explicable, yet alone justified. That the *Walsall Observer* does not understand why tinkers are hostile to it, is a remarkable example of wilful incomprehension. Local people are 'despairing'; in a state of 'fear' and 'alarm'. The report sets out to dramatize and maximize conflict; it adheres not at all to one of the essential creeds of the provincial press, the duty to be constructive in its reporting.

Thus, news stories and editorials are locked in an embrace of mutual legitimation, each confirming what the other is saying. The crux, as the editorial accompanying the above news story points out, is the status of the law (23 February 1968):

The law must be observed by all of us—and that includes the tinkers and their like. Giving the police instruction and full authority to carry out these instructions, would be a good start.

Tinkers are not at the mercy of the police, but vice versa, is the claim of the editorial of 19 April 1968 which interprets tinker conduct as challenging not only the law, but 'corporate authority':

It is time corporate authority was given some credence in Walsall. With all the law which is represented by the town council and the police, a handful of tinkers are holding it in complete contempt. The tinkers have not only been laughing at authority for weeks but almost contemptuously daring it to move them on.

There have thus been set up a whole series of paradigms through which the *Walsall Observer* seeks to interpret the tinker issue both in its editorials and its news reporting. These include those of the respectable citizens *v.* the irresponsible outsider, peaceful residents *v.* violent squatters, legality *v.* illegality and authority *v.* anarchy. Thus by the end of 1968 the *Walsall Observer* has set the scene for the dramatic confrontations of 1969. Plot and dialogue have been written long before the action begins.

A deputation of ratepayers to the Town Council in April 1969 is seen as legitimate in source, intention and proposals (18 April 1969):

The deputation was drawn from a complete cross section of the ratepayers. There was a group of the normal, self-effacing, acquiescent ratepayers, led by business people and introduced to the meeting by a Socialist councillor, making evocative statements in a grimly purposeful manner . . . That inoffensive ratepayers, whose height of public agressiveness is normally putting a cross in a different place on the polling paper, should take a direct protest line, is very significant.

It is especially significant for the *Walsall Observer*, which, ostensibly because of the legitimacy of the source of the protest, seeks to give legitimacy to its form. Here legitimation is offered through a not unsympathetic mention of the ratepayers' proposal to deport all 'tinkers' to Ireland forthwith. Earlier, there had been a conspicuous lack of editorial criticism of a councillor's forecast that unless something was done local residents would take matters into their own hands and a 'blood-bath', would ensue (1 December 1967). Later, organized and unorganized local opinion is seen as totally legitimate, however intense and extreme its expression, including, as we have seen, the advocacy of extermination.

The *Walsall Observer* has something of a problem here since many of the attitudes expressed clearly involve breaches of the law which, in the *Walsall Observer*'s eyes, is the bastion of civilization. Two techniques are employed to overcome this problem. The first is to portray such protest as expressing the feelings of the vast majority (5 September 1969):

In this age of protest, Walsall Action Group, whose sole endeavour is the removal of tinkers and their caravans from the town and the prevention of their ever returning, is in good company. The strange position exists, however that except for those MPs who approve the Caravan Sites Act which requires all towns to set up permanent sites for 15 caravans each and a relatively small body of like opinion in the country, the mass of people are heartily against tinkers.

Countless people in the locality have made protest in one form or another against tinkers—Walsall Action Group has alone collected over 7,000 signatures. Pheasey Action Committee has threatened violence to counter tinker violence, vigilante groups have been constituted in some areas, but still the tinkers have the whip hand.

The use of this kind of 'inferential structure' serves to legitimate almost anything which might be suggested or done. Since it is on behalf of the majority, and we live in a democracy, it must be right. What is wrong is the failure of government to recognize or reflect this majority feeling.

The second technique used to legitimate all local protest is to insist that the law may on this occasion be opposed, since it is not supported by the majority (10 July 1970):

A situation like this is a democratic parodox, for although the last government made the provision of sites compulsory, this was totally against local feeling both inside and outside the council. How can any law be a good law when the people upon whom it is imposed are virtually unanimously against it?

The Government must listen to an opinion which is held by an M.P., the borough council and the vast majority of the people who elected them both.

We cannot overemphasize the significance of the *Walsall Observer*'s editorial legitimation of local anxiety and extreme action, on the tinker issue. A different editorial stance would undoubtedly have affected the news reporting of the issue, and this in turn, given the communicative power of a local newspaper, would have altered the nature and effectiveness of the anti-tinker campaign. We shall briefly note in the next section some differences between reporting of travellers in the *Walsall Observer* and that in the four other papers in our sample. Before leaving consideration of editorial policy we wish, however, to suggest that the *Walsall Observer*'s editorial line on travellers parallels in many ways that of the *Smethwick Telephone* on race. There are clearly differences in specific arguments but overall several striking similarities arise. Both agreed that: (a) even if national action could not be taken, their's was a special case: (b) the town was shouldering a disproportionate share of the burden while others went scot-free: (c) in any case the council could not afford the necessary resources; (d) the minority expected privileged treatment; (e) local feeling was overwhelmingly hostile; (f) the everyday life of ordinary respectable citizens was being threatened by alien influences; (g) Whitehall was out of touch, over-influenced by the minority protest and indifferent to the sufferings of the local majority.

Traveller coverage by other papers

We did not measure or examine coverage of travellers in the other four newspapers in as much detail as that in the *Walsall Observer*. We shall therefore indicate the extent of the coverage by the number of items only (Table 69).

TABLE 69. Number of traveller-related items in four newspapers 1963–70 (excluding *Walsall Observer*)

	Birmingham Evening Mail	Coventry Evening Telegraph	Warley News Telephone	Wolver-hampton Express and Star	Yearly total
1963	0		1	5	6
1964	3			3	6
1965	0			4	4
1966	3		1	8	12
1967	2			0	2
1968	5	1		3	9
1969	5			3	8
1970	2		2	4	8
TOTAL (1963–70)	20	1	4	30	55

The larger sample of evening newspapers necessitates some adjustment for comparison with the *Walsall Observer*. They should be roughly halved. Thus, the traveller coverage in the *Walsall Observer* constitutes twice as much as all the other newspapers combined. The Wolverhampton *Express and Star* has the record highest coverage, but still only 18 per cent the number of items in the Walsall paper; the comparable figure for the *Birmingham Evening Mail* is 12 per cent. The *Coventry Evening Telegraph* produced only one item, a letter attacking an editorial in favour of Caravan Sites Act. The *Warley News Telephone* provided a graphic account of an eviction of travellers, a hostile letter from a councillor, and two pro-traveller letters in reply.

The *Birmingham Evening Mail*'s news coverage appears closest to that of the *Walsall Observer*. It habitually uses the 'tinker' label much earlier than Walsall—from 1966—and the label appears in 11 out of 20 headlines, 'gypsy' is used 4 times and the other 5 stories have no label. The overwhelming majority of the stories (70 per cent) were about local hostility; none were substantively pro-traveller. The 'traveller problem' was presented as occurring where redevelopment demolition had left derelict land: Newtown, Balsall Heath, Deritend and Duddeston. Opposition was occasional and fragmented. The council evicted wherever possible, but the issue did not appear hotly contested in local politics with the exception of a Deritend Conservative Councillor who resigned because of Council 'inactivity'. An appeal by the Public Works Committee for an expression of public opinion produced some virulently 'anti-tinker' letters in the middle of 1969, but the pressure was not sustained. Our sample yielded no editorials; judgement on the news presentation must be that travellers were seen as provoking local hostility on occasion, but were not a pressing problem.

The Wolverhampton *Express and Star* adopted a liberal and tolerant attitude. Two editorials in May and October 1966 advocated the provision of sites as the only constructive way to 'rehabilitate' travellers. The news coverage was influenced by this opinion. 'Local hostility' still provided nearly half the items, but was often set in the context of travellers' organizations and their efforts to get legislation implemented. One-fifth, six out of thirty items, were 'pro-traveller', including four news items as well as the two editorials. As for labelling, the Wolverhampton *Express and Star* settled for 'caravan dwellers' early on and for the main part stuck to it: one-third of the thirty items were headlined in this way, nine contained 'gypsy', one 'nomad, one 'vagabond', seven had no label at all, and two only contained the work 'tinker'. In both cases, the headline indicated attitudes held by local residents, one in a news story, the other in letters. This liberal stance is all the more at variance with that of the *Walsall Observer*, when dealing with the same material: two crimes, several debates on Aldridge-Brownhills Council and incidents such as the visit of Walsall M.P. Stanley Wells to residents living near a traveller encampment.

This brief review of other papers' coverage may indicate the very specific acts of selection and interpretation to which material about travellers was subjected. This is not a question of 'neutrality' or 'objectivity'. The Wolverhampton *Express and Star* and the *Walsall Observer* both construct their news values about travellers from editorial viewpoints, but do some from contrary opinions.

A more substantial analysis of the *Walsall Observer*'s coverage of travellers, and a comparison with that of the other papers, could only be possible on the basis of a complex historical reconstruction of what actually happened—where travellers went and why, how far they were more prevalent in Walsall than in Wolverhampton or Birmingham, and whether the crystallization of local opinion depended upon the kind of coverage given in the local press. This is clearly beyond our competence and brief. Our own experience, however, is that such a reconstruction is not helped, and may actually be obstructed, by access to a local newspaper.

Conclusion

We wish now to offer an interpretation of our findings. These we summarize as follows:

The relatively muted news and editorial coverage of race in the *Walsall Observer* appears to be partly attributable to its more extensive coverage of travellers.

There is a clear and dramatic increase in the *Walsall Observer* coverage of travellers in the last three years of the period (1968–70), as measured in the number and length of items.

The traveller-related material can be analysed by the same framework of content analysis as that used on race coverage. The main topics emerge as local hostility and legislation, the main reference themes as health, crime and immigration. These form a composite negative image of travellers as causing conflict, creating health hazards, committing criminal acts and as having special legislative rights and immunity from immigration control. News with any positive reference to any travellers activity is minimal throughout the period.

Developing hostility towards travellers on the part of the *Walsall Observer* itself is revealed by charges in the way travellers as a group are labelled in news headlines. Early on, the newspaper prefers denotative terms, such as 'nomad' or 'itinerant', or the contradictory connotations of 'gypsy'. These are dropped in 1967, in favour of the negatively connotative term 'tinker'. A differentiation between (English) gypsies and (Irish) tinkers is supported by news stories of gypsy-tinker conflict.

The terms in which the traveller debate is conducted in the pages of the *Walsall Observer* are analogous to those employed in the general West Midlands press discussion of race. The status of travellers as a foreign-born, culturally different, minority is used to raise questions of nationality, cultural conformity and majority interests. The analogy with race is made explicit by unfavourable comparisons of traveller behaviour with that of coloured immigrants, and by inferring that travellers exarcerbate Walsall's already existing immigrant problem.

Editorial standpoints constituted one-tenth of all traveller-related material. They were implacably hostile, mobilizing several paradigms to justify this hostility, notably those of respectable citizens *v.* irresponsible outsiders, peaceful residents *v.* violent squatters, legality *v.* illegality, authority *v.* anarchy and majority *v.* minority.

The use of such inferential structures together with the labelling process infused news reporting with a wholly negative image of tinkers and a wholly positive image of anti-tinker attitudes, however extreme.

The specific arguments made in the *Walsall Observer* to plead that Walsall was a special case with regard to travellers, are strikingly similar to those used in the *Smethwick Telephone* with regard to immigrants in Smethwick.

Other newspapers' coverage of travellers is minimal when compared with that in the *Walsall Observer*. The *Birmingham Evening Mail* adopts techniques similar to the *Walsall Observer* in its news reporting, though the scale is much diminished. The liberal editorial stance of the Wolverhampton *Express and Star* results in subtly different news reporting from that of the *Walsall Observer* even when the same events are being presented.

We wish to suggest that the interpretation of these findings depends crucially on the interchangeability of travellers and immigrants as topics of news in the local West Midlands press. We believe such interchangeability is to a large extent based on the following considerations:

The inverse relationship—both extent and tone—between the appearance of travellers and black immigrants in the *Walsall Observer*.

The parallel developments in the use of the 'tinker' and 'immigrant' labels.

The very fact that we were able to apply, without substantial modification, the framework of content analysis designed for race-related material, to the *Walsall Observer*'s coverage of travellers.

The similar terms of debate and explicit analogies between travellers and immigrants used in editorials and letters.

The emphasis in the image of 'tinkers' on their status as a foreign-born, culturally different minority group.

The strong similarities between the *Walsall Observer*'s coverage of 'tinkers' and the *Smethwick Telephone*'s coverage of race.

There remains of course the question of colour. A 'tinker' can conform by settling down, getting a job, and securing and education for his children, who may become indistinguishable from the rest of us. Such anonymity is impossible for those who bear their status marks on their skins. Yet though colour may be an irrevocable mark of social stigma, this does not mean that racial prejudice is simply a question of colour, or that other kinds of prejudice are without racial content. The assumed inherent inferiority of the Irish lay behind many 'anti-tinker' comments in the *Walsall Observer*, and many letters in the *Smethwick Telephone* were about differences of culture rather than those of race *per se*.

There may be then a continuum of outgroups in which racial minorities are marked off by their colour and by the significance of race in historical and international contexts. From the point of view of the hostile, racial minorities may be an easily identifiable target; but they may not be the only objects of abuse.

Social psychologists may offer the opinion that the authoritarian or prejudice-disposed personality will seize any outgroup upon which to project its own frustrations and inadequacies. When hostility occurs in a large proportion of a population, however, it implies that frustrations and inadequacies might be built into the social structure. The resulting public anxiety can then focus on a 'scapegoat group' which is seen as symbolic of all manner of social ills. It is this we suggest which constitutes the functional interchangeability of travellers and immigrants.

The best statement of this process, and one we find particularly illuminates the *Walsall Observer*'s presentation of travellers, is provided in a work by Stan Cohen, *Folk Devils and Moral Panics*. A study of societal reaction to the 'Mods and Rockers' phenomenon of the early and middle 1960s, it has more general applicability:[1]

Societies appear to be subject, every now and then, to periods of moral panic. A condition, episode, person or group of persons emerges to become defined as a threat to societal values and interests; its nature is presented in a stylized and stereotypical fashion by the mass media, the moral barracades are manned by editors, bishops, politicians and other right-thinking people, socially accredited experts pronounce their diagnoses and solutions, ways of coping are evolved or (more often) resorted to; the condition then disappears, submerges or deteriorates and becomes more visible. Sometimes the object of the panic is quite novel and at other times it is something which has been in existence long enough, but suddenly appears in the limelight. Sometimes the panic passes over and is forgotten, except in the folk-lore and collective memory; at other times it has more serious and long-lasting repercussions and might produce such changes as those in legal and social policy, and even in the way society conceives itself.

Those who are seen to provoke such panic are defined by Cohen as 'folk devils':[2]

In the gallery of types that society erects to show its members which roles should be avoided and which should be emulated, these groups have occupied a constant position as folk devils: visible reminders of what we should not be.

In the development of a moral panic, the media play an important role:[3]

A crucial dimension for understanding the reaction to deviance both by the public as a whole and by agents of social control is the nature of the information that is received about the behaviour in question. Each society possesses a set of ideas about what causes deviation . . . and a set of images of who constitutes the typical deviant . . . and these conceptions shape what is done about the behaviour. In industrial societies the body of information from which such ideas are built is invariably received at second hand. That is, it arrives already processed by the mass media and this means that the information has been subject to alternative definitions of what constitutes 'news' and how it should be gathered and presented.

Cohen offers an elaborate model of the development of a moral panic which it would again be beyond our brief to apply. We wish merely to note some of the main characteristics of a moral panic which we have already seen to emerge in the presentation of travellers in the *Walsall Observer*. An important step, for example, is the creation of a deviant stereotype in terms of which subsequent reporting is couched. This may involve 'emphasizing those new elements which confirm expectations and playing down those which are contradictory'[4]. There is also the *common rhetoric*. Cohen quotes the variations on the same theme: 'We won't allow

1. Stan Cohen, *Folk Devils and Moral Panics*, p. 9, Paladin, 1973.
2. ibid., p. 10.
3. ibid., p. 16.
4. ibid., p. 39.

our seafront/area/town/country to be taken over by hooligans/hippies/ blacks/Pakistanis.' Insert Walsall and tinkers and we have word for word more than one speech in the town council chamber reported in the *Walsall Observer*. Finally, there is the interpretation of the 'folk devils' as symptomatic or symbolic of social trends. Here the associations become quite specific. In the case of 'Mods and Rockers', the range of associations included youth affluence, permissiveness, drugs, and indiscipline. In the case of travellers, the immediate associations were dirt, violence, Irishness and evasion of rates and taxes. Behind them lay ignorance of the law, disregard for authority, and the helplessness of the silent majority against a central government oversensitive to vociferous minorities.

The last twenty years in the United Kingdom has seen a series of moral panics at national level. Youth has provided several: Teddy Boys at the end of the 1950s, Mods and Rockers in the early and middle 1960s and skinheads and football 'hooliganism' in the late 1960s, which also featured 'hippies' and students as a crisis of middle-class youth. Overlaying the youth theme has been a continuous concern with crime particularly of the more violent kind, and the issue of 'law and order' has been prominent in more than one General Election campaign. From the mid-1960s onwards, race takes on the dimensions of a moral panic resulting in widesweeping and discriminatory immigration control. After 1970 there is evident a tendency to collapse previously independent themes into composite images. Ongoing research at the Centre for Contemporary Cultural Studies has revealed a classic image of this kind in the 'mugging' panic of 1972–73. These folk devils turn out to be young, black and violently criminal.

At this national level the scapegoating of such groups appears to be a reaction to large scale and ambiguous social cultural and economic change. Affluence, permissiveness and the Welfare State are seen as knocking away society's moral props: work, family, discipline, a sense of national tradition.

At a more local level similar ideas are produced but given a particular local inflexion. The *Walsall Observer* portrays the 'tinkers' as the antithesis of normality: wandering around the country, evading taxes and rates, 'tatting' instead of working, their families dirty and uneducated, prone to crime and violence. From such a negative image we can read off our civic duties to pay rates and taxes, work to provide for our families and to live in peace with our neighbours.

The local inflexion is not necessarily explicit. It is best understood by considering the appearance of such a direct appeal to normality in the context of the local newspaper's cultural role. As we suggested in our section 'The Provincial Press as a Cultural Institution', local newspapers, especially the weeklies, have as their central function the presentation to the local community of its self-image. Its reports of council politics, the activities of voluntary organizations, weddings, sport and even petty crime, constitute rituals of conformity through which its readers can be assured that life does indeed go on as normal. As the Cox and Morgan study suggests, this continuous affirmation of communal stability may involve the suppression of real or potential conflicts of interest.

Yet such traditional normality may be under some strain. The great abstractions of the modern age such as 'affluence' and 'permissiveness' filter in insidious forms through to the local community if only in the activities of students at the local polytechnic. Geographical and social mobility may disrupt the sense of generational continuity on which traditional family life depends. Family pride in the winning of a university scholarship by one of its members, may be qualified by the knowledge that as a result of that success, he or she may never permanently return to Walsall again. Old cultural patterns evolved from outmoded patterns of neighbourhood and housing may weaken and no clear model replace them. Even the meaning of work may become unclear as a great gap opens in the economy between technologically skilled and manually unskilled jobs, the Black Country tradition of the small independent craftsmen may become only a memory. And so on.

Our point here is simply that the need to provide scapegoats who symbolize the potential undermining of traditional values may have particular salience for the self-conception of a local community and the newspaper which serves it. An alien group such as immigrants or tinkers may be used to overcome ambiguities and contradictions present within the community itself. As a symbolic challenge to the established local way of life and thus to the values of the local newspaper itself, such groups can be used to re-clarify the fundamental cultural bond of the local community. The polarization of civilized normality with uncivilized conduct may serve to eradicate conflicts, both overt and covert, about the changing definitions of the terms.

Such a context may help us to interpret the virulence with which the *Walsall Observer* opposed 'tinkers'. They were used as a negative symbol for all that was good and decent in local life. The issue was a managed threat to normality, managed because it was clearly chosen as an alternative to race as the focus of a local moral panic. For normality to triumph, challenges to it must always be limited or sporadic in nature. More than one symbolic challenge at any one time will leave too few manning the barricades of normality and even their status as the majority, may be challenged. There must always be more within the city walls, than without.

Thus, the *Walsall Observer* could not have run a double moral panic about black immigrants and travellers without losing its grasp of conformity as the norm. A choice had to be, and was made, between race and traveller coverage, but there is good reason to believe that either group, with some modifications, could have served the same purpose. Either could have been used as a negative reference point to uphold the values of cultural homogeneity, nuclear family life, sexual decency and the sense of citizenship as a set of obligations by which rights are earned—all those values in fact which are held to constitute the traditional British way or life, especially as it is lived in Walsall, Staffs.

A difference between the presentation of the two groups was that the travellers provided a more extreme antithesis to normality, since they lacked even the black immigrants' commitment to work and home. There was also little check on the expression of hostility since the travellers' own spokesmen were denied credence, the liberal establishment had a negligible local presence, and no local politicians showed any inclination to commit political suicide by siding with the tinkers. There was no need to become involved in elaborate arguments about statistics or the cause and effect chain in social problems of the kind which appeared in the race debate. Quite simply, the tinkers could be attacked for their inherently inferior life style; no voices could be heard defending their language, music, dress, or religion, especially when the differentiation from gypsies had been accomplished. They thus assumed, in the pages of the *Walsall Observer*, the mantle of the wilfully uncivilized, without possibility of reform or integration. What Cohen says of the Mods and Rockers treatment in the media can also be said of the presentation of travellers in the *Walsall Observer*: 'The response was as much to what they stood for as for what they did.'

The fundamental objection here is not that the *Walsall Observer* fabricated news stories or letters. There are certainly very specific criticisms we have already made of the way stories are handled, the willingness to publish letters of extreme intolerance, and legitimation offered by editorials to any form of local resistance. Neither are we denying that there are itinerant families of Irish descent, whose life style can and does interfere with that of those living near their encampments. There are also many travelling people who are not of this type, who the *Walsall Observer* conveniently forgets in its total opposition to any form of site. The main objection has to be that the *Walsall Observer* abuses its cultural power, it offers the 'tinker issue' as a closed subject: editorial letters and news stories provide only that information and opinion which fits the *Walsall Observer*'s overall encoding of the issue as the majority of law-abiding, decent, hard-working, local rate and tax payers, against a minority of criminal, shiftless, tax-evading, tinkers. The tinkers are thus stigmatized through the use of a stereotyped image. All tinkers behave like this; if any travellers do not behave like this, they are not tinkers. There is no way out of this definitional double-bind.

Even if, for the sake of argument, it is conceded that an identifiable number of travellers behave in this way, there are still many questions the *Walsall Observer* does not even ask, let alone answer. Among these are the reasons for the alleged expansion of tinker activity in the area and its exact extent; the genesis of government legislation about sites; any changes in the pattern of travellers' life styles; and why travellers choose such a life style and what alternatives are, or might be, open to them. The *Walsall Observer* never considers the historical and socio-economic explanations of travellers' life styles put forward by Father Griffiths in the 1965 news item—that travellers are forced to live off scrap because of the decline of casual labour especially in agriculture, that they never get the chance to settle or be educated because they are continually being moved on, that the activation of resentment and prejudice against them perpetuates rather than modifies their life style. The unique appearance of Father Griffiths demonstrates what kinds of debate and argument are ruled out by the closure of the moral panic. Cohen is again apposite.[1]

The central indictment of the way the mass media handles such areas as deviance, social problems and politics, is precisely that no such alternative explanatory frameworks are presented. It is not just a matter of bias, unreliability or unfairness, but the use of sterertypical modes of presentation and frameworks which virtually deny the possibility of the consumer obtaining a serious perspective on the underlying social content of what is being reported.

If this 'closed' coverage can be achieved at a national level in media addressing themselves to social issues clearly subject to conflicting and ambiguous interpretations, its operation at a local level is more marked and more transparent. The bias towards affirming 'normality' inherent in the weekly provincial press as a cultural institution and its increasing monopoly over local communication together enabling a powerful and unqualified mobilization of labelling and stereotyping, which determines editorial and news coverage of minority groups. In so doing, it lays itself open to the charge that, in the guise of pursuing the interests of the local community, it operates as a form of institutionalized intolerance.

1. Cohen, op. cit., p. 177–8.

Chapter 7

Summary and conclusion

Overseas news

Overseas news can be seen as race-related in three ways, offering information from: (a) countries where majority–minority race situations exist (South Africa, Rhodesia and the United States); (b) countries from which immigrants originate (West Indies, Indian subcontinent); (c) countries where black self-government is of recent origin (Black Africa).

In the evening papers, all overseas news accounted for 22 per cent of all race-related material. The majority of the news—62 per cent—was of the first kind (Rhodesia, 47 per cent; South Africa, 11 per cent; United States, 4 per cent); News from Black Africa amounted to 21 per cent of overseas material, with just 14 per cent of such news emanating from immigrants' homelands (India, 9 per cent; West Indies, 5 per cent).

There was a marked decline in the total amount of overseas news in the second half of the period, a decrease of one-third.

As judged by the relative lack of reference themes and of news forms other than 'hard' stories, overseas news was presented in a manner which was self-contained, superficial, and devoid of historical perspective.

Though published on the same day, the evening papers shared great differences in the amount and source of overseas news. The Wolverhampton *Express and Star* printed nearly twice as much proportionate overseas news as the *Birmingham Evening Mail*, with the *Coventry Evening Telegraph* holding an intermediate position. The Wolverhampton paper gave relatively greater coverage to the United States, while that of Coventry concentrated on Black Africa.

A special category was reserved for news from abroad which was conveyed through the activities or attitudes of British groups or individuals. This was called 'home-overseas news' to distinguish it from 'direct-overseas news'.

Such news frequently takes the form of political comment, pressure group or voluntary works, comments by churches, talks to local societies, etc.

'Direct-overseas' news accounted for two-fifths of all overseas news in the evenings, or 9 per cent of all race news. In the weeklies which carried no direct-overseas news, 3 per cent (Smethwick) and 7 per cent (Walsall) of all race news was of the 'home-overseas' type.

There was a strong element of support for white minorities overseas, especially in Rhodesia. The Smith régime was presented in terms of illegality, rather than racial oppression, and further negotiation with the régime was at all times supported by all the papers.

Presentation of the Third World emphasizes the role of voluntary and charitable organizations, and assumes 'development' to be an unproblematic programme.

The evenings

Topics in the evening papers

Crime stories at 18 per cent of all home news and human interest at 16 per cent jointly amount to over one-third of all race coverage. The presentation of race through such 'routinized' stories is thus of paramount importance.

Crimes presented are predominantly of a violent and serious kind.

Human interest stories do not always convey positive or neutral images of black people and may involve negative stereotyping. This is partly revealed by the kinds of frequent reference themes.

A further 22 per cent of all race-related material is covered by race relations (nine) immigration (eight) and white hostility (five) topics.

Race relations was essentially a residual category, but did reveal the considerable publicity accorded to liberal race-relations institutions.

Immigration was a crucial topic of race news and was defined mainly as an issue of control and political significance.

Housing (six), education (five) and cultural differences (five) amounted to 16 per cent of all race-related material.

Housing and education carried substantial and locally rooted images of black immigrants as causing social problems, especially overcrowding in houses and schools.

Cultural differences were presented in mainly negative terms. The assumption of conformity was further revealed in the amount of news space (4 per cent) devoted to racial integration, in which 'assimilation' was a more prevalent conception than 'accommodation' or 'pluralism'.

There is evidence of three 'levels' of race news: routinized news—crime and human interest, 34 per cent; political problem news—race relations, immigration, white hostility, 22 per cent; social problem news—housing, education, cultural differences, 15 per cent. These levels total 71 per cent of all race news.

Of the remaining 29 per cent the most important topics are discrimination (5 per cent)—discussed almost wholly in terms of individual cases and never as a pattern; immigrant organizations (3 per cent)—presented mainly when they impinge on white society, their work in ethnic communities went unnoticed; and sport and entertainment (4 per cent) mainly controversies over sport in South Africa.

There was little evidence of concern with the topics of health or numbers.

The problems and contributions of black people in the sphere of employment were rarely mentioned.

The relationship between black people and the police was presented as unproblematic and of minimal importance.

Reference themes in the evenings

The main reference themes were not the same as the main topics. Excluding human interest for which there was no reference theme and race relations because of its residual nature, the three major topics (crime, immigration, white hostility) and the three major reference themes (cultural differences, housing, education) are mutually exclusive.

The most important reference theme (12 per cent) was cultural differences. A quarter of these occurred in the context of crime. There was a heavy emphasis on language culture and West Indian parties.

With housing and education as reference themes, there is evidence of an even more negative emphasis, than in the topics.

There is some contrary evidence of a more 'negotiating' approach in the reference themes of racial integration, where accommodation and pluralism occur more frequently than in the topics, and race relations where 'anti-coloured prejudice' appears more frequently than in the topic.

Reference themes appear to offer a negative and locally-rooted set of inferences which operate as evidence for a debate about race conducted in terms of race relations, immigration and white hostility.

Variations in race in the evenings over time

Race coverage as a whole increases by 80 per cent in the second half of the period. Reference themes increase at a proportionally greater rate, and more than double.

Coverage of crime, human interest and housing, rises absolutely, but decreases as a proportion of race news; large absolute and proportional gains occur under the topics of race relations and sport and entertainment, smaller ones in immigration, white hostility, discrimination, racial integration, and immigrant organizations.

The graph of total race coverage shows a sharp increase in 1965 followed by a dramatic fall in 1966; an upsurge in 1967 to 1963–64 levels; a doubling in 1968, and only a slight fall in 1969 and 1970.

The peaks represent intensive 'anti-immigrant' lobbying in 1965 and 1968; the troughs can be interpreted as a deliberate saft pedaling of race news.

The expansion of race news does not involve great changes in the main topics and reference themes, but rather the expansion of the pre-existent news perspectives on race.

Differences between the evenings

The *Birmingham Evening Mail* carries substantially less race news than
might be expected based on population figures for immigrants. The
other two papers carry a percentage of race news which corresponds
almost exactly with the proportion of the local population, which is
black.

The papers' proportional coverage of topics and reference themes is
substantially the same.

The *Coventry Evening Telegraph* shows a much less variable distribution
of news over time than the other two papers.

In general, there is much less difference in news coverage between the
papers than might have been expected from the different socio-economic
and political factors at work in each city.

The Wolverhampton *Express and Star* carried more features (ten) and
editorials (twenty-six) than the other two papers combined. The
Birmingham Evening Mail had only five editorials but twenty features
which had the effect of collapsing the editorial/feature distinction. The
Coventry Evening Telegraph published seven editorials and just two
features.

The *Birmingham Evening Mail* concentrated on the issues of immigration
and neighbourhood decay in its features, and supported official
Conservative Party policy. Its objection to Powell's speeches, however,
were to their form rather than their content.

The Wolverhampton *Express and Star* declared its opposition to local
hostility towards black immigrants in both features and editorials,
though it could never break with the dominant definition of race as
an issue.

The *Coventry Evening Telegraph* declaimed the city's traditional virtue of
tolerance to an extent which appeared to deny the existence of any sort
of significant interracial problems.

The weeklies

Topics in the weekly papers

The distribution of topics and subtopics in the weeklies is substantially
the same as that found in the evenings, i.e. a predominance of
'routinized' news in crime and human interest stories; the essential
conceptualization of the race problem in terms of race relations,
immigration and white hostility; the 'second order' status of local
competition for resources and life styles in housing, education and
cultural differences; the underreporting of black employment and
black-police relationships.

Crimes reported are more varied in kind, but 32 per cent are in the
'violent' category.

Immigration is defined even more tightly in terms of control policies
(44 per cent) and election arguments (55 per cent).

In racial integration an even heavier emphasis on assimilation is apparent, and is the keynote of 70 per cent of items.

The total coverage, and subtopic distribution of white hostility, discrimination, housing, education, cultural differences and immigrant organizations show only marginal differences from the pattern of the evening papers.

The weekly papers give a much fuller portrayal of health issues, especially emphasizing the immigrant population as carrying infectious diseases and overstraining hospital services.

Sport and entertainment receives relatively little attention in the weeklies.

Reference themes in the weeklies

The number of reference themes per topic item (mean 0.74) was exactly the same as in the evenings.

Even more than in the evenings, the main 5 topics and the main 5 reference themes are mutually exclusive. Topics: crime (22), race relations (15), human interest (15), immigration (19), white hostility (5). Total 66 per cent. Themes: cultural differences (11), housing (11), education (7), employment (7), legislation (6). Total 42 per cent.

There was once again a strong association between cultural differences and crime, one-fifth of the former references occurring in the latter context.

Nearly a third of 'human interest' stories were found to have explicit reference themes, mainly those of education, employment, housing, white hostility and racial integration.

The tendency apparent in the pattern of reference themes in the evening papers towards a greater concentration on negative images was repeated in the two weekly papers.

Variations over time in the weeklies

There is a much smaller increase than in the evenings in the second half of the period, i.e. a much greater appearance of race news in the earlier period (48–52 per cent).

Topics show a somewhat contradictory development: the maintenance and rejuvenation of racial conflict over issues of education, immigration and cultural differences, yet a reassurance that day-to-day living is devoid of tension in human interest and racial integration topics.

It is difficult to make meaningful generalizations as the two papers' chronological developments are radically different.

Differences between the weeklies

The *Warley News Telephone* carries proportionally nearly five times as much race news as the *Walsall Observer*. As a percentage of news space, this represents an increase of two-thirds on the mean figure for the evenings; the *Walsall Observer* decrease is of the same proportion.

The Warley paper carries less on crime and human interest (29 per cent) and more on race relations (18 per cent) than any other paper. There is an especially dramatic change in the coverage of topics in the second half. Some topics decrease their share of news: housing (9 to 1 per cent), health (4 per cent to nil), white hostility (9 to 5 per cent)—while others increase: human interest from 10 to 16 per cent, racial integration from 1 to 20 per cent.

In the earlier period, the Warley paper structures its news coverage around the local anti-immigrant campaign and picked up the issues it defined as newsworthy. This is especially evident in the pre-election edition of 9 October 1964.

The changes in news coverage in the later period represent more than a return to 'normality' and may be interpreted as a conscious move to compensate for earlier coverage.

The *Walsall Observer* produces overall the highest proportion of human-interest stories (24 per cent). With a slightly below-average crime figure of 16 per cent, race news in this paper more than any other is predominantly of a 'routinized' kind.

In this paper, education (7 per cent) and housing (5 per cent) were well above the mean. Much less attention was paid to white hostility (3 per cent) and cultural differences (5 per cent).

The *Walsall Observer* was the only paper to give open and unqualified support to the activities of Enoch Powell, yet its overall coverage of race and especially that of white hostility, and cultural differences, was smaller than in any other paper. It was also the only paper to decrease its total race coverage in 1968.

This idiosyncratic pattern of coverage in the Walsall paper may be attributed to its sustained campaign particularly in 1968 against the presence of travellers in the town.

Special study

Travellers in the Walsall Observer

There is a clear and dramatic increase in the *Walsall Observer*'s coverage of the travellers' issue in the last three years of the period (1968–70), as measured in the number and length of news items. In 1968 this traveller coverage exceeds that of race, and is higher in all three years—1968, 1969, 1970.

The traveller-related material can be analysed by the same framework of content analysis as that used on race coverage. The main topics emerge as local hostility and legislation, the main reference themes as crime, health and immigration.

Developing hostility in the paper towards travelling people can be traced by the gradual abandonment of descriptive or ambiguous terms—nomad; itinerant, gypsy—in favour of the negative connotations of tinker.

Implicit and explicit analogies are apparent between travellers and black immigrants. The status of travellers as a foreign-born, culturally different minority is used to raise questions of national identity, cultural conformity and majority interests. Unfavourable comparisons are made of travellers' behaviour with that of coloured immigrants, and travellers are presented as a further aspect of an existing immigrant problem.

The specific arguments made in the *Walsall Observer* to plead that Walsall had a special problem of travellers, are strikingly similar to those used in the *Smethwick Telephone* to plead that Smethwick had a special immigrant problem, namely: (a) even if national action was impossible, theirs was a special case; the town was sharing a disproportionate share of the burden, while others went scot-free; (b) the council's resources were being drained; (c) the minority expected special treatment; (d) the extent of local hostility evidenced the need for action; (e) the everyday life of ordinary citizens was threatened by alien influences; (f) Whitehall was out of touch, overinfluenced by minority protests and indifferent to the sufferings of the local majority.

The other papers' coverage of travellers is minimal. The *Birmingham Evening Mail* adopts similar news techniques, through the scale is much dimished. The liberal editorial stance of the Wolverhampton *Express and Star* results in significantly different coverage of the issue, and even of the same events.

The conclusion is that both in the local community and in the local paper the issues of black-immigration and travellers are conceived and presented in the same terms: they are functionally interchangeable in what is essentially a scapegoating process.

The travellers coverage was thus a specific limitation on race coverage, if only because dual coverage would have presented the town as on the verge of complete cultural breakdown.

Conclusion

We hope to have made many of the essential connections between our various findings as we have gone along. Though the particular forms of race presentation in the provincial press are in many ways different from those of the national press, the overall effect is very similar:[1]

the way race-related material is handled by the mass media serves both to perpetuate negative perceptions of blacks and to define the situation as one of intergroup conflict.

If we can assume that we have established the main parameters of race as news in the provincial press, our concluding remarks can then attempt to suggest why race should come to be presented in such a way. From one angle, it is a question of how far British cultures can be described as racist, and how far the press reproduces and reinforces a racist tradition.

1. P. Hartmann and C. Husband, 'The Mass Media and Racial Conflict', *Race*.

This would require an examination of past and present cultures of both an official and unofficial kind which is beyond our brief. Our method would also not allow us to identify the particular inflexions which the press contributes to such an ideology. We comment on some of these problems in Appendix 2.

We can, however, value some comments here on the way in which race as an 'objective' social category comes to be taken up by the provincial press in its particular forms. This is the problem of news values which Stuart Hall amongst others has discussed, with special reference to news photos:[1]

By news values we mean the operational practices which allow editors, working over a set of prints, to select, rank, classify and elaborate the photo in terms of his 'stock of knowledge' as to what constitutes 'news'. News values are one of the most opaque structures of meaning in modern society. All 'true journalists' are supposed to possess it: few can or are willing to identify and define it. Journalists speak of 'the news' as if events select themselves. Further they speak as if which is the 'most significant' news story, and which 'news angles' are most salient as if they were divinely inspired. Yet of the millions of events which occur every day in the world, only a tiny proportion ever become visible as 'potential news stories' and of this proportion only a small fraction are actually produced as the day's news in the news media. We appear to be dealing, then, with a 'deep structure' whose function as a selective device is un-transparent even to those who professionally most know how to operate it.

In view of practising journalists' apparent unawareness of how and why news stories are selected, it may be useful to indicate some of the news values which appear crucial determinants of the presentation of race in the West Midlands press. In Chapter 2 we attempted to identify news practices distinctive of local as opposed to national newspapers: a parochial reference point inherently placing limits on potential news: a stress on the everyday normal and orderly; a conception of conflict as invariably soluble in a basically harmonious community; an overall effort to confirm the worth of respectability and to exemplify the values of existing institutions. The weekly newspapers adhered more closely to this code of cultural conduct than the evenings which made more connections with the dramatic abnormal anxiety—inducing news of the national press.

These differences should make us wary of generalizing too grossly about news values since the operation of categories of news present in all kinds of newspaper may have a particular inflection in the provincial press. If we examine the three kinds of news stories (routine, political and social problem) which dominated home news, we may begin to identify the criteria of news selection which help to determine how race is portrayed.

1. S. Hall, *The Determination of News Photographs*, University of Birmingham, Autumn 1972 (Working Papers in Cultural Studies, 3).

Routinized news (crime and human interest)

Our postulate then is that race as news cannot be fully understood unless the conception of routine news, independent of race, is first grasped. Certain kinds of dramatic crime, especially of a violent and/or sexual kind, have a long history as the staple diet of 'popular' newspapers. They enable a vicarious voyeurism of spectacular deviance, at the same time as providing a reminder, through the process of trial and sentence, of the penalties of transgressing the law. In the local context, however, it is much less clear why court reports of quite trivial crimes—drunkenness, driving offences, shoplifting—should be such an essential part of local newspapers. Some of the same functions are apparent: many such reports are a cautionary tale to the whole community of what may happen if they consume an excessive amount of alcohol. More than that, however, such reports stigmatize the offenders and formalize communal disapproval. It can be the report more than the court appearance itself which burdens the offender with a special sense of shame.

Such disapproval is powerful enough if heaped on one individual. If, however, there is a clearly recognizable group in the local community whose deviance from established conduct (in language, dress or religion) is already notorious, then the appearance of members of that group in court reports and in a regular association with crime has a cumulatively stigmatizing effect, and if reference is made in the court report to the arena of cultural differences, then the specific nature of the criminal act, whether objectively trivial or not, has been re-coded in a rather special way. The aberrant and idiosyncratic nature of routine crime has become an extension of the wilful deviance of a separate social group.

Human-interest stories are complex in their own right, before any racial connotations have been introduced. They hinge on a concept of normality or typicality without which they would seem uninteresting. As we argued earlier, their attraction in the local press is mainly that of ultra- rather than a typicality. People are presented as excelling at normal everyday routines which the presentation in the local newspaper signals to the community as important and significant. The relationship of blackness to typicality is clearly problematic; and it is this unhinging of normality which makes very few human interest stories involving black people simply analogous to those involving whites. Even the addition of an apparently innocuous photograph of a face which is not the normal white but the atypical black undermines the assumptions on which the whole story is balanced.

Both kinds of routinized news thus appear to depend for their newsworthiness on reference to a scale of normality and abnormality on which the story can be placed, and without which the story has no significance. Since we are arguing here that blackness is itself defined as an abnormality in the culture, the assumption cannot be made that black people appearing in them will be interpreted in the same way as white people. To use that justification for these practices—that these are just white people with black faces—is to delude oneself about the cultural significance accorded to colour. Wherever colour is explicitly invoked in the context of such stories the journalistic practice is an active collusion with racist definitions.

Political problem news (race relations, immigration, white hostility)

We have already noted the domination of race news by political definitions. What is especially striking here is the apparently automatic newsworthiness of statements on race by the already politically powerful. It may seem common sense that such statements by M.P.s or councillors should receive such extensive coverage, and as potential legislators or decision-makers their opinions are important. However, concentration on their statements tends to be exclusive, so that the opinions of the less powerful—in the case of race, black people themselves—go virtually unheard. Race as political problem news has as its source: white power. Immigration is an issue defined by white M.P.s, race relations a problem tackled by white middle-class liberals and white hostility an expression of white working-class feeling. It is possible to invoke the fact of a white majority in the total population to explain and justify the predominance of white opinion, but this is to accept that the press discussion of race has inevitably to be in white terms. That this is so, we have demonstrated; that it need not be so is evident from the unexplored areas of news such as employment and police. That black people are a problem for the police is inferred in the pattern of crime reporting; that the police are a problem for black people is rarely and grudgingly admitted.

The 'structure of access'—whose activities and opinions become defined as newsworthy—operates against black experience. There is no way any black group or individual could have come to have the same status, and thus press access, as Enoch Powell. Not the least consequence of this is a massive failure in the provincial press to communicate any sense of what it is like to be black in the United Kingdom—and more, what it is like to be black and British. The discussion of race is left largely to white opinion leaders who for the most part move throughout the period from 1963 to 1970 to progressively more hostile stances and policies.

The fact that the press automatically believes the utterances of the powerful to be newsworthy has the particular effect in the race issue of allowing the principle issues to be defined by white authority. Small wonder that black groups are largely suspicious of the local press.

Social problem news (housing, education, cultural differences)

The discussion of social problems touches a delicate nerve in the provincial press; the relationship between local and central government. As the discussion is mainly about resources and about money, the central argument is invariably about how far the locality can expect or demand special help from central government, or in the favoured imagery of the local press how far the 'burden' is to be allowed to 'fall' on the 'long-suffering ratepayer'. The reasons why the *Smethwick Telephone*'s assessment of the immigrants presence and the *Walsall Observer*'s reaction to race are so similar are not merely that they are carrying out similar processes of scapegoating (see summary pages 172–3). They are also because the social problems evident in any town or city are quite frequently handled in this way and that the only 'real' solution is for central government to recognize the locality as a special case, and to allocate it extra funds.

This framework of analysis has some validity in a situation where local government has an essentially outmoded and inequitable system of funding, and where local authorities are forced to compete with each other for government hand-outs. Again, however, the criticism to be levelled is not that the framework is wholly irrelevant, but that it becomes exclusive. Thus the cause of social problems in their local forms is the failure of national government to provide extra resources, as if the taxpayer was not the same person as the ratepayer. Since the lack of resources devoted to education and housing is a failure of central government, the larger problems of resource distribution—as in the inequality between the public and private domains of income and wealth—are largely ignored. Precisely what is ignored here is the relationship between private production and consumption, and the provision of public services.

It is thus not specific to the race topic, that stress on resources in housing and education is unrelated to employment. That West Midlands industries had in the early 1960s a crying need for male and female labourers whose families could be neither housed nor educated properly without expanding existing facilities seems to us to be the crucial factor. On occasion—as when Renee Short, a Wolverhampton M.P., suggested industry should provide hostels and nurseries for black immigrants—the connection was made, but this was a rare occurrence.

In part, then, the press treatment of black people in housing and education derived from non-racial discussions of those topics. There was a particular racial bent in the tendency to infer that immigrants caused rather than exacerbated deficiencies in resources and especially the negative connotations ascribed to cultural differences in religion, language and family life, which, as in the case of crime, provided a secondary problem factor. Not only did they live eleven or twelve in a house, but they appeared to want to; not only were they flooding the schools, but they could not speak or write English.

This use of cultural differences refers back to the provincial press's distinctive sense of a cohesive community dependent upon a conservative notion of homogeneity against which black groups are consistently contrasted. The cultural traditions of the local press could no more cope with the black immigrants than could those of the local inhabitants.

We have endeavoured in this conclusion to make some distinction between the kinds of news values which helped to determine the presentation of race in the press. Some appear to operate in all kinds of news and merely treat race as any other topic: a black immigrant protest demonstration may be handled in the same terms (e.g. violence and confrontation with the police) as one by students. Others appear peculiar to race, for example, the exploitation of cultural differences. We have then two sets of news values often intertwined but conceptually distinct: those of the provincial press defining news in general, and those of the white media defining the race issue.

This distinction is important if we are to adequately answer the question which inevitably arises in response to a study such as this: are you asking for special news treatment for race issues? The answer has to be no and yes. No, because some parts of the news values determining race coverage are applied to all news, and changing those parts of the news portrait of race must involve alterations in that more general conception of news. Yes, because there are parts of news values which appear particular to race, and require a special effort of comprehension and remedial action. To that effort we hope this report is a useful contribution.

Coding method

Overseas news

Topics and subtopics

South Africa
1. Pro-arms for South Africa.
2. Anti-arms for South Africa.
3. Anti-apartheid comment.
4. Pro-apartheid comment.
5. Black/white conflict—South Africa.
6. Detainees/trials—South Africa.
7. Race in South Africa—other/general.

Rhodesia
1. Unilateral declaration of independence—Rhodesia.
2. Pro-African majority rule or Anti-South.
3. Anti-African majority rule or Pro-Smith.
4. Detainees/trials—Rhodesia.
5. Black/white conflict—Rhodesia.

United States of America
1. Civil Rights Movement in the United States.
2. Black organizations in the United States.
3. United States riots and demonstrations involving blacks.
4. Efforts to calm the situation in the United States.
5. Other.

India, Black Africa or West Indies
1. Politics.
2. Underdevelopment (economic or cultural).
3. Internal riots and civil disorders.
4. War between existent or potential nations.
5. Natural disaster including accidents/famines.
6. Other.

Reference themes

As above plus home news themes, i.e. housing, cultural differences, etc.

Home news

Topics and subtopics

Housing
1. Association of coloured people with slums, overcrowding or multi-occupation.
2. Coloured people said to cause or aggravate the housing shortage.
3. Coloured people and council housing.
4. House occupancy by coloured people causing whites to move out.
5. Housing associations to provide housing for coloured people.
6. Housing for whites only.
7. Housing—no difficulties.
8. Immigrants as landlords.
9. Idea of neighbourhood decay associated with immigrant settlement.
10. Housing—other/general.

Education
1. Immigrants overcrowd schools or proportion of coloured pupils too high.
2. White children held back by immigrant children in school.
3. Dispersal of coloured children.
4. Coloured children making good school adjustment.
5. Immigrant children waiting for school places.
6. Special educational provision for immigrants.
7. Coloured children disadvantaged compared to white children.
8. Coloured children making bad adjustment to school.
9. Overseas students—in further/higher education.
10. Education—other/general.

Health
1. Immigrants with infectious diseases (e.g. typhoid).
2. Immigrants as health hazard to host population.
3. Strain on hospital and social services because of immigrants.
4. Psychological strain suffered by immigrants.
5. Health checks—needed, or set up.
6. Misconduct by coloured professionals.
7. Immigrants' use of birth control.
8. Health—other/general.

Employment
1. Coloured people take jobs, cause unemployment of whites.
2. Coloured people cannot get jobs, or cannot get jobs suitable for their qualifications (not discrimination).
3. Coloured people and strike action.
4. Coloured doctors and nurses employed in the health service.
5. Positive steps already taken or being taken to improve the employment situation for coloured people.
6. Coloured school-leavers seeking employment.
7. Levels of immigrant employment/unemployment.
8. Trade Unions/workers' organizations and immigrants.
9. Employment—other/general.

Numbers
1.   Size of coloured population in the United Kingdom—projections of future trends.
2.   Immigrant birth rates.
3.   Doubts expressed about accuracy of figures for immigrant population.
4.   Numbers as a source of conflict in the future.
5.   Repatriation of immigrants to solve 'numbers problem'.
6.   Size of population in West Midlands towns.
7.   Numbers, other/general.

White hostility
1.   Racial assualts by whites (different from crime).
2.   Verbal hostility towards coloured people.
3.   Protest demonstrations against coloured people or immigration.
4.   Hostile organizations.
5.   White hostility—other/general.

Black hostility
1.   Racial assualts against whites by blacks (different from crime).
2.   Black verbal hostility.
3.   Demonstrations by coloured people against white people.
4.   Hostility by coloured people against coloured people.
5.   Black hostility—other/general.

Discrimination
1.   Discrimination against coloured people (including discrimination in housing and employment).
2.   Discussion of discrimination as a general topic.
3.   Cases of discrimination referred to the Race Relations Board.
4.   Segregation of coloured people from whites.
5.   Discrimination—other.

Discrimination by coloureds
1.   Discrimination by coloureds against whites.
2.   Other.

Police
1.   Good relations between coloured people and police.
2.   Bad relations between coloured people and police.
3.   Coloured police.
4.   Police—other/general.

Racial integration
1.   Absorption and assimilation.
2.   Accommodation and adjustment (negotiation).
3.   Pluralistic integration.
4.   Minimal tolerance.
5.   Other/general.

Crime
1.   Coloureds accused/suspected of crime—violence against the person (not robbery).
2.   Coloureds accused/suspected of crime—sexual crime (not rape).

3.   Coloureds accused/suspected of crime—burglary.
4.   Coloureds accused/suspected of crime—robbery (including with violence).
5.   Coloureds accused/suspected of crime—theft.
6.   Coloureds accused/suspected of crime—prostitution.
7.   Coloureds accused/suspected of crime—drugs.
8.   Coloureds accused/suspected of crime—illegal immigration.
9.   Coloureds accused/suspected of crime—driving offences.
10.   Coloureds accused/suspected of crime—drunkenness.
11.   Coloureds accused/suspected of crime—offences associated with parties (e.g. noise, selling drink).
12.   Coloureds accused/suspected of crime—other crimes.
13.   General statements about relationship between coloured people and crime.
14.   Use of special punishments, e.g. deportation.
15.   Crime—other/general.

Human interest
Coloured people featuring prominently in the general run of news material as victims of accidents or crime, subjects of human interest or involvement in other news events.

Cultural differences
1.   Description of eating habits, religion, dress, etc.
2.   Language differences.
3.   Special cultural provision for coloureds—mosques, entertainments, etc.
4.   Differences in customs—marriage, voting, child-bearing.
5.   West Indian parties.
6.   Culture clash—negative evaluation of cultural differences.
7.   Maintaining original culture—positive evaluation of cultural differences.
8.   Cultural differences—other/general.

Celebrities
1.   Coloured politicians.
2.   Coloured sportsmen.
3.   Coloured entertainers.
4.   Celebrities—other.

Immigration
1.   Numbers of immigrants entering/leaving the United Kingdom.
2.   Immigration control.
3.   Right of entry of British passport holders.
4.   Coloureds refused entry to the United Kingdom.
5.   Illegal entry/forged passports (not convictions for those offences—crime).
6.   Kenyan Asians.
7.   Immigration as an election issue.
8.   Immigration—other/general.

Legislation
1.   Outline of legislation.
2.   Parliamentary debate on legislation.

3. Comment on legislation.
4. Legislation—other/general.

Race relations
1. Race Relations Board—general.
2. Community relations organizations.
3. General comment about race relations.
4. Speeches or statements on race relations with an anti-coloured tenor.
5. Positive steps to improve race relations.
6. Race relations as an election issue.
7. Anti-colour prejudice.
8. Race relations—other.

Immigrant organizations
1. Involvement in race relations.
2. Involvement in welfare of immigrants.
3. Involvement in cultural activities.
4. Involvement in British politics.
5. Other/general.

Sport and entertainment
1. 'Keep politics out' of sport and of entertainment.
2. Against South African Sports teams.
3. Demonstrations over race and sport.
4. South Africa and Olympic Games.
5. South African cricket tour.
6. Visits to South Africa or Rhodesia.
7. Controversies over television/films containing racial elements.
8. Sport and entertainment—other/general.

Reference themes

Housing
a. Association of coloured people with slums, overcrowding or multi-occupation.
b. Coloured people said to cause or aggravate the housing shortage.
c. Coloured people and council housing.
d. House occupancy by coloured people causing whites to move out.
e. Housing associations to provide housing for coloured people.
f. Immigrants as landlords.
g. Idea of neighbourhood decay associated with immigrant settlement.
h. Housing—other/general.

Education
a. Immigrants overcrowd schools or proportion of coloured pupils too high.
b. White children held back by immigrant children in school.
c. Dispersal of coloured children.
d. Coloured children making good school adjustment.
e. Immigrant children waiting for school places.
f. Special educational provision for immigrants.
g. Coloured children disadvantaged compared to white children.
h. Coloured children making bad adjustment to school.

i.   Overseas students in further/higher education.

j.   Education—other/general.

Health

a.   Immigrants with infectious diseases (e.g. typhoid).

b.   Immigrants as health hazard to host population.

c.   Strain on hospital and social services because of immigrants.

d.   Psychological strain suffered by immigrants.

e.   Misconduct by coloured professionals.

f.   Immigrants' use of birth control.

g.   Health—other/general.

Employment

a.   Coloured people take jobs, cause unemployment of whites.

b.   Coloured people cannot get jobs, or cannot get jobs suitable for their qualifications (not discrimination).

c.   Coloured people in strike action.

d.   Coloured doctors and nurses employed in health services.

e.   Positive steps already taken or being taken to improve the employment situation for coloured people.

f.   Coloured school-leavers seeking employment.

g.   Levels of immigrant employment/unemployment.

h.   Trade unions/workers' organization and immigrants.

i.   Employment—other/general.

Numbers

a.   Size of coloured population in the United Kingdom—projection of future trends.

b.   Immigrant birth rates.

c.   Doubts expressed about the accuracy of figures for immigrant population.

d.   Numbers as a source of conflict in the future.

e.   Repatriation of immigrants to solve 'numbers problem'.

f.   Size of population in West Midlands towns.

g.   Numbers—other/general.

White hostility

a.   Racial assaults by whites (different from crime).

b.   Verbal hostility towards coloured people.

c.   Protest demonstrations against coloured people or immigration.

d.   White hostility—other/general.

Black hostility

a.   Racial assaults against whites by blacks (different from crime).

b.   Black verbal hostility.

c.   Demonstrations by coloured people against white people.

d.   Black hostility—other/general.

Discrimination

a.   Discrimination against coloured people (including discrimination in housing and employment).

b.   Discussion of discrimination as a general topic.

c.   Cases of discrimination referred to the Race Relations Board.

d.   Segregation of coloured people from whites.

e.   Discrimination—other/general.

Discrimination by coloureds
a.   Discrimination by coloureds against whites.
b.   Discrimination—other.

Police
a.   Good relations between coloured people and the police.
b.   Bad relations between coloured people and the police.
c.   Coloured police.
d.   Police—other/general.

Racial integration
a.   Absorption and assimilation.
b.   Accommodation and adjustment (idea of negotiation).
c.   Pluralistic integration.
d.   Minimal tolerance.
e.   Other/general.

Racial tension

Crime
a.   Coloureds accused/suspected of crime—violence against the person (not robbery).
b.   Coloureds accused/suspected of crime—sexual crime (not rape).
c.   Coloureds accused/suspected of crime—burglary.
d.   Coloureds accused/suspected of crime—robbery (including with violence).
e.   Coloureds accused/suspected of crime—theft.
f.   Coloureds accused/suspected of crime—prostitution.
g.   Coloureds accused/suspected of crime—drugs.
h.   Coloureds accused/suspected of crime—illegal immigration.
i.   Coloureds accused/suspected of crime—driving offences.
j.   Coloureds accused/suspected of crime—drunkenness.
k.   Coloureds accused/suspected of crime—offences associated with parties (e.g. noise, selling drink).
l.   Coloureds accused/suspected of crime—other crime.
m.   General statements about relationship between coloured people and crime.
n.   Use of special punishments, e.g. deportation.
o.   Crime—other/general.

Cultural differences
a.   Description of eating habits, religion, dress, etc.
b.   Differences in language.
c.   Special cultural provision of coloureds—mosques, entertainments.
d.   Differences in customs—marriage, voting, child-bearing.
e.   West Indian parties.
f.   Culture clash—negative evaluation of cultural differences.
g.   Maintaining original culture—positive evaluation of cultural differences.
h.   Cultural differences—other/general.

Immigration
a.   Numbers of immigrants entering/leaving the United Kingdom.
b.   Immigration control.
c.   Right of entry of British passport holders.

d.	Coloureds refused entry to the United Kingdom.
e.	Immigration as an election issue.
f.	Illegal entry/forged passports (excluding convictions—crime).
g.	Kenyan Asians.
h.	Immigration—other/general.

Legislation

a.	Outline of legislation.
b.	Parliamentary debate on legislation.
c.	Comment on legislation.
d.	1962 Commonwealth Immigrants Bill/Act.
e.	1965 Race Relations Bill/Act.
f.	1965 White Paper 2739.
g.	1968 Race Relations Bill/Act.
h.	1968 Commonwealth Immigrants Bill/Act.
i.	1969 Immigrants Appeals Bill/Act.
j.	Post 1969 legislation.
k.	Legislation—other/general.

Race relations

a.	Race Relations Board—general.
b.	Community relations organizations.
c.	Speeches or statements on race relations with an anti-coloured tenor.
d.	Positive steps to improve race relations.
e.	Anti-colour prejudice.
f.	Race relations—other.

Immigrant organizations

a.	Immigrant organizations and race relations.
b.	Immigrant organizations and welfare activities.
c.	Immigrant organizations and cultural activities.
d.	Immigrant organizations and involvement in British politics.
e.	Immigrant organizations—other.

Sport and entertainment

a.	'Keep politics out of sport' and out of 'entertainment'.
b.	Against South African sports teams.
c.	Demonstrations over race and sport.
d.	Sport and entertainment—other/general.

Powell

Black power

British politics and elections

Second generation immigrants

Communism

Commonwealth

Churches

References to other countries coded under same subheadings as overseas news reference themes.

Appendix 2

A note on methodology

The basic method used in this study was inherited from the Leicester project on the national press. In that report the problem of analysing the press coverage of race seemed to be progressively scaled down to a point where the objective of the whole endeavour could be summed up in one disarmingly simple question—'What was the material about?' An oversimplified question invited an overly crude answer: the measurement and tabulation of the surface subject-matter of race-related stories. There is a significant disjunction here between the explicit theoretical position taken in the introduction and Chapter 3 ('Aims and Methods') of that report, and the method of analysis implemented in the study. It is to these theoretical and methodological problems that we address this brief appendix.

In order to study the presentation of race in the press, it is necessary to have some theoretical understanding of both racial attitudes and the mass media, before the relationship between them can be explored. On racial attitudes the Leicester statement prefigures the more substantial argument to be made later in *Racism and the Mass Media.*[1]

> We have reservations about the utility of the concept of prejudice, taken on its own, as a way of making sense of race relations situations. ... Our own study and research has led us to think that it may be more important and fruitful to ask about the social structural characteristics of situations in which prejudice thrives and about the overall understanding of these situations on the part of those who hold prejudiced, hostile or other attitudes towards minority groups.[2]

If racial attitudes should not be conceptualized in a one-dimensional manner, neither should the social significance of the mass media:

> Mass communications do not haphazardly impinge on social life from the outside. The mass media are social institutions integral to the society in which they operate. Their location within the structures must be assumed to influence their output. ... Newspapers are read within ongoing patterns of face-to-face communication. There is reason to think that one of their main functions is to influence the character of these ongoing communications by providing subject-matter for discussion and indicating the terms in which the discussion might be carried out. ... Newspapers make people aware

1. Paul Hartmann and Charles Husband, *Racism and the Mass Media.*, Davis-Poynter, 1974.
2. Leicester, op. cit., p. 20.

of certain things and suggest the degree of importance that different events and issues have by the amount and prominence of coverage that they give them.[1]

It is these two separate theoretical propositions—one about racism as located in the general culture rather than in pathological individuals; the other identifying the newspaper as one moment in a continuous process of presenting and interpreting information—which converge on to the crucial problem of definitions:

We suspect that attitudes and conceptions affecting race relations can be more usefully approached as cultural and subcultural phenomena, with the emphasis on conceptions or 'definitions of the situation'.[2]

From this it is a simple step to scaling-down the problem to one of relating such definitions to subject-matter. A method can then be adopted which measures subject-matter and identifies the definitions implicit therein: content analysis.

The problem is, however, that in the pursuit of a tangible objective, many components of the original theory have had to be abandoned:

There are a number of purposes for which press content might be analysed. Among these, two are perhaps most common. The first is from the point of view of its likely impact on public opinion, and the second is to gain insight into the personalities and procedures by which newspapers are produced. It should be made clear, however, that content analysis on its own cannot provide final answers to either of these questions. It may provide strong indications and hypotheses, but if we want to know about readers and newspaper production we must study readers and production, as well as content. . . . Just how all the factors and circumstances surrounding the production of newspapers shape their content is an important question, but it is not one that content analysis on its own can answer.[3]

. . . .

it may be misleading to maintain too sharp a distinction between events and issues on the one hand, and the news about them on the other. Events are reported because they are thought to be important; they are thought important because they appear in the news. The content analyst moves in an area of ontological uncertainties. He cannot claim to be studying events or their social consequences as such, nor can he claim to say much about what determines news output. He has to be content with saying something about what has been called 'events as news'—that is, the versions of the daily world laid before the public as a kind of suggested agenda for their thought, discussion and action. How these images originate and what kind of use is subsequently made of them are questions for further investigation by other means.[4]

The implication here is that content analysis is adequate for analysing the moment of 'the event as news', but that a full portrait of news as a process would need to go in two other directions—back to the actual journalistic practices which constitute news production and forward to the effect on an interpretation by the public of the news which reaches them. These two ends of the process have indeed been studied in two studies emanating from the Centre for Mass Communications.[5]

Valuable though that work is, we wish to dissent from the exclusiveness of this theoretical stance and its consequent methodological practices. First,

1. Leicester, op. cit., p. 3.
2. ibid., p. 20.
3. ibid., p. 2.
4. ibid., p. 4.
5. cf. Halloran *et al.*, 1970; Hartmann and Husband, op. cit.

though the selection-presentation-interpretation model of news is valid in its own terms, there are other terms in which news as a cultural product might be studied: specifically its role in the distribution and activation of cultural power. Secondly, we doubt whether content analysis, at least of the kind so far developed, is in fact an adequate method of analysis, even for just the 'event as news'.

If the news presentation of race is seen as one specialized part of cultural production in a society, it is more complex and particular than the Leicester report sometimes suggests:

In a complex society with multiple mass media, newspaper content has to be seen as one feature (though an important one) of the enormously complex patterns of inter-personal and impersonal communication by means of which the society is in a continual process of defining itself.[1]

If 'society defining itself' has any meaning at all, it refers to the public domain of definition. We wish simply to state that the power of public definition in this British society is not equally distributed, and that ruling groups have greater access to means of cultural definition. Indeed it is the amount of access to cultural power which in part helps to describe those who rule the society.

Thus the production of news may be seen as one part of the pattern of cultural domination and conflict. In one sense news is an integral part of the struggle between dominant and subordinate cultures (cf. Parkin); or more theoretically as a crucial means by which the ruling class seeks to maintain its own hegemony (cf. Gramsci).

In this sense it is possible to take news as a particular form of ideological production in a culturally stratified society. It can thus be abstracted from the surrounding process of production and reception and recontextualized as part of the dominant cultural system. (Should the relationship between newspapers and ruling groups be open to question, we would refer back to our discussion in Chapter 3 of the patterns of ownership apparent in the West Midlands press). A series of problems are then set up in the relationship between news and other parts of the cultural system, especially education but also other ideological constructs such as fiction and films, as well as more informal but equally ideological cultural transactions, such as jokes. And beyond such clearly delineated artefacts there are lived forms of the culture in more private arenas, such as family and work groups.

In practice, some of the best studies of race make these kinds of connections, however subjectively (cf. Dummett). Those interested in identifying the nature of racism as a cultural phenomenon must and do trace it in whatever forms it appears in the culture. Those who seek to delimit racism as a question of psychology or individual attitudes will always fall short of a satisfactory understanding since the theoretical premise about racism is incorrect (cf. Rose *et al.*). The point then is that though the selection-presentation-interpretation model of news is an important one, it is not the only one. And it may be a grave error to believe that observation of journalistic practice is more important as an effort of study than the tracing of definitional relationships throughout the dominant—and indeed the subordinate—culture.

This has implications for our methodology. The problem about the nature of the public discussion of race cannot be confined to its superficial form—of what it is about. For we are then merely confirming what is patently obvious—that race in this predominantly white society has been publicly

---

1. Leicester, op. cit., p. 4.

handled in arbitrary and politically motivated terms, and that the media reflect this definition.

What is really important to understand—if as we take it racism must be properly understood if it is to be thoroughly opposed—are the precise mechanisms by which this public definition has been carried out. What does it tell us if immigrant organizations receive more or less publicity than white hostility, or racial integration more or less than cultural differences? For this in essence is all content analysis achieves. The superficial form is less important than the deep structure. The topic is less important than the image. Sampling and coding should be a means of reading between the lines, of enabling the examination of linguistic typographic and photographic elements of news stories. As a method, straight content analysis does not and will not fulfil the Leicester project's hopes:

We hoped that this approach would allow us to see whether any central defining themes could be identified that might be taken as indicating the meaning and significance of race in the newspapers.

Significance is after all a word no media analyst should use loosely, in view of the development of semiotics and other related theories of signs and symbols. It is precisely this area of signification from which the Leicester team cut themselves off. In discussing the inadequacy of prejudice measurements, they make a point which is more generally applied in the study:

to elucidate and illustrate convincingly prejudiced tendencies and underlying assumptions requires a great deal of reading between the lines, and textual interpretation of a kind that could not effectively be applied to a representative sample of newspaper material over a period of eight years, at least not with a degree of inter-analyst reliability that we would find acceptable.[1]

The problem of 'inter-analyst reliability' arises in the given context of an essentially positivist conception of proof and evidence. While we cannot possibly enter into that wide-ranging debate here, we would merely point to some parts of this report as possibly indicating alternative methods of analysing press coverage of race which do not encounter problems of 'inter-analyst reliability' but which do attempt to unravel the mechanisms of racial signification in the press. The discussions of home-overseas in the weeklies, of features and editorials in the evenings, and of travellers in the *Walsall Observer* are sufficiently grounded we believe to identify modes of labelling, linguistic structures, and underlying assumptions, which cannot be penetrated by content analysis.

We are not suggesting here the abandonment of any kind of sampling, or the substitution of any oversimplified categorization of 'positive' v. 'negative' news such as that used by Bagley. And clearly financial constraints have operated on both the Leicester and the Birmingham reports: there is a limit to what can be done for a thousand pounds. Nevertheless, it does not seem necessary to us to foreclose theoretical concerns in order to arrive at a manageable methodology.

On balance it may be better to struggle on with more open methodologies which at least leave theoretical questions intact. This is in part what the recent work of the Centre for Contemporary Cultural Studies has been doing—in unravelling central ideological myths such as 'affluence' and 'youth'[2] in paying

1. ibid., p. 21.
2. cf. A. C. H. Smith, *Paper Voices*, Chatto & Windus, 1975.

detailed attention to the analysis of photographs and other non-visual signs[1] or tracing the covertly political role of the media in helping to create and manage moral panics.[2]

From these concerns, the method of straightforward content analysis has proved a diversion. We can only hope that in our modifications of the method and in explicitly raising here some broader theoretical questions we have kept alive the essential problems of conceptualizing and analysing forms of ideological production in their structural and cultural environs. For on the basic context we are at least agreed:

Elements of racial conflict in British society and the impingement of the mass media upon this process cannot be understood apart from the structure of the society as a whole and the major conflicts of interest that govern its course.[3]

1. cf. 'Working Papers in Cultural Studies, 3'.
2. cf. Clarke, Critcher *et al*.
3. P. Hartmann and C. Husband, op. cit., p. 206.

Bibliography

BAGLEY, C. Race Relations and the Press. *Race*, Vol. XV, July 1973.

BERELSON, B. *Content Analysis in Communication Research*. Hafner, 1971.

CHIMAN, E. *The Black Country*. London, Longmans, 1972.

CLARKE, J. *et al.* Newsmaking and Crime. (C.C.C.S. Stencilled Paper No. 37.)

COHEN, S.; YOUNG, J. (eds.). *The Manufacture of News: Deviance, Social Problems and Mass Media*. London, Constable, 1973.

COX, H.; MORGAN, D. *City Politics and the Press*. London, Cambridge University Press, 1973.

DUMMETT, A. *A Portrait of English Racism*. London, Pelican, 1973.

EVANS, H. *et al. Race and the Press*. Runnymede Trust, 1971.

FOOT, P. *Immigration and Race in British Politics*. Harmondsworth, Penguin, 1965.

GALTUNG, J.; RUGE, M. The Structure of Foreign News. In: S. Cohen and J. Young (eds.), *The Manufacture of News: Deviance, Social Problems and Mass Media*. London, Constable, 1973.

HALL, S. The Determinations of News Photographs. In: S. Cohen and J. Young (eds.), *The Manufacture of News: Deviance, Social Problems and Mass Media*. London, Constable, 1973.

HALLORAN, J. *et al. Demonstration and Communication: A Case Study*. Harmondsworth, Penguin, 1970.

HARTMANN, P.; HUSBAND, C. *Racism and the Mass Media*. Davis-Poynter, 1975.

——. Race and the Mass Media. In: S. Cohen and J. Young (eds.), *The Manufacture of News: Deviance, Social Problems and Mass Media*. London, Constable, 1973.

HIRO, D. *Black British, White British*. London, Pelican, 1973.

HMSO. *Sample Census 1966: Commonwealth Immigrant Tables*.

HOGGART, R. *The Uses of Literacy*. London, Pelican, 1958.

HOLMAN, R. *Socially Deprived Families in Britain*. Bedford Square Press, 1970.

JACKSON, I. *The Provincial Press and the Community*. Manchester University Press, 1971.

JONES, P. N. The Segregation of Immigrant Communities in the City of Birmingham. 1961. (University of Hull Occasional Paper.)

PARKIN, F. *Class Inequality and Political Order*. New York, Paladin, 1970.

PATTERSON, S. *Immigration and Race Relations in Britain*. Oxford University Press/Institute of Race Relations, 1969.

POLITICAL AND ECONOMIC PLANNING. *Racial Discrimination*. London, PEP, 1967.

ROSE, E. J. B. *et al. Colour and Citizenship*. Oxford University Press/Institute of Race Relations, 1969.

SMITH, A. C. H. *Paper Voices*. London, Chatto & Windus, 1975.

THOMPSON, D. *Discrimination and Popular Culture*. London, Pelican, 1964.

WILLIAMS, R. Radical and/or Respectable. In: R. Boston (ed.), *The Press We Deserve*. Routledge & Kegan Paul, 1970.

Working Papers in Cultural Studies, 3. (C.C.C.S., University of Birmingham, Autumn 1972.)

Part II

The Sikhs of Vancouver

**A case study of the role
of the media in ethnic relations**

Joseph Scanlon

Carleton University,
Ottawa

This study would not have been done if someone at Unesco had not decided the general topic of the media and immigrant groups was worth studying. It would not have been done if the Canadian Commission for Unesco had not found some money to make it possible. And it would not have been done if the author, because of some earlier connections with Unesco, had not had his arm twisted to do it.

Once that has been said, however, I should like to make absolutely clear that the entire study was run independent of any direction or control from Unesco or anyone else. The facts in it, the inferences drawn from them and the conclusions stated are all mine and no one else's. Certainly Unesco need bear no responsibility for them. I should also like to say I very much appreciate the original arm-twisting, because the study proved to be incredibly fascinating to do.

My acceptance of total responsibility does not mean, of course, that this study is solely a one-person effort. The content analysis, took Leslie Goddard endless hours of reading newspapers and microfilm. She also listened to the many, many drafts of the text. The field research was carried out with the help of a colleague Daniel Pottier and he, too, patiently listened to many of my half-baked ideas in our Vancouver hotel room and read the all-but-final draft making many valuable suggestions. And the analysis has been revised after some helpful comments by my colleagues Peter Johansen and Jay Weston. To all of them—especially Leslie and Danny—I owe my thanks.

It is also true that a number of persons made the research far more productive than might have been possible otherwise. They cannot all be mentioned but I must thank members of the Vancouver Police Department, especially Dave Randhawa and Ken McLarty, members of the Vancouver media, especially Pat Nagle, of the Sun; members of the Sikh community, especially Gurdeep Singh; and an old friend and always helpful colleague, Arnie Myers of the University of British Columbia.

Finally, because my style of writing and rewriting and my incredibly bad handwriting has driven more than one secretary insane, I should like to make clear that I appreciate very much indeed the endless patience and the willing help of Judy Poitras and the others in the journalism secretariat at Carleton.

As is always the case, I find at the end of a study, that I can think of innumerable references I should have read, innumerable interviews I should have conducted, and innumerable questions I should have also asked. No one is more aware than the author of the deficiencies of any piece of 'finished' research. Therefore, I should like to end these thank-you notes with the quite factual statement that I and I, alone, bear the responsibility for the remaining inadequacies.

T. JOSEPH SCANLON

Introduction

For most of its history, Canada has been able to control rather effectively just who was allowed to enter the country as an immigrant. The control was applied both to the kinds of people admitted and to their numbers and, for most of this century, it included implicit or explicit racial barriers. It is quite easy to document the fact that the country of Canada has tried very hard and very successfully to make itself a white man's country.

In the past decade, however, there appears to have been a change of attitude in Canadian immigration policy. Government regulations were gradually relaxed and it was declared that merit rather than place of origin or skin colour would determine entry. And the immigration figures for the last decade or so suggest that this change of policy did, in fact, have a significant effect. Between 1967 and 1973, immigration from Europe dropped from 71.8 per cent to 39 per cent of the total and during the same period immigration from Asia and Africa rose from 11.4 per cent to 28 per cent of all immigration. For the first time since the early part of this century, Canada was admitting substantial numbers of persons with a skin colour other than the customary Canadian white.

Most of these new coloured Canadians (as is true for all new immigrants) headed for the big cities, half of them going to Toronto, Montreal or Vancouver. There they made their homes adding a new tone to the existing population and, sometimes, changing the racial balance in the community. Their coming also often created a new set of problems and questions for these communities and made necessary a new round of adjustments.

This study is about one of these immigrant groups—about the East Indians.[1] In particular, it is about one element in that East Indian mosaic, about persons who call themselves Sikhs, persons whose origins are in the Punjab region of northern India but persons who may have come to Canada by a number of direct or indirect routes. As this study will show, this group is particularly interesting because, although the present group

1. The term is usually applied to those from India, Pakistan or Sri Lanka.

is largely of recent origin, Sikh experiences with Canada date back over three-quarters of a century.

But this study is not just about East Indians or Sikhs, it is about their experience in a particular community, the city of Vancouver, Canada's major west coast port, the Canadian gateway from the Orient. For it is in Vancouver that most of the Sikhs have settled and it is there they appear to have run into the greatest problems and it is there the problem began: it was in Vancouver that Canadians and Sikhs first clashed sixty years ago.

This study, however, is not just a study about the East Indians or Sikhs of Vancouver; it is a study of the mass media. It is an attempt to study how the local media have dealt with this latest large ethnic group and by analysing what has happened in one case study of the media and an ethnic group, to draw some general conclusions. As will be seen later, it would appear the choice of the Sikhs and Vancouver was a productive one: during the past twelve months, the Vancouver media have given considerable attention to East Indians, certainly enough to guarantee an adequate basis for analysis.

The basic technique used for this research is content analysis, an approach often used by the author in the past,[1] and one designed to provide a convenient classification system of media content. In this study, the author and his research staff have followed the classification system prepared by researchers at Leicester in the United Kingdom and attempted to identify all East Indian material in the two Vancouver daily newspapers according to these classifications.[2] They have also followed the guidelines of the later British studies classifying items that did not specifically refer to East Indians where the content appeared quite clear. (All male Sikhs, for example, use the name 'Singh' (lion): a reference to a person named Singh was assumed to be a reference to a Sikh.)

Content analysis is definitely useful for making comparisons within a media context. It is possible, for example, to trace the pattern of media coverage over time. It is possible to examine the differences between one medium and another. It is possible to see whether one group gets a different kind of coverage from another. Thus, through content analysis, it will be possible, by noting all material carried about East Indians, to see whether the pattern of coverage has altered over time.

But the methodology has its weaknesses: it does not provide any evidence as to the frame of reference from which the news was drawn; since it is an analysis only of published material, it reveals nothing about that which was available but rejected; and more important, perhaps, it provides no overall picture of reality from which the contents of the media can be evaluated. It is not possible using content analysis alone to make any significant comments about the quality of media or the

1. See, for example, Joseph Scanlon, 'Canada Sees the World Through U.S. Eyes: One Case Study in Cultural Domination', *The Canadian Forum*, September 1974, p. 34–9; and T. Joseph Scanlon, *A Study of the Contents of 30 Canadian Daily Newspapers*, Ottawa, Special Senate Committee on the Mass Media, 1969.
2. 'List of References Themes Grouped by Topic Heading', *Race as News*, Appendix 2, p. 171–3, Paris, The Unesco Press, 1974.

accuracy of their coverage. Doing this requires some outside points of reference.

It is this fact—that content needs to be evaluated in the light of other evidence—that explains why the first two-thirds of this section deals not with media content but with the story of the Sikhs in Vancouver. Only with such a detailed history—a history not available elsewhere—can a proper evaluation of media performance be made. Only in the light of such material is it clear whether the media have, in fact, reported an accurate and total picture of reality.

But there is another problem with content analysis. It does not help us assess impact. Research to date has not been able to establish that there is any proven connection between media content and attitude change. The evidence available about such things as selective exposure, selective perception and selective retention suggests people read what they want to read, see in it what they want to see and remember what they want to remember. Therefore, any findings on the basis of content analysis alone have some severe limitations.[1]

There is one media research finding, however, that does appear to offer some other productive area for content analysis. That is agenda setting—the finding that media may determine what it is that people think about even if they do not determine what those thoughts will be once the agenda has been decided.[2] The research in this area seems quite clear: if it should be shown that the media present a particular item on the agenda, then the audience will focus some attention on that item though, of course, they apply predetermined attitudes.

Finally there is some research that takes a step beyond this. It links content analysis to attitude change by suggesting that if the media focus on a subject, one already viewed by an audience as negative, then negative attitudes can be intensified by that focus. Furthermore, if the media link two subjects—both viewed by the audience as negative—then the level of intensity may rise still further.[3] There is evidence that this has happened elsewhere;[4] and it does not seem to be an inaccurate description of what this study shows about the media and the Sikhs of Vancouver.

This study is divided into a number of sections. First, there is a brief introductory chapter, 'The Early Years', a chapter which provides a short early history of the Sikhs. It is a story which is necessary to a complete understanding of racial intolerance in Vancouver, but it is a story which is not accompanied by any media analysis. Second, two chapters, 'The Quiet Years' and 'New People, New Problems', deal with the story of the Sikhs following the initial wave of immigration through to the present.

1. Joseph T. Klapper, *The Effects of Mass Communication*, New York, The Free Press, 1965. See Chapter 2.
2. Maxwell E. McCombs and Donald L. Shaw, 'The Agenda-Setting Function of Mass Media', *Public Opinion Quarterly*, Vol. 36, 1972, p. 176–87.
3. Ralph H. Turner and Samuel J. Surace, 'Zoot-Suiters and Mexicans: Symbol in Crowd Behavior', *American Journal of Sociology*, Vol. 62, 1956–57, p. 14–20. The events described here bear an almost frightening resemblance to those in Vancouver.
4. This may not be uncommon in racial situations. See, for example: Terry Ann Knof, 'Race, Riots and Reporting', *Journal of Black Studies*, Vol. IV, No. 7, March 1974, p. 303–27.

These chapters—matched for the most part by later content analysis—spell out a number of themes: (a) there is an era of relative tranquillity—the Sikhs become accepted as tolerated but inferior members of the community; (b) there is a period of relaxation of discrimination—the Sikhs win their legal rights; (c) the Sikh community, itself, splits into a Westernized and traditional group; (d) there is a new wave of immigration and a new set of problems both within the Sikh community and, once again, with the dominant white community; and (e) there are still more immigrants this time including educated professionals from Africa and this group provides still further strains.

The presence of these themes will emerge through Chapters 2 and 3. The question later is: How well did the media deal with them?

Chapter 4 deals with one specific aspect of the story of the Sikhs—the story of their relations with the Vancouver police and their involvement with various types of violent crime. This material is presented for two reasons. First, it provides a case study of the relations between the Sikhs and one official agency. It is, therefore, a basis for analysis of the media. Second, it provides important information for evaluation of media content for, as the following media chapter shows, the press have become preoccupied, in recent years, with crime and the East Indians. It is essential this preoccupation be evaluated in the light of the reality.

The last portion of the study takes advantage of the preliminary material by analysing and evaluating media content in the light of the earlier data. It will become apparent that the portrait presented by the media leaves quite a different picture than the portrait presented in the first two-thirds or this work. This contrast—and it is a vivid one—allows the final three chapters (6, 7 and 8) to deal with the essential questions: Why the difference? What can and should be done about it?

It seems likely that some critics will argue this part deals too much with the Sikhs, too little with the media. Perhaps this approach is necessary because the media have dealt too little with the Sikhs.

Chapter 1

The early years

Canadians like to pretend that their country is free of the racial problems and prejudice they see in the United States just south of the border; but the reality is, of course, somewhat different. There has been racial prejudice in Canada for over 100 years and it has been especially prevalent in British Columbia, Canada's Western-most province. The reason for this is, of course, easy to establish: British Columbia has been the home for more racial groups—particularly those with a distinctive colouring—than anywhere else in Canada. If racism was to exist, then British Columbia would, inevitably, be the place for it.

A climate of racism

Racism probably began in British Columbia with blacks coming north from the United States. Robin Winks in his book *The Blacks in Canada*[1] tells of a number of clashes between whites and blacks in British Columbia in the mid-nineteenth century just about the time of the United States Civil War. There was an attempt to segregate religious worship. There were criticisms in the mass media. There was discrimination in seating arrangements in public places and a riot when blacks attempted to break such barriers.[2] And there were various kinds of legal exclusions: blacks were barred from jury duty and then—except for those of British birth—denied the vote. Racial discrimination was clearly established in British Columbia.

But it was to be Asians rather than those of United States origin who would experience the full flower of prejudice in British Columbia. Not along after the first blacks arrived, Japanese and Chinese began to come to British Columbia as well. The Japanese went to work in the fisheries and in agriculture; the Chinese—in many cases—worked as labourers along the trans-continental railroad—the CPR. So many

1. Robin W. Winks, *The Blacks in Canada*, Montreal, 1972.
2. ibid., p. 284.

Chinese came that the provincial legislature passed a series of discriminatory acts against them and the federal government got involved as well with racial barriers to immigration. Among other things, the province of British Columbia managed to pass a law barring Chinese from voting even if they were natural-born Canadians;[1] and the federal government gradually raised the price of entry to Canada until Chinese paid $500 each to enter Vancouver.[2]

Neither provincial nor federal policies were apparently enough for Vancouver's white population. In August 1907, the labour unions organized an anti-Asiatic league. In early September that same year they marched on Vancouver city hall, burned the lieutenant-governor in effigy[3] and started a riot in Chinatown. The looting would have spread to the Japanese quarter as well; but the mob was driven back when the Japanese used guns to defend themselves.[4] In the early twentieth century British Columbia was a province of racial antagonisms and Vancouver was the centre of the disputes.

It was into this kind of tense racial atmosphere that the first East Indians came when they arrived in Canada around the turn of the century. According to some accounts, they began to arrive in 1886, but it seems more likely the immigration began after 1897 when a contingent of Sikh soldiers passed through British Columbia on their way home from Queen Victoria's Diamond Jubilee celebration.[5] These soldiers went home to the Punjab in northern India with stories about the opportunities in Canada and it was their relatives and friends—Sikhs from Punjab villages—who came to Canada as immigrants. In 1904, the British Columbia census showed only 258 'Hindus' (as they were often called incorrectly), but the number climbed to over 5,000 in 1908. Then the Sikhs, like the Japanese and Chinese, ran afoul of increasing government antagonism and the first wave of immigration was over: it would not resume for fifty years.

Treatment of the Sikhs

The Sikhs, who regarded themselves as British, tried very hard to distinguish themselves from the Chinese and Japanese whom they, too, saw as alien.[6]

People talk about these Oriental races, and the phrase is understood to include not only the Chinese and the Japanese, but the Sikhs as well, which is quite absurd. . . . They are British Subjects; they have fought for the Empire; many

1. Charles Price, '"White" Restrictions on "Coloured" Immigration', *Race*, Vol. VII, No. 3, 1966, p. 221.
2. One estimate is that the immigrants paid $18 million in head taxes for entering Canada up till 1918. W. G. Smith, *A Study in Canadian Immigration*, p. 168, Toronto, 1920.
3. He employed oriental labour.
4. Price, op. cit., p. 225.
5. This story shows up in a number of places. The material for this version was drawn from I. M. Muthanna, 'East Indians in B.C. (till 1910)', *The Indo-Canadian*, Vol. VII, No. 3/4, 1971, p. 4.
6. Dr Sundar Singh, 'The Sikhs vs. Canada', *Empire Club Speeches*, p. 113, Toronto, 1911–12.

of these men have war medals. . . . These Sikhs are the pick of their villages, they are not out here like the Japanese and Chinese.

But such appeals fell on deaf ears in British Columbia. In an article in the *Canadian Magazine* in 1907, Barclay Williams gave the common view of the Sikhs:[1]

The class of Hindu that have invaded British Columbia are commonly known as Sikhs, meaning the lower class, entirely dependent on their physical capabilities—those who have not set aim in life. They are the 'coolies of Calcutta'. . . . As Tradesmen, these East Indians do not seem to become apt scholars, and their knowledge of domestic duties is very limited. Physically, they are unfit for manual labor, their diet being so light and unsustaining as to have reduced them to weaklings. Not accustomed to the mode of labour as conducted in this country, they soon weary, and only by dint of force do they manage to hold through the day.

The condition of these deluded Hindus is a sad one. It is a daily sight to see them wandering here, there and everywhere, half-starved, half-naked, hording in wretched hovels, ordered here, excluded there and despised everywhere.

Williams was wrong in his background but his descriptive comments of Sikh life in Vancouver were not untrue. Writing in the same magazine, an East Indian, Saint Singh, commented:[2]

The City of Vancouver has grown rapidly and the house accommodation there is insufficient. Accordingly, the Indian immigrants on arrival have to put up with any sort of housing they can get. That most of these houses are poor, miserable shacks, ill-ventilated and badly plumbed, damp and unhygenic is unfortunately true. But for this the immigrants are not to blame.

Whatever the situation in Vancouver, itself, there is some evidence at least that the Sikhs did begin to find jobs and to settle in their chosen country. One author reports:[3]

They [the Sikhs] gradually started to supplant the Chinese and Japanese in the saw mills of British Columbia. The manager of the saw mill at Port Moody 'saw these strapping men only ask for a job then watch the mobs piles of lumber with ease'. Soon other mills started employing them.

This latter account makes sense, for many of the Sikhs came from lumbering areas of India and—in retrospect—the fact that some Sikh families now own mills suggests they prospered in the lumber business. According to a relatively unprejudiced observer who wrote some years later: The Sikhs who came to British Columbia 'proved remarkably tough, resourceful and determined'. He concluded:[4]

Most of them quickly found work as labourers in the lumber mills or in the logging camps, in many cases replacing the Japanese who were being driven out of the industry.

1. I. Barclay Williams and Saint R. Singh, 'Canada's New Immigrant', *The Canadian Magazine*, Vol. XXVIII, November-April 1906–07, p. 384–5.
2. ibid., p. 388.
3. Quoted in Muthanna, op. cit., p. 5.
4. John Norris, 'People of India and the Moslems', *Strangers Entertained: A History of the Ethnic Groups of British Columbia*, p. 231, Victoria, 1971.

Unfortunately for the Sikhs, success in their new country did not solve their problems. Discrimination against them was increasing and it was beginning to assume increasingly subtle and legal forms. In 1907, the provincial legislature passed an act which blocked Asians from entering a profession, serving on juries, obtaining government contracts and buying property in some parts of Vancouver.[1] And East Indians were included under the law: 'The expression "Hindu" shall mean the native of India not born of Anglo-Saxon parents.'[2] When the Asiatic Exclusion League was formed and led by persons such as Herbert Stevens, it too attacked the East Indian: 'Canada is best left in the hands of the Anglo-Saxon race ... it shall remain white and our doors shall be closed to the Hindus.'[3] And in 1908–09, the British Government proposed moving the British Columbia East Indians to British Honduras.[4] A delegation of four persons—J. B. Harkins of the federal Ministry of the Interior, W. C. Hopkinson of the Immigration Department (he was later to be murdered by a Sikh), Nagin Singh and Sham Singh—was actually sent to British Honduras to report on conditions there. The two Singhs reported to the rest of the community on their return that conditions were very poor indeed:[5]

The country was mosquito infested and malaria was rife. People lived miserably, subsisting on milk and vegetable diet, supplemented with coconut and coconut oil. Fresh water was not easily available and the cost of living was very high.

By this time, the Sikhs had established a temple and it was there, at a meeting, that they voted unanimously to reject the idea of any movement from Canada to British Honduras.

The Honduras incident was not, however, entirely over. The two Singhs alleged they had been offered a bribe by Messrs Harkins and Hopkinson of $3,000 to recommend the move to Honduras. (The two men denied the charges.) The Governor of the colony, Eric Swayne, was authorized by the United Kingdom to negotiate the move. However, the unanimous rejection of the idea by the Sikhs apparently convinced the Canadian government to drop the plan and it was abandoned.

The legal constraints

In the view of the federal government, however, there was a real problem: the Sikhs were not wanted in Canada but they were British subjects and Canada was a British country and the Sikhs therefore should have had some rights. Since Canada wished to avoid conflict within the Empire, a young Canadian civil servant was sent off to London to find a solution to the problem created by Sikh immigration.

1. Muthanna, op. cit., p. 8.
2. ibid., p. 8.
3. ibid., p. 9.
4. ibid., p. 12.
5. ibid., p. 12–13.

That man was William Lyon Mackenzie King (later to serve longer as Prime Minister than any other person) and he proved to be already a devious manipulator. Mr King came up with three means of attacking Sikh immigration without, apparently, imposing direct discrimination:[1]

1. An Indian (not a Canadian) statute prohibiting emigration of indentured labor was to be strictly enforced;
2. Immigrants from Asia were, in future, to be required to have $200 on hand rather than the usual $25; and
3. Immigrants, in future, would have to come to Canada by 'continuous journey and on through tickets from the country of their birth of citizenship'.

Mr King rationalized the first of these actions by arguing that Indian immigration to Canada was not spontaneous but the result of exploitation of the Indians. He said that some persons were painting glowing pictures of opportunities in Canada and persuading farmers to mortgage their homesteads at interest rates ranging from 15 to 20 per cent. He rationalized the second move—the increase in money needed—only by saying that if $25 was inadequate it should be increased. He did not really try to rationalize the third move; but it was clearly effective—there were no steamships making a direct passage from ports in India to ports in Canada. The requirement for continuous passage amounted to a total exclusion.

Mr King attempted to present his suggestions as in the interests of the Indians themselves:[2]

It was clearly recognized in regard to emigration from India to Canada that the native of India is not a person suited to this country, that, accustomed as many of them are to the conditions of a tropical climate, and possessing manners and customs so unlike our own people, their inability to readily adapt themselves to surroundings entirely different could not do other than entail an amount of privation and suffering which renders a discontinuance of such immigration most desirable in the interests of the Indians themselves.

But elsewhere in the same report, Mr King was more blunt about the reasons for the mission he had been given by the Prime Minister, Sir Wilfrid Laurier:[3]

That Canada should desire to restrict immigration from the Orient is regarded as natural, that Canada should remain *a white man's country*[4] is believed to be not only desirable for social and economic reasons, but highly necessary on political and national grounds.

Or, as Sir Wilfrid, himself, put it:[5]

were such immigration allowed to reach any considerable dimensions, it would result in serious disturbance to industrial and economic conditions . . . especially in the province of British Columbia.

1. Canada, Parliament, House of Commons, *Report* by W. L. Mackenzie King, p. 5–10 (Sessional Paper No. 360, 1908).
2. ibid., p. 7–8.
3. ibid., p. 7.
4. Author's italics.
5. King, op. cit., p. 5.

In short, the Sikhs were coming and the white population did not like that; so the Sikhs must be stopped. Canada's famed Stephen Leacock (a humorist who, as an academic, also wrote serious economic history), concluded:[1]

Hindu immigration to British Columbia was ingeniously side-tracked by the 'continuous voyage' rule, as smart a piece of legislation as any that ever disfranchised negroes in the South. The Hindus were free to come, but only on a 'through ship'; and there were no through ships.

Testing the law

It appears that, at first, the Sikh community in Vancouver did not entirely believe the 'continuous passage' rule or believe that it would be enforced against East Indians. And, at first, there were a number of reasons to justify this belief.

As early as 1908—just two years after the order-in-council was passed—the Sikhs got surprising media and community support when the immigration department tried to deport 200 East Indians who had run afoul of the regulation.[2] The reasons for the deportation order in this case were that those being held were in poor health, had insufficient funds *or* had not come directly from India. Even the *Vancouver Province*, not previously a supporter of the Sikhs, argued against such an action:[3]

The Hindus in question left Calcutta with the express intention of coming to Canada. They were compelled to sail by way of Hong Kong . . . to penalize them for a mistake or an act not their own, would be a monstrous injustice . . . we don't want Hindus in Canada . . . but between them and the Japanese, who would not take the Indians?

Hardly overwhelming praise, but it apparently influenced Canadian immigration and the decision was made to allow the 200 persons in custody to stay.

Other attempts to overcome the problem were made by appeals to the immigration department, by calls on shipping companies, by attempts to test the regulation and by delegations to Ottawa. Most of these efforts were in vain although there were occasional successes. The appeals to the immigration officers in Vancouver and Victoria (the British Columbia capital) simply brought a reply spelling out the wording of the order-in-council. Immigration, obviously, did not want to get into the debate.[4] The appeals to the shipping companies brought a sympathetic response (they

1. Stephen Leacock, *Canada: The Foundations of Its Future*, p. 13, Montreal, House of Seagram, 1941.
2. Muthanna, op. cit., p. 11.
3. ibid., p. 11.
4. Anon., 'The Position of Hindus in Canada', *British Columbia Magazine*, Vol. VIII, July-December 1912, p. 666-7.

would have liked the business) but a 'pass-the-buck' attitude. The companies did not want to have problems with Canadian immigration:[1]

We maintain that a journey on a through ticket by way of Hong Kong would constitute a 'continuous' journey as the regulation requires, and believe that immigration officers here are not justified in requiring the Hindu to come on a direct steamship, which is at present impossible. But it is the local immigration officers who meet our steamships and with whom we have to do business, not the Ottawa authorities. Therefore it is not to our advantage to go over the heads of these men.

The order-in-council, however, applied not only to those not yet in Canada; it applied as well to the families (wives and children) of those who had come to Canada legally and settled down:

Many Hindus had their wives and families awaiting embarkation in Calcutta when the order was made and the women and children are still in India living on such remittance as their men folk may send them, anxiously awaiting the removal of the restriction which keeps them from enjoying the company of their husbands and fathers as the case may be.[2]

Just at present there are two Sikh women confined aboard a boat at Vancouver; they came on the 22nd. One is the wife of a merchant, the other is the wife of a missionary. These men have been settled in this country for five years and are well spoken of. . . . On the 22nd they arrived here and the men are allowed to land (they had been previously in Vancouver) but the ladies are still confined as if they were criminals.[3]

When the priest of the Vancouver Sikh temple (the Sikh community in Vancouver had established itself) tried to bring his wife and child to Canada, they were refused admission on the basis of the 'continuous passage' rule. Mr Singh, the immigration department ruled, could enter Canada because he had established domicile in Vancouver. His wife and children—even though they had come to Canada on a through ticket—could not enter because there had been (admittedly of necessity) a stop in Hong Kong. In this case, one of the many appeals to the federal government in Ottawa brought a result. The priest's family was allowed to enter Canada after a delegation headed by Teja Singh went to Ottawa and pleaded for them. One other man's family was allowed in as well. But, the delegation was told, the act was not to be considered in any way as a precedent.[4]

In 1913, there was another minor test case involving some East Indians who entered Canada legally by following the letter of the regulations. When they were refused entry, they appealed to the courts and they got a favourable decision on the legal technicality—the regulations under which they had been excluded were in conflict with the act that authorized those regulations. They and a handful of others (about ninety in all) were granted admission that year.[5]

1. ibid., p. 667.
2. ibid., p. 665.
3. Sundar Singh, op. cit., p. 115–16.
4. Homie M. Engineer, 'East Indians in B.C. Since 1910', *The Indo-Canadian*, Vol. VII, No. 3/4, 1971, p. 21.
5. Eric W. Morse, 'Some Aspects of the Komagata Maru Affair, 1914', *Report*, p. 101, Canadian Historical Association, 1936.

But the Government of Canada was not about to allow its anti-India policies to be circumvented by any technicality in the law. That same year a new order-in-council (cabinet order) was passed stating that in view of the overcrowded conditions of the labour market in British Columbia, no 'artisans or labourers, skilled or unskilled' could enter that province. Such an order, if upheld by the courts, could be used to bar almost anyone, East Indian or otherwise.[1] It would allow Canada to continue to prevent the non-white entering via the Pacific while allowing white immigrants to enter via the Atlantic.

The *Komagata Maru*

Even as this decision was taking effect, another effort was being made to test Canadian discrimination against East Indians. A wealthy Punjabi, Gurdit Singh, arranged to charter a Japanese ship, the *Komagata Maru*, and to bring it to Canada carrying on it East Indians who had all sailed by continuous passage to Canada. Since none of these persons (almost all Sikhs) would be indentured, since all would have the necessary $200, since all would have met the 'continuous passage' regulation, all should be legally admissable to Canada. Such an action should test whether the Canadian Government was only prepared to hide behind a devious law or whether it was prepared to indulge in open and blatant discrimination against East Indians. The *Komagata Maru* sailed from the Far East in early 1914 and arrived in Vancouver on 23 May 1914, and the major incident in the history of Canadian immigration began.[2]

The Canadian Government took the first move: officials in Vancouver stopped the ship from docking—which prevented communication between the passengers and those on shore. Then health and immigration officials boarded the ship and began examining the passengers. First, the health officers gave all on board a medical examination and, after this, ruled that ninety of the passengers were medically unfit to land. Then, immigration started checking the documents of those who claimed Canadian domicile; and ruled that twenty of these claims (eventually twenty-two) were valid. Then all the other cases were heard and in each case the ruling was the same: the prospective immigrants were not to be allowed to land because they fell under the regulations that prohibited skilled and unskilled labourers from entering British Columbia.

As these examinations and hearings continued the situation on board the ship grew increasingly tense. The company that had provided the ship refused to give the passengers supplies and—though immigration provided some supplies—food, water and fuel were runnning low. Second, throughout the hearings, the Canadian officials continued to refuse to

1. ibid., p. 101.
2. ibid., p. 100–8. Many of the details of the aftermath are more clear in Emmaline Smillie, 'An Historical Survey of Indian Migration Within the Empire', *The Canadian Historical Review*, Vol. IV, 1926, p. 222–8. In Morse's views the presence of a man named Hardazal who was trying to organize a revolution against the British in India had left British Columbia's Indian community 'seething with sedition'. There is little evidence supporting this statement.

allow contact with the shore. Those who wished to seek legal advice were not free to do so. The impasse was broken only after a direct appeal was made to the Prime Minister, Sir Robert Borden. He agreed, in effect, to allow those on board the *Komagata Maru* access to the courts though he also told his officials, 'it is important to secure a hearing before a court which will give a reasonable construction to the Act and its regulations'.[1]

Finally the legal case was heard. The government argued that its actions were legal and that the restriction against unskilled or skilled labour had the force of law. The prospective immigrants argued that such regulations were *ultra vires*—beyond the power of the federal government. The key decision was made by the provincial court of appeal in Victoria, the provincial capital, and, as Sir Robert had hoped, it upheld the government. With the exception of the twenty-two persons found to have Canadian domicile, those on board the *Komagata Maru* were not to be admitted to Canada.[2] The ship would leave and they would go with it.

By this time—the whole affair dragged on for eight weeks in all—the atmosphere was becoming increasingly troubled. The Canadian Government was besieged both by complaints from India and in Canada. While the appeals from India were asking for permission for the passengers to land, the appeals from home were entirely opposed to allowing the passengers to disembark. Labour and religious groups, political and business associations and the provincial government all asked the federal government to keep the East Indians out of Canada.

Finally the passengers rebelled: 17 July, when the ship was due to leave, they mutinied and took control of the ship. When police and a party of 150 police and immigration officials tried to board they were repelled. The passengers used coal, wood or whatever else was moveable to keep off the authorities. The authorities, who had been told to avoid bloodshed, quickly fled and there were no serious injuries.

The problems on the ship were accompanied by problems on shore. The Sikhs in Vancouver, becoming increasingly annoyed at the proceedings, tried first to buy the ship—so it could dock—then, apparently, thought of using force to land the passengers. The day the officials were repelled from boarding the *Komagata Maru* there were also clashes on shore. Four Sikhs were arrested and 500 rounds of ammunition seized.

The Canadian Government decided, at that point, it would have to use force. It called on the *Rainbow*, one of the only two ships in the newly formed Canadian navy, to force entry on the *Komagata Maru*. The men on board were subdued and—though they were given food and medicine by the Canadian Government—they were forced to leave Vancouver. On 23 July 1914, two months to the day after it had arrived, the quays and house tops of harbour front Vancouver were jammed as the *Komagatu Maru* sailed. On board were not only its remaining passengers but a handful of Vancouver Sikhs who had decided to leave Canada in disgust.

1. Morse, op. cit., p. 103.
2. ibid., p. 104.

It would be nearly fifty years before as many East Indians would come to Canada again.

But the story of the *Komagata Maru* was far from over: in fact the violence related to it had just begun.[1]

None of the passengers were allowed to land (after leaving Canada) at Hong Kong or Singapore, not even those who had their homes there. She [the *Komagata Maru*] was compelled to leave for India. She finally arrived at Budge Budge Harbour. The passengers were ordered to board a special train that was to take them to the Punjab under police guard. They refused. They were fired at. Eighteen were killed, twenty-five wounded, twenty-eight, including Gurdit Singh (the man who chartered the ship) disappeared. The rest were rounded up, taken to the Punjab and put in jail. When they were finally released from prison, they become revolutionaires and fought against the British rule in India.

Even in Canada the story had not ended. During the time the *Komagata Maru* was in Vancouver harbour, Vancouver immigration was using the services of Mr Hopkinson (the same man who had gone to British Honduras), a former British police officer who could speak Punjabi, the language of the Sikhs. Mr Hopkinson had been fed information by an informant, a Sikh named Bela Singh. On 3 September 1914, one of Bela Singh's associates, Arjan Singh, was shot. Bela Singh thought the shooting had been intentional and on 5 September—two days after the first incident—he ran amok, killing two leaders of the Sikh community and injuring six others. He was put on trial for murder.[2]

The murder trial of Bela Singh appeared to have only one possible outcome, but that was not to be. William Hopkinson appeared for the defence apparently prepared to testify that his informant's life had been in danger and that Bela Singh had killed two men and injured six others in self defence. He was to testify on 21 October. The Hopkinson testimony was apparently the last straw for the Sikh community. On the day he was to testify, Mr Hopkinson was shot and killed by a Sikh priest, Mewa Singh. Mewa Singh was, of course, subsequently tried and convicted of the Hopkinson murder and executed. His body was taken from the place where it was hanged and carried through the city with honour. His name is now revered among Vancouver Sikhs. A plaque in the lobby of the new Sikh temple calls him a martyr and every New Year Mewa Singh day is celebrated.[3]

There were still other strange aftermaths. Bela Singh—the man who killed six Sikhs and injured six others in front of eye witnesses—was subsequently acquitted, despite the fact that his friend, Mr Hopkinson, never got to testify. And finally, some years later, the biographer of Canada's first Liberal prime minister, Wilfrid Laurier, noted that the *Komagata Maru* incident involved the first use of the new Canadian navy. It was ironic, O. D. Skelton wrote, that it was the first used to stop British subjects from landing on British soil.[4]

1. Gurdial Singh Pannu, 'Sikhs in Canada', *The Sikh Review*, October 1970, p. 33–4.
2. ibid., p. 44. There are conflicting versions about when this incident occurred.
3. ibid.
4. O. D. Skelton, *Life-Letters of Sir Wilfrid Laurier*, p. 352, New York, 1922.

Chapter 2

The quiet years

When the *Komagata Maru* sailed from Vancouver harbour in 1914, its departure marked the end of the first era of Sikh immigration to Canada. The next fifty years would be relatively quiet ones during which the Sikh population would gradually dwindle in size. It would be a period during which the Canadian Sikhs gradually adjusted to a new culture, giving up some, though not all, of their traditions. It would be a period during which some forms of racism continued in Canada but a period during which the Sikhs—and most Canadians of Indian origin were Sikhs—gradually won equal rights as citizens. But by the time it ended, the Sikh community had quietly split between those who were being assimilated into a new and somewhat distinct life style and those trying very hard to hold on to old traditions.

The disappearance of the Sikhs

The cut-off of immigration from India and other parts of the Asian world meant a great deal more than just that no more males arrived: it meant no more families arrived; it meant that no single females arrived to join the males already in Canada.[1] The immigration cut-off left Vancouver's Sikh community effectively isolated from the rest of the Indian and Sikh world.

This situation opened up a number of possibilities. The Sikhs could have given up and left Canada in search of a more congenial home. They could have remained as an isolated, mainly male community, carrying on a bachelor-like existence. Or they could have assimilated through intermarriage with other groups. The evidence available suggests quite a few chose the first alternative—to leave. Some, however, remained, and they remained as an isolated group; intermarriage was not acceptable to the Sikhs.

---

1. It is difficult to acquire accurate statistics but one estimate is that there were only 500 females among the 5,000-odd Sikhs who entered Canada prior to the First World War.

It is hard to tell how many left British Columbia during those quiet decades but it seems clear that some did go to the United States and others went back to India or elsewhere.[1] In any case, the population dropped from its peak of 5,000-plus around the First World War to about 1,100 just before the Second World War. Part of this drop may have simply been the result of death because those who did remain usually lived in very uninspiring conditions:[2]

Most of them are crowded into the poorer section of the cities. They have difficulty in procuring good houses. . . . Most of them live together in groups of four or six, sometimes even as many as twenty, in shacks, or barracks like boarding houses. They employ one of their number as cook, and usually the whole company eats and sleeps in the room where food is prepared.

Yet, despite the fall in numbers, those that did remain apparently maintained a fairly high level of visibility. Sikhs, by tradition and religion (as discussed later), wear turbans and beards and this, along with their brown skin, made them very visible in Vancouver:[3]

. . . the Indian sawdust truckers were a familiar sight in Vancouver in the 1930s and 1940s before oil fuel largely replaced sawdust as a domestic heating fuel.

And this visibility exposed the Sikhs to open forms of prejudice. They were called names like 'raghead' and—according to one source—in 'trams people will not sit beside them . . . they are not permitted to attend the picture show in their native dress.'[4]

The most notable characteristics of the Sikhs in Vancouver, however, was their resistance to any intermarriage with other racial groups. This has been noted by a number of scholars:

The Sikhs married only in their own faith . . . they kept and were kept to themselves . . . they made few concessions to western customs.[5]

East Indian opinion has been pretty consistent . . . despite the lack of East Indian women for the first decades of the community's existence, almost no intermarriage occurred . . . I was told that fewer than a dozen marriages have taken place between East Indian boys and Canadian girls. . . .[6]

As soon as ties with India became possible, the Sikhs arranged for boys of marriageable age to return to India and meet potential spouses. According to Mayer, about 80 per cent of the marriages in the immediate post-Second-World-War era involved a tie with India.[7]

1. 'East Indians', *The Canada Family Tree*, p. 90, Ottawa, Secretary of State, 1967.
2. Smillie, op. cit., p. 229.
3. Norris, op. cit., p. 233.
4. Smillie, op. cit., p. 229.
5. Norris, op. cit., p. 234.
6. Adrien C. Mayer, *A Report on the East Indian Community in Vancouver*, p. 28, University of British Columbia, 1959 (Working paper, Institute of Social and Economic Research).
7. Mayer, op. cit., p. 15.

Once or twice the Sikhs were given slight concessions by the federal government. In 1919, some already in Canada were allowed to bring in wives and children. There were also occasional admissions on compassionate grounds. And there were a number of illegal entries—a situation that reached the point that as the Second World War began in 1939 there were 218 Sikhs awaiting deportation. The pleas of a newly arrived Indian lawyer, D. P. Pandia, won this group a chance to stay in Canada subject to good conduct. They were eventually given landed immigrant status after the end of the war.[1]

But these concessions could not conceal the basic restraints and the legal barriers. During the years between 1914 and the end of the Second World War (1945) only a trickle of East Indians came into Canada; in fact, five times during those years there was not a single entrant. And those who did enter were clearly labelled as second-class citizens. They could not vote in federal, provincial or municipal elections. They could not serve on juries.

They could not hold property in some parts of the city of Vancouver and they could not enter professions such as law or medicine because they did not have full rights of citizens.[2]

Racism endures

Even though the long period during which the Sikh population in Vancouver gradually diminished may have been a quiet one in the sense that Sikh clashes with the rest of the community had dwindled, it was not in the sense that racism in general entirely disappeared. There are a number of pieces of evidence to show prejudicial racial attitudes and behaviour were common in Canada during those years and that they sometimes showed up in official regulations. Furthermore, there is some clear evidence in British Columbia, itself, of an enduring racial awareness. And, of course, the Sikhs, until well after the Second World War, were kept under a number of legal restraints because of race.

Racism and racial problems has not been an overly researched topic in Canadian scholarship but there are a number of studies to show the nature of discrimination. Robin Winks in *The Blacks in Canada* tells of racial attitudes in the eastern provinces and central Canada in the last two decades (including cases where restaurant proprietors have refused to serve blacks).[3] Charles Young and Helen Reid (in a book edited by Harold Innis) conclude in a study of Japanese Canadians that the only way to end continuing white-oriental racial friction would be for Japan to stop emigration to Canada.[4] Franklin J. Henry found blacks in Hamilton, Ontario, subjected to various forms of discrimination,

1. Norris, op. cit., p. 233.
2. ibid., p. 233.
3. Winks, op. cit., Chapter XIV: 'Self-Help and A New Awakening 1930–1970', p. 413–69.
4. Charles H. Young and Helen R. Y. Reid, *The Japanese Canadians*, p. 191, Toronto, University of Toronto Press, 1938.

denials of service and name calling.[1] Harold Potter reports the government maintained racial barriers in selecting air crews during the war:[2]

I have had some correspondence with the minister and also spoken to him about you. I learned that only those of pure European descent could be accepted for appointment to commissioned rank and for enlistment in air crew.

Douglas MacLennan found that the Canadian wartime job referral operation—selective service—collected racial data and allowed employers to use it.[3]

If any employer declared that he did not want a Jew, a Negro, a Roman Catholic or a Protestant that was listed, a Selective Service Worker heeded the employers' wishes.

But the major event involving race occurred in 1942 when—under pressure from British Columbia—Canada decided to move all those of Japanese descent from the West coast.[4] These persons were taken into internment camps. Not only that, their property was sold at prices well below market value. Even those who later volunteered and served with the Canadian forces during the Second World War found that their property was gone when they wished to return to British Columbia after the war. It would have been hard for the East Indians to be unaware that racist attitudes still surrounded them.[5]

Despite this, the Sikhs, themselves, enjoyed a partial freedom from some pressures during the Second World War. Because there were too few of them to justify the formation of special units, they were excused from compulsory military service because the military could not meet their needs of special food and clothing.[6] But the basic legal restriction against them continued. Until 1947, only East Indians who had fought in the First World War were allowed the vote (a provincial law that barred them from voting provincially also applied in federal elections). Finally, that year, thanks to the active support of the Co-operative Commonwealth Federation (a socialist political party) the East Indians won the vote in the province of British Columbia and thus the federal vote. One year later, in 1948, they won the right to vote in municipal elections and the right to serve on juries and run for public office.[7] After forty years, they had finally gained the rights most British subjects enjoyed on arrival.

1. Franklin J. Henry, 'The Measurement of Perceived Discrimination: A Canadian Case Study', Race, Vol. X, No. 4, 1969, p. 459.
2. Harold H. Potter, 'Negroes in Canada', Race, Vol. X, No. 4, 1969, p. 47.
3. Douglas MacLennan, 'Racial Discrimination in Canada', The Canadian Forum, October 1943, p. 165.
4. H. F. Angus, 'Asiatics in Canada', Pacific Affairs, p. 404, 1946.
5. The expulsion of the Japanese was justified on military grounds, a justification the author finds hard to accept. Some of those evacuated were Japanese Canadians who had served with the Canadian forces in the First World War.
6. Angus, op. cit., p. 402.
7. Mayer, op. cit., p. 3.

Why the turbans

Given the new and rather unfriendly environment the Sikhs encountered in Canada, one might well ask: Why did they maintain their strange (to Canadian eyes) appearance? Why did so many of them continue to wear turbans and refrain from shaving?[1] Why did they congregate together? The answers to these questions are found in the answer to another question: What is a Sikh?

The first chapter (and many of the documents quoted in it) used the terms 'East Indian', 'Hindu' and 'Sikh' as if they were interchangeable. That was because that was the way such terms were used in British Columbia and it simply seemed easier to begin by following the existing usage. In fact, of course, the three terms are distinct and, later, these distinctions sometimes become important.

The term 'East Indian' is one that carries both regional and racial overtones. It applied generally to those from a particular part of the world—now mainly Pakistan or India and Sri Lanka—and to those who have a particular colour tone, brown skin. The term 'Hindu', in contrast, is a religious one applying to persons of a particular religion. Since most of these who are Hindus are from India most are also East Indian but this need not be the case.[2] The term 'Sikh' is, like 'Hindu', a religious term. Once again, most Sikhs are East Indians—in fact they are from the Punjab, a particular region of northern India—but since Sikhism is a religious rather than a racial term, Sikhs can be (and sometimes are) many colours other than brown. Some prominent converts are white.

It is not difficult to get agreement among those who call themselves Sikhs about certain aspects of their religion. All would agree that Sikhism was expounded by a series of Gurus (wise men or prophets) starting with Guru Nanak (1469–1539) and ending with the tenth and last Guru, Guru Gobind Singh (1666–1708). All would agree that Sikhism is supposed to be a religion which, unlike Hinduism, is without caste barriers: all Sikhs are to be treated as equals; all are welcome at the Gurdwara or temple. In fact, the tenth and last Guru, Guru Gobind Singh made a point of welcoming those of different classes or castes when he created the Sikh brotherhood or Khalsa.

Certain other aspects of Sikhs' life are also tied to the religion. Sikhs are expected to live monogamous married lives and not to have sexual relationships before or outside of marriage. Sikhs are not to use stimulants such as tobacco or alcohol. Many are also vegetarians, or, at least, like Hindus, they do not eat beef. Sikhism is a very ascetic religion. Although the temple contains paintings of the Gurus, it is basically a very simple place. The worshippers sit on the floor (men on one side, women on the other); there are no chairs. The walls are plain. The focal point is the

---

1. All did not continue these habits. Saint Singh, op. cit., p. 387, wrote in 1907 that 'the picturesque Sikh-dress is fast disappearing among the advanced section of the immigrants'.
2. The East Indians objected very strongly to the label 'East'. They point out it was 'the result of a historical blunder made by the first explorers of the North American continent': *Brief presented by the 'East' Indian community of the Commission on Multiculturalism, Vancouver, March 9, 1972.*

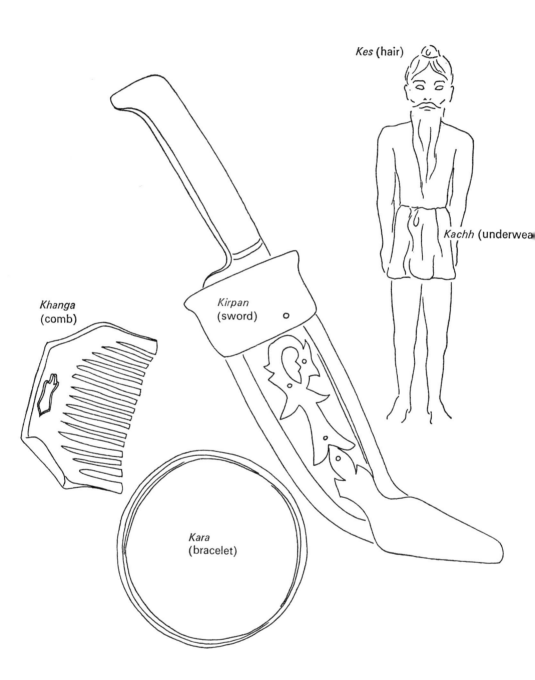

FIG. 1. The *Kakka* or five Ks.

altar which contains the writings of the Gurus and others in a Holy Book, a book that is itself revered, because of its contents, as a Guru. This book, the Guru Granth Sahib is 1,430 pages long and contains 6,000 verses not only the writings of the Guru but also Hindu and Muslim beliefs and sayings. Adrien C. Mayer described the Sikh religion as one of 'ritual simplicity and of equality among members. . . .'[1]

Sikhs also carry some other visible characteristics. The tenth Guru, Gobind Singh, advocated creation of the militant Sikh, the warrior saint, the person who believed he should fight for his beliefs, and Guru Gobind Singh called upon Sikhs to demonstrate their faith by five visible signs of their devotion:

Sikhs do not remove any hair but keep it 'long, intact and natural'. (This applied to—as do all rules—males and females.) This explains the beard of the male Sikh and the long hair of the female. (Sikhs also cover their hair: for males this means wearing a turban in public.)
Sikhs carry a special religious sword.
Sikhs wear a special iron or steel bracelet around their wrist.
Sikhs wear a wooden or ivory comb in their hair.
Sikhs wear a special kind of breeches or underwear.

When all of these elements are called by their Punjabi names: they all have the same first letter: hair (*Kes*); sword (*Kirpan*); bracelet (*Kara*); comb (*Khanga*); and underwear (*Kachh*). Thus they became known as the *Kakka* or five Ks (see Fig. 1). For the traditional Sikh, these five Ks, or *Kakka*, are obviously an essential part of their religion. They are as much a part of Sikhism as the crucifix is to Roman Catholicism or the Star of David to Judaism. To many Sikhs, to be without the *Kakka* is to be without a critical symbol of faith.

A Sikh, Canadian style

Despite these Sikh religious traditions, many Canadians of Sikh origin began to change as they adapted to their new homeland. They removed their turbans and shaved.[2] They took on more and more attributes of others in the community. As Pushpinder Puri explained in an article in the *Sikh Review* in 1973:[3]

At present, Sikhism is defined in a slightly different way than it is defined in the native Punjab. A Sikh, especially a young one, considers that so long as he expresses his faith in the teachings of Guru Nanak or Guru Gobind Singh and considers Guru Grath Sahib as the holy scripture of the Sikh religion, he is a Sikh. The hint is clear, he is not prepared to accept the traditional physical

1. The material in this section was taken from a number of documents about the Sikh religion. See, for example, P. M. Wylam, 'An Introduction to Sikh Belief', undated pamphlet published by Khalsa Diwan Society in Vancouver; Dr Edward A. De Bellancourt, 'From Quietest Acolyte to the Fighting Sikh', undated pamphlet, Khalsa Diwan Society; Anon., 'Sikh Dharma Brotherhood Principles of the Dharma', mimeographed document signed by Mukka Singh Sahat and Philip Singh Hoskins, certifying it reflects principles of Sikhism.
2. Mayer, op. cit.
3. Pushpinder S. Puri, 'Sikhs in Canada', *The Sikh Review*, Vol. XXII, No. 231, p. 238.

outlook of a Sikh, which was made compulsory by Guru Gobind Singh, by imposing on the Sikh the five Ks. He advocates the essence of Sikhism in the script and soul and not on the physical requirements.

To others, such an explanation was not acceptable and Puri's article brought an immediate and scathing rejoinder from another author, Kapur Singh:[1]

It is not easy to sympathize with a point of view which arrogates to itself the authority to define 'Sikhism' in a 'slightly different way, from how it has been defined by the founders of Sikhism. . . . This arrogation is escapist cowardice . . . the very claim which the young Sikhs of Canada thus make of redefining Sikhism for themselves is not only highly presumptuous but it also constitutes a defiance of the starting point of Sikhism. . . . The belief therefore of the young Sikhs of Canada that they can diverge from the culture of the older Sikh generations nurtured in Punjab and yet can remain whole Sikhs is shown to be altogether fantastic. . . . Sikhs remain Sikhs in spite of every pressure and temptation.

Clearly there was a conflict among the Sikhs in Vancouver as to just what was or was not acceptable and as will be seen it could easily become a serious conflict for it revolved around a matter of religious principle.[2]

For a long time, however, the disagreement was restrained by the fact that the Sikhs, despite what the Gurus said about equality, were very much aware of social class or caste. Normally, they married only within their class although they associated with other classes at the Gurdwara.[3] In Vancouver, the community was fairly well knit and caste differences did not create any real problems because, just as the East Indians who settled in Vancouver were mostly Sikhs, the Sikhs who settled in Vancouver were largely from two main regions of northern India and from two main social groups:[4]

In the early days, news about Canada was sent by people to their relatives, and it was they or their neighbours who came to the new country. Later marriages were made in India with relatives or go-betweens, and so took place in other villages of the same regions. When in recent years, the close relatives of Canadian residents were allowed to emigrate, these were people of these localities.

In other words, the original immigrants came from one or two areas and were from one or two particular groups. Those who came later were required (because of immigration controls) to be relatives. They, too, therefore, belonged to the same groups. Immigration policy reinforced the tight little island nature of the group of Sikhs in Vancouver.

---

1. Kapur Singh, 'Sikh Symbols and the Sikhs in Canada', *The Sikh Review*. This article is obtained as a reprint of an article by the Khalsa Diwan Society in Vancouver in 1973.
2. The Canadian Sikhs are not the only ones to respond to pressure. A study in the United Kingdom reported that 'the turban and the untrimmed beard . . . both in India and elsewhere . . . are becoming less common. . . . About 70–80 per cent of the Sikh men in Southall are cleanshaven . . .', Narindar Uberoi, 'Sikh Women in Southall', *Race*.
3. Michael M. Ames and Joy Inglis, 'Conflict and Change in British Columbia Sikh Family Life', *B.C. Studies*, No. 20, Winter 1973–74, p. 36.
4. Mayer, p. 9.

Most of the Vancouver Sikhs came from the Doaba and Malwa regions of northern India, two contiguous regions of the Punjab. Although Sikhism is allegedly a religion without caste barriers, most of them were members of the Jats or land-owning agricultural caste, a caste regarded by its members at the top of the hierarchy. The other largest group was composed of Rajput Sikhs, a castle mainly from one of the northernmost districts. The evidence available suggests that each of these groups used the temple regularly and tended to mingle more freely with each other. More important, perhaps, the caste identities were reinforced by the fact that caste members tended to marry within their own social group. Those who brought wives from India or went there to find them married only within their own region and their own caste.

The first dispute[1]

Despite all this, the disagreement about Sikhism—especially about the five Ks—inevitably led to some disagreement within Vancouver's Sikh community, disagreements which eventually led to a split. The first quarrel came in 1952 when the majority of the Khalsa Diwan Society objected to the ageing priest waving an unsheathed sword about at ceremonies in the temple. The decision was taken to a vote and a majority voted that it should stop. The decision was a bitter one for the traditionalists because it marked for them a first formal step away from what they saw as traditional Sikh values.

The real break came shortly afterwards. This time, the debate was whether anyone who was clean-shaven—and had, therefore, broken one of the five Ks—could serve on the temple executive. Once again a vote was taken. Once again, the traditionalists lost. The Westernized Sikhs and their attitudes were now dominant in the Khalsa Diwan Society. The decision, however, was too much for some traditionalist elements to take: they decided to split from the society and form a new and more traditional Akali Singh Temple. The old temple became, therefore, the place for the new attitudes: the new temple, a home for the traditionalists.

The split, of course, reflected more than just religious disagreement. The Akali Singh group included many of the old, early settlers, the ones who had help found and build up the community. The new group—now dominant in the old temple—were the Westernized, Canadianized Sikhs. This meant there were socio-economic gaps because the old group (now at Akali Singh) were largely ill-educated, the new leadership (at Khalsa Diwan) were the new, educated class, including the professionals. They provided an appearance of achievement and knowledge which gave them an aura for leadership.

Despite the difference between these two groups—and the creation of a second temple—there was a continuing liaison. Together, representatives of the two temples created an East Indian Canadian Citizens Welfare Society, which was to act as spokesman for the two groups and to look

1. The rest of the material in this chapter is drawn directly from interviews.

after those who needed help whatever their temple allegiance. (This association was probably not entirely a Sikh initiative: government officials had already objected to hearing two separate voices claiming to represent the Sikh community.)

In 1952, when the split occurred, Vancouver's Sikh community was still relatively isolated from the rest of the Sikh world. There were, of course, the ties with India but these represented ties to the old village and to the same social groupings. If this isolation and these infrequent contacts had continued as the only ones, it seems likely the situation would have stabilized. The traditionalists would have remained in the Akali Singh Temple and gradually died out. The Westernized group would have become gradually assimilated. The Gurdwara would have become more a social than a religious home. Indeed there were signs that this was happening. During the years immediately after the split, the Westernized group in the older temple began to stick less and less to traditional Sikh customs. Many of its adherents ignored the custom, for example, of covering one's head in the inner part of the temple. The majority rather than just some of the executive became clean-shaven and entered the temple bare-headed. The Sikhs had gradually become a smaller and smaller element in Vancouver society. They had begun to assimilate Canadian style. Many of them had made their way into business and the professions. And they were not being reinforced by any substantial immigration. Removal of their turbans and long hair had eliminated their visibility. It appeared they would be very soon almost out of sight and very much out of mind.

If the isolation of the Sikh community in Vancouver had continued, then the tiny Sikh population might have been little heard from again. But this did not happen. In 1951, the year before the split in the Khalsa Diwan Society, the winds of change began to blow. The federal government began to relax its immigration regulations and the flow of East Indians began to rise sharply. Not only that, for a brief period, there was a sudden and unexpected arrival of Sikhs from Africa, part of the group of Asians expelled because of racial disputes. The result from all of these new arrivals—new problems. There were more serious conflicts in the Sikh community. There were clashes between the new immigrants and the established residents. There were problems of discrimination. And there was some crime. The last few years have been troubled ones for the Sikhs and all East Indians in Vancouver.

Chapter 3

New people, new problems

In 1951, Canada and India agreed that 150 unnominated skilled and unskilled Indians could enter Canada. In 1956 (five years later) that number was raised to 300. In 1957, there was still another relaxation: now, residents, not just citizens, could nominate spouses, unmarried minor children and aged parents and bring them to Canada as immigrants. The doors were opening and East Indians were coming through them: the 1957 relaxation meant that not only could men immigrants come, but that they could establish themselves and their families very quickly.

In 1962, there was a slight tightening of immigration regulations but then in 1967 Canada began to open its doors wider than ever. All immigrants—including those from Asia—were to be judged on merit. A relationship with someone already in Canada would be an asset, but the merit test (a point scale) would be the critical factor. For the first time, East Indians would be able to come into Canada on the same basis as everyone else and this time—it appeared, to some extent—that is what happened.

The second wave

The opening up of immigration to persons other than those nominated by relatives had a particular effect on the Sikh community. The Sikhs had been fairly close knit coming as they did from one of two areas and one or two distinct groups. The custom of sending children back to find a spouse had maintained the connection with India and kept the East Indian community in Vancouver almost entirely Sikh. Now the opportunity was opening up to others. The Sikh community would no longer be so homogenous.[1]

1. Most authorities seem to agree that the East Indian community in Canada was composed mainly of Sikhs until the last decade. Ames and Inglis say that as late as 1966, about 80 per cent of British Columbia's East Indians were Sikhs (p. 17). Nash Gill estimated the percentage of 95 per cent in his paper, 'The East Indian People of British Columbia', p. 8, Vancouver, The British Columbia Human Rights Council, 1971. Gurdial Singh

According to the Minister of Manpower and Immigration, Robert Andras, Asian immigration went up two and one-half times in the six or seven years following the relaxation of regulations. According to the immigration figures available, his figures would appear to be accurate. While the figures are not entirely clear because of changing definitions (Pakistan, Sri Lanka and India, once grouped, are now shown as separate countries), the figures do show a rapid climb in East Indian immigration to Canada:[1]

1952	172	1960	691	1967	4,726
1953	140	1961	772	1968	3,932
1954	177	1962	830	1969	6,579
1955	249	1963	1,131	1970	6,947
1956	332	1964	2,077	1971	6,449
1957	334	1965	3,491	1972	7,184
1958	459	1966	2,943	1973	9,203
1959	741				

This rapid increase in the population seems to have worried even the Sikhs themselves. In February 1974, the East Indians Canadian Citizens Welfare Association, presented a brief to the Minister of Manpower and Immigration, Robert Andras, arguing that Canada needed more immigrants and that Indians would make good immigrants but it added:[2]

allowing for a sudden flow of immigrants from one country is an undesirable practice, inasmuch as it produces with equal suddenness, difficulties in the country's social, economic and human affairs, in addition to needlessly taxing the public exchequer.

The figures for the past few years show a total far higher than that for the early wave and—since British Columbia proved second only to Ontario—the largest province—as an attraction to East Indians, Vancouver's East Indian population rose rapidly. It is now estimated at between 20,000 and 30,000. (Figures are hard to establish because there is no reliable source of statistics.)

Equally important, the East Indian immigration was not confined to persons from India, Pakistan or Sri Lanka. The problems in Africa drove many East Indians from their homes there—from places like Tanzania, Kenya and Uganda. In the first nineteen years after the war (1946–65), there were less than 10,000 total immigrants coming to Canada from Africa—about 500 per year on average. In the past few years, immigration from one country, Uganda, has been over 2,000 in a single year (1973) and many of these persons were East Indians, some of them Sikhs.

Pannu states that until the early 1960s, 95 per cent of East Indians in Canada were Sikhs: 'Sikhs in Canada', *The Sikh Review*, Vol. XVIII, No. 203, October 1970, p. 45. A document prepared by the Canadian Citizenship Branch, Secretary of State Department, gave the 95 per cent figure in 1967: 'East Indians', *The Canadian Family Tree*, p. 89, Ottawa, Queen's Printer, 1967.
1. The figures are taken from Ames and Inglis, op. cit., p. 19, and from the quarterly reports on immigration published by Canada Manpower and Immigration.
2. East Indians Canadian Citizens Welfare Association, Brief on Canadian Manpower and Immigration, February 1974, p. 2.

A new mixture

But the impact of all these immigrants was not created by numbers alone. The new Indian immigrants ranged from skilled professionals to completely unskilled persons who came in as relatives of citizens or residents. The new African immigrants came in as experienced businessmen or professionals or as educated persons, such as teachers. The East Indian community in Vancouver, once a tightly bound community composed mainly of two Sikh castes, soon became a polyglot Sikh community. There were the old originals, unskilled, uneducated; the new Canadianized Sikhs who had adapted to Western custom, shaved off their beards, abandoned other traditions and made their way into business and the professions; the new unskilled traditionals from India; and the new Asian group, orthodox but also well educated, confident in their manner because of their previous success in business, anxious to establish themselves quickly in their new homeland.

Even before the last group—the Asian Sikhs—arrived, there were increasing problems in the temple. The orthodox Sikhs among the newcomers began to demand a return to orthodoxy in the Khalsa Diwan temple. They objected to the casual disregard of what they saw as the need for head covering and to the presence of clean-shaven persons on the temple executive. They challenged the Westernized leadership which, in their view, had turned the temple more and more into a social rather than a religious centre and they began to insinuate that these Westernized community leaders had made personal profit out of the construction contracts of the new temple.[1]

By the early 1970s, this group from India was being vigorously reinforced by the new arrivals from Asia, other Sikhs who had also adhered to the religious traditions. The public reason for the growing conflict was tied to the use of head-covering in the temple. The traditionalists argued that head-covering was a necessity. The Westernized group—the ones still in control—objected strongly to this view. The fact is that the disputes were based on much more serious problems. There was a clear difference in caste between many of the old-timers (Westernized or not), and *some* of the newcomers. There were social and economic differences as well, and most important, a challenge to the established leadership by an orthodox merchant class which by its adherence to Sikh traditions had attracted the support of less well-educated Sikhs.

Whatever the underlying cause, the internal disputes at the Khalsa Diwan temple reached the point that there were occasional physical clashes between the various factions. Several times the police were forced to intervene. As will be seen later, the factions became so quarrelsome that an outside mediator was needed at one point to resolve a violent row over the election of temple officers.

---

1. There were a number of problems in the workmanship of the new building including some problems with some pieces of lumber. The fact so many Sikhs were involved in the lumbering business made them especially observant and critical of such problems.

Finally, although this is still smouldering under the surface, the Asian influence has started to show in another way. A Sikh group known as the Rhamgaria (carpenters), a caste that formed its own community in East Africa, has now begun to try to organize itself in Vancouver. Sikhs who are members of this group are now on the executive of both temples but they are also meeting privately among themselves in an effort to found a third temple. So far they include about thirty families many of them leaders in the community.

At this point, it is hard to say where the disputes will lead. The Rhamgaria may split off letting leadership at the Khalsa Diwan temple fall once again into the hands of Westernized professionals. The Westernized group may leave the Khalsa Diwan temple and form a new Sikh social centre. Continuing immigration may reinforce the traditionalists giving them an increasing say in temple affairs and bringing about an increasing demand for orthodoxy. The slowing down of immigration could lead to a gradual Westernization of the entire community.

Whatever the trend, the problems are obviously complex. They intertwine social and economic conflict with caste conflict with religious tradition. The stability of fifty years of assimilation and peace has obviously gone and gone for good. The Vancouver Sikh community has entered into a period of internal conflict and change. And—because of the religious nature of some of the quarrels—it seems clear that some of the disputes will be vigorous, even violent. One executive member at the Khalsa Diwan temple said he could 'not compromise fundamental religious principles no matter what image the public gets of our feuds'. Finally, it also seems clear that these disputes (as will be indicated later) have caused the outside community grave concern. A judge commented at one point: 'if they can't meet at a religious temple without violence, they should go elsewhere . . .'.[1] The East Indian community publicly criticized him, but he obviously reflected a growing reaction to Sikh conflicts.

External conflicts

The problems of conflict within the Sikh community are, of course, partly a reflection of the fact the Sikhs in Vancouver run into problems with the dominant white community. Some of these are simply the result of adjustments from life in a small village in the Punjab to that of a big city in Canada. Others are the result of cultural clashes between two different sets of social values. Some are the results of harassment or deliberate discrimination. All of these create pressures that are reflected in the struggles at the temple between those who wish to preserve religious traditions and those who wish to conform to the conflicting demands of Canadian society.

Life in a village in the Punjab is, to say the least, a great deal different

---

1. 'Judge's Comments Attacked—East Indians Claim Prejudice in Supreme Court', Vancouver *Province*, 26 February 1973, p. 34.

from life in a large metropolitan Canadian city like Vancouver. The normal Indian village has very few of what would be known in Vancouver as modern conveniences. In the Punjab, only a few homes would have indoor plumbing facilities, flush toilets. In Vancouver, these are ordinary. In the Punjab, such appliances as washers, dryers, dish washers, etc., would be non-existent. In Vancouver, they are common. In the Punjab, telephones are confined to officials or to a village phone. 'My daughter's father-in-law was a judge so he must have a telephone at home.' In Vancouver, in contrast, the home without a phone is a rarity. In fact, about the only things common to both a Punjabi home and a home in Vancouver are bicycles (even though these are used for quite different reasons in the two societies) and radios: 70 per cent of homes in the Punjab would have a radio; just about every home in Vancouver has at least one if not two or three.[1]

Let us begin with a commonly held notion. India is a land of villages: 80 per cent of the people live in villages. But even this figure does not convey the rural character of Indian society. Of the 20 per cent urban population, 12 per cent live in towns of less than 20,000. Towns of this size can only with considerable amount of imagination be called towns. Certainly they have few of the characteristics of town or cities in Canada. In these cities there is hardly any industry to speak of, few metalled roads, no sanitation and sewerage facilities, seldom any running water and electricity is a luxury few of the residents can afford. Most of the houses have thatched or impermanent roofs or mud walls, few of the streets are suitable for motorized traffic, both because they are narrow (sometimes only a few feet wide) or because abutting houses are not aligned to form uninterrupted passage.

There is no zoning and few by-laws governing the development of these towns. People build as they live, to standards they can afford. There is no building inspection to speak of since there are no building standards or codes. As such the town is a conglomeration of individual decisions. In a sense, therefore, the city comprises a physical framework expressing, within economic constraints, the way of life of the people. The environment and city form is not mediated by institutionally prescribed codes, standards, practices and by-laws. These cities are literally built by the people for themselves.

In contrast a Canadian city is an expression of the institutional framework: the municipal by-laws, the city grid, the standards and codes, the constraints imposed by service facilities: roads, sewer lines, etc. In other words, the non-human demands have primacy over strictly human needs in a Canadian city.

Then there is the language problems. The men learn English at government expense as heads of households. The children learn it at school. But the women, trapped at home, often do not learn it at all and become separated from the rest of their families.

But the real problem is that of cultural adjustment—the pressure society puts on immigrants to conform. These pressures operate on Sikhs at work, on Sikh children at school. They create conflict between old

1. J. I. Richardson, 'Culture and Family', one of a number of unpublished papers prepared for a teachers' seminar in Vancouver, sponsored by the Centre for Continuing Education, University of British Columbia and the Khalsa Diwan Society.

values and new customs and cause stress in the family because they affect different members in different ways. The whole process of immigration for anyone, not just Sikhs, causes a complete re-examination of life style and value system.

There are other problems too. East Indian women are used to shopping in speciality stores and dealing with a storekeeper known to them. In Vancouver, most shop at multi-purpose supermarkets. This phenomenon is so confusing to those unfamiliar with it (especially those who have language problems as well) that one community group arranged to take East Indian women on group trips to supermarkets so they could become accustomed to them. The same group arranged to take women on the public transportation system because it, too, was new and confusing:[1]

Just imagine. You have to get a bus going the right way. Then to buy a strip of tickets. You rip off one and put it in the ticket box. You then ask the driver for a transfer. You watch where you are going so you can get off at the right place. You then must find another bus going the right way. You get on that bus and hand your driver the transfer.

Two researchers who have studied the Sikhs in British Columbia—Michael Ames and Joy Inglis—have reported some differences among what the Sikhs visualize as the traditional pattern of Sikh family life (the way it was supposedly in India), the intermediate pattern of Sikh life in Canada (how it should be in Canada) and what the Sikhs see as the way Canadians live (how Canadians appear to be). They report that Sikh life in India is somewhat different than the way it is perceived by the Sikhs: India is changing and in some ways the traditional Sikhs are not aware of those changes.[2]

The research done for this narrative certainly suggests the idea that Sikh customs in Canada are sometimes compromises with Indian life styles. Quite often, for example, only part of the family unit emigrates, and, therefore, only part of the unit can group itself in Canada:[3]

We have two brothers and both families. We live together. All our property is held jointly. We would both rather live together. We are more happy. We don't like living separately. I like living with my mother and father.

I am living with the family of my youngest brother and I have no problem. I don't have to wash my clothes or do my cooking. Because I am the oldest of all the family, the children show me more respect than even to their father. The eldest brother is considered most like his father.

The problem is that while such arrangements are considered normal and natural to the Sikhs, they violate Canadian norms. Canadians consider such dual family arrangements as overcrowded and, therefore, a violation of municipal by-laws which restrict some areas to 'single families' by which is meant single 'nuclear' families. Sikh customs therefore come

1. From an interview.
2. Ames and Inglis, op. cit.
3. These quotes and all subsequent quotes are from the many interviews conducted by the author and Dan Pottier with members of the East Indian community in Vancouver.

into conflict with Canadian law even though political pressure (other immigrant groups follow the same patterns) has kept that law from being enforced.

As Ames and Inglis have also noted, the domination by the man is customary among Sikhs and the male in Canada attempts to enforce his dominant position: 'The man is boss; the woman does what the man wants.' In some families you will hardly see any women doing the grocery shopping. The men are along with them. 'The role of men in the society? Boys are like lords: their say is final.' This control is such that the group mentioned earlier trying to orient women to Canadian things such as a supermarket found resistance from Sikh husbands:[1]

We both pick them [the women] up, bring them to the centre, then drop them back. The women won't come on their own . . . they, the women, are dependent. They can't come on their own. We have to make two trips sometimes to bring these women to the centre.

The male domination sometimes reaches the point that the women are abused. Even then it appears many of them simply accept male domination:

Most women will not go out. They will suffer in the house. Even if they are beaten they will do all the work at home. A few cases, the husbands beat up their wives. They know they do not want to separate. Divorce or separation is considered a disgrace to the family.

This woman came to us. She had come here from India. When she got here, the man she was to marry was already married, so she married an older brother. But they've had problems. He beat her. She came for help but all the time we talked she was ashamed because *her* marriage had failed. She couldn't leave; she had no one.

Perhaps it is not surprising that the conflicts at the temple have led some males to object to their wives participating in activities there:

The husbands . . . they don't like their women to go there [the temple]. If they go regularly they say people just go there to fight not to worship.

The problem is that education or acculturalization leads to conflicts between women and their husbands. As Sikh women in Canada are forced to go to work, as they acquire education and as they move around more on their own in a large community—observing the comparatively free behaviour of the Canadian women—they tend to demand equality at home.

Even some of the males interviewed have begun to object to male domination and argue for more freedom for their wives:

The role of [Sikh women] compared to Canadian women is different. Their attitude toward their husband is generally submissive and they are very faithful. Even sometimes when they get no proper treatment they tend to hold on. The women who are in Canada, they must be educated to be more free.

1. From an interview.

As mentioned earlier, Sikhs still arrange marriages for their sons and daughters. This was partly the result of the past necessity whereby the absence of unmarried women in Vancouver forced Sikhs to send their children to India to find a spouse or to bring a spouse to Canada sight unseen. But it is also the custom in India:

The parents want to have their choice. They want to select a husband for their girl and their own daughter-in-law. They don't want the children to get involved.

These arranged marriages do not in any way suggest that Sikh parents are not concerned about finding a satisfactory relationship for their children or that they are not committed to making the marriage work:

When the parents arrange a marriage they try to trace the background and history. If there are problems the parents interfere. They would try to patch up the quarrel.

Probably the most serious conflicts of all, however, arise between Sikh parents and their children, especially the female children. Whenever Sikh girls go out, they see a more open society than they have been used to and than their parents wish for them. They wish to participate in this society, but their parents object. The result can be a good deal of tension:

As they go to high school, Indian girls feel that other girls have more freedom. Indian girls are not allowed to go out and stay late. The children move into a different world. When in the schools, they are in a different world. It's really rough for them. They are always afraid they may not adapt to the Canadian culture.

In schools, the girls want to go out with boys. The parents say, 'no way'. There's such a gap. Girls are not supposed to talk to boys. In this case the mother said, 'no more'. They [the parents] are afraid. In India, they don't believe in dating or courting.

Sometimes when they come into this open society they see freedom between the boys and girls, sometimes they do not know how to behave.

They [the parents] see all the girls to have the freedom. They don't want their children to have that freedom. Some of the girls are not allowed to visit their girlfriends. If they want to go shopping their mother takes them. It [their home] is just like a jail to them. Some of them are very rebellious.

Some of them, of course, do rebel. Girls skip school to be with their friends. Others run away from home. Others break many of the Sikh cultural rules even going to the point of sexual intercourse. Then, they approach an even more severe conflict. They are not able to talk to their parents because the parents would neither understand nor accept this.

One case, a 13-year-old-girl. She was sure she was pregnant. Just pity the children. They can't talk of all these things to their parents.

If a social worker or other person goes to the parents, the family feels disgraced. They usually plead that the matter should not be talked about.

They are especially worried that the story might get back to their relatives and friends in India.

While these kinds of conflicts can become very serious, many of the problems arise through sheer ignorance. In the schools, for example, teachers are often unaware of the taboos. They treat Sikh children as they treat other children and the results are sometimes disturbing to the teacher.

A teacher trying to help children in her class learn English arranged for two children to try a simple conversation, such things as 'hello', etc. The two children invited to take part in this discussion were an East Indian boy and an East Indian girl. The next day the girl's father was in to complain to the teacher that she had compromised his daughter's chances for marriage.

A teacher arranged for children in her class to exchange valentines. One valentine went from a white boy to an East Indian girl. The white boy was subsequently threatened by the girl's brother.

In each case, the teacher unknowingly violated East Indian norms and the result was conflict. Such conditions make it difficult for the best-intentioned to overcome cultural gaps.

Richardson concluded two opposite tendencies may develop. The child who makes progress in English may win support of teachers and friends and suppress their native culture and avoid Punjabi-speaking children. Those who do not retreat into their families, fraternize with those who speak Punjabi and drop out of school.[1]

The problems the Sikhs have in Vancouver, however, go beyond problems of cultural adjustment. They extend to taunts aimed at customs and dress and to harassment or discrimination.[2]

Outright discrimination

The difference in cultural norms between India and Canada may easily lead Sikhs in Vancouver to perceive discrimination where none exists. Parents, for example, as shown earlier, may perceive treatment given their children in school as offensive when in fact it is standard. Yet although difficult to document, it is hard to avoid the conclusion that there is a good deal of discrimination against the Sikhs in Vancouver. This ranges from teasing to harassment to discrimination in accommodation and employment to actual physical attacks on Sikhs and their residences and places of worship.

Some children can handle the simple teasing that comes with being different—whether it's being Sikh or being fat:

Just a few names here and there. 'Hey Punjab.' I made a joke myself, 'what flies over India at night? Peter Punjab.' Everybody used to play with me and they used to invite me into their homes.

1. Richardson, op. cit.
2. In a paper prepared for a teachers' seminar, J. I. Richardson cites a comparable example: 'Children taking lunches to school find themselves the object of curiosity at best and derision at worst because of the form and smell of their food.'

But others find it more difficult:

A boy told his parents he could not stand the constant taunts about his turban. He said, 'either we go back to India or I take off my turban'. He came home from school crying every night. Finally, he couldn't stand it any longer and took off his turban. His parents were very upset but they didn't know what to do.

And sometimes it is the simplest things that cause problems. Indian parents traditionally put a herbal preparation in the eyes of their children: it is used to prevent sore eyes. It is called *surma* (powder) or *kajal* (liquid). The problem is that it gives the appearance of mascara and boys who use it are teased and told they are using make-up.

But the problems—even for the children—go far beyond taunts.

There have been in the past racial discrimination. Children in the schools beaten up. Goaded into fights, being called names. Children tell me 'the boys in the school they beat me'.

And for the adults it is much worse:

Whether we will reach a destination without passing any comments. While Canada is a free country, we don't feel safe. . . . Two East Indians were coming from a sawmill. There were white guys on a motorcycle. They stopped the motorcycle and they beat one guy. The other ran away. They beat one guy without any reason.

The biggest pressure on the adult is, of course, to conform in order to get employment. It is a pressure that is understood and discussed by those who have conformed and those who have not:

The people who wear turbans have special problems. The general attitude is 'no job unless you take off your turban'. When I came to Canada in 1954, I went to the employment office in Montreal, 'you can't get a job unless you take off your turban'.

It's a question of survival. They come over here with the intention of becoming good Canadians. But they can't get jobs unless they shave off their beards and take off their turbans. This is a big demoralizing effect, then they try to find some excuse to break the Sikh commandments. They then start talking against religion.

In the area of employment, the story is often, 'don't call us, we'll call you' and calls never come. 'You apply and the foreman says, "you don't speak English". You go to the union and he says, "we'll see". You go back and the job has been filled.' Sometimes Sikhs learn to lie about their education attainments in order to obtain employment.

In that case you don't need to fill in master's degree. We just fill in grade 10 education. I know if I fill in, 'I got a master's degree' I don't get job.

Even when Sikhs do get jobs they run into prejudice. They are diligent, industrious, hard-working. They normally do not drink or smoke. They are faithful in attendance. (Sometimes if illness strikes, they will be replaced by a relative or friend.) This means employers who do hire them prefer them to the young unskilled and less committed Canadians.

Not surprisingly, these persons, finding themselves displaced and no longer wanted, attack the Sikhs using race as an excuse for their own lack of commitment. There have been a number of racial feuds in and around Vancouver started by young, unskilled workers who resent the industrious brown-skinned immigrants.

In the area of housing virtually every Sikh has a story about the apartment advertised for rent that was filled when he arrived. One Sikh married to a white was told quite bluntly, 'if your wife wants to stay she can but you can't. We don't rent our place to East Indians or Indians.' (This identification with Canadian Indians rankles Sikhs when it occurs: most of them regard themselves as upper caste and therefore above what they see as Canadian Indian social status.)

Finally, there are some cases where community attitudes about Sikhs have blown up into violence. There have been a number of instances of harassment of Sikh families and a few years ago there were a series of incidents at the Akali Singh Temple. At one point the people responsible for human rights in the province concluded:[1]

There has developed an atmosphere of tension and fear in the East Indian community in Vancouver as the result of a number of incidents affecting East Indians.

And there are occasional public outbursts. During the annual 'Miles for Millions' walk in Vancouver in 1973 there was a vitriolic attack on the project—children get sponsors at so many cents a mile and go on long mass walks to raise money for Oxfam:[2]

If the participants 'running around' Alderman Pendakur [Hindu] and M. L. A. Banes [Negro] want to be useful, why don't they run all the way to Asia and Africa and donate their talents to people they belong to. . . . Pendakur could have been much more useful in India in the sacred war against holy cows.

Gunnar Myrdal once classified the kinds of discrimination possible. He rated them in order—although this order was later challenged:[3] economic; legal; political; public facilities; personal relations. The Sikhs of Vancouver have fully experienced three of these five barriers; and there is also a social, though, not a legal, taboo on intermarriage, although this is imposed as much by the Sikhs as by others.

Feuds

Many of the Sikh problems in Canada reflect the intolerance of Canadians and the failure to understand the life styles of a different people. One aspect of life in India that has apparently been transferred to Canada and Vancouver is less understandable. There is some evidence—from a

1. From unpublished statement.
2. This material is quoted from a mimeographed sheet that was distributed to the participants in the 'Miles for Millions' walk in Vancouver on 5 May 1973.
3. Gunhar Myrdal, *An American Dilemna: The Negro Problem and Modern Democracy*, p. 60, New York, 1962.

number of instances in the past year or so—that there has been an outbreak of violence among the East Indians themselves. It is difficult to comment on these cases—many of them are still before the courts—but the evidence appears to be that they often arise because someone had come into conflict with Indian moral standards—unmarried persons are living together or someone tries to establish an extra-marital relationship—and the reaction is violent.

It was mentioned earlier that a boy felt it necessary to defend his sister's honour where he saw an affront. This attitude (the need to defend family honour) is one that is, of course, held by adults as well and held rather strongly:

It's very common to take revenge. Naturally the girl's family will not sit quietly. They will do anything in anger.

We know that East Indian people take revenge. An East Indian will never start a fight. But even if he doesn't want to fight he will fight when other people compel him. Then he will start to fight and he will never care whether he will be killed or other people will be killed.

Most East Indian people will seek revenge. If someone killed my brother, I would seek revenge.

This does not mean that all East Indians in Vancouver would accept revenge or that the vast majority would accept it in Canada. It just indicates that there is an understanding of why it happens, an understanding that is not shared by others living in Vancouver. But it is also true that there is a great deal of uneasiness about such events. Many East Indians, in interviews, said Canadian laws were not harsh enough, 'there is not enough punishment here'. Others said those involved in the crimes had harmed all those who were identified as East Indian. 'I feel that everyone starts looking at you as if you were the murderer.' 'It is very tragic because it victimizes me. I don't know the people. I don't have any connection with them, but I'm there.'

There were some attempts to use community pressure to stop such feuding. But the social control possible in an Indian village is not possible in a city like Vancouver. The East Indian community is relatively concentrated in some areas—in the Oak Ridge area, for example, near the new temple on Ross Street at Marine Drive. But there are no East Indian ghettoes and (as the previous material makes clear) there is no united East Indian community. The East Indians in Vancouver now represent a large, diffuse group (some estimated 20,000 to 30,000 persons): they cannot act as a cohesive community against those who violate community norms.

And some members of the community are concerned because this diffusion makes it impossible for the community to speak out in condemnation of what has happened. There is a feeling among some at least that the community should make public statements attacking the unacceptable behaviour.[1] 'Why this death-like silence? Why are all the religious, social

1. Quoted from an article in Welby *Parwertan*, translations supplied by editor Karan Singh, 21 June 1974.

and political leaders silent?' The answer is that the community—once coherent— now lacks a focus and a voice.

Finally, it seems quite likely that here, as elsewhere,[1] the increasingly diffuse nature of the Sikh and East Indian communities has made it increasingly difficult for the dominant whites to relate to them. Once it was easy to relate to a Sikh: he was poor, ill-educated, wore a beard and a turban and worked in a lumber yard. Now it has become difficult. He may or may not be poor—some Sikhs are lumber barons. He may or may not be ill-educated—some Sikhs (male and female) are university graduates. He may or may not wear a beard or a turban. And the lumber yards are no longer the sole source of employment—there are Sikhs in insurance, travel agencies, real estate, banks, industry, teaching and the professions. And many of them (especially the African group) are competent and confident, an attitude that the existing community describes as 'pushy'—a phrase that reflects its inability to deal with what was once a unified group.

---

1. This point is made by Anthony A. Richmond in 'Sociological and Psychological Explanations of Racial Prejudice. Some light on the Controversy from Recent Researches in Britain', *Pacific Sociological Review*, Fall 1961, p. 64.

Chapter 4

The police
and the East Indians[1]

During the quiet years of low East Indian immigration, the Vancouver Police attitude towards East Indians was one of casual awareness. But in recent years, that attitude has changed. Conflict between East Indians and others, conflict within the Sikh community and a new problem—serious crime—has demanded increasing police attention. The description of that new situation and of the problems being faced provides a case study of how a government agency has tried to cope and an insight into the complexity of these problems. It also serves as useful background to the discussion of media attention to East Indians in the next chapter: for the media have become somewhat preoccupied with East Indians and crime.

The problems of racial conflict

At one time, the Vancouver Police had a fairly simple view of Sikhs: they were a convenient insurance policy for a policeman needing an arrest. Old-timers in the department recall that by stopping a Sikh driver, they could almost guarantee he was someone for whom a warrant was outstanding. Sikhs being notorious for their refusal to pay tickets or to respond to subsequent summons, the police—needing an arrest—looked for a Sikh to find a wanted person.

In interviews, spokesmen for the Sikh community said this phenomenon was easy to explain. Sikhs are frightened of contact with the police, regarding it as a disgrace. Therefore, when stopped for a traffic offence, they were extremely relieved when they were allowed to go after receiving only a piece of paper. They were also completely unwilling to initiate any further contact by responding to any kind of legal notice.

However one views the implications of such a relationship and such an explanation, it is no longer possible to describe police/East Indian relationships in such simple terms. The Vancouver Police have found that

---

1. The author wishes to thank members of the Vancouver Police Department for their assistance in obtaining the information in this chapter.

racism (or complaints of racism) are becoming an increasing problem. They are also finding it extremely difficult to deal with—for it is often extremely hard to classify.

Some incidents are fairly straightforward even if the solution is not obvious. Recently an orthodox Sikh was refused admission to traffic court because (as part of the five Ks) he was wearing his traditional dagger or *kirpan*. When it was forcibly taken away from him, he went on a hunger strike in the lobby of the courtroom, wearing a sign saying, 'hunger strike for my *kirpan*'. Eventually a compromise was reached: the man agreed to enter court without the *kirpan* on the understanding it would be returned the instant his case was concluded. The incident attracted some local publicity, but it left some of those involved a little confused. Would the same treatment have been accorded to someone wearing, say, a Christian symbol such as a crucifix?

The *kirpan* incident at least had the merit of clarity and the compromise proved acceptable to both sides. Other incidents have been less clear. In one case, for example, an East Indian complained his children were being subjected to gibes by a neighbour. The police listened to the complaint but found it hard to deal with. Do you jail a man who is alleged to have called someone a raghead? The complainant, seeing no action, decided to act himself: he told the neighbour 'leave my children alone or I'll kill you'. The neighbour complained. The police came again, this time obliged to warn the East Indian against violence. He saw the police response as racist. They do not know what to say: they realize their inability to deal with the initial complaint provoked a violent response but—in their view—the first incident was not a crime, the second, a threat, was.

Sometimes this escalated response causes more serious difficulties. In autumn 1974, there were problems with white youths harassing with verbal abuse persons at the Sikh temple on Ross. Finally some of those at the temple decided to respond. Two white youths were physically attacked, one suffering a broken arm.[1] An East Indian was subsequently charged with an offence. Again, the police felt powerless to deal with the verbal abuse but had to intervene when the physical violence occurred.

Sometimes where incidents have occurred at a special location the police have been able to act. Recently, there have been scuffles between whites and East Indians at a tavern and at a restaurant. A police team (one white, one Sikh) visited both locations and warned those present against any continuation of the violence. By identifying regulars and threatening immediate arrest if scuffles occur, the police are, sometimes, able to head off the more physical aspects of future relations between racial groups at such locations.

At other times, the police have had to step in and discuss an adjustment of surveillance procedures as a result of a series of incidents. In early 1973, for example, the officers of the Akali Singh Temple complained there had been a lot of window breaking and other vandalism. Police promised additional patrols in the area. The vandalism was eventually stopped.

1. There is some evidence that those beaten were not doing the harassing.

But sometimes vandalism is impossible to control. An East Indian has complained that his windows have been broken on numerous occasions. Police have not been able to locate those responsible. The man now threatens to reply by shooting at those who attack him. Police have warned him against this but they have also said they cannot watch a private home 24 hours a day to stop windows from being broken. The incident is a continuing one: the man, so far, has not shot at anyone but he has lost his insurance. The insurance companies refuse to keep paying for continuing breakage.

But the problem for the police is not just in dealing with the incidents but also in assessing their character or cause. Is it always a racial dispute when there is a fight between an East Indian and someone who is not? Is it always a racial problem when the windows of an institutional building are broken? Is it always racism when someone steals hubcaps off a car or rips out the wiring if that car belongs to an East Indian? Is it a racial incident if there is a scuffle in a schoolyard and one of those involved is wearing a turban?

Police have tried to investigate such incidents by assigning a two-man team to the Oak Ridge area and asking them to follow up on incidents involving East Indians. They have also tried to keep statistics about racially related crime. Both efforts are well-meaning. Neither is completely satisfactory. The team has had some success because one of its members is a Punjabi-speaking Westernized Sikh. He can usually guarantee that those who have difficulty in English or those who lack understanding of Canadian customs are given adequate explanation. He, with his partner, can guarantee that those who abuse persons for racial reasons can see that the police intend to give equal treatment to all. But he and his partner cannot be everywhere. The statistics are intriguing—53 per cent of incidents involving East Indians have also involved whites—but they are also impossible to interpret. If the East Indians operated in a racially impartial way—committing crimes against East Indians and whites in proportion to population—then they should be mainly involved in interracial incidents. In fact, the proportion of East Indian against East Indian crimes is higher than normality would suggest: perhaps the statistics suggest racial incidents are lower than could be expected?

Finally, the police have one further problem in relating to the East Indians themselves. Police can only act in a situation in any forcible way when they believe the law has been violated and, even then, can only start the process: the courts must make the final decision about whether the law really has been violated and what the penalty should be. At a public meeting the East Indians complained that the police were neglecting their complaints and provided a list of grievances. The police answer was that all the complaints were in hand. The police were, in fact, able to follow up with specific charges and the courts with specific penalties. But the process seems rather slow to those who complain.

Meetings and mediation

The police concern with East Indians, however, does not stop with investigation of specific incidents however unclear those incidents might be. The police also have become involved in trying to prevent violence by acting as mediators in the disputes at the Sikh temple. They also have been asked to participate in a series of meetings of various public agencies concerned about East Indian problems in Vancouver. Police records of concern with East Indians look more like a set of minutes than like any sort of normal police incident reports.

In three months, in early 1973, for example, the police were involved in six separate meetings with various feuding groups at the temple. Twice the police simply kept an eye on events to make sure things went peacefully. Then they set up a meeting between the feuding factions; and worked out a voting procedure acceptable to both groups as an approach to a new constitution. Then they attended a meeting of people at the temple and spoke to them. Then they went out and persuaded an outsider (an outsider to both the Sikhs and the police) to step in and offer to mediate. Then they chaired another meeting to win acceptance for that mediator. Finally, the mediator chaired a series of meetings that finally resulted in an arrangement whereby the temple elections could proceed without disturbance.

Just a few months after these negotiations, police personnel were involved in a host of other meetings about East Indian problems:

15 November 1973: human rights meeting considers East Indian problems; police asked to participate.

21 November 1973: first meeting of human rights committee; police are in attendance.

25 November 1973: public meeting on East Indian problems; police questioned about handling of cases; demonstrations disrupt the meeting.

18 December 1973: meeting convened at City Hall to discuss East Indian problems.

17 January 1974: human rights and police personnel meet Sikh leaders then take part in another City Hall meeting.

8 May 1974: another general discussion of East Indian problems at City Hall; civil liberties groups and representatives of the Canadian Council of Christians and Jews take part.

The list appears to be endless. On top of this, the police attempted a number of tactics to reduce the problems. Police officers attended functions at the temples. Police officers spoke to women's groups. The mixed team—one Sikh, one white officer—called on neighbours when there were complaints of harassment. Police began to take part in special radio broadcasts aimed at the East Indian community.

The involvement reached the point that a number of police began to question the nature of the involvement. One officer asked to be transferred to other duties. Others began to consider whether it was time the Sikhs in particular were told future relations would assume a straight law-and-order function. One officer, in fact, warned those at the temple he would simply enforce the law by locking up those involved in any further violence. Having made the statement, he continued to attempt to act as an arbiter and avoid problems. By this time, however, concerns about the East Indian community had begun to shift as a new problem emerged—violent crime.

Violent crime

In 1974, it appears—on the surface anyway—that police had to face a new East Indian problem. The East Indians seemed to be involved in a series of feuds among families and among neighbours, feuds often leading to violence: there was some evidence of continuing vendettas. Furthermore, these feuds—perhaps because of their violence—were reported by the media as if they were linked: on 6 July the *Sun,* for example, had an interview with the then Alderman Setty Pendakur (an East Indian) about what the story called 'a recent rash of violent crimes in the Vancouver area involving East Indians'.

The incidents began outside Vancouver with crimes in the suburbs of Delta and Burnaby.

On 26 April, Ramesmmar Singh Grewal of North Delta was hacked to death with an axe. Another East Indian, Santokh Singh Atwal, of Delta, was charged with his murder. On 21 May, Rajinder Rai, a housewife, was found dead, strangled, in her home in Burnaby. Her husband, Teja Rai, was charged with the murder. (Both had come to Canada from India about two years earlier.) Neither incident would normally be considered part of a study of East Indians within the city of Vancouver, but they are included for two reasons. First, they were linked because of race by the Vancouver media; second, and more important, the Rai murder actually did become connected with another violent incident which took place within the city.

The first violent crime to take place within the city itself happened on Wednesday, 5 June 1974, just two weeks after Mrs Rai's death. A 30-year-old East Indian, Harbhajan Singh Hayre, was involved in a dispute in front of the Captain George's Restaurant on Marine Drive. Eyewitnesses said there were four persons involved and that all four were East Indians. According to these eyewitnesses (diners in the restaurant) one of those attacking Mr Hayre had carried a machete, the other a club. The dispute went on for several minutes before Mr Hayre was left, dying, on the sidewalk in front of the restaurant. Later, three men, Kuldip Singh Dhillon, Gurmail Singh Biring and Surjit Singh Presto were all charged with non-capital murder. At the trial there was some conflicting testimony, but it appeared clear there had been previous altercations between Mr Hayre and the others. (The man's widow said her husband had been threatened. The accused said the slain man (6 foot 2 inches, 230 pounds) had assaulted one of the accused, Mr Presto (5 foot 2 inches, 130 pounds).) Whatever the case, a continuing feud was obviously involved: the group shared accommodation.

The second incident in the city did not involve actual violence, but it did involve another East Indian. According to testimony at the trial, Nirmal Singh Walia (later convicted) had tried to hire another man, Lloyd Harris, to murder a third man, Reggie Virk. Virk had been living with Walia's sister-in-law. Harris (the man approached about the murder) decided to take the matter to the police: they gave him a briefcase concealing a tape recorder and the subsequent trial included the playing of tapes containing conversations about a gun, a getaway and a $4,000 fee. The judge, in convicting Walia, said the crime was 'one of the most vile and loathsome crimes in the Criminal Code'.

That incident had barely appeared in the media—the charge was laid in the last week of June—when a new incident took place, again one involving what appeared to be a family vendetta. The incident was connected to the death of Mrs Rai (the woman who was strangled in Burnaby). It is difficult to recount a matter still before the courts but—as far as can be determined (and told)—this incident involved an attempt at revenge, an attempt that failed.

What happened, apparently, was that a relative of Mrs Rai (the murdered woman) attempted to get revenge on two relatives of Mr Rai (the man charged with his wife's murder). According to the information available, Mrs Rai's uncle, Gurdev Singh Gill, had waited at the place where two of Mr Rai's relatives—Muscan Rai and Darshan Dhillon—work. (Muscan Rai is Mr. Rai's brother; Darshan Dhillon is Mr Rai's brother-in-law.) Mr Gill, armed with a shotgun, opened fire on Mr Rai and Mr Dhillon as they left work. In the scuffle that followed, Mr Rai suffered head cuts. Mr Dhillon suffered gunshot wounds and Mr Gill was killed. A pathologist testifying at the inquest said Mr Gill had died after being beaten six or seven times. Mr Rai and Mr Dhillon were subsequently both charged in connection with Mr Gill's death.

To the police, the incidents appeared to be a series of similar events. All involved quarrels among families or neighbours and the last one (the ambush) appeared to involve a vendetta. Police have some indication (reports to this effect have been published) that the vendetta in the Rai case may not yet be over. There may be yet another attempt to take revenge. Such matters are of particular concern because they are very hard to control: police cannot, because of personnel limitations, maintain a permanent watch on someone whose life may be threatened.

The impact of these crimes has been to increase the police concerns about violence at the temple. It has led them to contact immigration officials because they are concerned that the feuds might escalate and persons from India might come to participate. And it has preoccupied Dave Randhawa, the Punjabi-speaking officer: he has spent a great deal of time on violent crime, thus reducing his ability to deal with other matters involving contact and negotiation.

Chapter 5

Vancouver media
and the East Indians

As the preceding chapters show, the story of the East Indians in Vancouver is a complex one and a not altogether happy one. It is a story of an industrious people who, when they immigrated to a new country, ran into racial intolerance, discrimination and legal barriers. It is the story of a group that—faced with the problems of cultural conflict—ran into difficulties within its own community and with its neighbours. The question asked in this chapter is: How well did the press of Vancouver deal with this story? The answer is: not too well.

Print content over the years

Vancouver is served by two daily newspapers, the afternoon *Sun* (city circulation: 158,992) and the morning *Province* (city circulation: 65,521). The two papers share the same quarters and are joined by an agreement under which they are operated by the same company. But—despite this union—they are each part of a different newspaper group; the *Sun* belongs to Free Press Publications, a group that includes some of the largest newspapers in Canada including the Montreal *Star* and the Toronto *Globe and Mail*; and the *Province* is part of the Southam group, until quite recently (when Free Press Publications expanded) the dominant group in the country. Both groups allow their members a fair amount of editorial freedom and both Vancouver papers use this freedom. The *Sun* tends to be very partisan Liberal (thus supporting the present political party in power in Ottawa); the *Province*, Conservative (the opposition party in Ottawa). Neither paper has been particularly happy with provincial politics since the government has been dominated, in recent years, by two minor parties, Social Credit, a right-wing group and now, the New Democratic Party, a social democratic one.

In the initial stages of this study, it was decided to select thirty issues of the *Sun* for every third year commencing in 1944, a total of 330 issues. The papers were to be selected on a structured basis to guarantee that at least two and no more than three papers would be read for each month.

The returns from this sample—in terms of stories about the Sikhs—were so low that, as the study continued, it was decided to read sixty (rather than thirty) issues of the *Province*, in this case every third year starting in 1946. These issues were selected on a pure random basis. In both cases, if a sample date turned out to be a holiday the day immediately following was read or, in the case of consecutive holidays, the first publishing day.

In the case of both papers, all stories relating in any way to East Indians and Canada were noted. These included stories in which names like Singh were used even though the story did not specifically use the appellation East Indian. It did not include stories about India that had no relation to such matters as immigration or shipments of clothing or something else that tied such a story to Canada's East Indian population.

What this study showed was that, over the years, the attention given to East Indians gradually dropped to rise again during the past decade: 1945–49, one story per fourteen issues; 1950–54, one story per twenty issues; 1955–59, one story per thirty-six issues; 1960–64, one story per thirty issues; 1965–69, one story per thirty issues; 1970–74, one story per nine issues.

The attention (though not heavy) appears to be in line with historical data. Right at the end of the war there was some attention to the struggles of the East Indians to gain the vote. Once these struggles ended, the interest in the community (and its profile) dwindled; but, as immigration doors began to open, the East Indian profile and the media attention to it began to rise again.

Over the years, as well, there have been three dominant themes for stories about East Indians: there have been stories about crime, stories about cultural differences and stories that appeared to deserve the label of 'normal'.[1]

The crime stories cover the gamut of topics that have appeared in other press about an immigrant group. There are stories about murder, stories about a marriage racket involving illegal immigration, stories of assaults and bribery and rape. There are no stories about East Indians being involved in petty crime other than assault charges.

The stories about cultural differences are mainly those about Indian dancers, Indian musicians and Indian clothing. There are one or two items relating to sport including an incident involving an injury during a male field hockey game and one or two about religion. Two stories appear to call attention to cultural problems: one about an East Indian being called to the bar; another about a girl (presumably white) who wanted to wed a Sikh. There are no stories in this category explaining the kind of cultural problems that face an immigrant from an Indian village trying to adjust to life in a Canadian city.

The 'normal' stories cover the range of human interest stories. There was a story about a Sikh thought dead who turned out to be sunning himself, a story about a boy making a long trip and a story about East Indian boys (like other Canadian boys) playing marbles in the springtime.

---

1. It has been questioned whether any story that includes a racial mention can ever be considered 'normal', but this category was used in the Vancouver study.

And there were the stories where East Indians simply became part of the run of news—obituaries, accident and inquest reports and a story about a bus driver who was fired after leaving a couple of his passengers behind.[1]

TABLE 1. Sample dates

	1945–49	1950–54	1955–59	1960–64	1965–69	1970–74	Total
Crime	2	1	2	1	—	8	14
Cultural differences	3	3	1	1	3	1	12
Normal	1	1	2	3	1	3	11
Discrimination	1	1	—	—	—	2	4
Celebrities	2	—	—	—	—	2	4
Legislation	2	—	—	—	—	—	2
Housing	—	—	—	—	—	1	1
Employment	—	—	—	—	—	1	1
White hostility	—	—	—	—	—	1	1

Outside of these stories, there are a number of others covering various areas of human activity, most of them dealing with conflict. There are stories about discrimination, about housing problems and about legislative barriers to East Indian equality. The total content is low enough that it is difficult to see a trend except possibly in the area of crime coverage. In the final period, 1970–74, there were eight stories concerned with crime out of nineteen turned up by the sample, 42 per cent. Until that period, stories of a normal character or stories about cultural differences had always had or shared the lead. However, the total volume of stories is so low that any such conclusion is suspect.

Print media—1974

Any doubts about the concentration on crime stories can be quickly eliminated, however, by an examination of total print media content in 1974. While the number of stories about East Indians was in line with the sample data for the past five years (one story every nine issues) the number of stories dealing with crime was sharply higher. Of the sixty-four stories read, thirty-seven (just under 60 per cent) dealt with crime. And both papers had this emphasis: there were eighteen stories in the *Sun* and nineteen in the *Province* dealing with crime.

The concentration on crime and violence becomes even more apparent in an examination of headlines of East Indian stories carried on the front page throughout the year:
'Fall Kills 6-yr. Old' (*Sun*, 28 March).
'Man Hacked to Death in Street' (*Province*, 6 June).

---

1. This story points out one of the major problems of content analysis: it could have been treated as a derogatory story but it was not. Yet the driver's race (not critical to the story) was mentioned.

'Dragnet out for Slayers' (*Province*, 6 June).
'3 Questioned in Knifing Death' (*Province*, 7 June).
'Street Death—3 Charged with Murder' (*Province*, 8 June).
'Man Bent on Revenge Beaten, Shot to Death' (*Sun*, 5 July).
'Bus Driver Fired After Hike Mix-up' (*Province*, 25 September).
'2 Youths Injured, Man Held in Row Outside Sikh Temple' (*Sun*, 28 October).
'Family Stoned out of Home' (*Sun*, 20 November).
The image is hardly a positive one.

This portrayal of crime and problems as the dominant topic does not mean there was no 'normal' coverage. As Table 2 indicates, there were some normal stories—a couple of items about an East Indian boy acting as mayor of the city for a day, a photo of an East Indian who won a house in a draw at the annual Pacific National Exhibition, and a couple of accident reports which covered only the accident and made no racial implications (though race of the driver was mentioned).

TABLE 2. Coverage (1974)

	Sun	*Province*	Total
Crime	18	19	37
Normal	2	4	6
White hostility	3	1	4
Discrimination	—	3	3
Cultural differences	2	1	3
Race relations	2	1	3
Immigration	1	1	2
Celebrities	1	1	2
Housing	1	1	2
Education	1	—	1
Employment	—	1	1

But the bulk of the other stories (even though the numbers in each category were quite small) was also concerned with problems. There were stories about families being evicted, stories about beatings and fights outside the Sikh temple, stories about accommodation being refused a man because he was East Indian, stories claiming a high level of racial tension in the community.

Once again, what was missing was the kind of story to put this situation in context. The crime stories dealt with crime—not with the special police efforts to resolve East Indian problems. The other stories dealt with hostility, not with attempts to overcome it. There were no stories about cultural adjustment problems, no stories about how teachers were trying to learn to help immigrant children, no stories about the stresses and strains of a (Sikh) community now become a very complex one. Instead the East Indians were still by and large portrayed as a homogenous and troublesome group.

Indeed there appeared to be growing acceptance that East Indian racial conflict and violence is part of the Vancouver scene. Many of the stories simply assumed this and stated it as a fact.

State Man Steps Into Race Mess

The federal state department is becoming actively involved in helping to settle racial disputes and discrimination against East Indians living in Vancouver.[1]

East Indian Says White Shot At Him

More racial violence broke out Monday at the Sikh temple . . .[2]

Family Stoned Out of Home

A family is moving out of the Killarney section of southeast Vancouver because of racial conflict—the fourth such family to be forced out of the area in the past 18 months.[3]

East Indian Violent Crimes

Pendakur cites over-reaction:

Ald. Setty Pendakur said Friday that no single factor can be blamed for a recent rash of violent crimes in the area involving East Indians. . . .[4]

Vancouver Grapples With Racial Tension

The city of Vancouver is grappling with the ugly tensions of racial intolerance. . . .[5]

All of the stories above assume race tension exists. The last one, incidentally, was the first story to point out that the 'East Indian' community is now far from homogenous. The bylined story (by Patrick Nagle and Neale Adams) stated:

To further add to the complexity, it is not even correct generically to describe the brown-skinned community—estimated at 15,000 persons in southeast Vancouver—as 'East Indians'. They have arrived here from the United Kingdom, Africa, Fiji and the Caribbean.

A story of murder

On the basis of the material presented so far, two conclusions seem inevitable. First, over time and during the past year, the two newspapers seemed to have ignored a substantial portion of the story of the East Indians in Vancouver. Second, the press seems to have emphasized one aspect of that story, the story of crime. The first conclusion—the absence of some material—is supported by the earlier part of this study and is reinforced by analysis later in this chapter. The second conclusion is more difficult to support: perhaps the East Indians are more involved in crime than other racial groups?

In an effort to test this proposition, a search was made for statistics about crime. These were not available. The police do not keep racially based statistics; they are not even allowed to keep 'mug' books showing persons of the same race—books which allow witnesses to attempt to

1. *Province*, 23 November, p. 8.
2. *Province*, 29 October, p. 27.
3. *Sun*, 20 November, p. 1.
4. *Sun*, 6 July, p. 39.
5. *Sun*, 23 November, p. 9.

select, from a group of likely looking people, the one with whom had come into contact.

Since the statistical approach was not possible another one was tried. Figures were gathered for racial participation in one area of criminal activity—murder. (The choice was made because there were twenty-three murders in Vancouver between 1 August 1973 and 31 July 1974, enough to provide reasonable basis for analysis without becoming overwhelming.) The media reports were checked. By comparing the actual racial involvement with the reported racial involvement, it would be possible to see if East Indians were reported as criminally active out of proportion to their actual involvement.

An analysis of the twenty-three murders showed that a number of races had been involved in these crimes during the twelve-month period. A couple of the murders involved East Indians. Four others involved Canadian native people—Canadian Indians. Four others involved still other races—immigrants from Europe, two from the United Kingdom, one from Yugoslavia, one from the Netherlands. The variety of races offered the media a fair chance to demonstrate racial impartiality; if anything the concentration should have been on native Indians rather than East Indians.[1]

The media analysis of murder coverage went a step beyond the previous media check. It covered not only the files of the two daily newspapers, the *Sun* and the *Province*, but also those of the Canadian Broadcasting Corporation (CBC) public television station and of the Canadian Television (CTV) private network affiliate in Vancouver. Each outlet was checked for all coverage of murders both at the time they occurred and on surrounding dates. (The excellent filing systems at the outlets made it easy to check the coverage.)

What the files showed was that in print there is a great deal of media coverage of murder. The *Sun* carried 103 stories about the 23 murder cases; the *Province* carried 93 stories. Both papers were exceptionally interested in one case involving a millionaire—a total of 20 different stories appeared in the 2 papers. But in neither paper did race really enter the picture. The Yugoslavian, the Dutchman, never got mentioned. The native Indians made it once into the paper and only in the form of a quote from an attorney in court. The only other mention of race—apart from a reference in the *Sun* to a man from Wales—was to East Indians. They get considerable play.

The *Sun* mentioned East Indians several times in its coverage of murders involving East Indians. On 6 June, it carried a story describing the assailants in the murder of a man named Hayre as 'East Indian'. On 5 July, as a result of coverage of the murder of a man named Gill it listed the 'East Indian' murders. It also quoted, on 16 July, a man as saying: 'I saw two East Indian men chasing another East Indian male.' The *Province* (covering the Hayre murder) mentioned that the assailants

---

1. It was possible that the coverage given the stories would reflect other characteristics of crimes—their public nature, the amount of violence involved, etc. But race still should have shown up.

were 'East Indians'. On 8 June it described Hayre, himself (the victim) as East Indian. On 7 June, it carried a lengthy story about feuds in the East Indian community. On 6 July, covering the Gill murder, it mentioned the 'slaying of an East Indian'. There was no further mention of East Indians in coverage of the Gill murder.

CBC and CTV, however, gave very little coverage to murder—no matter who was involved. CBC had only three items about murder in the twelve months, CTV seven. The racial characteristics, however, matched: each station mentioned race just once—each time the race mentioned was East Indian.

Self-evaluation

In addition to the content analysis itself, a number of interviews were conducted with media personnel to get their evaluation of media performance. The persons interviewed were all at the executive level in news and those talked to included persons at the *Sun*, the *Province*, the CBC and CTV television outlets, and the three leading radio stations in terms of audience. In each case, the persons interviewed were guaranteed anonymity—the same guarantee given to all others involved in this study.

The basic question was: how would you evaluate the performance of media in Vancouver in relation to ethnic groups and particularly in relation to the East Indian population? The answer was virtually identical in each case: the media managers themselves were very critical of media performance:

I don't know of any branch of the media that is doing a halfway adequate job.

The present media have fallen down very badly.

Media performance? I suggest it has been lackadaisical.

All of the media personnel interviewed said they had no specific news personnel assigned to ethnic or cultural affairs; only one had ever had a newsperson with any competence in an East Indian language. And when asked about contacts in the East Indian community all were aware of only one or two of the élite, mainly the Westernized élite.

The principal explanation given for this highly critical assessment was that the nature of news means that the focus is on the dramatic rather than the ongoing and also that in-depth reporting is extremely difficult. One media manager said native Indian problems were getting a great deal of attention.

The native Indians are making noise and the media dwell too much on native people's problems because they are so visible.

In his view, East Indians, because they have not been noisy (noisy in the sense they have demanded attention to their problems) have not received the same kind of attention. But, in any case, the managers said in-depth reporting was very difficult. 'It's very difficult to make people understand other people have their own culture.' And, in the case of radio and television, staff shortages were given as an added explanation for the lack of suitable in-depth reports.

One news manager said the East Indian story was particularly difficult to deal with because of the internal conflicts in the community. One person said it was just too confusing to report. And still another said experienced personnel tend to avoid stories about factions:

Unless it is a very compelling story they tend to stay away. No matter what you say, you are likely to offend at least half of them.

In any case, according to one person, there was not much appetite for detailed, explanatory stories:

The NFB [National Film Board of Canada] could put together a film that explains the cultural background . . . what makes these guys take meat cleavers to each other.

Some media personnel expressed the view that more detailed news reports about the East Indians might be counter-productive:

Let's face it, there is an underlying bias against the East Indians in the community. It would be stupid not to admit it. Anything we said at greater depth would tend to inflame things.

All media said they did not deliberately include the name of a racial or ethnic group unless it was vital to the story. But there was awareness that the East Indians had got some mention. The problem appeared to be that East Indian news has related to disputes at the Sikh temple (so 'East Indian' or 'Sikh' is mentioned) and to news of murders involving feuds so again East Indian gets mentioned.

Unless it is vital to the story, it would not be mentioned. Feuds among different families and religious groups among the East Indians, it would be mentioned.

The same sort of policy was followed when the news involved conflict along racial lines:

I have on occasion included the fact the person was an East Indian when it would further the understanding of the story. When it is white violence against East Indians I draw the distinction along racial lines.

The problem appears to be that most recent media stories about East Indians have fallen into the categories where the tag 'East Indian' is attached. East Indians, therefore, get an especially high level of ethnic mentions in the media.

Chapter 6

An evaluation—
the particular case

The Sikhs of Vancouver are extremely sensitive about news media treatment, particularly about recent crime coverage. They also have some complaints about media performance—complaints of inaccuracy, unfair use of 'East Indian' identification in stories and distortion. An evaluation of media performance—based on the evidence obtained for this study —suggests some but not all of these complaints are justified. But the real problem appears to be not so much what the media do but what they do not do.

The Sikh complaints

Although there were any number of general comments about the media by the Sikhs there was only one complaint of a gross nature. A spokesman for the Ross temple said that in 1971 the *Province* had, by implication, tied the Sikhs to starvation in Bangladesh. The paper had run a story about the problems in Bangladesh and run with it a picture of an attractive new Sikh temple in Vancouver. The complaint was accurate but a check showed the incident was simply a totally inexplicable error by the paper and that the *Province* had immediately printed an apology. No other serious errors were located.

However, the major complaint was not that the media are inaccurate, but that they label East Indians in a way they do not label other racial or ethnic groups:

If there is any murder by any European, then they don't name his country of origin after his name. They would never let us become Canadians. Unless we overcome that, I will always be an East Indian. I want to be a Canadian.

What I object to are the headlines mentioning, 'East Indian'. Many of these so-called East Indians may be long since Canadian citizens. This type of head-line definitely causes feelings among other groups in the community.

As the analysis of the media coverage of Vancouver murders suggests, this complaint seems to have some basis in fact. At the moment, East Indians are labelled as such and, apparently, other races are not. Furthermore, the label is used in a general way with no attempt to distinguish among the various persons who can attract that label.

It is very tragic because it colours the whole bloody 50,000 people. I don't know the people. I don't have any connection at all. But I'm there.

The dilemma however is that, to some extent, a case can be made for such labels. Certainly in stories about the temple feuds within the community it is impossible to avoid the linkage to the Sikhs. Certainly when it appears that when family feuds or quarrels are involved it would appear such a label has some meaning. And—as the Sikhs themselves admitted—it is difficult to disguise the identity of a person named Singh. Most of the audience for print, television and radio would have identified the murders as East Indian whether or not racial tags are used. However, if this is the case, it then seems pertinent to ask why did the media so often add a racial label as well?

Another complaint often expressed was that coverage of East Indian matters is blown up or distorted. On the surface this complaint appears to have some justification. There has been considerable front-page coverage to East Indian activities in the Vancouver media during the past year. However, an examination of the events so covered have the basic elements of front-page news. They have, for example, included: (a) an incident involving an attempt to arrange a murder with a hired killer; (b) violent disputes and fights at a place of worship; (c) a revenge ambush in which the attacker becomes the attacked; and (d) the public beating to death of a man in front of a restaurant.

Such events whould probably get front-page coverage no matter which racial group was involved.

It is hard for a professional journalist to avoid the conclusion that the East Indians in Vancouver have been news-makers during the past year. There is clear evidence of racial clashes. There is clear evidence of family feuds or vendettas. There is clear evidence of violent conflict within the community. Such stories, by any professional judgement, are newsworthy; it is not surprising they have got considerable play.

The real problem

As mentioned earlier, the real problem is that, except for one story, the media have concentrated on this aspect of East Indian and Sikh affairs. They have not included the explanatory material that might have made these problems understandable. This becomes increasingly evident after one reviews the dominant trends in the post-war years.

Five dominant themes emerge from the historical data presented in the early chapters of this study. Only two are properly dealt with.

The first theme is the struggle of the Sikhs for equal status and legal rights. This struggle ended just as the post-war period began. It is reflected in the stories turned up by content analysis for that period.

The second theme is the conflict between the Westernized Sikhs and the traditionalists, the conflict that led to the split in the temple, and the establishment of the Akali Singh temple. This story is entirely missing from the material turned up through content analysis. In fact, as a careful check of the stories shows there is virtually no attempt to describe either the many pressures that exist when Sikhs adjust to Canadian society or the fact that many of them have made a successful adjustment.

The third theme is tied to the new wave of immigration and the problems created when culture clash occurs. This involves the stories of difficulties of language and attitude, of the strains created when moral standards seem to disintegrate and when customs, seen as normal, are hooted at by those who do not understand. It is also the story of racial intolerance and discrimination. This theme does appear sporadically in the media, usually in the form of a report about a racial clash. It rarely takes the form of an insight into cultural difference. The few stories that tackle this problem deal with trivia—'Indian Musicians Delight Audience' or 'Saris Could Make The Scene'.

The fourth theme involves the wave of African immigration—the arrival of a new and educated group of persons in the East Indian community. It meant those in Vancouver would have to face a new kind of East Indian, one—based on stereotypes—they would see as pushy. This story, too, is missing. It seems likely that some stories about the Ugandan Asians were carried as part of the general run of news. But it seems clear (given the extent of the sample) that the story of the changing nature of the community has not been well told if told at all.

The fifth theme of course is the story of crime, the problems of racial violence in clashes between whites and East Indians but, more important, in crimes among East Indians. It involves fights about moral standards and feuds among families and among neighbours. This story has been told but told in headline form. The clashes were reported. The underlying problems have not been.

In short, the portrait by the media for the years 1944 to 1974 is a very distorted one.

Some suggestions

Even in the particular case of Vancouver one can see some possibilities for an improved media performance. The media can and should try to get what in journalistic parlance is known as the story behind the story. The ethnic groups in Vancouver are large enough now that such specialized reporting is worth while and necessary. Such material could make the front-page news more understandable. It could also build up a group of journalists who unlike the present one would be completely aware of the Sikh community.

Some communities (Toronto in the 1950s) have ethnic beats, reporters who specialized in ethnic affairs. These journalists usually write of festivals and get-togethers, of success stories. There was no attempt at understanding. This is not what is being suggested. What is needed is not necessarily a fantasy of the Sikhs, but an accurate picture of reality. It took Pottier and Scanlon just two weeks—journalists could well afford to spend an equal amount of time.

And certainly, the backgrounder or interpretative story is becoming more and more the norm in journalism. A move in Vancouver towards this kind of copy would only be an extension of an approach not at all uncommon on major metropolitan papers.

Chapter 7

A discussion

At first glance, this study appears to fulfil the objectives set out in the introduction. It provides a picture of the Sikhs and/or East Indians in Canada as portrayed in the media. It provides an independent picture of the same people from other sources. And it gives an assessment of media performance based on that comparison, an assessment which indicates the media appear to report mainly conflict, leaving out the background material necessary to an understanding of that conflict.

Such a finding would appear to provide very strong support for the ideas advanced by Paul Hartman and Charles Husband in their article, 'The Mass Media and Racial Conflict', for they conclude media coverage of racial relations take place 'in a way that causes people to see the situation primarily as one of actual or potential conflict'. Furthermore, they argue that the media do not provide the background necessary for understanding that conflict:[1]

While the media seem to play a major role in establishing in people's minds the association of colour with conflict, their role of providing any kind of background information that would help make the race relations situation, including its conflict elements, more understandable, is relatively small.

The study also fits in very nicely to the model of agenda setting and related attitude change also discussed in the introduction. The Sikhs and/or the East Indians have, in the past year, been linked mainly to stories of violence including criminal violence. They are being portrayed as a dangerous and violent people, one who cannot keep order even within their own place of worship. Such a linkage (between race and violent behaviour) certainly provides a striking item for the public agenda, an item which would inevitably engender a negative reaction. Since there is no explanation of conflict (nothing even, for example, about the cultural reasons underlying conflict in the temple) it seems

---

1. Paul Hartmann and Charles Husband, 'The Mass Media and Racial Conflict', *Race*, Vol. XIII, No. 3, 1971, p. 279.

inevitable that, as other studies have suggested, the general community will have an increasingly strong negative reaction to East Indians.

Perhaps the reason for this is that the media focus on conflict no matter what the subject. Reports about race relations only fit into a general framework of conflict. News is made whenever conflict occurs, whether that conflict is: (a) between individuals (a boxing match or a presidential election); (b) between groups (team sports, labour-management disputes or race riots); (c) between nations (war—hot or cold); or (d) between man and nature (natural disasters).

Perhaps the conflict model really needs to be applied to all media reports rather than just to reports of race or ethnic matters. In short, James Halloran is right: 'News reporting is person centred and negative events are preferred to the positive events.'

Certainly, such an argument gains weight when the self-evaluative comments of media managers (reported in Chapter 5) are reviewed. The media managers made very clear there is no system whatsoever to their coverage of race relations. They have no personnel assigned to the Sikhs or for that matter to any other ethnic groups. They have no personnel with experience in such areas and none with the necessary languages qualifications. They have no contacts except with a few of the élite. They cover ethnic news as part of the general run of news.

But what does that mean? Where does the general run of news originate? Quite simply, it surfaces where there are events of a public nature or where events attract official attention. This means the media will report meetings (the Attorney General meets the public), public statements (the human rights people make a statement), charges (an alderman says there is discrimination) and public disturbances (the police are called in). They will also report matters when the law is formally involved (civil as well as criminal cases before the courts). These matters all take place at society's pressure points and result from conflict. More important, all such events are created by persons other than the media. The media act only in a Pavlovian sense: they respond to certain alarms. They report only what is called to their attention. They rarely, very rarely, initiate. Given such a situation, it is easy to see why the stories reported are mainly about conflict. Those are the ones forced upon the media. It is also easy to see why background stories are missing. These require individual initiative.

There is another syndrome which is also becoming evident and that is the protective syndrome—the 'I don't want to get beaten' syndrome. It has been pointed out in a chapter prepared for a book on the media (and in private interviews) that media personnel are not (as sometimes portrayed) in the business of scooping their competitors. They are in the business of preventing themselves from being scooped. As long as everyone follows the same, clear formula then all goes well. If someone deviates from that formula and strikes out on his own then he must face it with an independent judgement. It is much easier to avoid such risk-taking. The researchers at Leicester identified this standard framework; they only failed to spot the herd-like instinct that creates it.

Finally, there is significant evidence that the media can and do use colour as a basis for a stereotype. The East Indians in Vancouver are composed of a number of varying groups; the Sikhs, themselves, are a mixed assembly. But reports in the media usually describe persons of brown colouring as 'East Indians' or—in the case of stories about the temple—as 'Sikhs'. There is no attempt to differentiate. This failure explains why the East Indians find it so disturbing when one of them is headlined in the news.

There are, however, some problems with some of these conclusions. It is true the media in Vancouver have highlighted conflict but it is also true that conflict is not the kind of conflict Hartmann and Husband portrayed in their study. They were talking about intergroup conflict, conflict between two races. The Vancouver media are reporting mainly intragroup conflict, conflict among Sikh factions at the temple, conflict and violence among family groups. Interracial clashes have been reported, but they have not dominated the news.

None of these points are, of course, dramatically new. They are exactly the problems outlined by Halloran in the Unesco publication, *Race as News*:[1]

The sameness of presentation across the media, the lack of variety, the interpretations within set frameworks . . . the heavy stress on events and on negative aspects, and the lack of background material, emerge as the main findings.

The media makes us see all members of the labelled group as more alike than they really are.[2]

The conclusions quoted above are directly from Halloran's comments. They could just have easily been written for the present commentary. What is happening in Vancouver is largely what is happening in the United Kingdom. The carefully drawn perspective of history and the detailed portrayal here of events treated sketchily in the media only underlines how serious these problems really are.

Solutions

The inevitable question is: Are there any solutions, or even any helpful signs? Are there any approaches to an improvement in the present unsatisfactory situation?

The answers to this are outlined in the next chapter, a brief personal note.

1. James Halloran, *Race as News*, p. 20, Paris, The Unesco Press, 1974.
2. Halloran, op. cit., p. 26.

Chapter 8

A personal note

Perhaps, however, it would be useful if I added my own comments as a professional, an undetached observer, rather than as an academic. Subjective reactions are always present. They are better, in my view, presented rather than hidden.

First, I am full of admiration for the carefully controlled and responsible way the police in Vancouver have handled a difficult and touchy problem. The police relations with the Sikhs have been complicated. They have also been demanding. On the whole, however, the story is a pleasing one. I am embarrassed, however, by the contrast between the enormity of the police involvement and the fact that the press has not done the sort of digging, interpretation and backgrounding that, in my opinion, was so obviously needed. I believe—and this is why I am where I am—that because of the increasing professional standards in journalism through professional education, some of the journalistic limitations will be overcome. Professional standards in my view, are rising steadily as are educational levels.

The revolution of professional education which began in the United States is now spreading to places like the United Kingdom and Europe. It is no longer uncommon to find specially trained and qualified professionals on major metropolitan newspapers and at the top.

There are also outside pressures on the press—journals of commentary ranging from the pacemaker, *The Columbia Journalism Review*, to the more sarcastic local publications, including the rather muted Canadian one, *Content*. There are press councils—in Canada they are not yet very vocal, but they exist in Quebec, Alberta and Ontario, though not in British Columbia. And there is an increasingly articulate vocal press consisting of small community weeklies, special-interest publications, etc.

These are all hopeful signs.

But there are some failures.

The real failures, in my view, are those of community agencies (the schools, the police, the immigration department and all the others) to tell their own story and to insist that the media pay attention to them. The police are doing a good job, in my view, in relation to the Sikhs, but the media are not aware of it. The teachers are trying very hard, but the media are not really aware of that. It is certainly a media failure that the positive story is not being told, but it is a community agency failure as well.

Most important, the pressures for change in the media must come at all levels. They must come from agency heads to agency heads (chief of police to publisher) and further down the line as well. They must come from an increasing openness that will guarantee the newsperson has no excuse for telling only a partial story.

The media are only one agency in a society and they are, in many ways, a reflection of that society's value systems and approaches. The media may be failing to do the kind of job that needs to be done but, as a journalist, I would like to suggest that some of this blame be cast on the society itself.

Appendix

Headlines from the Vancouver dailies, 1943–74

Vancouver *Province* 1943–73

Discrimination

11 March 1946, p. 5	FORUM BLASTS RACE BARRIERS
26 February 1973, p. 34	JUDGE'S COMMENTS ATTACKED—East Indians Claim Prejudice in Supreme Court

Crime

26 September 1949, p. 13	'ENEMY' SHOT MISSED CITY MERCHANT BY INCH—Murder Attempt Follows Fire in Office
2 February 1955, p. 11	RAPE TRIAL AT ASSIZES
8 July 1955, p. 11	RAPE TRIAL AT ASSIZES
13 January 1964, p. 21	MURDER UNLIKELY CORONER BELIEVES
7 August 1970, p. 24	COMMITTED FOR TRIAL
15 October 1970, p. 10	ASSAULT TRIAL OF CITY DOCTOR HALTED
22 May 1973, p. 9	WITNESS ACCUSED OF BRIBERY BID

Normal

14 June 1949, p. 3	SIKH NOT SICK, JUST RESTING
17 January 1955, p. 4	HINDU MARRIAGE DISSOLVED
9 June 1958, p. 10	OBIT FOR KARAM SINGH
6 April 1961, p. 17	FELL UNDER TRUCK, Jury Blames Husband in City Woman's Death
27 June 1961, p. 17	2 INQUESTS SET FOLLOWING FATAL CRASHES
14 March 1964, p. 1	SNOW, RAIN OR SHINE, IT'S MARBLE TIME AGAIN [*Photo*]
28 March 1967	EAST INDIAN COMMUNITY LEADER DIES
24 September 1973, p. 37	DRIVER DIES IN CRASH. Wife and son Injured

Cultural differences

15 August 1949, p. 2	CITY SIKHS CELEBRATE ANNIVERSARY
14 February 1952, p. 12	CITY REFUSES EAST INDIAN'S BID FOR LAND

11 January 1958, p. 6	HINDU 'BIBLE' LECTURES SET
2 September 1961, p. 20	UNIVERSITY PLANS SERIES IN FAITH
28 April 1967, p. 10	STICK INCIDENT COSTS PLAYER $2,200 AWARD

Celebrities

3 November 1949, p. 3	NEHRU IN VANCOUVER [6 photos]
3 November 1949, p. 21	NEHRU ENTERING TEMPLE [Photo]

Vancouver *Sun*, 1944–73

Discrimination

12 March 1944, p. 5	EAST INDIANS TO SEEK MEETING WITH PEARSON
22 March 1944, p. 10	PEARSON APOLOGY FAILS TO SOOTHE EAST INDIANS
27 July 1953, p. 9	RATEPAYERS APOLOGIZE TO EAST INDIANS

Discrimination by coloureds

26 February 1971, p. 7	EAST INDIANS END HIGH COURT BATTLE

Crime

11 September 1947, p. 1	MURDER HUNT IN DEATH OF EAST INDIAN
17 May 1950, p. 29	SIKH FAMILY DISAPPEARANCE BEING PROBED
30 November 1950, p. 39	B.C. BOY ENDS LONG AIR TRIP
1 February 1971, p. 1	300 MEN INVOLVED—Marriage Racket Cracked
7 April 1971, p. 12	THE BRAHACHARI SAYS—'TURN TO MEDITATION' TO TURN OFF DRUGS
12 July 1971, p. 8	FOR WORKING ILLEGALLY—POLICE HUNT EAST INDIANS

Cultural differences

26 February 1944, p. 3	16 YEAR OLD GIRL WANTS TO WED SIKH
1 February 1947, p. 18	BASIL MATHEWS TO SPEAK ON INDIA
30 November 1947, p. 15	400 ATTEND CELEBRATION—East Indians Mark Birth of Religion
7 December 1950, p. 31	INDIAN MUSICIANS DELIGHT AUDIENCE
16 July 1953, p. 8	EAST INDIAN READY FOR CALL TO BAR
24 October 1968, p. 73	SARIS COULD MAKE THE SCENE

Legislation

2 June 1947, p. 9	INTERNATIONAL NIGHT—to Celebrate Extension of Franchise to Chinese and East Indians of B.C.
24 October 1947, p. 13	EAST INDIANS MAY VOTE HERE

Celebrities

20 September 1971, p. 9	INDIAN PARLIAMENTARY SPEAKER TO VISIT

Vancouver *Province*, 1974

Housing

24 May, p. 35   TURN THAT HEAT BACK ON—Landlord
                             Ordered to Behave

Employment

17 June, p. 27   'FARM WORKERS' TREATMENT QUESTIONED

White hostility

29 October, p. 27   EAST INDIAN SAYS WHITE SHOT AT HIM

Crime

4 January, p. 25   2 QUESTIONED IN MAN'S DEATH
2 February, p. 11   PAIN NOT GUILTY OF EXTORTION
29 April, p. 27   DELTA WORKER KILLED WITH AXE
22 May, p. 22   WOMAN FOUND STRANGLED
6 June, p. 1   MAN HACKED TO DEATH IN STREET
6 June, p. 1   (Later edition): DRAGNET OUT FOR SLAYERS
6 June, p. 1   FEUD SPELLS DEATH
7 June, p. 1   3 QUESTIONED IN KNIFING DEATH
8 June, p. 1   STREET DEATH—3 CHARGED WITH MURDER
9 July, p. 21   INQUEST SET FOR FIGHT VICTIM
17 July, p. 23   AMBUSHER'S DEATH STRUGGLES DESCRIBED
24 July, p. 10   MURDER SUSPECTS TO HIGHER COURT
31 July, p. 25   INQUEST ENDS ABRUPTLY WHEN
                             SUMMONS SERVED
9 August, p. 7   TRIAL ORDERED FOR MURDER TALK
13 December, p. 14   WIDOW SAYS MEN TOLD HER
                             'WE FINISHED HIM TODAY'
14 December, p. 14   6 YEARS IN JAIL FOR HIRE-KILLER PLOT
14 December, p. 14   ACCUSED TESTIFIES AT MURDER
                             TRIAL—Carrying the Knife, fell on top
                             of him
17 December, p. 23   TRIAL ORDERED FOR DHILLON
18 December, p. 38   MAN FELL ON KNIFE

Discrimination

26 January, p. 60   TECHNICALITY—RACIAL CHARGE
                             WITHDRAWN
3 September, p. 7   NDP EXEC. POWER WON BY ISLAND
                             MEMBERS
23 November, p. 8   STATE MAN STEPS INTO RACE MESS

Normal

14 August, p. 27   IN THE MAYOR'S CHAIR—YOUNGER BLOOD
16 August, p. 16   MAYOR PHILLIPS WITH 2 EAST INDIAN
                             BOYS WHO ASKED TO BE MAYOR FOR A DAY
                             [*Photo*]

4 September, p. 31	WINNER OF DREAM HOME AT EX-JOGINDER SINGH BUBRA [*Photo*]
25 September, p. 1	BUS DRIVER FIRED AFTER HIKE MIXUP

Cultural differences

24 August, p. 33	MALL'S IMAGE OF INDIA
27 August, p. 23	CRAFTS OF INDIA ADAPTED FOR U.S.

Race relations

3 October, p. 54	EAST INDIANS' TENSIONS EASE, RIGHTS COMMITTEE REPORTS

Immigration

30 December, p. 7	EAST INDIANS LEAVE CITY

Vancouver *Sun* 1974

Housing

17 January, p. 8	EVICTED FAMILY FINALLY FINDS APT.

Education

9 January, p. 10	IMMIGRANT MOTHERS GET ENGLISH CLASS

White hostility

28 January, p. 13	MAN'S NOSE, JAW BROKEN IN BEATING
28 October, p. 1	2 YOUTHS INJURED, MAN HELD IN ROW OUTSIDE SIKH TEMPLE
20 November, p. 1	FAMILY STONED OUT OF HOME

Crime

7 January, p. 9	2 MEN CHARGED IN RICHMOND DEATH
6 June, p. 39 (Later ed., p. 1)	DINERS WATCH MAN KILLED
7 June, p. 9	POLICE CHARGE TRIO IN STABBING DEATH
11 June, p. 3	3 MEN FACE MURDER CHARGE
5 July, p. 1	MAN BENT IN REVENGE BEATEN, SHOT TO DEATH
6 July, p. 8	AUTOPSY FINDS BEATING KILLED MILL AMBUSHER
6 July, p. 39	REVENGE 'MOTIVE' IN MAN'S DEATH
10 July, p. 19	AMBUSHERS DEATH PROBED
16 July, p. 2	WITNESS DESCRIBES DEATH BY BEATING
31 July	SCHEDULED WITNESS FACES DEATH CHARGE
19 September, p. 2	APOLOGETIC BANDIT RETURNS HIS LOOT
9 December, p. 10	2 PLEAD NOT GUILTY
12 December, p. 53	WITNESS IDENTIFIES 'MAN CARRYING KNIFE'
13 December, p. 37	WIFE TOLD—'WE FINISHED HIM TODAY'
14 December, p. 9	WIDOW'S CREDIBILITY QUESTIONED BY DEFENCE IN MURDER TRIAL

17 December, p. 7	TRIAL ORDERED IN DEATH CASE
17 December, p. 14	I WAS ATTACKED
19 December, p. 6	TWO GIVEN LIFE TERMS IN STABBING

Normal

| 28 March, p. 1 | FALL KILLS 6-YR. OLD |
| 1 April, p. 13 | MAN, 27, DIES IN CAR PLUNGE |

Cultural differences

| 7 January, p. 17 | COLORFUL PUNJABI FOLK DRAMA DELIGHTS QUEEN E. AUDIENCE |
| 24 December, p. 67 | BRIDES HEADING BACK TO INDIA |

Celebrities

| 5 July, p. 7 | SIKH LEADERS BEGIN 10-DAY VISIT |
| 10 August, p. 12 | SIKH LEADER TO VISIT CITY |

Immigration

| 1 November, p. 13 | HEARING URGED TO HALT LABOUR BOSSES 'WHO SHIP IMMIGRANTS LIKE CATTLE' |

Race Relations

| 6 July, p. 39 | EAST INDIAN VIOLENT CRIMES—Pendakur Cites Over-reaction |
| 23 November, p. 9 | VANCOUVER GRAPPLES WITH RACIAL TENSION |

Bibliography

Books

GILL, Nash S. *The East Indian People of British Columbia.* Vancouver, The British Columbia Human Rights Council, 1971.

HALLORAN, James C. (ed.). *Race As News.* Paris, The Unesco Press, 1974.

KLAPPER, Joseph T. *The Effects of Mass Communication.* New York, The Free Press, 1965.

LEACOCK, Stephen. *Canada: The Foundations of Its Future.* Montreal, 1914.

MYRDAL, Gunnar. *An American Dilemma: The Negro Problem in Modern Democracy.* New York, Harper & Row, 1962.

NORRIS, John. *Strangers Entertained: A History of the Ethnic Groups of British Columbia.* Victoria, The B.C. Centennial, 1971.

SKELTON, O. D. *Life and Letters of Sir Wilfrid Laurier.* New York, Century, 1922.

SMITH, W. G. *A Study in Canadian Immigration.* Toronto, The Ryerson Press, 1920.

WINKS, Robin W. *The Blacks In Canada.* Montreal, McGill-Queen's University Press, 1972.

YOUNG, Charles H.; REID, Helen R. Y. *The Japanese Canadians.* Toronto, The University of Toronto Press, 1938.

Journals

AMES, Michael M.; INGLIS, Joy. Conflict and Change in British Columbia Sikh Family Life. *B.C. Studies*, No. 20, Winter 1973–74.

ANGUS, H. F. Asiatics in Canada. *Pacific Affairs*, 1946.

ANON. The Position of Hindus in Canada. *British Columbia Magazine*, Vol. VII, July-December 1912.

ENGINEER, Homie N. East Indians in B.C. Since 1910. *The Indo-Canadian*, Vol. VII, No. 3/4, 1971.

HARTMANN, Paul; HUSBAND, Charles. The Mass Media and Racial Conflict. *Race*, Vol. XIII, No. 3, 1971.

HENRY, Franklin J. The Measurement of Perceived Discrimination: A Canadian Case Study. *Race*, Vol. X, No. 4, 1969.

KNOPF, Terry Ann. Race Riots and Reporting. *Journal of Black Studies*, Vol. IV, No. 7, March 1974.

MacLENNAN, Douglas. Racial Discrimination in Canada. *The Canadian Forum*, October 1943.

McCOMBS, Maxwell E.; SHAW, Donald T. The Agenda-Setting Function of Mass Media. *Public Opinion Quarterly*, Vol. 36, 1972.

MUTHANN, I. M. East Indians in B.C. (til 1910). *The Indo-Canadian*, Vol. VII, No. 3/4, 1971.

PANNU, Gurdal Singh. Sikhs in Canada. *The Sikh Review*, October 1970.

POTTER, Harold H. Negroes in Canada. *Race.*

PRICE, Charles. White Restrictions on 'Coloured' Immigration. *Race*, Vol. VII, No. 3, 1966.

PURI, Pushpinder S. Sikhs in Canada. *The Sikh Review*, Vol. XXI, No. 231.

RICHARD, Anthony H. Sociological and Psychological Explanations of Racial Prejudice: Some Light on the Controversy from Recent Researches in Britain. *Pacific Sociological Review*, Fall, 1961.

SINGH, Kapur. Sikh Symbols and the Sikhs in Canada. *The Sikh Review*, 1973. (Published by Khalsa Diwan Society.)

SMILLIE, Emmaline. An Historical Survey of Indian Migration Within the Empire. *The Canadian Historical Review*, Vol. IV, 1926.

TURNER, Ralph H.; SURACE, Samuel J. Zoot-Suiters and Mexicans: Symbol in Crown Behavior. *American Journal of Sociology*, Vol. 62, 1956–57.

UBEROI, Narindar. Sikh Women in Southall. *Race*.

WILLIAMS, J. Barclay; SINGH, Saint R. Canada's New Immigrant. *The Canadian Magazine*, Vol. XXVIII, November–April 1906–07.

Miscellaneous

EAST INDIANS CANADIAN CITIZENS WELFARE ASSOCIATION. Brief to Canada Manpower and Immigration, 23 February 1974.

MAYER, Adrien C. A Report on the East Indian Community in Vancouver. Institute of Social and Economic Research, University of British Columbia, 1959. (Working Paper.)

RICHARDSON, J. J. Culture and Family. One of a number of unpublished papers prepared for a teachers' seminar in Vancouver, 14 March 1974.

SINGH, Karam (ed.). *Parivertan* (weekly). The issue quoted was 21 June 1974.

Newpapers

The Vancouver *Sun*, 1944–74.

The Vancouver *Province*, 1946–74.

Reports

CANADA. PARLIAMENT. HOUSE OF COMMONS. *Report*, by W. L. Mackenzie King. 1908. (Sessional Papers, No. 360.)

MORSE, Eric. Some Aspects of the Komagata Maru Affair. *Report*. Canadian Historical Association, 1936.

Part III

Reporting Northern Ireland

A study of news in Great Britain, Northern Ireland and the Republic of Ireland

Philip Elliott

Centre for Mass Communication Research,
University of Leicester

The funding for this study came from two sources, Unesco and a federation of German churches. I am very grateful to Professor Halloran, Director of the Centre for Mass Communication Research, for negotiating this support, to Unesco, and Brian McGuigan, Brian Walker, Dr Eric Gallagher and Rev. Desmond Wilson who acted as trustees on behalf of the German churches.

Particular thanks to Brian McGuigan who has been a continual source of help and encouragement and to all the other people I have met on various visits to Northern Ireland and the Republic of Ireland who have gone out of their way to help my understanding of affairs in Ireland, north and south. It goes without saying that they, like the others whose help I gratefully acknowledge, are not responsible for the use or misuse to which I have put it.

Various people collected and recorded material. The Ulster Television output was recorded by Eric Peak at Magee College, Londonderry. I am grateful to him and Professor Edwin Rhodes who made it possible. Pat Morrow arranged for the Northern Ireland newspapers to be sent to England. In Leicester, George Clements of the School of Education enabled me both to record material and play it back. Particular thanks to my friend and colleague, Adrian Wells, who took all these affairs in hand at various points. Without him I should have had little to work on.

Other colleagues—Peggy Gray, Derek McKiernan and Sue Middleton—helped at a later stage with coding. They also provided many useful comments on the research and earlier drafts of this report. So too did Peter Golding and Paul Hartmann.

Others outside the centre have given me helpful advice at various stages. In particular I should like to thank Professor Rex Cathcart, now at Queens University, Belfast, Professor Richard Rose at the University of Strathclyde, Ciaran McKeown of the Irish Press and W. D. Flacks of the British Broadcasting Corporation (BBC).

Finally my thanks to the secretarial staff at the centre for their patience and perseverance in dealing so efficiently with the demands this study has put on them.

PHILIP ELLIOTT

Chapter 1

Introduction: problems and methods

Community conflict in Northern Ireland

The recent 'troubles' in Northern Ireland brought the province to the attention of the world's news media. Even though Northern Ireland is part of the United Kingdom this was particularly true in Great Britain. The Irish question bedevilled British politics in the late nineteenth and early twentieth centuries. The question developed into one of how to accommodate the descendants of the Protestant settlers of Scottish stock in the north of the island, in any settlement which gave independence and self-government to the Celtic, Catholic south. The solution embodied in the Government of Ireland Act, 1920, was the partition of the island with an independent State of twenty-six counties in the south and a separate parliament at Stormont to administer the six northern counties.

After partition, the British press and later broadcasting followed British politicians in treating the Irish question as closed. Affairs in the north were left in the hands of the Stormont Parliament, with its built-in unionist majority. The Unionist Party represented those who had campaigned to maintain the link with Great Britain. Its support was drawn from the whole social spectrum in the north, landowners, industrialists, the commercial and professional middle class and the industrial working class around Belfast. They were united by a common religion of Protestantism, a common opposition to the Catholic Church and a common loyalty to the British crown. Attempts to break up this common allegiance and to introduce class interest into the structure of northern politics were largely unsuccessful. The Northern Ireland Labour Party (NILP),[1] for example, never achieved wide support even in the industrial areas of Belfast.

Instead, northern politics has been dominated by the issue of the border. Partition created a State in which there was a built-in Protestant majority in support of the union, but only so long as it was not divided over other issues. The Unionist Party, therefore, had to keep the allegiance

---

1. A full list of abbreviations used in this work is given in the Appendix, p. 374.

of the Protestant population and at the same time counter any threat from the Catholic minority within the new country. This was done by keeping the border issue in the forefront of Northern Ireland politics. The political leaders of the Catholics refused to accept the constitutional legitimacy of the State of Northern Ireland. The republican views of most members of the old Nationalist Party meant that most took no part in the political institutions of the north. This helped the unionists to convince the Protestants that continued vigilance was necessary to ensure Northern Ireland's survival, vigilance which took the form of support for the Unionist Party, the Orange Order and other organizations expressing the solidarity of the Loyalist community. In some areas west of the River Bann, notably the city of Londonderry, appeals to majority solidarity were not enough. Catholics outnumbered Protestants in the particular locality. Protestant, unionist supremacy was secured by such means as the gerrymandering of ward and constituency boundaries, restrictions placed on the franchise in local government elections and voting irregularities.

In England it was an open secret that such practices were going on in part of the United Kingdom. Until the civil rights campaign began in the mid-1960s, constitutional abuse and fraud at the polls in Northern Ireland was a subject of which no one spoke in public, but many joked in private. The meaning of such slogans as 'bring out your dead' or 'vote early and vote often', was quite clear, but the issue received little public attention through the news media. In broadcasting the uneasy relationship between the local administration and the local BBC organization meant that reporters from the mainland could be kept out of the province until 1965 as, for example, happened to Alan Whicker and a *Tonight* team in 1959 (Smith, 1972).

Various dates in the 1960s could be taken as the start of the present troubles in Northern Ireland. In 1963 Terence O'Neill became Prime Minister, the third unionist Prime Minister since partition, but one cast in a different mould from his predecessors—the two viscounts, Craigavon and Brookeborough;[1] in 1965 there was an indication of some of the policy differences between O'Neill and his predecessors when Sean Lemass, Taoiseach of the Republic of Ireland visited Belfast, the first Prime Minister to do so; in 1967 the Northern Ireland Civil Rights Association was founded and in 1968 the initial civil rights demonstrations began. Subsequently more than a thousand people have died as a result of violent conflict in the province. (The total up to and including May 1976 was 1,537.)[2] In 1969 the British army was sent in to help the civil power in Northern Ireland to maintain order. In 1972 the provincial government was suspended and direct rule by the United Kingdom Government

1. Between them, these two ruled Northern Ireland for forty years. There was a brief interregnum of three years during the war, when John Andrews was Prime Minister. Harbinson, the historian of the Unionist Party divides its leaders into two types, those like the two viscounts, who followed the short-term strategy of waving the flag and banging the drum, to keep the loyalists united, and the others, including Carson as well as Andrews, O'Neill and Chichester-Clark, who tried to follow a more long-term strategy to unite the society.
2. *Fortnight*, 4 June 1976.

introduced. In spite of various attempts to reintroduce a local adminis-tration, the problems of drafting a new constitution, acceptable to all the parties involved, has proved intractable and direct rule continues. So, too, has the presence of the British army. Initially, the army was sent to protect the Catholic minority from Loyalist rioting; subsequently it became involved in a guerilla war with the Provisional IRA; most recently official policy has been to play down the quasi-war situation existing in the province and play up the individual criminal aspects of the continuing violence.

Throughout the troubles, any account of events has been regarded as tendentious by one or other party to the conflict, let alone any attempt to assess motive and responsibility.[1] In the early days, for example, the authorities were inclined to put the civil rights demonstrations down to Republican agitators and subversives, the people whom they had held responsible for any threats to the established order in the province in the past. The demonstrators, however, argued that they were simply pressing for rights enjoyed by their fellow citizens in other parts of the United Kingdom and that their movement was not sectarian. Nevertheless, it was mainly Catholics who did not enjoy full civil rights. Bands of extreme Loyalists met what they regarded as Catholic demonstrations with violent opposition. The demonstrators, as at the bridge at Burntollet, could look for little protection from the police and civil authorities.

The IRA had been largely dormant since the collapse of the terrorist campaign it had mounted from its rural strongholds between 1956 and 1962. Its quasi-military activities and preparations had been run down in favour of the development of a socialist political programme for Ireland. The organization's lack of readiness in the face of Loyalist threats to the Catholic minority led to a split between those who favoured a more militant military line, the 'Provisionals', and those who continued to support the socialist programme, the 'Officials'. The Provisionals soon moved from defence of the Catholic community to attack on the State of Northern Ireland and subsequently on the British Government and army when they took over direct responsibility for the province. In spite of the welcome the army received at first as protectors of the Catholic community, relations between the British army and the Catholic minority soon soured. Arms searches and harassment by the army in the face of attacks on soldiers and security personnel produced a situation of mounting tension. The Unionist administration, by then led by Brian Faulkner, decided with army support to introduce internment without trial, a policy which had helped to control previous terrorist campaigns both north and south of the border. On this occasion however, the level of violence was not controlled but increased.

The nature of the troubles changed from the early days of marches, demonstrations and riots in which many participated, to bombing and sniping incidents, each carried out by a few, though this is not to judge

---

1. The account which follows draws heavily on the efforts of the *Sunday Times* 'Insight' team to keep pace with contemporary history both in their book, *Ulster*, and subsequent reviews published in the paper. It goes without saying, however, that they are not respon-sible for this selection.

how wide was the support for either type of activity. Subsequently, another type of violence developed, the sectarian murder.[1] Mainly, extreme Loyalists have been responsible for these murders, trying to eliminate Catholics, on the grounds that all are potential subversives. By so doing they hope to intimidate the minority community in general. But the IRA has also been responsible for some assassinations of individual civilians in spite of its protestations that its policy is to oppose the authorities and particularly the British, not to wage sectarian war in Ireland. There have also been periods when feuds between the different paramilitary groups within each community have reached such a pitch that members of rival groups have killed and injured each other.

This brief survey of the troubles in Northern Ireland has concentrated on violence as this is the main focus of attention in the news coverage to be reported below. It shows some of the problems journalists have faced in picking their way through a confused situation in which rival accounts abound. Nevertheless, it is important to go beyond such a historical review into a brief analysis of the various developments which upset the previous stability of the Northern Irish political and social structure. As we shall see in later chapters, such an analysis is missing from the news coverage except in the sense that repetition of the same treatment of similar events amounts to an implicit explanation of the situation.

After the events of the past seven years, it looks as if the stability of Northern Ireland was always precarious. Nevertheless, the Unionist régime at Stormont had survived the earlier IRA campaign in the 1950s without British assistance and maintained its own hold on power since partition. In the terms used by Rose (1971), the Unionists relied on the compliance rather than the consent of the Catholic minority, keeping power in their own hands and away from those whose allegiance to the State was in doubt. With O'Neill's accession to the premiership signs developed of a change in this policy. By concentrating on economic development within the province, encouraging ecumenical contact between the churches and cross-border contact with the Government of the Republic of Ireland, O'Neill hoped to create a society in which consensus might replace enforced compliance, in which the minority might come to accept the constitutional legitimacy of the State in which they lived. O'Neill was encouraged to adopt this policy by the increasingly outward-looking policies of the government in the republic; by the rapid economic growth achieved in the south; by the Unionist government's own success in putting down the 1956–62 IRA campaign aided by the lack of popular support for the campaign in the province and the republic and by the ecumenical movements in the various Christian churches which made the religious differences between Protestants and Catholics, main symbol of the difference between the two communities, seem less significant. Nevertheless, even the early tentative moves the O'Neill administration made were opposed vigorously by Protestant

---

1. On this, see Dillon and Lehane's careful analysis in another Penguin special, *Political Murder in Northern Ireland*, Harmondsworth, Penguin, 1973.

fundamentalists in the Loyalist community, one of whose leaders was the Reverend Ian Paisley.

But if there was change on the Unionist side, the same was true for the minority. The growth of the civil-rights movement showed that the minority, led by a growing professional and educated middle class, were becoming less concerned about the border and more concerned about the system of political, economic and social discrimination which had enforced their compliance for half a century. Instead of continuing the old Republican tactic of non-participation, representatives of the minority began to demand the same civil and political rights as those enjoyed by other citizens of the United Kingdom. Throughout 1968 and 1969 the civil-rights movement campaigned on a reform programme, many of which were conceded by O'Neill in a package of measures introduced at the end of 1968. But the civil-rights movement's attempt to appeal across the sectarian divide and unite all the disadvantaged in Northern Ireland on the basis of their common class position fell on deaf ears. As the government was forced to make concessions by demonstrations and protest, so Protestant opinion hardened in the face of what it had begun to see as a threat to its security and way of life. Claims that the civil-rights movement was non-sectarian were soon overtaken by events. The violent opposition with which it was met by fundamentalists on the Loyalist side and the methods used by the unionist government and the police in the province to enforce order suggested that once more the majority had fallen back on the tactic of repressing the minority.

One set of explanations for these developments puts most weight on external influences, emphasizing the various ways in which Northern Ireland, previously a closed society, came into contact with the outside world at this time. Some of these contacts were of the Unionist administration's own choosing, as, for example, in the attempts to expand trade and tourism and to establish links with the south. Some were the result of developments outside Northern Ireland itself, as, for example, in the growth of the ecumenical movement in the church or the change in the style and agenda of politics which occurred in the 1960s. The Unionist Party in Northern Ireland was linked to the British Conservative Party, the party in power in the United Kingdom during most of the time Northern Ireland had been in existence. In 1964 the Conservatives lost power and though the incoming Labour government took no immediate interest in the affairs of Northern Ireland, its election was one indication of a changed mood in British society. The era of an unquestioning acceptance of authority, embodied, for example, in the predominance of an aristocratic ethos in the previous Conservative administrations, was over. The questioning opposition to authority which took its place led many groups to a sense of common identity and grievance and attempts at united action to right their wrongs. This process was an international one in which the example of developments among the black community in the United States and among European students was particularly influential. So far as Northern Ireland was concerned, the model of an oppressed, disadvantaged group was readily applicable to the situation of the Catholic minority and some of the methods and rhetoric used by the civil-rights movement to proclaim its case seemed similar to those used by other groups overseas in their own campaigns.

Barritt and Carter (1972) in their account, *The Northern Ireland Problem*, first written before Northern Ireland had become a problem in the sense accepted now, drew attention to the various ways in which the province was becoming less isolated. There was a simple physical process by which increased travel and communication, developments in trade unionism, cultural activities, sport, higher education and the churches all provided more opportunities for contact between citizens of the province and those outside and all contributed in Barritt and Carter's view to the erosion of the old ideas, a process much accelerated in the 1960s with the advent of television. As Carter notes in a postscript to the second edition: 'the equilibrium ended at a time when violent demonstrations, or violence in breaking up peaceful demonstrations, were common features in the news from many parts of the world.' He goes on to suggest that: 'what happened may therefore owe something to the infection conveyed so quickly by the mass media from other countries, as well as to memories of Ireland's own violent past' (Barritt and Carter, 1972, p. 159). The idea of television spreading the infection of protest around the world is an extreme example of the direct stimulus, 'hypodermic needle' account of media effect which has been severely criticized in the research literature.[1] Nevertheless, it implicitly includes two more specific accounts of media influence, that methods of demonstration were adopted by imitation or for their proven publicity value elsewhere and an account of media news values; that such demonstrations were regarded as newsworthy because of what happened at them, and their similarity to other events already judged newsworthy elsewhere. These are among the issues in the continuing controversy over media performance and effect in a situation of social conflict which provides the background to the present study.

But looked at as an explanation of the development of the troubles in Northern Ireland, accounts like Barritt and Carter's which emphasize processes of external influence are extremely idealist in their view of social behaviour. Complementary explanations based on social and economic change in the province have already been hinted at in the reference to the development of a Catholic middle class as important in the growth of the civil-rights movement. British imperialism has been in decline in both the forms in which it was originally practised in Ireland, garrison control and colonization. Instead the emphasis has shifted to commercial and economic relationships. The interest shown by the O'Neill administration in economic development, one of the factors which laid the province open to external influence, followed from the fact that the old mixed economy of heavy industry and landed estates was no longer viable. The same process of accommodation as occurred in Great Britain between the landed aristocracy and the commercial and industrial bourgeoisie has been played out in miniature in Northern Ireland with the difference that

---

1. See, for example: J. D. Halloran, *The Effects of Television*, London, Panther, 1970; J. G. Blumler and E. Katz (eds.), *The Uses of Mass Communications*, Vol. III, Sage Annual Review of Communications Research, 1974.

the working class there has not developed separate organizations comparable to the British Labour Party and trade-union movement. The continuing external threat, real or imagined, has provided a basis for common organizations, like the Orange Order and an ideology of loyalism which stretches across social class boundaries.

There have been recurrent differences between upper-class and lower-class Unionists which have found expression in the formation of various breakaway parties and organizations. Harris (1972, p. 182), pointed out in her study of *Prejudice and Tolerance in Ulster* that 'the basic political problem of the poorer Protestant was that to secure his independence from the Irish Republic he had to support politically those whom he neither liked nor trusted'. More recently the Loyalist paramilitary organizations have drawn most of their support from the Protestant working-class areas in and around Belfast. The rhetoric of working-class Unionists includes derogatory descriptions of their upper-class colleagues such as 'the fur coat brigade', some of which were mentioned in the election campaigns covered in this study. But generally such differences have not prevented the Loyalist community maintaining a united front against the minority and its representatives. Nelson (1976, p. 165) has observed that

most working-class Protestant activists who were beginning to talk during 1973 and 1974 of 'fifty years of misrule' and 'the fur coat brigade' nevertheless hold to the belief that a small group of IRA members organized the 'civil rights' after a long and careful period of preparation. They will admit that discrimination existed against both sections of the working class, but not that it was disproportionately anti-Catholic.

If it is difficult to produce an uncontentious account of recent events, these questions of the course of social change in Northern Ireland and of the nature and causes of community conflict there, are even more matters of dispute. In a review of recent social scientific studies of Northern Ireland, Lijphart (1975) identified no less than ten different theories of conflict implicitly or explicitly employed. Much of this theorizing turns on the question of whether the situation can be described in terms of its apparent characteristics, as, for example, a difference between religions, between nationalisms (Rose, 1971) or as a racial difference between tribes (De Paor, 1970) and how far such differences themselves need explanation. Marxist analysis of the situation in Ireland, which is mainly to be found in various polemics, holds that such differences have been created and maintained by British imperialism and its allies, the local bourgeoisie, to obscure the common class interests of the workers in Ireland and so keep them under political and economic control.[1] In moving towards causal explanations, account needs to be taken not just of the nature of internal divisions but of such external relationships between Northern Ireland, Great Britain and the Republic of Ireland. But these can be

1. An example of such a polemic is 'An Analysis of the Significance of the Ulster Workers' Strike' by the editorial staff of *Red Patriot*. This includes several references to the part which 'the British imperialist propaganda machine' plays in propagating such differences while suppressing an account of class divisions within the society.

described in various ways to emphasize not only British colonialism, but also Irish nationalism or comparisons between Loyalists in Northern Ireland and other beleaguered groups of settlers in 'fragment societies' like the Boers in South Africa.[1] Harold Jackson emphasized the reciprocal relationship of dependence and dominance in his account of Ireland as a double minority problem with Protestants dominating Catholics in the north and vice versa in the south. The notion could be extended to include the dependent relationship between both parts of Ireland and Great Britain to give three interrelated levels.

The prime interest of such concepts and models for this study, however, is not their efficacy in explaining the situation in Northern Ireland so much as their use, implicitly or explicitly, in popular debate and news reporting. There is no reason to suppose that the traffic in concepts and explanations is one way through the popularization of academic or literary work, in the press and on television. Social scientists showed little interest in affairs in the province before it became a centre of attention for the world's news media. Given the characteristics of modern, market-oriented media and the style of journalism practised by them, however, such concepts and accounts are likely to be implicit and simplified in day-to-day news reporting. Nevertheless, one aim of this study is to examine the way in which such beliefs about the nature of the conflict and the role of the various participants are made available to those same participants through the various news media.

The mass media in Northern Ireland

As well as the question raised at the end of the previous section of the images and perspectives on the conflict contained in news reporting, another aim of this study was to investigate how different media and the journalists working for them reported a situation of continuing violence, conflict and dispute. These two aims provided guidelines for selecting the media to be included in the study. To cover the first, it was necessary to include those press and broadcasting outlets most widely used in the province. To cover the second, other media, different in style, technique or place of publication were included for comparison. In both cases, the study concentrated on news reporting rather than other material such as editorials, features and letters.

Two morning papers are published in Belfast, the *News Letter* and the *Irish News*, as well as an evening paper, the *Belfast Telegraph*. At the time when this study was carried out two organizations were broadcasting locally, BBC Northern Ireland, using both radio and television, and Ulster Television. More recently, local commercial broadcasting has been introduced. Radio and television channels are part of the British national networks controlled by the BBC and the IBA. They carry the news services provided nationally by the BBC and ITN. The British national

---

1. See for example B. Schutz and D. Scott, 'Patterns of Political Change in Fragment Regimes: Northern Ireland and Rhodesia', in I. Crewe (ed.), *The Politics of Race. British Political Sociology Year Book*, Vol. 2, London, Croom Helm, 1976.

press also circulates widely throughout the province. Five of the British national dailies, the *Daily Mail, Daily Mirror, Daily Express, Daily Telegraph* and *Guardian*, publish separate editions for Northern Ireland which are variants on the papers' northern editions. The national press and broadcasting services of the Republic of Ireland are also available in the north but are less widely consumed than their British or local counterparts.

General circulation and readership data for the daily papers published in Belfast, London and Dublin are shown in Table 1. In 1970 59 per cent of the adult population of Northern Ireland read the *Belfast Telegraph*, 33 per cent the *News Letter* and 21 per cent the *Irish News*. The best-selling British daily, the *Daily Mirror* was read by 30 per cent, the *Daily Express* by 12 per cent and the *Daily Mail* by 9 per cent. Since that time there has been a general fall in the circulation of the popular press except in the case of the *Sun* whose circulation has increased substantially in Northern Ireland as well as Great Britain.

In 1970 readership of the British quality press was at a similar low level to readership of the Irish papers. Data from Richard Rose's survey, reported in *Governing Without Consensus*, showed that the Dublin papers were read almost exclusively by Catholics in the north. The British papers on the other hand were read extensively by people of both religions. More than 90 per cent of the readers of the Dublin papers among those

TABLE 1. The circulation and readership of the press of Great Britain, Ireland and Northern Ireland in Northern Ireland

Press	Circulation (1975) (000s)	Readership (1970) as percentage of Northern Ireland population[1]
GREAT BRITAIN		
Daily Mirror	56.6	30
Daily Express	20.6	12
Daily Mail	13.3	9
Daily Telegraph	7.2	4
Guardian	1.6	1
Sun	44.8	n.a.[2]
The Times	n.a.	1
IRELAND		
Irish Times	4	2
Irish Press	n.a.	4
Irish Independent	5	2
NORTHERN IRELAND		
News Letter	67.8	33
Irish News	54.4	21
Belfast Telegraph	178.1	59

1. The estimated adult (15+) population of the province at this time was 1,070,000.
2. The *Sun* did not start distribution in Northern Ireland until October 1972.
Sources: Northern Ireland Readership Survey, 1970. ABC and publishers statements quoted in Ulster Television, *Marketing Guide to Northern Ireland*, 1975.

sampled were Catholics while just under half of the readers of the British papers were Catholic, just over half Protestants. Extrapolating from these results to the population at large, Rose points out that a higher proportion of Catholics than Protestants read the British press. He goes on to suggest that they read the popular British press for its entertainment value rather than for its political content.

Rose's survey also demonstrated the sectional appeal of the two Belfast morning papers. Whereas the *Belfast Telegraph* was read by roughly the same proportion of members of each religion, most readers (87 per cent) of the *News Letter* were Protestants and nearly all readers of the *Irish News* Catholic (92 per cent). Boal (1969 and 1971) reports similar results from surveys with smaller samples in various areas of Belfast. Boal was particularly concerned with comparing the relative extent of differences based on religion and social class. The *Belfast Telegraph* had a high readership in every area regardless of religion or social class. The *News Letter*, however, was read more widely in the middle-class Protestant areas than in the working class ones. There, the *Daily Mirror* was particularly popular. Boal's two studies show that propinquity is no guarantee of community. In both cases there was a high level of integration within each area which was homogeneous in terms of religion and class, but both factors acted as an almost complete barrier to interaction between adjacent areas. Boal (1969) noted that the common readership of the *Belfast Telegraph* gave it 'an important role as an integrator operating across the religious community boundary'.

Others have noted this integrative potential of the *Belfast Telegraph*. Barritt and Carter cite the progressive policies of the then editor of the *Belfast Telegraph*, John E. Sayers, as another factor which helped to expose Northern Ireland to the outside world. Lord Windlesham (1975, p. 87) is among many observers who have thought Belfast 'fortunate to have an evening paper which has been remarkably independent and tolerant in its outlook'. His view that 'television and radio are also moderating influences' seems to be less widely shared, particularly within the province itself; a point which Windlesham recognizes when he continues 'the same programmes are seen by both sides and blamed by both sides'. Rose's study suggested a particularly high level of consumption of news and current affairs programmes in Northern Ireland among members of both communities, a point confirmed by more recent analyses.

Cathcart (1976) suggests this high level of news consumption can largely be explained by the instrumental value of knowing what incidents have taken place recently, whereas Rose (1971, p. 343) notes that 'watching television news and current affairs programmes exposes Ulster people to opinions that they might not hear, or not hear discussed sympathetically, in their immediate environment'. But he found that viewers of news and current affairs programmes did not differ from non-viewers in their political attitudes to Northern Ireland and so concluded that such programmes mainly reinforced existing views. Similarly, 'analysis of political outlooks by newspaper readership, controlling for religion, shows that there are no substantial differences about political outlooks among the major readership groups' (Rose, p. 344). Again Rose concluded that this showed selective perception and evaluation of newspaper content rather than influence by the paper's political position.

This quiet and sober analysis of media influence contrasts strikingly with the repeated criticism of broadcasting and the press by politicians and public figures in Great Britain and Northern Ireland. Admittedly, too much weight cannot be placed on results from a few questions in a correlational survey. Nevertheless, the contrast does suggest a need to explain official and public concern over media coverage and its possible influence as much as to investigate questions of media effect further. The latest official expression of this concern is to be found in the report of the Gardiner Committee (1975) on measures to deal with terrorism in Northern Ireland. In the committee's view the news media encourage terrorist activity in Northern Ireland by giving publicity to terrorist leaders in broadcast interviews and press advertisements, by sensational reporting of violent incidents which give a false glamour to the events and those involved in them and by giving credence to ill-founded allegations against the security forces. Throughout the troubles the authorities in Great Britain and Northern Ireland have made similar charges that the media were glamourizing and encouraging dissidents, but hindering the police or the army in their attempts to control the situation. For example, in November 1971 a group of Conservative back-benchers, led by Lieutenant-Colonel ('Mad Mitch') Mitchel, complained of biased and hostile reporting against the British army.

Other observers have been more impressed with the support the British media have given the authorities and particularly the British army since its introduction to the province. Eamonn McCann remarks on the change in British press reporting once British troops went in. Instead of being generally favourable to change, though patronizing to those trying to bring it about, the press recast the situation into one in which rioters were 'baddies' and the troops, 'goodies'. McCann recounts the logic behind this. If the troops were there to keep the peace and were above suspicion, then the riots must be provoked by some sinister influence, left-wing extremists or the IRA. Earlier attempts by Stormont ministers to blame the troubles on such influences had been treated with contempt as mere political special pleading. With the introduction of British troops, however, McCann claims the press began to attribute violence to the IRA without evidence, before the IRA itself became active but in line with information fed to it from official sources.

The earlier period, however, when media coverage was more sympathetic to demands for change in Northern Ireland has left a legacy of bitterness among Loyalists in the province (Nelson, 1976). Martin Dillon and Lehane (1973, p. 283) quote in full a press release written in 1973 which they regard as 'the most eloquent statement of the case of Ulster's Protestant militants given throughout the course of the troubles'. Much of this is critical of press coverage which has cast extreme Protestants

in the role of wicked 'heavies', the 'bad guys' of the story, the narrow-minded bigots of Ulster, the cause of all the present troubles. . . . It seems a lifetime ago that our competent, if partisan, government came under fire from a Civil

Rights movement which, it has to be admitted, did have a justification for many of its grievances. Cast inevitably in the role of St. Bernadette came a pint-sized lady of fiery oratory and poverty-stricken background. . . . You, the press, made a heroine of this girl and you bear a heavy responsibility for what followed. The blundering, incompetent and seemingly repressive antics of our leaders confirmed your attitude that she and her associates were right and that we were wrong. The B-Specials, the reactions of our police forces and the so-called ambush of Burntollet, hardened your views which, in turn, hardened ours, and the die was cast.

The statement goes on to outline the beleaguered isolation of the Scots-Irish of Northern Ireland, 'second-class Englishmen, half-caste Irishmen', traditionally betrayed by English politicians, threatened by the southern Irish and unable to count on overseas support like the IRA. The statement returned to the theme of press coverage in the end (Dillon and Lehane, 1973, p. 280–3):

You turned an adulterous little slut into a revolutionary saint; a soft-voiced failed priest fanatic was called a moderate and you gave a terror organization all the publicity it desired. . . . We, the Scots-Irish, are fighting for survival.

Official concern about the publicity given to terrorists has also been expressed in the Republic of Ireland. In Great Britain, there have been occasional consultations between government ministers and the chairmen of the two broadcasting authorities to draw their attention to official concern over aspects of the coverage. The government in the Republic of Ireland has taken more vigorous action. RTE, the Irish broadcasting corporation, has always enjoyed less of the titular independence from government accorded to the BBC and the IBA in Great Britain. In October 1971 the Provisional IRA terrorist campaign was really under way in the north, so the government in the south activated Clause 31 of the Broadcasting Authority Act 1960 in an attempt to control the publicity given to the acts of the IRA. This clause provides that the minister may direct the authority in writing to refrain from broadcasting on a particular subject. In October 1971, the topic so proscribed was 'any matter that could be calculated to promote the aims or activities of any organization which engages in, promotes, encourages or advocates the obtaining of any particular objective by violent means'. The organization the government had in mind was the IRA. In November 1972, an interview with Sean MacStiofain, then Chief of Staff of the Provisional IRA was broadcast by RTE. In reprisal, the government dismissed the authority. As in Great Britain, there is less scope legally and constitutionally for government interference in the press. However, when the editor of the Provisional Sinn Fein newspaper was jailed by the Special Criminal Court in Dublin, other editors were quick to point out that some of the charges brought against him under the Offences against the State Act, such as handling seditious documents, could equally well have been brought against them.

On both sides of the Irish Sea such cases of official interest and interference have created suspicions that the news from Northern Ireland is directly censored. In Great Britain such suspicions gained further credence from cases where programmes and items on the north were postponed or dropped by the broadcasting authorities, as for example the *World in Action* programme, *South of the Border*, produced by Granada. Within the broadcasting corporations the machinery for internal control over programme decisions was continually reorganized until there was a situa-ation in both networks in which controllers were closely involved in day-to-day news and current-affairs programme decisions. Smith's view in 1972 was that in so far as this had introduced censorship, it was through the ascendancy of the narrow, objective news-reporting view of the journalist's function over the more active, speculative and investigative concept associated with current affairs.

Other commentators, however, were prepared to take a wider perspec-tive, accusing the government of censorship and explaining its behaviour as the result of its need to maintain control at home in the face of the general economic crisis of capitalism overseas. An article in *Open Secret*, the journal of the Free Communications Group, argued that

because of the vicious nature of the armed terror being used to try to quell the revolt against rule by Stormont and Westminster, the ruling class have been forced to conceal the full facts from the British public. The Tories fear that too great an exposure of their aims and methods would create far too much political enlightenment at home for the comfort of their continued rule. . . . But to achieve this news suppression, the Tories have needed to do more on this occasion than simply rely on the normal middle-class bias of the gentlemen of the press and television. They have had to resort to more and more blatant censorship. This has appalled liberals of all kinds, including a lot of 'uncommitted' journalists who were already on the move politically anyway.

The article goes on to point out that the economic crisis of capitalism and the resulting development of revolt in its peripheral dependent areas like Chile and Northern Ireland had already troubled such people and though they were never going to be in the front line of any fight against capitalism, they could start to question the system. It then went on to report a meeting held at the ICA to protest against Northern Ireland censorship in which they 'did just that'.

In recent years much of the heat has gone out of this debate about censorship and bias, but it still provides an important background to the present study. Within Northern Ireland itself, the disaffection which there has been on all sides with the general media coverage of the troubles and with the way the case of particular groups has been presented or ignored, led to a growth of 'underground', 'alternative', 'partisan' or 'community' journals and pamphlets. This development, like the use of mass public protests and demonstrations, was also contemporaneous with similar developments elsewhere. Many of these journals have only had an ephemeral life, related to some particular group or issue in the conflict. Others have established themselves as continuing organs serving some particular cause or section of the community. A study of such journals would clearly be important in any analysis of the competing ideologies and perspectives on the conflict available to people in the province. It falls outside the scope of the present research, however, which is concerned with those images, perspectives and ideologies which are made available to the general public through mass media run by public or commercial organizations and staffed by professional journalists. Both the Belfast morning papers come close to the border of such a distinction. Each finds its audience almost exclusively in one of the two sections of the community in the north, but both are public news media. One of the themes which runs through the following chapters is an attempt to identify and analyse the nature and extent of sectionalism and partisanship in the *News Letter* and the *Irish News*.

They differ from each other and more conventional newspapers in appearance as well as content. The *Irish News* is printed on poor-quality paper with uncertain layout and typography. Bernadette Devlin recalls the paper with its stories of Catholic festivals, Irish sports, nationalist politics and careful recording of the saints days as part of the background to her Northern Ireland childhood. The paper is both cheaper and shorter than its rivals. Much of the limited editorial space is devoted to sport and it carries few features or photographs. It also carries little advertising. Apart from the usual entertainment and consumption advertisements, most directed specifically at the Catholic minority, it also carries official jobs adverts and information notices and occasionally adverts and notices from republican groups drawing attention to their activities. Among the typographical errors and poorly aligned columns of the *Irish News*, it is possible to find some very odd stories apparently lifted straight from the wire services and included as fillers.[1] On 10 October 1974 the only news story on its editorial page was a two-line report that at least fifteen Calcutta dock workers had been arrested to break the go-slow at the port, according to the Dock Labour Board. Two days early it reported on its front page that a young couple, killed five days before their wedding, had been married posthumously at Tonjong Karang, Southern Sumatra, according to the Antara News Agency in Jakarta.

This item was also front page news on the same day in the *News Letter*. The *News Letter* has less problems with layout and typography, carries more photographs and features than its rival, presumably has more staff and resources and generally looks more like a modern newspaper. It too, however, has been ridiculed by metropolitan journalists for its apparent lack of professionalism in the reporting and presentation of stories. The paper specializes in lead stories with banner headlines proclaiming some new threat to the majority community in no uncertain terms. The sectionalism of the two papers is often clear from their headlines and choice of front-page leads. Gay Firth in *Fortnight*, for example, noted the reporting of the findings of the Scarman Tribunal as a striking case of divergent interpretation. While the *News Letter* led with 'B Specials Exonerated', the *Irish News* headlined 'B Specials-Murderers'. Her conclusion at that time was that while the *Irish News* was often confused because it tried to incorporate all shades of Catholic and nationalist

---

1. It is a little unfair on the *Irish News* to single out this practice for comment when it is not unknown in the conventional British local press and also occurs in the *Belfast Telegraph*. For example, both the *News Letter* and the *Belfast Telegraph* carried a brief report one day that the New Zealand Minister of Tourism, Mrs Whetu Tirikatene-Sullivan, had given birth to a boy after having labour pains in her office.

opinion, the *News Letter* was more single-minded in its opposition to Catholicism and more inclined to print speculative stories, only tenuously linked to the course of events. Even the camera can be made to lie. Nelson (1976, p. 165), notes that when Unionist and Loyalist leaders were trying to identify the civil-rights movement with republican or 'extreme socialist' agitation as a 'front' for a well-planned IRA campaign, the *News Letter* 'revealed its skill at hunting down the lone tri-colour flag in a civil-rights march and printing photographs of it'.

Both these two papers are locally owned. The third, however, the *Belfast Telegraph*, is part of the Thomson Group. It is a commercial evening paper with a substantial amount of space devoted to classified advertising, much like any other to be found in the larger cities of the United Kingdom. Perhaps it is this sense of familiarity which has made the metropolitan journalists who ridicule the morning papers turn to it with relief.[1] More than that, however, throughout the troubles the *Belfast Telegraph* has received a series of accolades for the professionalism of its reporting in difficult circumstances.

Charges of censorship, bias and distortion tend to be applied very widely to all media or general classes of media such as television or the press. Implicitly, however, most charges refer to British-based or British-owned media, partly because they are the most prominent and partly because of Great Britain's colonial role in Irish history. There is an assumption that the Irish press and broadcasting services take a different view, again mainly because of their country's different involvement in past history and the present crisis. The Irish daily papers vary between themselves in political outlook and particularly in their view of the north and republicanism. There are three morning papers published in Dublin. The *Irish Press* is most closely identified with Fianna Fail, currently the main opposition party in the republic and historically the party of republicanism. The *Irish Independent* is generally associated with Conservative Catholicism while the *Irish Times* puts more value on the Anglo-Irish link than many Irishmen, certainly more than many of the correspondents to its letter columns, who regularly accuse it of being soft on the colonialists. RTE radio carries a lunchtime news programme, *News at 1.30*, modelled on the BBC radio programme, *The World at One*. The new format for radio news was introduced in the 1960s to allow items to be dealt with at greater length and depth in a feature section following the conventional bulletin.

Sample and method

The previous section described the newspapers and news bulletins included in this study and set out the principles by which they were selected. The media may be divided into three main groups: British, Northern Irish and Irish, according to their place of publication. This is the main basis

---

1. As for example Simon Winchester (1975) in his account of the time he spent in Northern Ireland as the *Guardian*'s correspondent.

of comparison used in the following chapters. There are, however, important differences within each group, and, cross-cutting the differences in location, the technical and organizational differences between broadcasting news media and the press. So far as the British media are concerned, there are individual differences of style and policy between different papers and programmes, as well as broad differences between the popular and quality press. Similarly in Northern Ireland, while each medium has its own characteristics, the two Belfast morning papers have been grouped together as the 'sectional press' on the grounds that their appeal is mainly to one section of the community. In Great Britain again the *Morning Star*, the daily paper linked to the Communist Party, is so different from the rest of the press and the broadcast media that, when appropriate, it has been dealt with separately. References to the British media or British press in this report should always be read as excluding the *Morning Star*. The other inter- and intranational differences are elaborated in later chapters.

The press and broadcast bulletins were studied for two three-week periods. The first, from 23 September to 11 October 1974, included the British general election of 10 October 1974. The second, from 21 April to 9 May 1975, included the elections for the Northern Ireland Convention on 1 May 1975. A common criticism of the coverage of Northern Ireland, indeed one which is often made generally about the whole range of subjects included in the news, is that reporting skates over the surface of events taking no account of history, social context or the social processes leading into the future.[1] In the Northern Ireland case, a further related charge has been that the news media concentrate almost exclusively on violence. The intention in picking two election periods was to minimize both these characteristics by ensuring there was more political material available to report than usual.

One important difference between the two periods was that the Provisionals were actively pursuing their campaign in the autumn of 1974, but then a ceasefire was arranged during the winter which was still in operation at the time of the second period. The level of violence in the province varied little, however. Table 2 shows the number of deaths, explosions and shooting incidents in Northern Ireland resulting from

TABLE 2. Violent events in Northern Ireland in the study periods

Date	Deaths	Explosions	Shooting incidents
September 1974	12	28	222
October 1974	19	32	271
April 1975	36	26	199
May 1975	10	17	121

Source: Fortnight.

1. This is one of the main conclusions of a comparative study of television news carried out at the Centre for Mass Communication Research. See Golding *et al*. (in press).

the troubles in the relevant months of 1974 and 1975. Though the rates for May 1975 were generally lower than those for the two months of the previous year, those for April, the month leading up to the Convention election, were particularly high. It is more appropriate to leave a discussion of why this should have been so until after we have considered the explanations which emerge from the news coverage.

As well as these incidents in Northern Ireland, one major incident, the bombing of two pubs in Guildford, occurred on the British mainland in the first period. The bombings, together with the general election, provided the British press with most of its lead stories in that period. The second period, however, coincided with the fall of Saigon and that provided a major focus of attention for the national media in both Great Britain and Ireland. Ireland also had some internal problems at that time including a major strike of petrol delivery drivers.

So far as the British and Irish media were concerned, all news which was in any way connected with Northern Ireland was included. In the Northern Irish media this was restricted to news in any way connected with the troubles. Table 3 records the average number of Northern Ireland related stories in the British media. The level of attention was low in the radio and television bulletins and those newspapers which did not have special Northern Ireland editions. Such editions were obtained

TABLE 3. British media sample
(including the *Morning Star*) (both periods)

Newspapers	Issues included	Issues missing	Mean number of Northern Ireland related stories			Total stories
			Period I	Period II	Combined	
POPULAR PRESS						
Daily Mirror	34	0	6	6	6	209
Daily Mail	34	0	6	3	5	155
Daily Express	34	0	3	1	2	69
Sun	34	0	15	15	15	51
QUALITY PRESS						
Daily Telegraph	33	1	5	4	5	155
Guardian	33	1	4	3	3	109
The Times	34	0	3	2	2	81
BROADCAST MEDIA[1]						
BBC TV *9 O'Clock News*	36	2	1	1	1	36
ITN *News at Ten*	33	5	1	1	1	32
BBC Radio 4 *World at One*[2]	19	0	1	—	1	21
COMMUNIST PRESS						
Morning Star	34	0	1	1	1	49

1. Includes equivalent programmes at weekends.
2. Period I only.

for those papers which published them. There were some supply problems, however, and, when necessary, the sample was made up with editions available in Leicester. The proportion of 'Leicester' as compared to 'Northern Ireland' editions included in the sample for each of the five papers is shown in Table 4. The two papers most affected by the supply problem were the *Daily Express* and the *Guardian* in the second period. The fourth and fifth columns of Table 4 show that editioning made little difference to the numbers of Northern Ireland related stories in the *Guardian*. There were fewer such stories in the 'Leicester' editions of the *Daily Express*, however, by a factor of 3 to 1. Apart from Northern Ireland editions missed, various newspaper and broadcasting organizations were involved in industrial disputes during the study periods. In the case of newspapers, only odd copies were lost, but there were a series of strikes by journalists in commercial television in the first period. Five editions of ITN's *News at Ten* and five of UTV's *Ulster Reports* did not appear. A few other broadcast bulletins were missed because of technical problems. Most seriously affected was the sample of RTE's *News at 1.30* because of poor reception conditions in Leicester.

TABLE 4. Different editions included in British press sample (both periods)

Newspaper	'Leicester' editions[1]	'Northern Ireland' editions[1]	Total number of issues included	Mean number of Northern Ireland related stories	
				'Leicester' editions	'Northern Ireland' editions
Daily Mirror	3	31	34	...[2]	6
Daily Mail	2	32	34	...	5
Daily Express	19	15	34	1	3
Daily Telegraph	2	31	33	...	5
Guardian	12	21	33	3	3

1. The papers vary in the names they give to these editions. These terms have been used to provide a common indication of the location in which the editions were available.
2. ... = too few issues of that edition to provide a meaningful average.

The number of missed editions for the Northern Ireland and Irish media are shown in Tables 5 and 6. In the first period, only the *Irish Times* and RTE's *News at 1.30* were studied. Preliminary analysis, however, suggested that there were important differences between these and their British counterparts so the other Irish papers were added in the second period to widen the scope for comparison. Again, however, there were supply problems. The *Irish Press* sample was particularly affected. These tables also record the mean number of stories from each of these media included in each period. The level of attention to Northern Ireland and related news was much higher in the Irish media than the British. In Northern Ireland itself, the *Irish News* is a good deal smaller than the other two Belfast papers. On the average, the space available for news in the *Irish News* was about half that available in the *News Letter* and less than half of the space in the *Belfast Telegraph*. The fact that it carried fewer stories related to

TABLE 5. Northern Ireland media sample (both periods)

Newspaper	Issues included	Issues missing	Mean number of 'troubles related' stories			Total number of stories
			Period I	Period II	Combined	
Belfast Telegraph	32	2	25	21	23	732
News Letter	34	0	25	21	23	783
Irish News	34	0	19	20	19	660
BBC TV *Scene Around Six*	29	1	8	7	7	216
UTV *Ulster Reports*	25	5	8	9	8	212

TABLE 6. Irish media sample (both periods)

Newspaper	Issues included	Issues missing	Mean number of Northern Ireland related stories			Total number of stories
			Period I	Period II	Combined	
Irish Times	32	2	15	17	16	509
Irish Press[1]	12	5	—	11	—	130
Irish Independent[1]	17	0	—	11	—	187
RTE Radio *News at 1.30*	28	10	5	7	6	154

1. Period II only.

the troubles than its rivals reflects the smaller space at its disposal, not a difference in philosophy.

It is noteworthy that there was a general tendency for the level of attention to Northern Ireland or the troubles to drop slightly from the first to second period in the British media and British-oriented media in Belfast (*News Letter* and *Belfast Telegraph*). In the *Irish News* and the two Irish media for which comparable data are available the level of attention was maintained. Anticipating later chapters in which it will be argued that there is a broad difference in the way these two types of media interpret the violence of Northern Ireland, it may be that this is related to the fact that the Provisionals were active in the first period, formally inactive in the second.

Individual stories as separately presented in each of the media studied were taken as the basic unit of analysis. Most of the attention counts presented in the tables in later chapters are based on counts of individual stories. Most types of story vary in length so that proportional counts based on numbers of stories produce similar results to counts based on measures of space. In his studies of British press reporting of race and industrial relations, Hartmann showed there was a high correlation between measures of space and story counts. In this study, particular attention has been paid to those types of news in which this was not the case, as, for example, reporting of court cases related to the troubles discussed in Chapter 2. The story unit, however, particularly in the press with its headlines, spatial boundaries and accompanying illustrations is both a unit used in the work of journalists researching, writing copy and making up the paper and also a measure of prominence for readers. Story counts provided a measure of the attention given to a particular subject but more than that the story unit enabled comparisons to be made across media in their treatment of the same story.

There is a problem in the choice of the media defined story as the unit of study. Separate stories, in the sense of reports of discrete incidents or developments are often run together in the press, occasionally in broadcasting, to produce a composite story. The problem is not avoided by measuring attention in terms of space. Indeed, it is one which standard coding procedures largely ignore. Sometimes such composite stories were explicitly presented as round-up accounts of the news on a particular topic. The Belfast newspapers, for example, commonly treated election news and minor violent incidents in this way, giving round-up accounts of both on a daily basis. Sometimes, however, there was no clue in the headline or first paragraphs of the story that it would move on to other topics later. In most cases the later incidents reported were of the same type as the first so that they were effectively round-up stories. In some cases, however, and particularly in the British quality press, it was Northern Ireland itself which provided the focus of the round-up so that the reporter's piece would deal with all the important developments of the day in Northern Ireland—violent, political or whatever. In all cases counts reported in this study are based on the media defined story unit, taking as the subject of the story the topic which appeared in the headline and first few paragraphs. Substories (the incidents reported in later paragraphs) were separately recorded for study, however. This was important to allow comparison of the way the same incident was treated in different papers and broadcast bulletins.

Conventional content analysis techniques record the incidence of different types of content using a previously prepared coding schedule. Their strength lies in producing frequency counts of different types of content which can be further cross-tabulated to show the interrelationship of different themes and subjects, as for example in Hartmann, Husband and Clark's survey of *Race as News*. The result can be a comprehensive and analytic survey of the general way in which the subject is treated in the media studied.

Such techniques, however, are not well adapted to dealing with the treatment of particular stories. It is difficult to set up categories in advance to differentiate between various treatments of the same story. Inevitably such reports overlap in many of the facts included but diverge in nuances of emphasis, presentation and selection. It can be argued of course that the similarities are more important than the differences, but that would be more appropriate as a conclusion than as a presumption.

The method adopted for this study was designed to record both the general treatment of the subject, as measured by basic frequency counts, and the detail of the way individual stories had been handled in particular papers and bulletins. Each media-defined story unit was recorded on two sheets, the media sheet and the story sheet. The media sheet was designed to record frequency of occurrence by medium. It was divided into rows horizontally by media and columns vertically by type of news, location of news event and actor identifications used in some types of story. The story sheet was designed to record the teatment of the particular incident or development by different media. It was divided into columns which recorded which media covered the incident, the date on which their report appeared, the space, prominence and any pictorial illustration given to it and then a synopsis of their account. If a newspaper or broadcast bulletin only reported a particular incident as a substory, their treatment of it was recorded on the story sheet but not the media sheet. Subsequent analysis was carried out by hand by summing frequencies on the media sheets and sorting and resorting the story sheets. These sorts are equivalent to the codes put into the initial schedule in the traditional type of analysis. The method has the advantage, however, of keeping the researcher close to the original material and allowing him to reformulate the coding frame in the light of experience with it.

The synopses recorded on the story sheets were divided under four headings—actors, event, news angle, commentators and comments. The first two are largely self-explanatory. Under 'actors' particular attention was paid to the way each medium identified or described those involved, looking for the labels used to classify particular types. Standard identifications in general news reporting include age, sex, occupation and eminence or position, but in Northern Ireland actors may be identified with one or other section of the community, a particular organization involved in the conflict or simply described as a participant in a violent act as, for example, by the term 'gunman' or 'bomber'. By 'news angle' was meant that aspect of the event which had been singled out for special emphasis by the particular medium. For example, a *Daily Mirror* lead story headlined 'Cave In' reported not some underground disaster but the authorities' decision to reintroduce privileges for internees and detainees at the Maze Prison. The headline and initial presentation of assassinations, often paid particular attention to the personal characteristics of the victims. Reporting inquests and court cases, the media often paid more attention to the accounts of the past events reported at the hearing than to the outcome of the hearing itself. Similarly with political developments, some media built their story around subsequent reactions, dealing with the development itself later in the presentation. Frequency counts were based on what the story was about in the sense of the event or development reported, not the particular news angle adopted. The main area in which the alternative strategy would have altered the counts was in the classification of court reports as 'law enforcement news' rather than 'violence' even though the report was angled around the original incident of crime.

Under the fourth heading, 'commentators and comments', were listed all those whose views on the event were quoted, including the views which the medium itself supplied without any other attribution. Violent events, for example, are commonly condemned by politicians and other community leaders. Inquests and court cases regularly give law officers an opportunity to pass comment on the cases before them. Stuart Hall (1975) has referred to such people in broadcast news and current affairs programmes as primary definers, drawn from the major institutions of society and authorized to provide a reaction on behalf of the society to some threat of conflict or change. Hall's analysis stresses the homogeneity and stability of British society and the support it receives from the broadcast media. He has argued elsewhere (1972) that recent crises in British broadcasting have been prompted by an increased heterogeneity in the society. The writ of the primary definer no longer runs for all members of the society. This is even more likely to be true in a case like Northern Ireland where there are clear social and political divisions. If a large proportion of the population does not accept the basic legitimacy of the society, there would then seem to be little scope for primary definers. On the other hand, when the demonstrations gave the civil-rights protesters and their supporters a platform in the media, Protestants found themselves powerless to counter the views except by giving vigorous expression to their anger and frustration. Each section of the community in Northern Ireland may be able to produce its own definers to give its own particular view, but these are likely to be more acceptable to some media than others, introducing another aspect of sectionalism in news reporting. Such sectionalism might appear in the selection of commentators to give reactions to all types of development including both violence and political news. It might also be supplied by the medium itself in the form of estimates of the reaction to an event or development. 'Waves of horror' in reaction to violence or 'furious rows' in politics are as much a product of the phrases journalists use to write stories as of any realistic assessment of public or elite reaction. This means that the journalist or his paper has some scope in deciding how much weight he should give to such reactions in particular cases. In Northern Ireland this means playing up or playing down the views of a particular section of the community.

The next three chapters each deal with a particular type of news related to Northern Ireland to investigate the accounts and perspectives on Northern Ireland and the troubles provided by the various media in their news coverage. More detailed definitions are provided in each chapter of the broad categories which were used as the basic measures of media attention. Even with the limited scope available on the media sheets, more categories were provided initially than proved useful in analysis. In subsequent presentation these have been reduced to four—violence, law enforcement, politics and other. This reduction has effectively ironed out most problems of ambiguity in the coding frame provided on the media sheets. These ambiguities that remained were in the division between law enforcement and violence news and this is one reason why the two types are discussed together in the next chapter. Chapter 3 deals with political news and Chapter 4 with other types of news. This last heading of other news brings together several different types of story which were originally counted separately on the media sheets. The analysis in Chapter 4 is mainly based on the story sheets, however, as the attempt to subdivide other news produced small numbers of cases under ambiguous headings. A more general survey of the various images of the province and its troubles apparent or implicit in the coverage of the different media and an account of their origin in the practice of journalism is to be found in the Conclusion (Chapter 5).

Chapter 2

Violence and law enforcement news

Definitions

All media news related to Northern Ireland or the 'troubles' there was grouped under four main headings—'Violence', 'Law Enforcement', 'Politics' and 'Other'. There was some overlap between news in the first two categories to be discussed in this chapter in cases where it was ambiguous whether the story dealt with the aftermath of a violent event or with security operations following it. Stories were classified according to the main news point presented in the headline and the opening paragraphs. The technique of summarizing reports on story sheets enabled event, aftermath and follow-up stories to be examined together and then compared across media. The two types of news 'Violence' and 'Law Enforcement' were defined as follows for the media sheets:

Heading	Subdivision	To include
Violence news	Events	All acts of violence, hoaxes or potential acts of violence (except those which occurred in the course of collective protest).
	Aftermath	The aftermath of such acts, including inquests and compensation awards.
	Threats	Predictions or threats of future violent events.
Law enforcement news	Against the Provisional IRA or other Republican	
	Against Loyalist paramilitaries	Security operations, investigations and arrests. Remand proceedings. Court proceedings.
	Against other, unattributed or unknown	
		The deployment and activities of the security forces. Security forces personnel and their activities.

The majority of the stories included under the heading of law enforcement reported remand proceedings and court cases.

British media

The first column in Table 7 shows that these two types of news accounted for nearly two-thirds of the stories in all the British media. Within this overall figure, however, there was some variation in the attention different types of medium paid to the two types. Stories about violent events received most attention in the national television news bulletins, less in the popular newspapers and least in the quality press. Law enforcement stories, however, made up a larger proportion of the output of both types of newspapers than of the television news bulletins.

TABLE 7. Main types of Northern Ireland story in the British media: periods I and II

Type of story	Number of stories (percentages)			
	Press and television ($N=897$)	National television ($N=68$)	Quality press ($N=346$)	Popular press ($N=483$)
Violence	30	50	26	30
Law enforcement	33	22	32	35
Politics	24	22	31	19
Other	14	5	12	17
TOTAL[1]	101	99	101	101

1. In this and subsequent tables, totals may not equal 100 because of rounding off.

The first finding seems to support the claim that the news on television over-emphasizes violence. It is doubtful, however, whether the results also support the argument which often accompanies such a claim, that violence is attractive to television, a visual medium, because it is a visual phenomenon. For the first period data is available for the BBC radio programme, *The World at One* (see Table 8). This radio programme

TABLE 8. Main types of Northern Ireland story in British and Irish media: period I

Type of story	Number of stories (percentages)					
	British television ($N=44$)	British quality press ($N=193$)	British popular press ($N=280$)	BBC Radio *The World at one* ($N=21$)	RTE Radio *News at 1.30* ($N=75$)	*Irish Times* ($N=255$)
Violence	61	28	30	62	29	14
Law enforcement	23	29	35	14	31	25
Politics	11	31	20	19	31	39
Other	5	13	15	5	10	23
TOTAL	100	101	100	100	101	101
Mean number of stories per issue/bulletin	1	3	4	1	5	15

carried an even larger proportion of violent incident stories than the two national television bulletins. Apparently, it is not the visual aspect of violence so much as its immediacy that is important in accounting for the emphasis on violence. Radio is the fastest medium, bringing up-to-date news of the latest events. Violent incidents are sudden unexpected events which lend themselves to this type of immediate reporting. Many television news stories, including many reports of violent incidents, were simply read by a newsreader to camera and so could be regarded as visual radio news of much the same immediate type.

Another qualification to the argument that television carries violent events because they are visual is that only rarely can television show the occasion of violence itself. Generally, all that can be shown on the screen is some aspect of the aftermath of the event—pictures of property damage, subsequent security operations or interviews with victims or witnesses. The longest violent event stories on television were those which included such interviews. This was true regardless of how serious the incident was. Again an immediacy factor seems to be important, as if the aim of the news story was not just to say what had happened, but also to tell what it was like to be there.

Commentators have often suggested that a gradual escalation of terrorist violence is inevitable because there is a macabre calculus of publicity values according to which property damage is worth less space than a death and one death less than many. Deaths were more likely than other sorts of incident in Northern Ireland to get a mension on national television news but they did not necessarily get more space. The same was true of the British press coverage.

These points were graphically illustrated by the incident in Northern Ireland which took up most space in British press and television in the first period. This was an abortive hijacking and bombing mission which did not result in injury, damage or even the arrest of those concerned. Gunmen hijacked a light aircraft from a private flying school in Ireland and forced the pilot to fly over Northern Ireland where they dropped a home-made bomb. The British media were in no doubt that the IRA were behind the operation, but were somewhat divided over its significance. Some suggested the aerial attack was intended to back up a contemporaneous ground attack on an army post at Crossmaglen. Others linked it with the Provisional Sinn Fein conference being held in Dublin that same weekend as a token show of enterprise and daring, while others saw it as a response or warning to Enoch Powell currently campaigning in South Down. The *Guardian* thought the whole affair was a bit of a joke, pointing out that the plane did not reach its target, the bomb did not go off, and the ground attack on the army post was no more than firing heard in the distance, according to the army. The popular papers and the *Daily Telegraph* made much of the fact that the hijacked pilot of the plane was not just an Englishman, but a wartime pilot decorated for his service in Lancaster bombers. He even looked the part, complete with handlebar moustache, when he told his story on television. The *Daily Telegraph* billed him as the brave silent Englishman, suitably reticent about his courage. The *Sun* headlined 'My IRA Bomb Run by the Wingco'.

Both newspapers and television featured pictures of the plane as well as its pilot.

In general, the story was a good example of an incident which achieved prominence because of the various ways in which it could be developed and presented. It was not quite the story which had everything, in the sub-editor's phrase. No women, no children and no animals were involved. But it certainly had plenty, an appeal to British folk memories of the war and an opportunity to make the IRA look both sinister and ridiculous. In contrast to the general run of violent stories from the north, there was more to report than simply that the incident had happened. Moreover, although there was some doubt about the significance of the incident, neither that nor its attribution to the Provisionals were particularly contentious.

In other incidents, attribution, the identity of victims and the significance of the events are often highly ambiguous if not contentious. For example, again in the first period, a British army colonel was shot and injured by a single gunman at his home in Wiltshire. The *Daily Express* immediately concluded that this was the work of the IRA. The colonel led a regiment which had served in Northern Ireland even though he had not served there himself. The *Sun*, however, reported unequivocally that detectives and army chiefs 'do not believe the IRA were involved', that the would-be assassin did not have an Irish accent and so identified him as a 'grudge' gunman. Other British papers reported that police were looking for a motive, as did the media of Ireland and Northern Ireland though with the added information that an Irish connection had been ruled out.

A few days later, after the Guildford pub bombings, the police announced they were now looking for a man, 'the man in black', in connection with that event. In Great Britain most papers and the broadcast news bulletins began to speculate whether the same man was involved in both incidents. In Northern Ireland itself, both the *Irish News* and the *News Letter* carried the story in spite of the earlier account both had given of the shooting of the colonel. It seems clear that it was the police themselves who started this press speculation. What is less clear is why they did so. The case illustrates news-media dependence on the police and security forces to make sense of events for them, in particular to supply information on the identity of the victims and the perpetrators and also, implicitly or explicitly, a motive. It also illustrates a tendency on the part of British popular newspapers to jump to the socially acceptable conclusions about such details, i.e. that the Provisional IRA was responsible for any violence. The example of the *Sun* shows, however, that this tendency, while clear, was not entirely consistent.

Table 9 shows that in all British media most attributions of responsibility for violence were to the Provisional IRA or some other republican group. Compared to television, the press carried a larger proportion of attributions in its stories of violence. Presumably this reflects the greater caution exercised by television newsmen in not jumping to conclusions on an aspect of the event on which it might be difficult to secure accurate information, but which might turn out later to be highly contentious. By contrast, relatively few television stories did not identify the victims of

TABLE 9. Attribution of violence in Northern Ireland in the stories
of the British media: periods I and II

Group	Number of stories (percentages)			
	Popular press (N=144)	Quality press (N=89)	National television (N=34)	Press and television (N=271)
Provisional IRA or other Republican	38	39	18	35
Loyalist paramilitary or Protestant	10	8	12	6
Law enforcement	3	1	0	2
No attribution, other or unknown	49	52	70	57
TOTAL	100	100	100	100

violence as members of the security forces or as members of one or other religious community. Such information is both more accessible than attributions, in the sense that if a victim's identity is known, his religion or membership in the security forces can easily be checked and more likely to be available in the case of the major incidents which make up most of the television coverage.

There was a paradox implicit in the general consensus of the British media that most of the violence could be attributed to the Provisional IRA or another republican group and that most of the identified victims were law-enforcement agents or members of the Catholic community. The consensus was that 'Catholics' were both the main perpetrators and one of the main victims of violence. This suggests it is a poor version of the truth, though of course it has not been unknown for members of different republican groups to attack each other and there were several such incidents in the second period. The paradox was implicit, however, in the sense that it emerged only from a numerical analysis of the detail of the stories and not from an immediate reading of the news angles the British media used to report the violence.

Such news angles did include attribution to the IRA, particularly in the headlines of the popular press. But when victims were identified with one of the two religious communities this was done in the course of the story, not as the main news angle. Most often it was an individual attribute of the particular incident or victim that provided the most prominent news angle. Such attributes as the particular misfortune of the individuals involved, for example, that they were pregnant, about to leave the province or should not have been there at the time; the ordinariness of the occasion—that it happened at work, on the way to work or as the family relaxed at home; the particular bravery of someone involved or the particular horror of the act itself, provided the material for the headline writers to differentiate one incident from another. By contrast, when the victim was a member of the security forces, this fact was likely to appear immediately in the headline. A surface reading of the immediate news points would lead to the conclusion that violence related to Northern Ireland was carried out by the IRA against members of the security forces and that many other people were suffering apparently at random. A more detailed accumulative reading would show that many of these others were Catholics and a further detailed, sensitive exploration would reveal that Loyalists were responsible for some of the violence.

This analysis is based on the different aspects of the conflict which appear to be most salient at different levels in the content. It does not depend on identifying different readers with different levels of attention, to whom the various images are apparent. Rather it is an account of the way the different aspects were presented in the news reports. None of the British media seemed inclined to make capital out of the fact that one section of the community rather than another was suffering. Membership of the security forces, however, was likely to provide a main news angle. In the case of the British media, this was not simply a consequence of the fact that such information was more easily and speedily available than a victim's religion. It built into an impression of the security forces' role in the province which might be summarized as brave, inactive suffering.

From the British press reports almost the only active part the security forces played in events in the province was issuing warnings of expected terrorist activity. Otherwise, their members were involved in incidents but invariably as targets though occasionally they returned fire; soldiers and policemen won awards for bravery, took part in public parades, occasionally helped ordinary citizens and were compensated for injuries received. All the compensation cases reported in the British press in both periods involved members of the security forces except one which was a record award to the widow of a magistrate who had been assassinated. The only smudge on the British army's reputation in the account given of its action in the British press were a few reports of court cases involving individual soldiers.

The British media did not entirely ignore the fact that some of the perpetrators of the violence in the provinces were Loyalists. In each period, the emergence of a new Loyalist group claiming responsibility for a series of murders was a news event in its own right. Nevertheless, the British media did tend to use the ambiguous label 'sectarian' to identify those incidents in which Protestant extremists were involved and to couple reports of murders by such groups with explanations in terms of Loyalist anger, reprisals or a Protestant backlash.

The two new Loyalist organizations which emerged were the 'Young Militants' in the first period who telephoned RTE in Dublin with the claim that they had killed several Catholics and the 'Protestant Action Force' (PAF) who telephoned the *Belfast Telegraph* with a similar claim in the second period. In the telephone call the 'Young Militants' announced that they had been forced to act because the authorities had not put down the IRA. In the first stories in the British press on 28 September, this justification was taken up by all the papers except *The Times* and the *Guardian* which simply reported that a new group had emerged, and the *Sun* which did not have the story at all. Over the next three days, two more Catholics were killed and a Protestant injured. The *Daily Express* and the *Sun* attributed the violence to Loyalists, but also provided them with justifications—'fanatical protestants angered by the IRA murder of two law chiefs are thought to have been responsible' (*Daily Express*, 30 September 1974). BBC TV *News*, the *Daily Mail* and *The Times* described the killings as sectarian. The *Daily Mirror* managed to transform the story into 'Concern over Action by IRA', reporting that the army now feared some big IRA action after the reprisals carried out by Loyalist teenagers provoked by the actions of young IRA assassins who had killed the judge and the magistrate. In the second period, the emergence of the PAF was only reported by the *Guardian* and the *Daily Mirror* among the British media.

The guarded and ambiguous treatment of Loyalist violence in the British media contrasted with the treatment of republican violence. This was presented partly as if the events were related to a planned campaign, as if there really was a war in progress but also as if they were simply senseless random and unpredictable events. The view of terror as a planned campaign was presented in various references to who or what were now regarded as legitimate targets by the Provisionals. In the first period, for example, several British papers carried a story, apparently originating in the *News Letter*, that following the murder of Judge Conaghan and Magistrate Birney the IRA were now threatening civil servants in Northern Ireland. According to the *Daily Mail*, this sinister new development was aimed at destroying the Northern Ireland judiciary and meant that even girl typists would be at risk. The *Daily Express* reported that the authorities were not taking the story seriously, the *Daily Telegraph* that they were. Such 'threat' stories were much more apparent in the British press in the first period when they accounted for just over 7 per cent of all violence news stories. In the second period, there was only one such story in all the British papers. The difference seems to be that the Provisional IRA had declared a ceasefire before the second period. The security forces had less need to warn the public to be on their guard and were less concerned about putting out scare stories implicating the IRA in some new villainy. The British press was less concerned to print them. In the first period, however, the 'threat' stories carried with them the idea that the IRA was waging a campaign and aiming at targets with a purpose.

Explicitly, however, very little attention was given to that purpose. Provisional Sinn Fein held its annual conference in Dublin in the first study period. There were two stories about it in the national BBC television bulletins, but both dealt with security aspects. The *Daily Express* gave the security aspects of the conference a passing mention, while *The Times* referred to the policy proposal for 'an autonomous Ulster within a federally-structured state' at the end of another story. Only the *Guardian* and the *Daily Mirror* reported the conference as a story in its own right, the latter under the paradoxical headline 'IRA's Fear—Secret Pullout of Army'. The fear was that a sudden withdrawal might precipitate a Congo-type situation. The Northern Ireland *News Letter* headlined its conclusion from the conference that there was no hope of a ceasefire as the Provisionals planned to keep up their campaign. As reported in the *Guardian*, Rory O'Brady, President of the Provisional Sinn Fein, urged the British Government to emulate De Gaulle's phased withdrawal from Algeria not Belgium's withdrawal from the Congo. He also complained that Sinn Fein's policy for an independent Northern Ireland within a federal Ireland was either ignored or censored by the media. In Ireland itself, the *Irish Times* reported the conference on its front page and published the whole text of O'Brady's speech inside, and RTE derobed more than a minute of its lunchtime bulletin to the story dealing both with the speeches and the security aspects. In Great Britain, however, these few reports of the conference were the only accounts of the aims of Provisional Sinn Fein carried by the media in both periods.

Instead, the tendency of the British media was to report violent events as simply irrational and horrid. Indeed, the relationship was usually portrayed as causal rather than simply conjunctive. Such events were irrational because they were horrid. The clearest example of this was in the reports of the Guildford bombings. These were headlined in terms which emphasized the youth, feminity and innocence of the victims as well as their being members of the British army. Much attention was paid to the story's human interest aspects such as those mentioned generally above. The aspects which made news were lucky escapes, the irony of being bombed in the middle of a birthday celebration or even simply while taking a drink, the bravery of an ordinary landlord and his good fortune in clearing his pub. The military campaign account of IRA activities was present in the coverage as, for example, in the *Daily Mail* which announced 'IRA Wage War on Women'—'Sinister New Move in Campaign of Terror'. But so too was the view that such acts were irrational. All the British media quoted the comments of Roy Jenkins, the British Home Secretary, who went beyond an expression of horror, condemnation and sympathy, to describe the event as 'a perversion of human reason which showed the dark forces of violence and terror at work'. This was a particularly graphic statement of a recurring theme in the comments made on such events. An expression of horror was run together with the suggestion that the act was irrational—a conflation perhaps best expressed in the double meaning attached to the word 'senseless'.

The reporting of the Guildford bombings also clearly illustrated the British media's preoccupation with events on the British mainland as compared to those occurring in Northern Ireland. In the first period, twice as many people were killed in Northern Ireland as died at Guildford and, as well as incidents involving fatalities, there were a series of other incidents in the province resulting in injury, property damage or simply a disturbance of the peace. The Guildford bombs, however, took up two-thirds of all the space in the British media reporting violent events in the first period. The remaining third was devoted to incidents in Northern Ireland (see Table 10). In the *Morning Star* and the two Irish media studied for this period, the *Irish Times* and RTE's midday radio news bulletin, these proportions were reversed.

The Guildford bombs were also unique in that, unlike any other

TABLE 10. Space devoted to violent incidents in Great Britain, Ireland and Northern Ireland: period I (percentages)

	British television ($N=2,088$)[1]	British popular press ($N=2,002.5$)	British quality Press ($N=1,206$)	Morning Star ($N=51.5$)	Irish Times ($N=449$)	RTE Radio News at 1.30 ($N=1,087$)
Great Britain	68	63	71	35	32	30
Ireland	0	0	0	0	0	8
Northern Ireland	32	37	29	65	68	61
TOTAL	100	100	100	100	100	99

1. $N=$ Column inches or seconds.

violent incident in either period, they became a running story. The bombs went off on the night of Saturday, 5 October, and the first news appeared in the television bulletins, the same evening. All the papers led with the story on Monday except the *Guardian* and the *Daily Express* in which it figured prominently on the front page. This was in spite of the fact that it had by then been reported on radio and television on Sunday and in the Sunday newspapers. At the end of the week, the last day of the study period, all the British papers except the *Daily Mirror*, and one television station, the BBC, were still reporting follow-up stories. By contrast, few killings in Northern Ireland in either period were reported on for more than one day in the British press. Those that were were cases like the shooting of the official IRA leader Billy McMillan or the bus inspector, UDA Captain Millar, when the victim's funeral was a news event in its own right. At McMillan's funeral, Cathal Goulding, Chief of Staff of the Official IRA, gave the funeral oration; at Millar's, the Belfast bus crews came out on strike.

The contrast between the prolonged attention given to the Guildford bombs and the staccato procession of incidents in Northern Ireland does not simply reflect the importance which British news editors attached to events on the mainland as against those in the province. It also reflects much more fundamentally the different societies in which these events were taking place. The follow-up stories showed British society united against an external threat. After the bombings, there were messages of horror and sympathy to be reported from such leaders of British society as the Queen, the Prime Minister and the leader of the opposition. The Mayor of Guildford set up a relief fund for the victims to which the breweries owning the pubs contributed. Reports were published about the condition of the injured in hospital, the funerals of the victims and the impact of the incident on the life of the town.

Two political issues developed as a result of the bombings, first, the question of whether capital punishment should be reintroduced for murder in terrorist cases, second, the question whether the Price sisters would be transferred to a jail in Northern Ireland to serve their sentences for other terrorist offences there. Both these issues were taken up most vigorously by the more conservative papers, the *Daily Telegraph* and the *Daily Mail*, presumably because they saw an opportunity to make political capital, and by the BBC, both on television and in its radio news programme, *The World at One*. In practice, none of the party leaders tried to exploit these issues in the election and they were left to Conservative Party mavericks and the papers themselves. Nevertheless, the story provides a good example of the general phenomenon noted elsewhere (Elliott and Golding, 1973) of the way in which Parliament and the party system quickly becomes involved in any type of social conflict in Great Britain. Their role as agencies of conflict resolution is reinforced by the attention it receives in the news media.

After the incidents in Guildford great attention was paid to the police hunt for the bombers. This first centred on two girls whose identikit pictures appeared in the papers but who were found and eliminated. It then turned into a hunt for 'the man in black', a name for the public to conjure with like the 'black panther' whom the police had been looking for earlier in connection with a kidnapping and several murders of sub-postmasters. From the similarity of the reports appearing in the different papers and the attributions made to police sources, it is clear that the police themselves supplied most of this information about the progress of their inquiries including the possibility of a link with the army colonel's attacker, though, as mentioned earlier, the police appeared to have ruled out any 'Irish connection' in that case. The point is that both the police and the press seemed to want to keep the story alive, presumably to show that the forces of law and order were fully mobilized against the threat and that the leaders of society and those connected with it were at work expiating the outrage. The only sour note in the coverage was various reports that the remaining pubs in Guildford were thinking twice about serving service personnel, a policy of which the papers did not approve. The stories reporting it carried defensive quotes and denials from publicans and the breweries.

The function the news media perform after such incidents by keeping the story alive almost regardless of the intrinsic news value of the events themselves which occurred in the follow-up period, might be termed social cauterization. Each day society applied a new dressing to the wound. This is possible in a society in which there is fundamental unity and stability, in which the dignified and efficient elements of the constitution, to borrow Richard Crossman's terms, can act together on such occasions of external threat, in which there is general support for the forces of law and order and political mechanisms for pursuing and resolving marginal disputes arising from the threat. All these conditions are missing in the divided society of Northern Ireland. The result in the British news media is that incidents occurring there are reported and then dropped. Where the society does not mobilize, the news media cannot cauterize. The form this takes within the province itself will be further discussed below in the section on the media in Northern Ireland.

Another aspect of the mobilization of society against the threat posed by terrorist activities is the trial and conviction of those involved. The clear-up rate for terrorist offences has been much higher on the mainland than in Northern Ireland, though, overall, there have been many fewer incidents and so subsequent court cases. Again, the British media paid much more attention to such cases before the English and Scottish courts than in the province itself. Reports of cases related to the troubles before the courts on the British mainland took up four-fifths of all space devoted to court cases in the British popular press, rather more in the quality press and all the time given to terrorist court cases on the national television news bulletins. If anything Table 11 understates this concentration as the only papers which reported cases in Northern Ireland at any length were the *Daily Mirror*, the *Daily Mail* and the *Daily Telegraph* presumably because these were the papers with the most distinctive Irish editions.

TABLE 11. Location of court cases covered in the British media

	Television ($N=490$)[1]	Popular press ($N=1,779.5$)	Quality press ($N=890$)
Great Britain	100	82	88
Ireland	0	6	4
Northern Ireland	0	12	8
TOTAL	100	100	100

1. N=column inches or seconds.

In all, eight trials took place or were immediately pending in England and Scotland in the two periods studied. One of these, the Coach Bomb Trial in Wakeford of Judith Ward, accounted for most of the coverage. The reporting of this trial continued the process of cauterizing the wound to society by recounting the horrors of the incident within the context of massive security operations for the trial itself and revelations of the way the police had tracked down their suspect. Judith Ward herself was treated both as a callous monster (she was reported as laughing in a pub at the time the bomb went off) and as a rather pitiful inadequate (there was plenty of detail about her chequered employment record in the WRAC and as a stable-girl with a circus). Though there were passing references to her as an 'IRA girl' or the 'IRA bomber', the reports only established personal links with the organization such as she had Republican literature, a Republican boyfriend, made Republican jokes rather than treating her as the visible tip of a much wider conspiracy. In so doing, of course, the news media were simply following the form of the trial in British justice which holds individuals not organizations responsible.

Nevertheless, it seems likely that the process of social cauterization is better served by showing a monstrous but fallible individual being brought to justice than by any reminder that the cause and organization for which she worked still has the support and strength to act again. Just as in the reporting of violent incidents, it was the human interest aspects of the event and its victims which provided the main news points, so in the court reports, it was human interest details about the accused, the

victims, the survivors or the event itself rather than the blow dealt to
the terrorist organization to which the accused belonged by her arrest
and trial. Table 12 shows that in a large proportion of law enforcement

TABLE 12. Identification of groups against whom law enforced
in law enforcement stories in the British news media: periods I and II (percentages)

Group	Television (N=15)	Popular press (N=167)	Quality press (N=110)
Loyalist organizations	0	10	8
Provisional IRA and other			
Republican organizations	80	48	45
Unidentified or other	20	42	47
TOTAL	100	100	100

stories in the press no explicit mention was made of who the enforcement
was directed against. In those cases in which it was, the same proviso
applies as to the figures for attributions and victims, reported in Table 9
and 13. Identifications usually occurred in the body of the story rather
than as the main news angle.

TABLE 13. Victims of violence in Northern Ireland in the stories
in the British media: periods I and II

Victims	Number of stories (percentages)			
	Popular press (N=144)	Quality press (N=89)	National television (N=34)	Press and television (N=271)
Law enforcement	28	24	32	27
Catholic	28	24	35	27
Protestant	10	9	12	10
Other or unknown	34	43	21	36
TOTAL	100	100	100	100

The *Morning Star*

As mentioned in the introduction, the *Morning Star*, the British daily
newspaper associated with the Communist Party, has not been included
with the other British media in this analysis. Reference has already been
made in this section to the consensus view to be found in the British
press and television on the nature of the troubles and on the primary
importance of any mainland events or connections. Reference has also
been made to the exceptional instance of the *Morning Star* in its relative
lower interest in the Guildford bombs (Table 10). The *Morning Star*,
however, was more than a vehicle for a few exceptional cases. Taken as
a whole, its coverage represented a complete alternative view of Northern
Ireland and its troubles from that to be found in the other British media.
So far as the reporting of violence and law enforcement is concerned,

this took the form of playing down the role of the IRA, playing up that of violent Loyalists and portraying the Catholic community rather than law-enforcement agents as the chief victims of continuing violence. The *Morning Star*, however, did not report the conflict in religious or sectional terms but in political terms as a conflict of Unionists and Unionist extremists against anti-Unionists. In all, the paper carried fifteen stories of violent incidents in the two periods. In seven cases, violence was attributed to Unionist extremists, in two to the IRA and in one to the British army. In six cases, the victims were identified as anti-Unionists, in one as Unionist and one as a member of the security forces. Similarly, the seven stories reporting law enforcement included one in which the enforcement was reported as being against a Unionist extremist, one against a member of the IRA. Behind these figures was a consistent interpretation of violence in the province as Unionist extremist intimidation of the anti-Unionist population of the province. For example, in the first period the *Morning Star* took the emergence of the 'Young Militants' claiming responsibility for the assassination of Catholics as clear evidence of a diehard Unionist campaign to intimidate anti-Unionist voters. In the second period, the paper took a similar line on the feuding between various Republican groups in which Billy McMillan, the Official IRA leader was killed, reporting that British intelligence was involved in an attempt to frustrate the election activities of the official Republican movement.

For all the *Morning Star*'s interpretation looks odd, given the consensus to be found elsewhere in the British media, it is not completely implausible: in Northern Ireland in the periods included in this study fifteen Catholics were killed, six Protestants, one member of the security forces and one other.

Northern Ireland media

In the two sectional newspapers in Northern Ireland, the *Irish News* and the *News Letter*, violence and law enforcement news did not account for the majority of Northern Ireland stories or 'troubles-connected' stories.

TABLE 14. Main types of 'troubles' story in the Northern Ireland media: periods I and II (percentages)

Type	Number of stories				
	Irish News (N=660)	*News Letter* (N=783)	*Belfast Telegraph* (N=732)	BBC TV *Scene Around Six* (N=216)	UTV *Ulster Reports* (N=212)
Politics	39	37	26	22	16
Law enforcement	20	25	38	31	43
Violence	19	19	22	33	31
Other	21	19	14	14	10
TOTAL	99	100	100	100	100

Table 14 shows that about 40 per cent of all stories in these two papers came under these headings as compared with 60 per cent in the *Belfast Telegraph*, 64 per cent in the BBC local television news programme and 74 per cent in the commercial equivalent, *Ulster Reports*. The three newspapers carried about the same proportion of violence news stories, but the proportion of law enforcement news was much larger in the *Belfast Telegraph* than in the sectional press. The proportion of violence news stories in the two television programmes was larger than in the press and so was the proportion of law-enforcement news. This proportion was strikingly large in UTV's *Ulster Reports*. Law enforcement news accounted for more than 40 per cent of its stories.

The predominant types of law-enforcement news were court reports of cases connected with terrorism ranging from arms offences to murder and wounding charges. There were also some cases of armed robbery, theft and extortion which were related to the troubles in that they had been carried out to raise funds for paramilitary organizations on one side or the other and not for personal gain. It was occasionally ambiguous as to whether such cases were 'connected with the troubles' and so should be included in the study. As a general rule, ambiguous cases were included rather than excluded.

On television, these court reports were presented in a routine format as a succession of brief items, lasting between 10 and 20 seconds, read by the newsreader to camera. Out of a total of 158 law-enforcement stories on both channels in both periods only twelve dealt with cases in Great Britain or in Ireland (Republic). The two local television news programmes followed a national news bulletin on each channel. *Scene Around Six* was also part of the BBC's national, local news programme, *Nationwide*. To have covered trials in Great Britain, therefore, would have been to reduplicate the national coverage. The few stories which did appear picked up some particular local news angle from the defendant's past or the events recounted in the trial.

Reports of trials in Northern Ireland itself were not only brief but routine in style, reporting the offence, a summary of the events, the decision of the court, the age, sex and area of residence of the defendants, occasionally giving their occupation and other trial details. As shown in Table 15, it was unclear from most of the court reports on both television channels whether defendants belonged to one of the paramilitary organizations and, if so, which. Such information usually emerged from the case itself if the defendant was charged with membership of the Provisional IRA or from demonstrations in court by the defendants or their supporters. Neither television programme paid much attention to the details of the proceedings, reporting few of the statements of judges and magistrates condemning the criminals and their crimes and the pleas in mitigation or alternative accounts of the case given by the defence. One of the few cases in which the television reports included such condemnations and excuses involved a Protestant whose defence to an arms charge, conducted by Desmond Boal QC, was that he had been preparing for the doomsday he expected when the British army withdrew. Otherwise, legal comments were only quoted regularly in those cases in which

TABLE 15. Identification of groups against whom law enforced in law enforcement stories in the media in Northern Ireland: periods I and II (percentages)

	Number of stories				
	Irish News (N=133)	*News Letter* (N=198)	*Belfast Telegraph* (N=278)	*BBC TV Scene Around Six* (N=66)	*UTV Ulster Reports* (N=92)
Loyalist organizations	17	13	14	11	9
Provisional IRA and other Republican organizations	34	31	28	24	22
Unidentified or other	49	56	58	65	69
TOTAL	100	100	100	100	100

the accused were found not guilty, apparently to explain why such a verdict was appropriate.

Such stories were usually among the longer reports together with other cases which were 'unusual' in other ways. These included odd crimes, such as a man who burnt his own taxi as a protest against continuing assassinations and the man who was preparing for doomsday; odd cases such as a murder trial in which an elderly lady testified about the general atmosphere of violence in Andersonstown and one in which a policewoman was praised for her bravery in preventing an assassination and cases which involved special points of law such as whether a magistrate had the power to stop the publication of the address of the accused.

Court reporting in the Belfast newspapers followed a similar pattern. Most cases in Northern Ireland were reported in a brief, routine fashion. Table 16 shows that the average length of case reports was 6 column inches in the two sectional papers and 9 inches in the *Belfast Telegraph*. The same odd and unusual stories were covered at greater length in the newspapers as on television. The *Irish News* also covered a few cases

TABLE 16. Total and mean length of court reports from different locations in the Northern Ireland press and *Irish Times*: periods I and II

	Irish News		*News Letter*		*Belfast Telegraph*		*Irish Times*	
	Mean	Total	Mean	Total	Mean	Total	Mean	Total
Great Britain								
Coach bomb trial	6[1]	6	27	245.5	33	330.5	18	129
Other	11	113.5	15	224	13	194	11	96
Ireland (Republic)	8	38.5	6	35.5	11	115.5	12	255.5
Northern Ireland	6	620	6	610	9	1,587	4	92.5[2]

1. One report of pre-trial security.
2. Excludes one 'unique' case (see pages 317-18).

which involved Loyalist paramilitaries at greater length. For example, in the first period it carried two stories over 20 column inches long reporting, first, the conviction of a UVF man for the murder of his Catholic workmate and, second, the refusal of bail to a UDA man who beat up a Catholic who refused to contribute to a collection he was making for the association. These stories were reported in the *News Letter*, but much more briefly (13 column inches in all) and without the emphasis on Loyalist paramilitary involvement. Three headlines from the second period neatly illustrate this apparent sectionalism. A story which appeared in the *Irish News* as 'Life for 2 Loyalist Assassins' appeared in the *Belfast Telegraph* as 'Murderers Toured City Looking for Victims' and in the *News Letter* simply as 'Life for Murder'. However, the *Irish News* was by no means consistent in playing up Loyalist involvement. A similar story in the second period which appeared in the *Belfast Telegraph* as 'Murderous Two Get 15 Years for Wounding' was only reported in the *Irish News* as a sub-story to an IRA explosives case. Neither the *Irish News* nor the *News Letter* in its report mentioned that the two men had been connected with the UVF, though there were demonstrations of support in court.

Apart from this tendency—itself by no means consistent—for the *Irish News* to play up Loyalist paramilitary involvement and the *News Letter* to play it down, there was no other sign of sectionalism in the press coverage of the Northern Ireland court reports. The *Irish News* carried a few lengthy stories in which the accused clearly belonged to the IRA. For the most part, membership of that organization or a Loyalist paramilitary group had to be deduced from the text of the report in all three papers. The same factors as in the television news reports provided the basis for such deductions—charges of membership of the IRA, refusals to recognize the court and demonstrations by the accused or their supporters. Table 15 shows that on this basis there was no striking difference between the three papers in the proportion of stories they carried reporting law enforcement against one side or the other. Compared with the television stories, however, the newspaper stories were more likely to include the details from which a deduction could be made.

The newspapers also carried more detail in that they were more likely to report the 'condemnations' and 'excuses' that emerged in the course of the trials. The *Belfast Telegraph* carried more of these than the other two papers, but then it also reported more court cases at greater average length. As can be seen in Table 17, the number of condemnations and excuses carried was not large even in the *Belfast Telegraph*. The distribution of those that did appear, however, does not suggest sectionalism between the different newspapers so much as that defence pleas in mitigation were more likely to be entered or at least more likely to be reported when the accused did not appear to be associated with a paramilitary organization.

The *Belfast Telegraph* again appeared to be more 'professional' than its rivals in the sense that its news judgements in this type of reporting were based on similar criteria to those of the national media and the local

TABLE 17. 'Condemnations' and 'Excuses' appearing in the Northern Ireland court reporting of the Northern Ireland media: number of cases

	Irish News	News Letter	Belfast Telegraph
'Condemnations' of			
Members of IRA or other Republican group	1	1	5
Members of Loyalist paramilitary group	3	3	4
Members of the security forces	1	–	2
Other	1	1	5
'Excuses' for			
Members of IRA or other Republican group	1	–	1
Members of Loyalist paramilitary group	2	2	3
Members of the security forces	1	–	1
Other	6	3	14
TOTAL	6	5	16
TOTAL	10	5	19

broadcast media. The longest Northern Ireland court report to appear in that paper in the two periods was an account 33 column inches long of a case in which a trooper in the British army was cleared of the manslaughter of a wedding guest. This was one of the few cases to become a running story and then it appeared on only two days. In all it took up a total of 75.5 column inches in three stories in two days in the *Belfast Telegraph* compared to a total of 22 column inches in the other two papers. The story was a good example of the professional criteria of news value in that it was unusual—a member of the security forces had been charged; it had human interest—the soldier had shot a guest at a wedding and authority was upheld—the judge said the soldier had not been negligent.

The way the *Belfast Telegraph* shared these criteria with the national media was also apparent in the coverage it gave to the coach bomb trial in England in the first period. As can be seen in Table 10, its longest report of a case in Northern Ireland was only as long as the average of the reports the paper carried on the coach bomb trial. To put it another way, on average a report of the coach bomb trial was nearly four times as long as a report of a case in Northern Ireland. The coach bomb trial reports were very similar to those in the British press, recounting the horror of the event, the security at the trial and the personal history of the accused, Judith Ward. The *News Letter* also reported the trial at length and in the same vein, but the *Irish News* ignored it, carrying only one brief story about the security measures being taken before the trial. The *Irish News* only reported at length on three of the other trials in England and Scotland connected with terrorism. Two of these were cases in Scotland against men associated with Loyalist paramilitary groups and the other was the extradition of Kenneth Littlejohn, known almost universally in all the press as 'the so-called British spy', to face bank robbery charges in Dublin. The two Loyalist trials in Scotland were both reported at length in the *News Letter* and the *Belfast Telegraph*, but so, too, were various other cases in England involving members or sympathizers of the Provisional IRA. Very few stories about terrorist cases in the Republic of Ireland appeared in any paper. Those that did were reported in the same brief style as the Northern Ireland cases.

It will be apparent from this discussion that sectionalism in this area mainly took the form of the *Irish News* playing up its coverage of trials involving Loyalists at home and abroad and playing down those involving republicans in England. Sectionalism in the reporting of violent incidents was also restricted to a few aspects of the subject. Prominent among these was the attention given to Catholic victims in the *Irish News*, the lack of attention they received in the *News Letter* as well as lack of attention to Loyalist paramilitary groups as perpetrators of violence. Otherwise, the media varied little in the proportion of stories carrying attributions of violence to one of the three sources, republican, Loyalist or law-enforcement agency. Attributions to both types of paramilitary groups were higher on the television programmes than in the press, presumably because television coverage concentrated on the most 'important' events which resulted in the loss of life, injury or property damage, cases in which attributions were clearer or even claimed by those involved. A similar explanation would account for the fact that the television programmes also identified proportionately more victims than the papers. In all media except the *News Letter*, the largest proportion of victims identified were Catholic (Table 18). Members of the security forces made up a smaller proportion, though still larger than Protestants in all media except *Ulster Reports*. In the British media, it will be remembered (Table 4) that the proportion of Catholic victims identified was roughly equal to that of law-enforcement victims and the incidents themselves were much more uniformly attributed to the Provisional IRA or other republican organizations.

Table 19 also shows that the *Irish News* carried a relatively large proportion of stories reporting violence attributed to the security forces. Most of these took the form of verbatim allegations of the harassment of election workers, demonstrators or ordinary citizens from local branches of the Provisional or Official Sinn Fein. One story, however, at the end of the first period went beyond such routine retailing of complaints, reporting an army raid on a home in the Falls Road area of Belfast. Headlined 'No Glory in Gloster Raid', the story told how the young mother of a seven-month-old baby sobbed at the home of a neighbour. She had been made homeless by the third army search of her house in a week. As if to point up the difference from the usual harassment stories it carried, the *Irish News* was at pains to point out that the paper had sent a reporter who had found the house in a shambles. He also found a local councillor prepared to condemn the troops as animals and their behaviour as a most outrageous act comparable to the Falls curfew. A neighbour was quoted as saying the troops should pick on someone their own size, not a mother and her baby whose husband had been recently imprisoned for twenty years. This harassment story was unique in both periods in that details of the incident were reported, but it only appeared in the *Irish News*.

TABLE 18. Victims of Northern Ireland violence in the stories in the media in Northern Ireland and Ireland: periods I and II[1] (percentages)

				Number of stories			
Victims	Irish News (N=123)	News Letter (N=150)	Belfast Telegraph (N=164)	BBC TV Scene Around Six (N=72)	UTV Ulster Reports (N=65)	Irish Times (N=37)	RTE Radio News at 1.30 (N=22)
Law enforcement	15	17	17	22	15	24	27
Catholic	42	15	24	36	37	19	4
Protestant	13	13	13	12	18	13	4
Other or unknown	30	55	46	30	30	44	65
TOTAL	100	100	100	100	100	100	100

1. Except for Irish media in which case period I only.

TABLE 19. Attribution of violence in Northern Ireland in the media of Northern Ireland and Ireland: periods I and II[2] (percentages)

				Number of stories			
Group	Irish News (N=123)	News Letter (N=150)	Belfast Telegraph (N=164)	BBC TV Scene Around Six (N=72)	UTV Ulster Reports (N=65)	Irish Times (N=37)	RTE Radio News at 1.30 (N=22)
Provisional IRA or other republican	15	15	12	17	21	13	14
Loyalist paramilitary or Protestant	11	4	7	17	11	13	4
Law enforcement	12	3	7	0	3	0	0
No attribution, other or unknown	60	78	74	66	65	74	82
TOTAL	98	100	100	100	100	100	100

1. Except for Irish media in which case period I only.

Otherwise, on two occasions news conferences were called by different branches of the republican movement to present evidence of British army involvement in harassment and spying on the civilian population. Both of these received wider attention.

One was reported extensively in the British press following an incident in which a soldier in plain clothes was shot and injured while sitting in a car in a Catholic area of Belfast during the weekend immediately prior to the second study period. Among the British papers, the *Sun* had no doubt that this was an 'IRA Ambush'. Most of the other papers, however, reported that the Provisional IRA denied responsibility, that the army said the man was on administrative duties, but that local people thought he was a spy. By Wednesday, the British press reported that the Provisionals had admitted responsibility, and the following day that they had played some tapes found on the soldier to journalists to prove their claim that he was a spy and so that the army had broken the ceasefire. The Irish papers took the allegations further, reporting the claims of Provisional Sinn Fein spokesmen that the information on the tape showed that the British army was operating assassination teams.

The story received a good deal more attention in the British and Irish press than in the Northern Ireland media which scarcely covered it until the Provisionals admitted responsibility for the shooting. On the following Tuesday, there were long stories on both local television news programmes reporting the Provisionals' claim that the army had breached the ceasefire. These were followed on Wednesday by reports of the press conference at which the tapes were played together with the further IRA claim that the soldier was a member of a 'murder squad' and subsequent army denials. The story received most attention in the Belfast press on Wednesday when each paper printed a rather different version. The *News Letter* led with the story that Rees had condemned the Provisionals' attempted murder as a breach of the ceasefire and went on to recount all the breaches of the ceasefire to date before finishing off with the Provisionals' statement that they had tape recordings to prove the soldier was a spy. The *Irish News* gave less prominence to a story that while the Northern Ireland office claimed the soldier had been on administrative duties, the 'Provos' claimed to have tapes to prove he was a member of an SAS team. The *Belfast Telegraph*, publishing later, was able to report that the tapes had been played. It also carried a further story reporting government denials that four-man SAS assassination teams operated in the province and a restatement that the soldier was on administrative duties checking the ceasefire. The story provides a rare example of a Provisional IRA statement and press conference, beyond a simple denial or claim of responsibility, being taken seriously by media other than the *Irish News*, presumably because it was backed up by the evidence of the tapes.

The incident also illustrates some aspects of the sectionalism to be found in the *News Letter*'s reporting of violence. At this time the *News Letter* seemed to have adopted a definite policy of trying to expose what it persistently dabbed 'the so-called ceasefire'. In its first report of the incident in which the plainclothes soldier was injured, it quoted comments from two prominent loyalists. A Unionist convention candidate said that it showed the reality of 'the so-called ceasefire' and a spokesman from the Orange Lodge that it showed the need to retain Sir Frank King as GOC Northern Ireland. If he were to be dismissed then it would be further evidence that British policy was to appease the IRA. (In fact King was replaced a few days later.) The paper picked up comments from members of its own section of the community and used them to tie the incident into the wider concerns of that section.

Table 19 shows that the *News Letter* printed relatively few stories in which the violence was clearly attributed to loyalists. Nevertheless, when the two new paramilitary groups, the 'Young Militants' and PAF, revealed that they had been waging an assassination campaign against Catholics, the *News Letter* carried both stories, though not at great length and on an inside page. In both cases, the paper quoted condemnations from Alliance Party politicians. No Unionist politicians were quoted and the only Loyalist to give his views was the Grand Master of the Orange Lodge who condemned PAF unreservedly as a sinister development on the eve of the (convention) election. The 'Young Militants' declaration in the first period specifically referred to an incident for which they had been responsible in which a priest had been injured the day before. This had been the lead story in both the *Irish News* and the *News Letter*, both of whom quoted condemnations from two Protestant churchman and the leader of the Alliance Party. Reporting the Young Militants' declaration, both papers again agreed in quoting first a comment from a spokesman for the security forces that they hoped this sectarianism would only be a 'flash in the pan' and then quoting condemnations by 'centre' politicians from Alliance and NILP. In general, neither of these declarations was featured prominently and extensively in any of the Belfast media including the *Irish News*, though PAF claims formed the basis for a lengthy news story on both television channels. In contrast to the coverage given to them in the British press, the Northern Ireland media, including the *News Letter*, did not quote the justifications which the claimants gave for their acts—that they were trying to make up for the inadequacies of the security forces. Nor did the Belfast media supply them with others, such as that a Protestant backlash was to be expected following the assassination of Judge Conaghan and Magistrate Birney.

The shooting of the priest and the Young Militants' declaration provided a comparatively rare example of agreement between the *Irish News* and the *News Letter* on whose views they should quote. Table 20 shows that it was more usual for the two papers to quote comments in condemnation from politicians associated with their own section of the community. Nevertheless, there was some overlap in the centre. The *Irish News* carried seven condemnations from politicians in Alliance, UPNI or NILP, the *News Letter* nine. There was also some similarity in the quotation of the views of church leaders (both papers quoted more Catholics than Protestants) but this was largely because the *News Letter* quoted condemnations, such as the Pope's statement following the Guildford bombings, as if to underline that even leaders of the Catholic Church had been moved to speak out.

TABLE 20. Sources quoted in the media of Northern Ireland and Ireland (Republic) in condemnation of violent incidents and developments: periods I and II

	Irish News	News Letter	Belfast Telegraph	BBC TV Scene Around Six	UTV Ulster Reports	Irish[1] media
Politicians						
UUUC	—	7	5	1	1	2
NILP	1	4	1	—	—	—
UPNI	1	—	1	—	—	2
Alliance	5	5	—	—	—	5
SDLP	14	1	4	4	4	18
Republican[2] clubs	8	1	1	1	1	6
Church leaders						
Catholic	9	4	3	32	1	7
Protestant	2	2	—	2	—	—
Relatives, friends, witnesses or otherwise connected	6	3	8	6	7	4

1. Includes the *Irish Times* and RTE Radio *News at 1.30* both periods and *Irish Independent* and the *Irish Press* period II only.
2. This table does not include condemnations of harassment by the security forces. The cases included were condemnations of incidents resulting from the feuding between republican groups in the second period.

Too much should not be made of the results shown in Table 20 as the figures are small. Nevertheless, two other comments can be made. First that the non-sectional media quoted politicians from both sides, though the sectional papers made most use of Alliance spokesmen as if they provided a common meeting ground between the two sections of the community as all-purpose condemners of violence, not linked to either section. Second that the non-sectional media made more use of statements from relatives, friends, witnesses or others connected with the victim. This seems to indicate the greater attention these media paid to the twin values of human interest and accurate reporting of the immediate incident. A curious consequence of the attention given to the latter news value, particularly on television, was that many incidents were described as motiveless because in the immediate aftermath police spokesmen were not prepared to say why a particular victim had found him or herself subjected to violence. This was reinforced by the comments of friends and relatives who were regularly quoted as being baffled why such a terrible thing should have happened to such a pleasant, unassuming and uninvolved person. An example of this occurred towards the end of the second period on 2 May 1975 when a bus inspector was shot dead in Belfast. Reporting the incident the next day, the *Irish News* noted that the inspector had belonged to the B-specials, but it was not until the *Belfast Telegraph* appeared in the afternoon that it was publicly reported that inspector Millar had been a captain in the UDA. The *Belfast Telegraph* picked this information up from a death notice published that morning in the *News Letter*. The *News Letter*'s own report of the incident made no mention of it. Both television programmes had carried the story the previous evening before the UDA connection became apparent. Three days later when the busmen had decided to strike on the day of Millar's funeral in protest against the lack of security for bus crews, *Scene Around Six* reported their plans at length. A busman's leader was quoted as saying the incident showed there was something wrong with security if such a thing could happen to the inspector as there had never been any sectarianism on this job, never any trouble among bus crews. The following day *Scene Around Six* carried another story on the strike and reported the large military-style funeral which the UDA had held for Millar.

To call an incident in Northern Ireland 'motiveless' can only be true in a very specific, technical sense. But the notion has a similar general application to the notion of 'senselessness' discussed earlier in connection with the British media. The day after the assassination of the inspector, four British papers reported the incident, including the *Daily Mirror* which quoted police sources as saying there was no apparent motive for the attack. Later the *Daily Mirror*, *Daily Telegraph* and *Guardian* reported the funeral and the strike. The latter noted that the motive for the murder had not been established. Millar might have been a victim of the feud between the UDA and UVF, but the police had not ruled out possible IRA involvement. The *Guardian* was the only national or local medium in Great Britain to canvass these possible explanations for the incident except the *Morning Star* which also reminded its readers that no group had claimed responsibility, but that there had been continuing violence between the UDA and UVF.

In other cases, other media, both national and local, adopted the strategy which the *Guardian* used in reporting Millar's funeral of laying possible explanations side by side. In Northern Ireland all the media made use of police accounts of incidents, but the sectional press were particularly likely to challenge or interpret these according to their own line on violence in the province. For example, soon after the killing of the plainclothes soldier at the beginning of the second period, three Catholics were killed by a bomb planted in a farmhouse which they were renovating near Dungannon. Two theories were canvassed to explain this incident, one that it was an IRA booby-trap bomb intended for troops searching empty property, the second that it was a Loyalist bomb planted as part of a continuing campaign against Catholics in area which had come to be known as the 'murder triangle'. The local television news reports referred to it as a booby-trap bomb though they recorded that the police had an open mind on the two theories. So did the *Belfast Telegraph*, the *Irish News* quoted various Catholic spokesmen who had no doubt it was a Loyalist sectarian attack. A local priest complained that the television reports had left the question open when there could be no doubt because of other incidents in the area. The *News Letter*, on the other hand, reported only Royal Ulster Constabulary (RUC) speculation that it might have been a booby-trap intended for British troops. All the British papers except the *Daily Telegraph* reported the incident as a probable sectarian attack, most attributing this view to the police. The *Daily Telegraph* reported the theory that it might have been intended for the army, but then also quoted denials from the local IRA unit. Both television bulletins, however, described the incident as an intended attack on soldiers, in one case attributing this view to the army, in the other to the police. Nine days later, when the PAF declared itself, the bombing of the farmhouse was one of the incidents for which it claimed responsibility. Both local television programmes reported the PAF declaration, including this claim, but neither pointed out to their viewers that this was somewhat at odds with the story they had been told on both channels when the murders themselves had been reported. It seems to have been a case in which the television news organizations, both nationally and locally, played safe when reporting the incident, both in the sense that they followed the official version and in the sense that as that was itself ambiguous they emphasized the most acceptable version, according to which Northern Irish violence is primarily caused by the IRA. At the time of the incident, the *Irish News* came out unequivocably with an attribution to Loyalist extremists, but that was the line to be expected from the paper and its commentators from the Catholic community. The testimony of the local priest, Father Desmond Faul, for example, could be discounted on the grounds that he was well known as being in sympathy with the republican cause. By the time it was clear that on this occasion the *Irish News* was right, the incident had passed into history. The immediacy factor in news values, together with each medium's desire to maintain its credibility, ensures there

is little scope in the news for rewriting the past, however recent.
— Discussing the coverage of violent incidents in the British media, a contrast was drawn between the staccato presentation of incidents in Northern Ireland and the extended attention paid to those in England as British society cauterized its wounds. In the Northern Ireland media, incidents in the province itself were covered in the same staccato fashion as the British press. This seems to underline the point that this is a consequence less of styles of presentation adopted by the media than of the means society in general has for coping with internal violence. Immediately prior to the first period, two prominent Northern Ireland law officers, Judge Conaghan and Magistrate Birney were assassinated. These murders were followed up in all the media with stories about police attempts to pursue the killers, with condemnations from various community and religious leaders and with a statement from the judge's daughter in which she hoped her father's death would bring people to their senses so he would not have died in vain. The *News Letter* also ran two stories about sinister new threats from the IRA posed by the murder of the law officers. This follow-up was not extensive by comparison with the aftermath of the Guildford bombs, but it was remarkable within Northern Ireland in that no other incident in the two periods received similar treatment. The difference seems to be that in this case an attack had been made on the 'establishment' of the province which brought some of the same mechanisms into play as were activated by an attack against the more united English society.

Apart from this case, there were other incidents in which the victims funeral or some other event provided the occasion for subsequent news stories. The funerals, however, such as that of the official IRA leader Billy McMillan or the UDA Captain Millar were very clearly occasions on which sections of the community mobilized, not the society as a whole. In two cases the other events reported subsequently were the arrest of those responsible, but these were quite brief formal announcements. Only in the case of the judge and the magistrate were there news stories about the lines of inquiry the police were following after the crime. In the second period, there were also a few brief announcement stories of the recent rate of arrests for terrorist crime. These were couched in terms such as '35 Travelling Gunmen Arrested' so there was no indication whether the clear-up rate was improving or which recent cases, if any, had been solved.

Another type of aftermath story were reports of inquests, and awards made for compensation or for bravery. The delay between the incident and the inquest meant that many inquest stories became repeat stories of the incident, so much so that it was only apparent towards the end that these were inquest reports. The television programmes carried few reports of inquests and compensation cases and then mainly in the same brief, routine format as the court reports on television. The *Belfast Telegraph* carried most of this type of story. In its account of inquests it usually quoted the coroner's condemnation of those responsible. It was not usually known, however, who they were and the inquest hearings did not pay much attention to the question which group or section of the community might have been involved. The coroner's statements, therefore, were simply general condemnations of violence.

Apart from follow-up stories about particular incidents, there was one other form of continuity in the coverage through the repeated use of various concepts and labels. At the least specific level, there was a continual repetition of the labels used to describe the perpetrators of violence either in terms of age—'youth', 'man'—or in terms of the technique of violence employed—'gunman', 'bomber'. The continuity supplied by such terms was simply repetitive violence. More specifically, however, some incidents were differentiated from this repetitive stream and labelled by date or location. In the first period a man injured by the Abercorn bomb—the bombing of a restaurant in Belfast—had recovered sufficiently to be able to marry. These labelled incidents generally had a particular sectional connotation so that the Abercorn bomb, like 'Bloody Friday', was an occasion when bombs apparently planted by the IRA resulted in extensive death and injury among the general population. They symbolized the IRA threat to the (Protestant) civilian population. On the other side, there were labelled dates and incidents symbolizing the threat to the Catholic community posed by the security forces and Loyalist extremists. Pre-eminent among these were the incidents of 'Bloody Sunday' in Derry. Reference has already been made to a comparison with the Falls Road curfew in an *Irish News* story and to the currency which that paper and others gave to the concept of the 'murder triangle' around Portadown and Dungannon. In the *Irish News*, 'murder triangle' meant an area with a high incidence of the sectarian assassination of Catholics, but the *News Letter*, supported by various Loyalist politicians, tried to redefine it as an area in which there had been a large number of attacks on members of the security forces.

Such concepts and labels are also interesting for the way they reveal a common stock of knowledge available in a community. Journalists are able to make use of this stock simply by repeating a concept without needing to reiterate on each occasion what it stands for. At the beginning of the first period the *Belfast Telegraph* reported at length on a court case which involved murder and assault apparently committed in the course of paramilitary disciplinary proceedings in a UDA 'Romper Room'. This term, which has had some currency in the British as well as the Northern Irish media, would clearly mark out the case as one involving the extra-judicial disciplinary procedures of a paramilitary group. The story was unusual, however, in that it contained this specific cue. This subject was one with which all the news organizations seemed to have difficulty in dealing. There were occasional references to such general processes as intimidation and extortion. A number of reported incidents involved knee-cappings, tarring and feathering, scarring and general beatings which are the extra-judicial punitive measures characteristic of one or other paramilitary group, but the implication was rarely drawn out in the reports of the incidents. Such reports were not written to cue the readers to bring their stock of common knowledge into play, so much as in reliance on the existence of such a common stock even though it could not be publicly recognized.

The Irish media

The information available on the media from Ireland (Republic) is less extensive than that on the British and Northern Ireland media discussed in the two previous sections. Nevertheless, Table 21, summarizing the main types of Northern Ireland story to be found in the study Irish media, suggests both a similarity between the various Irish media and a difference between them and most of the British and Northern Ireland newspapers and broadcast bulletins discussed so far. In general, the Irish media carried fewer violence and law-enforcement stories than the comparable British news media. For example, these two types of story made up only 37 per cent of the output of the *Irish Times* as compared to 58 per cent of the output of the British quality press (Tables 7 and 21).

TABLE 21. Main types of Northern Ireland story in the Irish media (percentages)

Type	Number of stories		
	Irish Times[1] (N=509)	RTE Radio *News at 1.30*[1] (N=154)	*Irish Press* and *Irish Independent*[2] (N=317)
Politics	39	39	32
Law enforcement	20	21	21
Violence	17	29	25
Other	25	10	22
TOTAL	101	99	100

1. Periods I and II.
2. Period II only.

Nearly 40 per cent of stories in the *Irish Times* were political and 25 per cent dealt with other types of news as compared to proportions in the British quality press of 31 per cent and 12 per cent respectively. A similar comparison between the British and Irish broadcast media in the first period is shown in Table 8. The proportion of violence stories in the BBC Radio 4 news programme, *The World at One* was more than double that of its counterpart on RTE, *News at 1.30*, while the BBC programme carried only about half the proportion of political stories.

One explanation for this difference is that the Irish media generally paid much more attention to affairs in the north than did the British media. Reference to the figures for the average number of Northern Ireland stories per issue, given for the first period at the bottom of Table 2, shows that the Irish media carried more stories than their British counterparts at a ratio of about 5 : 1. It is not, however, simply a question of greater interest but of the form that interest takes. In the British and Northern Ireland media, with some qualification so far as the sectional Belfast press is concerned, the 'problem of Northern Ireland' is seen mainly as one of violence. In the Irish media, the problem acquires an important political dimension. This difference of emphasis seems to reflect differences in the way the problem is regarded in the two political systems involved and differences in the social function of the news media.

The function of the British media is to contain and counter an internal threat and cauterize its consequences. The Irish media, however, in most of its coverage is simply reporting and commenting on an external situation.

The different emphasis given to violence in the broadcast news put out in Great Britain and Ireland (Republic) clearly demonstrates the importance of considering political factors involved in the relationship between a medium and the society of which it is a part as well as technical factors about the style and content of news appropriate to a particular medium. Discussing the high proportion of stories about violence to be found in the national television news bulletin in Great Britain reference was made to an immediacy factor. The explanation seemed particularly powerful given that the proportion of violent news on the most 'immediate' medium, radio, was even larger. The further comparison between the two radio news programmes suggests that the concentration on violence cannot be explained simply by technical factors such as speed or style of presentation. A comparison across the Irish media shown in Table 21 suggests such technical factors do play a part. Irish radio news carried a larger proportion of stories about violence than any of the newspapers. But reference must also be made to political factors and, in particular, to the way the subject is defined in the political culture of the society.

RTE Radio made relatively few attributions of violence, presumably reflecting the caution characteristic of broadcast media which was noted in the British case. Attributions were more frequent in the newspapers. In the second period in all papers most of these were to the Provisional IRA or another republican group. This was largely a consequence of the feuding going on between various republican groups at the time. Ignoring the stories of feuding, there were as many attributions to Loyalists as to Republican groups in the second period, a finding confirmed for the *Irish Times* in the first period in Table 19. There were very few stories in any medium in either period about violence or harassment committed by the security forces in Northern Ireland and those there were reported Provisional or official IRA allegations.

Not only did the distribution of attributions vary from those in the British press, so too did the style in which they were made. The overall tendency of the British press was to simplify by writing the IRA into the headlines, as the popular papers did in the first period, by following the official police or army versions or by grouping an incident under a collective label like 'feuding' or 'sectarianism'. Reports in the Irish newspapers were more complex. More attention was paid to the way in which any particular incident fitted in with current trends. More emphasis was placed on assessing responsibility, not simply in the sense of reciting alternative versions, but in the sense of deciding which was more likely to be correct. The Irish papers were less likely to quote official sources unless they contributed to this process of validating a version of the event. Official sources were simply one among others providing accounts, all of which were to be assessed in the light of what the journalists thought made sense.

For example, the story of the shooting of the plain-clothes soldier began quietly in the Irish papers as elsewhere, but in its first story the *Irish Independent* headlined 'Army Tight Lipped' as if to signal that the important story was not what had happened so much as why and whose account was going to be believed. Two days later, all three Irish papers covered the story, reporting the allegations of Provisional Sinn Fein and British army denials. The next day, the papers reported the playing of the tape and the Provos' news conference, but dropped the British army denials. Similarly, in the reporting of the farmhouse bombing near Dungannon, the only references to army and police suggestions that the bomb might have been a booby trap intended for the security forces were in a lengthy quotation of the Provisionals' denial in the *Irish Press* and a story in the *Irish Independent* a day later quoting a local priest's criticism of the police for not accepting that the victims were entirely innocent, the *Irish Times*, also quoted that part of the original Royal Ulster Constabulary statement in which the police had said they had not found any evidence of the farmhouse being used as a bomb factory. Two days after this incident a bomb concealed in a transistor radio went off in a Belfast chip shop, injuring four children. Reporting the incident, the Irish papers all noted that this was not the first attack on the family. Next day, reporting on the children's injuries, the *Irish Independent* also noted that the security forces in Northern Ireland had alleged that the chip shop was a bomb factory. The *Irish Independent* quoted this version not because it believed it, but to show its readers what the official sources were putting about. Describing this as an allegation was particularly significant as normally, in all media in both countries, only republican sources made allegations, official sources made statements. On another occasion after the bombing of an Orange Hall in Belfast, the *Irish Times* followed up its report of the incident with an account of the various claims which had been made justifying the attack and the denials and counter claims these had produced. After each successive assassination attempt on a Catholic in the first period, the *Irish Times* reminded its readers of the number of killings perpetrated since the IRA had murdered the judge and the magistrate.

On occasions the Irish papers also provided a longer historical dimension. After the bombing of the farmhouse in Dungannon, the *Irish Press* took up Austin Currie's complaint that no Protestant clergy or Loyalist politicians had come forward to condermn yet another killing of Catholics by Loyalists in the 'murder triangle' as a cue to provide a history of 'the troubles', starting with the civil rights campaigns and leading on to the subsequent sufferings of the minority community. The *Irish Independent* took the first anniversary of the Dublin bombs as an occasion for a lengthy retrospective report. Before the convention election it published a general story reviewing the escalation of terror prior to the poll, an escalation which made it the most violent election campaign since the 1920s.

Most victims identified with one section of the community in the second period were Catholics, but again this was partly a result of the feuds between the Republican groups going on at the time. Ignoring the feuding, most identified victims were Catholic, though there were as many identified as Protestants or law-enforcement agents, taking the two categories together. In the *Irish Times* and on RTE radio in the first period (Table 18), the order was more comparable to that found in the British media—law-enforcement agents first, Catholics second and Protestants third. The identification of victims brings out another difference in style between the British and the Irish media. Instead of concentrating on the human interest in the horror of each incident, the Irish media reports tended to be straighter and less sensational. For example, although the *Irish Independent* reported the Dungannon farmhouse bombing as 'Mother-to-be Horror Blast Victim', the *Irish Times* had simply 'Three Killed in Bomb Blast' and the *Irish Press* 'IRA Deny Bomb'. When three men were killed in a Catholic darts club, the *Irish Times* used only 6 column inches of its front page to report the news, the *Irish Independent* 4, but these stories were followed up subsequently with reports of condemnations, police inquiries, the escalation in violence of which this was a part and the victims' funerals. Overwhelmingly, condemnations of violent incidents quoted in the Irish media came from Catholic clergy and policitians associated with the minority. As shown in Table 20, twice as many condemnations were quoted from SDLP spokesmen as from Unionist and Centre Party representatives combined. The feuds between the various republican groups attracted a good deal more attention from the Irish papers than terrorist and sectarian incidents. All the papers reported the killing of Billy McMillan, the Official IRA leader, on their front pages using a total of 174 column inches of space. All the papers carried pictures, but most of the space was taken up with assessments of who might be responsible, in particular with IRSP denials in which they implicated the British army. The next day, the *Irish Times* and the *Irish Independent* reported the Official IRA's disbelief in the IRSP denials followed a day later by reports of the funeral in which Cathal Goulding, Official IRA Chief of Staff, again laid the blame on the IRSP. Eight days later, an attempted assassination of a leader of each group again prompted extensive coverage, reporting of the claims and counter-claims of those involved and assessing the current state of the feud.

The comments and accounts given of violence in the Irish media seemed most concerned to give a minority perspective, though not usually the one put out by the paramilitary groups associated with the minority. Their concern over the feuding reflected a similar interest in developments within the minority. It was particularly noticeable that in the period covered by this study the concept of the minority was no longer used by any medium except those of Ireland and, occasionally, the *Guardian*. The only politicians still using it were those in the SDLP and Ireland.

The proportion of law-enforcement stories was low in all the Irish media. Reports of court cases in Northern Ireland appeared most often in the *Irish Times* and were universally short routine accounts as shown in Table 16. The only exception among the stories covered in this study was a lengthy account of a case in which two youths, one Protestant and one Catholic, had been prosecuted for singing in the street. The police considered it a foolhardy, if not, provocative act. The burden of this report in the *Irish Times* was not to make light of the troubles as was common in the British press, but to underline the essential sadness and stupidity of the situation. In the second period, there were few reports of trials in Great Britain though the *Irish Times* carried several stories about the coach-bomb trial in the first. Reports of trials in Ireland itself were longer and more detailed than those of cases in the north. One of the longest was a whimsical account in the *Irish Independent* of the trial of a typist who had been seduced into passing secrets to a Provo. In general, there was little in these reports to suggest a process of social mobilization and cauterization in Irish society comparable to that occurring in England. The only hint of the Irish media performing such a function was in the *Irish Independent*'s account of incidents in Limerick in the second period. A warning was given, the bombs found, and no injuries caused, but the *Irish Independent* gave the incident 91 column inches reporting the local mayor's condemnation of the act as showing a 'twisted mentality', the gardai's (police) praise for the way those evacuated kept calm, the lines of investigation they were following, the extra security mounted at the nearby jail holding, among others, Bridget Rose Dugdale, and a lengthy discussion of the code given with the warning to prove its authenticity. There were no major terrorist incidents in Ireland in the course of this study such as might have involved the Irish media in a more extensive process of cauterization.

Conclusion

The general features and implications of the results presented in this chapter will be further discussed in the concluding chapter of this report. Rather than reiterate the points made above about media from different locations, this section will concentrate on a number of general points as an introduction to further analysis in the last chapter. First a word of warning is in order about the limitations which necessarily surround such generalizations. Various references have been made in this chapter to particular examples which were not entirely consistent with the general case being presented. For example, there was a tendency, particularly in the first period studied, for the British popular press to lay the responsibility for violence on the IRA, but there were particular cases where individual newspapers missed or contradicted this view, even though their rivals thought it applied to the case in question.

In so far as a general image of the conflict emerges in the British media, three factors would seem to be mainly responsible for it. Two of these are features of the way news is presented in the British media so as to be both simple and of immediate human interest. Both these features are most characteristic of the popular press, but they extend into the quality press and the broadcast media. Simplicity involves both a lack of explanation and a lack of historical perspective; human interest, a concentration on the particular detail of incidents and the personal characteristics of those involved. The result is a continual procession of unique, inexplicable events. The third factor behind the production of a common image is the reliance on official sources to provide accounts of incidents, to identify victims and attribute violence. These sources and the way they are used by the media seem to be ambivalent as to whether the conflict in the north should be laid at the door of the IRA, so as to emphasize its similarities with a conventional war, or whether it should be left as a meaningless series of incidents in which people are killed and injured and homes and businesses destroyed almost at random. In the first period, for example, prior to the ceasefire, there were several stories of possible new threats from the IRA or new examples of their devilish cunning which apparently originated from British army sources. Official sources also made the most of opportunities to show the violence as indiscriminate by emphasizing the innocence of victims or the lucky escapes of bystanders, particularly children. Politicians condemning particular outrages were inclined to take the line that violence was meaningless and senseless.

These factors were all less important in the Irish media. RTE apparently exercised considerable caution in making any explicit links between the IRA and violence. But generally the Irish papers were much more open about the information available to them, the relative value they put on it and so the account of events which seemed most plausible to them. In Great Britain, scepticism of the official account was rarely shown. Such accounts were usually explicitly identified so the reader was presented with them on a take-it-or-leave-it basis. The Irish papers often went further, not just printing alternatives but dropping versions, including official versions, they no longer believed and taking on themselves the responsibility of pointing the reader in the right direction. Moreover, the Irish media were less inclined to concentrate on simplicity and human interest in their presentation of the news. Partly this was because they were less preoccupied with the single story of violence in the north and more concerned about political developments and the political future of the province.

In Belfast itself, the non-sectional media were broadly comparable to the British media, in the sense they tended to select events according to similar criteria and present them in a similar way. There was a sharp difference, however, between the apparent social function performed by the British media when faced with a case of terrorism in Great Britain. Following the Guildford bombs, the British media orchestrated a process of social cauterization for which there was no parallel in Northern Ireland. There, the staccato repetition of particular incidents continued. There was some indication that local journalists may have been more hindered than helped in producing news about the conflict, by themselves being members of the community. For example, in reporting the role of the paramilitary groups, it seemed likely that they knew more than their metropolitan counterparts, but could report less. The two sectional papers varied from each other less in the facts they reported about the incidents than in the context in which they put them. Whereas in Great Britain the process of translating conflict into political, parliamentary debate is one of conflict resolution, in Northern Ireland political comment on violence tended to become a source of tension in itself, with arguments developing over who was prepared to condemn what sort of violence.

Chapter 3

Political news about Northern Ireland

The British media

About a quarter of the Northern Ireland stories in the British media were concerned with politics. Both study periods included elections so it is a safe assumption that the overall proportion of political stories outside election periods would be lower. The proportion of political stories was lowest in the popular press, highest in the qualities. In papers of both types, the proportion of political stories fell slightly between the first and second periods. The amount of space devoted to political news fell more sharply as the overall attention given to Northern Ireland news was lower in the second period compared to the first. In the national television bulletins, for example, there were nearly twice as many Northern Ireland stories in the first period as in the second. There was a much higher proportion of political stories in the second period, just over 40 per cent as compared to just over 10 per cent in the first.

For some time the British political parties have maintained a united policy on Northern Ireland. Its cornerstone has been that government in the province should be broadly acceptable to both communities there. In practice, this means some form of power sharing between the Unionist majority and representatives of the Catholic minority. The convention for which elections were held on 1 May 1975, was another initiative to achieve this aim, designed this time to let the Northern Ireland politicians work it out for themselves. Only the province itself, therefore, was involved in the convention election in the second period. In the first period, however, the election of the twelve Northern Ireland MPs was a relatively unimportant part of the British General Election of 10 October 1974. So far as the major parties were concerned, Northern Ireland was not an issue in the election, most seats were held with enormous, unassailable Unionist majorities and the Unionists had lost their traditional link with the British Conservative Party. From the perspective of British party politics almost the only point of interest in the elections in Northern Ireland was that Enoch Powell was standing for the United Ulster Unionists. Largely because of Powell's involvement,

TABLE 22. — Political stories in the British
and Irish media: period I (percentages)

	Number of stories				
	Popular press (N = 56)	Quality press (N = 60)	National television[1] (N = 5)	Irish Times (N = 99)	RTE Radio News at 1.30 (N = 23)
Northern Ireland Loyalist parties	64	52	4	25	30
Northern Ireland anti-Unionist parties	11	7	. . .	21	30
Northern Ireland centre parties	7	3	1	17	17
British politicians	9	22	. . .	11	4
Politicians in Ireland (Republic)	9	13	. . .	15	4
General	0	3	. . .	10	13
TOTAL	100	100	(. . .)	99	98
Political stories as percentage of total	20	30	11	39	30

1. Except for the final figure in this column these are raw figures as there were too few case
on which to base percentages.

the general election in Northern Ireland was treated in a much more
partisan way in the British media than the convention election. In the
first period most political stories in all media were about Unionist
politicians, as shown in Table 22. In the second, shown in Table 23, most
were general news and reviews of the convention elections. Even so,
there were more stories about the Unionists than any another political
party in Northern Ireland. The SDLP, the main anti-Unionist party,
received little attention in the first period and less in the second.

General election coverage—the phenomenon of Enoch Powell

Colin Seymour-Ure (1975), reviewing the general treatment of the
October 1974 general election in the British press, noted that Enoch
Powell received more attention than all the other politicians in minor
political parties put together. His dominance of the political news from
Northern Ireland was even more striking. Table 24 shows that nearly
two-thirds of the space on Northern Ireland politics was devoted to Enoch
Powell as compared to just over a quarter dealing with other Northern
Ireland politicians. The remainder—less than 10 per cent—was taken up by
stories about British and Irish politicians. Apart from Enoch Powell, the
only other continuing interest in the Northern Ireland elections for the
British media was whether Harry West, the leader of the official Unionist
Party, would manage to keep his seat in Fermanagh and South Tyrone.
Stories about this took up very little space however.

These general figures mask some important differences between

TABLE 23. Political stories in the British and Northern Ireland media: period II (percentages)

Type	Popular press (N=34)	Quality press (N=46)	National television[1] (N=10)	Irish News (N=137)	News Letters (N=143)	Belfast Telegraph (N=111)	BBC TV Scene Around Six (N=18)	UTV Ulster Reports (N=21)
				Number of stories				
Ireland (Republic) politicians	15	15	...	1	4	7	0	0
British politicians	18	22	...	7	10	21	33	24
Northern Ireland centre parties	12	9	...	24	13	11	0	9
Northern Ireland anti-Unionist parties	0	2	...	47	11	11	11	9
Northern Ireland Loyalist parties	15	13	4	2	45	22	6	14
General/mixed or other	41	39	6	19	17	28	50	43
TOTAL	101	100	(...)	100	100	100	100	99
Political stories as percentage of total	17	30	42	40	39	31	19	16

1. Except for the final figure in this column these are raw figures as there were too few cases on which to base percentages.

TABLE 24. Space devoted to various types of Northern Ireland political news: British media, period I (percentages)

Type	Popular press $(N = 887.5)$[1]	Quality press $(N = 712)$	Television $(N = 908)$	Morning Star $(N = 46)$
Enoch Powell and related	66	66	51	21
Other Ulster	33	19	49	33
Northern Ireland politics in Great Britain	0[2]	7	0	38
Northern Ireland politics in Ireland (Republic)	1	8	0	9
TOTAL	100	100	100	100

1. $N =$ column inches or seconds.
2. Less than 0.5 per cent.

individual newspapers. In three papers—the *Daily Express*, *Daily Telegraph* and *Sun*—stories about Enoch Powell took up more than 90 per cent of all space devoted to Northern Irish politics. In three others—the *Daily Mail*, *Guardian* and *The Times*—Enoch Powell took up about half the space and in the other national daily, the *Daily Mirror*, about three-quarters. These four papers all gave more space than the others to Northern Ireland politics, the *Daily Mail* strikingly so, carrying nearly double the number of column inches as appeared in each of the other three. As well as carrying campaign features on Enoch Powell, the *Daily Mail* also carried one on his SDLP opponent, Sean Hollywood; on Ian Paisley, leader of the Democratic Unionist Party within the UUUC, and Gerry Fitt, leader of the SDLP. The extent and the range of its coverage of Northern Irish politics were unrivalled in the British press. In contrast the *Daily Telegraph* focused almost exclusively on Enoch Powell. A number of stories on other subjects included apparently gratuitous references to him, for example the account of the IRA hijacking mentioned earlier in the section on violence. The *Daily Telegraph* also carried a feature discussing Powell's leadership potential in Great Britain as well as stories about his leadership chances in Northern Ireland. Altogether, the *Daily Telegraph* seemed concerned to keep Powell before its readers as a potential British as well as Northern Ireland politician, though after his two speeches on the Common Market and his implicit advice to vote Labour he received less attention.

Powell's leadership potential both in Great Britain and in Northern Ireland was only one reason why he provided such a fascinating focus of attention for the British media. He was a controversial figure. In the course of the campaign, he made two speeches in England against the Common Market. Implicitly at least he repeated the advice he had given the British electorate in the February General Election to vote Labour, a sentiment not shared by his former political colleagues in the Conservative Party or his current ones in the UUUC. Towards the end of the campaign, it became clear that his views also diverged from those of his new colleagues on the question of whether or not State aid should be given to the Belfast shipyard of Harland & Wolf. On Northern Ireland itself, he accepted the view that the conflict was a territorial war and also the consequences that the Catholic population in the north would have to give up its territorial aspirations, but that those currently fighting for them were equivalent to combatants in other wars which had been officially declared. Both views prompted strong reactions from other politicians in Great Britain and the province.

But Enoch Powell had more to offer the media than leadership potential and continuing controversy. His face and figure were well known to the British public. In the course of the election, every national newspaper carried at least one picture of him and most considerably more. Many of these had no particular news angle, but simply recorded Powell's campaign as if he were himself a variety act. Powell playing the recorder, Powell walking by the seashore, Powell speaking, watched by a girl blowing bubble gum. This same variety act quality came over in the variety of labels or identities which could be given to Powell to provide the basis for a quick picture caption if not a more extended story. As well as the various political positions he had held and views with which he was associated, a remarkable range of non-political labels were available with which to identify him. He had been an academic, a professor, a classical scholar, a soldier, a brigadier, as well as having a reputation as a biblical scholar, a practising Christian, a poet and, at least in the recorder-playing incident, a musician. The *Sun*, in a rare comment on politics in Northern Ireland, also reported that he ate black pudding for breakfast.

The media are not unaware of the part they play in creating such prominent public personalities as Enoch Powell or, in earlier periods, Brian Faulkner and Bernadette Devlin. This awareness tends to appear as resentment when their protégé rounds on them and attacks their coverage. In the course of the election campaign, Powell received some critical coverage from some journalists when he objected to questioning on why he had not made a more extensive tour of Newry, a town variously described as a Catholic or IRA stronghold. In some papers the affair reached the proportion of a blazing row in which another feature of the Powell persona featured prominently—his 'hard cold eyes'. If this incident illustrates the way in which journalists are ambivalent about their own power to create such persona, a story in the *Daily Mail* headlined 'Whatever Happened to Bernadette?' illustrates their continuing fascination.

The same preoccupation with Enoch Powell can be seen in the national television coverage. A major part of the coverage which both organizations gave to the election in Northern Ireland was a constituency survey of South Down in which Powell was the UUUC candidate. Martin Harrison (1975) in his general survey of the broadcast coverage of the election has noted that Powell was the only Northern Ireland politician whose views were quoted on either channel.

Harrison (1975, p. 142) has also noted the peculiarities of election reporting in the broadcast media which make it an unmemorable type of journalism, 'a highly stylized genre in which, however much news editors protest to the contrary, considerations of balance prevail over "news value" '. The constituency survey is one such reporting technique founded on the requirement of balance. Because there were so few stories on the election in Northern Ireland in the national broadcast media, the full range of these techniques and the way they were deployed in the Northern Ireland situation only became apparent in the provincial news bulletins. Nevertheless, it seems that these considerations, together with the fact that Northern Ireland policy itself was not regarded as an election issue by any of the major parties, contributed to the lack of attention given to politics in the province by the national broadcast media.

The fact that Northern Ireland policy was not an issue meant that there was little to report in Great Britain about Northern Ireland politics. The Northern Ireland Civil Rights Association put up candidates in some English Labour seats. Communist Party candidates campaigned in Northern Ireland and were reported as doing so in the *Morning Star*. Mr Wilson was heckled at one public meeting about the Irish question. But, except in the view of the *Morning Star*, these were all events outside the mainstream of politics in Great Britain. Only after the Guildford bombings did political issues arise related to the troubles. Demands for the reintroduction of the death penalty and the question of whether the Price sisters should be sent to a jail in Northern Ireland to serve their sentences were apparently pursued by some papers, notably the *Daily Telegraph*, because they offered the prospect of (Conservative) Party advantage. Nevertheless, it was more of a campaign for the Conservative Party the *Daily Telegraph* would have liked to see, adopting a hard line on capital punishment and the imprisonment of terrorists, than for the existing Conservative Party, whose leadership largely eschewed the opportunity to make political capital out of the Northern Ireland troubles and the terrorist campaign.

The Convention Election

The UUUC was expected to be as successful in the Convention Election as they had been in the General Election the previous year. Nevertheless, the coverage given to the Convention Election by the British media was quite different. Instead of concentrating almost exclusively on the Unionist Coalition and its candidates, newspapers and television carried many more general stories reviewing prospects for the election or the convention itself.

Enoch Powell was not a candidate for the convention. No other politician was given the full public personality treatment such as he had been accorded in the first period. There was also a technical difference between the two periods selected for study. Whereas the election came at the end of the first period, it came at the middle of the second. The second period, therefore, did not cover all the campaign period, but included just over a week after the election in which the first moves were made to set up the convention and decide on procedure.

The distribution of coverage over this time period suggests that the British media were relatively uninterested in the election campaign. The election itself and the subsequent arrangements made for the convention to meet received more attention. In other words, the British media seemed less interested in the contest for power in the convention than in the assembly itself as a mechanism which might resolve the constitutional position of the province. There was little optimism, however, that it would prove to be effective and the attention given to the convention seemed to follow more from a sense of duty that it was the British Government's initiative and as such should be reported rather than from any sense of enthusiasm that it would break the political deadlock. The *Daily Telegraph* headlined one story as a 'Convention Ray of Hope'. This reported that Glenn Barr, 'architect of the strike which brought the Northern Ireland assembly to its knees', was prepared to work with anyone whose allegiance was to Northern Ireland. But most reported that the Unionists were committed to no power sharing, a policy apparently unacceptable both to the opposition in Northern Ireland and the British Government. Announcing the election, the *Daily Mail* reported that prospects for success were dim; the *Daily Telegraph* that the convention was already doomed; and the *Daily Mirror* that prospects were gloomy. By contrast there was some attempt to build up the importance of the elections as: 'a sincere attempt to solve Ulster's problems' (*Daily Telegraph*); 'another desperate gamble for peace' (*Sun*); 'the most important ever final chance of finding a peaceful solution' (*The Times*). The 'last chance for peace' formula seems to be a recurring theme used by British and Northern Ireland politicians to describe each new initiative in the province, one which is regularly taken over by the media in their coverage of the development.

Another contrast between the two periods was that many more stories in the second period reported the activities of British politicians. Most of these occurred after the convention election. The British governments' policy was one of non-intervention in the election campaign as it was later in the course of the convention itself. But Merlyn Rees was widely reported at the end of the campaign when he urged people in Northern Ireland to take seriously the opportunity to vote. After the election journalists were able to report more general comments by Rees on his hopes for the convention. They also covered the activities of other British ministers as they went about the legislative and administrative duties involved in 'direct rule' over the province and in combating terrorism in Great Britain in general. During this time a bill to prohibit discrimination in employment in Northern Ireland was introduced and the act giving the Home Secretary special powers to deal with terrorism was coming up for renewal.

More interesting as a reflection of the nature of media coverage, however, was the attention which the British media gave to signs of dissent from the bi-partisan policy among British politicians. Leo Abse's statement at a 'Troops Out Movement' news conference that loyalists should realize further intransigence would lead to British withdrawal was hardly noticed by the British press, being mentioned by

The Times and the *Daily Mirror* in the course of other stories and only carried as a separate story by the *Daily Telegraph* on its back page. The suggestion that the Conservative Party might be changing its line on Northern Ireland, however, in such a way as to threaten the bi-partisan policy, received considerable attention from the quality press. There were two aspects of policy over which the Conservatives were uneasy, the release of more detainees and the continuing attempt to force power sharing on an unwilling Northern Ireland majority. The *Guardian* reported government concern at these threats to the bi-partisan policy. It felt these sprang from Conservative spokesman Airey Neave's unfamiliarity with the Irish problem and his closeness to the Protestant right wing.

In general, it can be argued that the news media in Great Britain are very dependent on the parliamentary system and inter-party debate to air political issues and policies. When party conflict is removed, as it has been on Northern Ireland policy since Northern Ireland came under direct rule, the scope for handling such issues within a news format is much reduced. It was largely for this reason that the main political news points in the British media in the convention election period were such procedural items as that the elections had been held and the convention would meet. National television coverage in the second period was devoted almost exclusively to these formal events.

Northern Ireland media

As shown in Tables 23 and 25, there was more difference between the individual newspapers and television bulletins in Northern Ireland than in Great Britain, but less difference between the way each election was

TABLE 25. Political stories in the Northern Ireland media: period I (percentages)

Story	Number or stories				
	Irish News (N=123)	*News Letter* (N=146)	*Belfast Telegraph* (N=83)	BBC TV *Scene Around Six* (N=29)	UTV *Ulster Reports*[1] (N=13)
General/mixed or other	6	14	16	52	10
Ireland (Republic) politicians	2	6	8	3	...
British politicians	2	4	8	0	...
Northern Ireland centre parties	32	16	26	14	...
Northern Ireland anti-Unionist parties	50	11	14	10	1
Northern Ireland Loyalist parties	8	49	26	21	2
TOTAL	100	100	98	100	(...)
Political stories as percentage of total	39	35	22	24	16

1. Except for the final figure there are raw figures as there were too few cases on which to base percentages.

covered. Looking at each medium separately, attention was distributed in a similar way between the various parties involved in the two elections. Each used much the same techniques of reporting and presentation to cover both. In the television programmes election coverage took four main forms: constituency reviews, general reviews of the election prospects and results, round-ups of the campaigning, reports of each party manifesto as it was published, and reports of other campaign events or incidents. As the second period extended after the convention election, there were also some stories about other aspects of politics altogether, largely the activities of the British ministers responsible for Northern Ireland and election reaction stories—the post-election equivalents of the pre-election general reviews and round-ups.

In the press, election coverage was less formalized, but again some characteristic techniques could be identified. All three papers reported the ordinary run of campaign speeches extensively. In the *Irish News* these tended to be grouped together by party, while both the *News Letter* and the *Belfast Telegraph* carried long stories with points from all the election speeches either headed with a general title such as 'Election Forum' or with a headline derived from the point quoted from the first speech. Some speeches, party news conferences and other statements by candidates were also treated as individual stories by all three papers. The *News Letter* and the *Belfast Telegraph* carried constituency reviews and picture stories of individual candidates campaigning. There were two innovations in the second period. The *News Letter* gave about half a page on different days in the campaign to the leader of each party contesting the election to state their case. This included both Gerry Fitt of the SDLP and Malachy McGurran of the Republican Clubs. The *Belfast Telegraph* called for readers to write in with their views on the convention. Apart from these discernible techniques, most of the coverage in all three papers simply took the form of news stories. The *Irish News* carried very few feature articles of any sort. There were none on the elections and politics so the range of techniques was much narrower in that paper than in the other two.

Tables 23 and 25 show that the two 'sectional' newspapers clearly concentrated on the views and activities of politicians associated with the section of the community they represented within Northern Ireland. For the *Irish News*, this meant the Republican Clubs, the Social Democratic and Labour Party, the Alliance Party with some attention going to the Northern Ireland Labour Party and the Unionist Party of Northern Ireland, counted as 'centre parties' for the purposes of this research. The *News Letter*, on the other hand, paid most attention to the candidates of the three Unionist parties within the UUUC and then some attention to the centre parties and little to the anti-Unionist parties. The way attention in these two papers peaked at the Unionist and anti-Unionist extremes but overlapped at a lower level across the centre provides some justification for the national spectrum implicit in the coding frame. The *Belfast Telegraph*'s political coverage was more widely spread than that of the two 'sectional' papers, but its moderate Unionist traditions were clearly reflected in the general distribution of its coverage. The paper paid most attention to the Unionist Coalition and Brian Faulkner's

Unionist Party, the UPNI, both in terms of the overall number of stories and in terms of the more detailed analysis of points from party speeches in the convention election campaign (Fig. 1).

The *Irish News* and the *News Letter* differed, however, in the degree of sectionalism they showed. Points from the speeches of Republican Club and SDLP candidates were included in the general round-ups of election speeches in the *News Letter*, even though they rarely provided the news point for the headline or were given much priority in the order. As mentioned before, the *News Letter* introduced a new feature in its coverage of the convention election when it gave a similar platform to the leaders of all the parties involved—though the Unionists qualified for three as the leader of each party within the coalition was treated separately. Overall there were more stories about the anti-Unionist parties in the *News Letter* than about the Unionist Coalition in the *Irish News*. All the parties' election manifestos were published within the first study period and all were reported as separate stories in the *News Letter*, the SDLP manifesto in particular taking up 90.5 column inches. But picture stories of candidates campaigning in the *News Letter* almost without exception featured Unionist candidates.

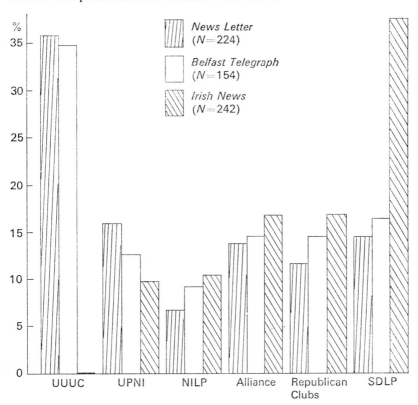

FIG. 1. Points reported from Party speeches—Convention Election campaign. (In the *News Letter* and the *Irish News* another 3 per cent was taken up with points from Communist Party candidates and in the *Irish News* another 8 per cent with points from Provisional Sinn Fein statements.)

The *Irish News* rarely reported any Unionist coalition candidate speeches. Only points from SDLP, Republican Clubs and Alliance speeches were reported in a routine way. Statements from Provisional Sinn Fein organizations were also carried regularly in the second period when the Provisionals campaigned more actively for a boycott of the election. In the first period the publication of the UUUC manifesto took up no more than 9 column inches at the end of another political story. For the most part the *Irish News* reported politics in Northern Ireland as if the Unionist coalition did not exist. When the paper did recognize its existence, the point of the story was usually to prophecy the coalition's failure or to underline dissension within its ranks.

Both these papers went beyond sectionalism, however, in the sense of paying selective attention to their section of the community, to partisanship in the interpretation and presentation of political stories to support the politicians and parties representing their section and to further their views. In the general election there was most doubt about the outcome in the constituency of Fermanagh and South Tyrone where the anti-Unionists finally agreed to support one independent candidate, Frank Maguire, against Harry West, leader of the official Unionist Party within the UUUC. Each newspaper confidently reported that the candidate representing their section of the community would win. The *Irish News* referred to Enoch Powell as the cuckoo in the Unionist nest in the general-election campaign. When Powell made his first anti-Common Market speech in England the *Irish News* reported 'Big Three Furious at Powell's Labour X', whereas the *News Letter* headlined 'Unionist Blessing for Powell Attack'. In this campaign there was at least one example of one of these newspapers printing a partisan story that turned out to be based on false information. On the Tuesday before the election the *News Letter* reported that the Official Sinn Fein in Dublin had put out a statement urging its supporters in Great Britain to vote Labour. 'Our executive has agreed', so the statement ran, 'that Harold Wilson is the best friend the IRA ever had', and it went on to list individual Labour MPs thought to be sympathetic to republicanism. The statement turned out to be a forgery. The next day the *News Letter* did report Official Sinn Fein's claim to that effect, together with the news that the fraud squad of the 'Eire police' [sic] were investigating.

In the Convention Election the *News Letter* made much of the rumour of a voting pact between the parties in favour of power sharing, in particular between the UPNI and the SDLP, presumably in the hope that this would tar the Faulkner Unionists with the brush of republicanism. On election day itself its lead story was headlined 'Eve of Poll Furore Flares' over a report that while both parties had denied any such pact, the Unionist Coalition regarded it as an attempt to frustrate the will of the pro-British majority. However, the *News Letter* did carry at least one story under another vigorous headline 'SDLP Slams Stay-at-Homes', putting the SDLP case against the Provisional Sinn Fein boycott. Towards the end of the story it also reported accusations of intimidation against the UVF in West Belfast. In the *Belfast Telegraph* story the two accusations were reversed, under the headline 'Thugs Take over Claim'.

In both elections the *Irish News* and the *News Letter* were incorrigibly optimistic about the prospects of their own side.

Both papers also carried reaction stories—accounts of how prominent figures in the parties associated with their section of the community had reacted to some new development. These were more frequent in the *News Letter*, perhaps simply because more space was available, than in the *Irish News*. For example, the day after the publication of the SDLP general-election manifesto, it reported an attack on it by William Craig, leader of the Vanguard Party within the UUUC and by two NILP candidates. The same story, however, took up a good deal more space and was more prominently featured in the *Belfast Telegraph*. After the Convention Election the *Irish News* gave a good deal of space to SDLP leaders' reactions to Dr Conor Cruise O'Brien's reactions to the election results. The SDLP's continuing demand for power sharing provided the lead story while another reaction story was also given prominence on the front page. This reported that a clash was now expected between the Loyalists and the Westminster Government and quoted statements by Brian Faulkner (UPNI), Gerry Fitt (SDLP), Napier (Alliance), the Provisional Sinn Fein and the Republican Clubs. Dr O'Brien's interview on RTE radio also provided the *News Letter* with its lead story, under the headline 'Face Facts SDLP Told'. In the course of the story it reported Unionist leaders' reactions not only to the original O'Brien interview, but also to the SDLP leaders' reactions.

These reaction stories provide an example of the public nature of Northern Ireland politics. This has been noted by political commentators as a general feature of politics in Northern Ireland (Windlesham, 1975), a feature which must have been exaggerated by the suspension of political institutions within the province itself. Nevertheless, the media play a prominent part in the process by publicizing immediate political opinions and reactions. The *News Letter*'s treatment of such stories was particularly noticeable for the air of strife and conflict in which politics was conducted. In the *News Letter* no politician simply reacted to his opponent; rather they 'flayed' them, 'slammed' them or 'slapped them down', 'furiously', 'angrily' or 'explosively'. At the least this involved a 'row', but it may have been a 'furious row' or even a 'furore'. It is an interesting speculation as to whether these metaphors of conflict in the *News Letter*'s political coverage are related to the military slogans such as 'No Surrender' which form such a prominent part of the Loyalist ideology.

One further aspect of sectionalism between these two papers appeared in their treatment of stories about political developments in Ireland (Republic). The *Irish News* in fact paid these proportionately less attention than the *News Letter* though they achieved little prominence in either paper. Again, it seems likely that this was a consequence of limited space and resources at the *Irish News*, keeping its attention restricted to the local area of the province. In the *News Letter*, however, when a story from the republic did not directly support a position acceptable to the Loyalists in the north, it was made to do so. Either southern politicians were portrayed as agreeing with the Unionist views against the anti-Unionists in the north, as, for example, in the report of Dr O'Brien's interview referred to above, or political events in the south were interpreted in such a way as to support existing Loyalist reasons for wanting no truck with the republic. For example, during the second period a criminal justice bill was debated in the Irish Senate providing for the trial of fugitive terrorists from Northern Ireland or Great Britain. The *News Letter*'s lead story on 25 April 1975, headlined 'Shock Move on Border Issue', reported that the paper had received a letter from Rory Brucha, the Fianna Fail spokesman on Northern Ireland, stating that the law could only apply to the republic unless others elsewhere agreed. The *News Letter*, helped by statements from Unionist politicians, turned this into a 'shock move' by linking it to the articles in the constitution of the Irish Republic which provide for the government of the republic to exercise jurisdiction over the whole of the island, a continuing source of irritation in Northern Ireland Unionist circles. When a southern politician said something clearly unacceptable to Unionist opinion, then the *News Letter* could use the same technique of reaction reporting as it applied to domestic political developments. For example, after the Convention Election, the republic's Prime Minister, Liam Cosgrave, reiterated his government's unequivocal support for power sharing and the 'Irish dimension'. This appeared in the *News Letter*'s lead story as 'West Raps Meddling by Eire'. Cosgrave's unacceptable statement was thus treated quite differently from O'Brien's earlier remarks which fitted unionist views.

By contrast, the *Belfast Telegraph* handled this story by separating the reactions from the statement itself. One story reported Cosgrave's statement, contrasted it with the impression given by Dr O'Brien in his radio interview and quoted the reaction of Jack Lynch, the Leader of the Opposition in the republic, who wondered whether the government had a policy on the north other than to confuse and bewilder its own people. In another story it reported political reaction in Northern Ireland, quoting West's opposition to the republic's intervention and Hume's reaffirmation that the SDLP would put forward these policies in the convention. The story provides another example of the 'professionalism' of the *Belfast Telegraph* as compared to the two sectional papers. The *Irish News* simply reported Cosgrave's statement under the headline 'No Change on Power Sharing' with no reference to the O'Brien interview which had preceded it or the various reactions the statement itself provoked. The *News Letter*'s story was made up of elements similar to those of the *Belfast Telegraph* account. It reported Hume's welcome for the statement and that it followed Dr O'Brien's interview, but these were all mixed in the same story, starting with West's reactions. This blurred the distinction between the two political systems involved. The *News Letter* treated Cosgrave's statement simply as an intervention in the affairs of the north, whereas the *Belfast Telegraph* presented it in the context of the republic's own political system and dealt with northern reactions separately.

In general, it was remarkable how little attention all the press and television outlets in the north paid to politics in the republic and, indeed, to other aspects of life in the twenty-six counties. The cases quoted, however, do show some of the ways in which the *Belfast Telegraph* differed from the two sectional papers. These are relevant to other types of stories. In the case of Cosgrave's statement, for example, it gave more of the context of the event than the *Irish News* and unlike the *News Letter*, started its report from the event. In many stories in the *News Letter* it was difficult to disentangle what had happened from subsequent reaction and interpretation. Pride of place went to Unionist reactions or to some angle on the event which fitted in with Unionist interpretations. These were not necessarily intransigent as, for example, in the *News Letter*'s lead story on the first meeting of the convention. This announced that there was optimism as the Loyalists had left the door open. The paper attributed this view to Gerry Fitt. It went on to support this interpretation with West's undertaking that the majority would not use their power to kick the minority around. This interpretation was in marked contrast to the other two papers, both of which headlined intransigence as the two sides restated their positions.

Both the sectional papers indulged in wishful thinking, running speculative stories with predictions which had less basis in fact than in what would suit that section of the community. In the general election campaign, for example, the *Irish News* repeatedly predicted a split in the Unionist coalition because of the activities of Enoch Powell. After the Convention Election, it assured its readers that a clash between Westminster and the Loyalists was now expected. The *News Letter* ran a story before the first meeting of the convention speculating on whether the Queen and Harold Wilson would send messages with their good wishes for opening and bemoaning the fact that there were no signs so far, nor of any neighbourly greetings coming from the President of the Ireland. It is a nice point whether neighbourly greetings would have become unwarranted interference if any had actually been received. By contrast, the *Belfast Telegraph*'s speculations were more safely based as, for example, on predictions of Loyalist success at the polls, or such more routine, ones as security alerts or low turn-outs at the elections.

A similar observation applies to speculative stories in the two television news outlets. The leaks and speculations reported on television were well founded, predictable and uncontentious. This applied to most of the speculative political stories carried on both channels. In both elections there were speculations about the rate of polling, particularly before the convention election when all media feared apathy. Presumably the fear was compounded by the fact that the Provos and the IRSP were campaigning for a boycott, but this was rarely explicitly stated. Both programmes carried stories about a possible split in the British Conservative Party following the Convention Election results, a speculation which was also carried by most newspapers; both carried Brian Faulkner's prediction of a split among the Unionist leadership once the convention was established; UTV based a story of a possible pact to share votes among the power sharing parties on Dublin press reports. In the last two cases, the news medium was covered by reporting what someone else had said or reported first.

Another technique, used extensively by the BBC, was to employ a special political correspondent, someone who could provide the newsroom with advance warning of likely developments as well as assessments of events and who could present these to the public in general overviews of the situation. The predominant form of coverage on the BBC programme *Scene Around Six* were analyses by their political correspondent, W. D. Flacks, while on UTV's *Ulster Reports* there were more roundtable discussions or successive interviews with politicians.

Because of the conventional nature of election reporting on television, it was possible to group the political stories under a few main headings. Before the convention election, there were general reviews and round-ups as well as reports of news events. Before the general election, these were supplemented by constituency surveys and, on *Scene Around Six*, reports of each manifeso as it was published. By contrast, *Ulster Reports* only featured the manifestos of the two main parties—the UUUC and the SDLP. In other respects, too, UTV's coverage was less extensive than that of the BBC. BBC *Radio Ulster* included various other types of election programme in its output during both campaigns. So far as news was concerned, in the general election period *Ulster Reports* carried only two news stories about developments in the election, both of which appeared in *Scene Around Six* together with five others.[1] A similar though less marked difference applied in the second period.

This difference in the breadth of coverage may be one reason why the BBC attracts more criticism for irresponsibility within the province than UTV. Among the events reported on *Scene Around Six* there were several which were presumably uncongenial to important sections of Northern Ireland opinion. These included a short story in each election period reporting allegations of harassment by the Republican Clubs and, after the Convention Elections, reports of the activities of Leo Abse M.P. and the 'Troops Out Movement' in England and of an NCCL statement that the act aimed at controlling terrorism in England should not be renewed. Nevertheless, among the UTV stories which were not dealt with extensively on *Scene Around Six* was a report on the Provo's post-convention election press conference at which they claimed that the boycott had been a success. After the Guildford bombs in the first period, *Ulster Reports* carried a story questioning whether the Provisionals were split on the policy of bombing in England. Both programmes reported the call for a boycott of the convention election which came from another republican group, the IRSP.

These examples suggest that both programmes covered a similar spectrum of stories. In so far as the BBC was different, it was simply that it carried more of all sorts. The same point can be made by examining those stories which did not deal, however obliquely, with unconstitutional opposition. In the general election campaign *Scene Around Six* reported Lord Brookeborough's call for the reintroduction of capital punishment and in the convention campaign it took up the questionnaire devised at the Corrymeela Peace Centre for deciding which politicians were men of goodwill and invited replies from politicians.

In the course of the two campaigns twenty-five political news events

1. It must be remembered a strike blacked out five editions of *Ulster Reports* in the first period.

provided the basis for a story on one or both channels. Too much, therefore, should not be made of the difference between them. This is all the more the case given the basic agreement on presenting constitutional initiatives in a favourable and optimistic light, for example, by emphasizing the importance of each election, the need to avoid a low turn-out and the amicable atmosphere apparent at the first meeting of the convention. Similarly, both gave extensive coverage to appeals from official sources for an end to violence even though in terms of news values an appeal from Merlyn Rees and the Chief Constable was neither novel nor more likely to be effective than those made in the past. The fact that the rhetoric of news values such as importance, significance and novelty are used occasionally to defend the selection of a story outside the official perspective should not be allowed to obscure the fact that that perspective provides the underlying theme of the coverage, almost regardless of the novelty of the particular events which illustrate it.

More political parties participate in the political process in Northern Ireland than in Great Britain generally. This creates particular problems for the broadcast media used to maintaining a balance between two main political parties. To some extent the Unionist Coalition and the SDLP are equivalents of the two main British parties on the mainland, but as political differences are grounded in community divisions, there is no expectation that the two will alternate in power or even in electoral success. With the suspension of the institutions of government in Northern Ireland, these two parties do not fill the role of government and opposition either. Both stand in a subordinate relationship to the British Government. In the broadcast coverage this aspect of the political process predominated, with most attention going to Unionist policy in relation to British Government policy, some attention being given to SDLP policy as the voice of the other section of the community, to Brian Faulkner as the last ex-Prime Minister and then to the other minor parties.

So far as the press is concerned, an interesting comparison may be drawn from the points which the newspapers carried from the election speeches. To an extent reports were a reflection of what was said and so of the style of campaign adopted by the candidates or the party in the election. In the general election, for example, a major plank in the Republican Clubs' platform was opposition to sectarianism in Ulster politics, while David Bleakley, leader of the NILP, directed most of his attention to attacking Brian Faulkner and the UPNI because he stood most chance of picking up votes from them. Similarly, in the convention campaign, the SDLP candidates directed a good deal of their effort to trying to secure their own 'tribal vote' against such different threats as the Provisionals' boycott, the Republican Clubs and the Alliance Party. The Unionist Coalition, too, had to direct some of its attention to attacking Brian Faulkner and the UPNI, a potential threat to its own 'tribal vote'. Election campaigns in Northern Ireland, therefore, involved different parties jockeying for position within each section of the community as much as an overall contest between the two sections carried out by the major parties representing each. This aspect of the campaigns was more apparent in the two sectional papers than in the *Belfast Telegraph*, particularly in the *Irish News* during the convention campaign in which many of the points quoted from speeches were attacks by one party on their rivals for the support of the Catholic community.

More generally, a distinction could be drawn between the 'politics of policy' and the 'politics of posture', the former involving statements about party programmes, the latter appeals for support or attacks on rivals. Again, as Table 26 shows, the two sectional papers carried proportionately more 'posture' points from speeches than the *Belfast Telegraph*. The distribution of points quoted from different parties in each paper reinforces the analysis presented earlier of the different attention paid to each party in each paper. Figure 1 shows that there were nearly three times as many points from Unionist coalition candidate speeches as

TABLE 26. Points from party speeches—Convention Election campaign (percentages)

	Belfast Telegraph (N=156)	*News Letter* (N=224)	*Irish News* (N=242)
Postures within Northern Ireland politics	22	40	45
Policy and other	79	60	55
TOTAL	101	100	100

from candidates of any other single party in the *News Letter*; in the *Belfast Telegraph* the proportion was reduced to 2 to 1; while in the *Irish News* SDLP candidates predominated. Nevertheless, while the *Irish News* clearly avoided reporting UUUC candidates' speeches, in the *News Letter* SDLP speeches made up the third largest group followed by Alliance and the Republican Clubs. The *Irish News* was the only paper to quote the statements of Provisional Sinn Fein. All these, except one, were 'posture' statements—attacks on the SDLP or the Republican Clubs or reports that the boycott was going well. By contrast, few of the Republican Clubs' speeches were 'posture' statements in any paper, an observation which says more about the campaign style of the official republican movement than media coverage itself.

As well as the Provisional Sinn Fein, 'posturing' was most generally characteristic of the two 'main' parties, the UUUC and the SDLP and of the UPNI. The 'postures' included in this analysis were those internal to Northern Ireland, not statements of position in relation to the British Government and direct rule. It could be argued that such posturing is a consequence of the public nature of Northern Ireland politics and the current lack of any local organs of government. Regardless of that general point, however, there does seem to be a difference in the emphasis placed on it in the different newspapers. Further, it must be emphasized that 'the politics of posture' is not a pejorative term. To understand Northern Ireland politics, it is just as important to know where each party stands in relation to others, particularly those with whom it may be directly competing for votes, as to know the details of its policies or its position in relation to the British Government.

Irish media

The previous two sections have shown the different perspectives on Northern Ireland politics used by local as against national media. The main concern of the British media was with national British politics and they tended to assess Northern Ireland politics in that light. The local media, however, were more concerned with the political system of the province itself. The press and radio of Ireland (Republic) recognized the importance of this local political system but also introduced another perspective of their own based on the political system of the republic. Table 27 shows that reports of the activities of politicians in the republic took up between one-fifth and two-fifths of all political stories related to

TABLE 27. Political stories in the Irish media: periods I and II (percentages)

	Irish Times (N=198)	RTE News at 1.30 (N=60)	Irish Press and Irish Independent (N=93)[1]
Ireland (Republic) politicians	21	17	37
British politicians	11	10	19
Northern Ireland centre parties	12	7	6
Northern Ireland anti-Unionist parties	19	20	12
Northern Ireland Loyalist parties	20	17	3
General/mixed or other	16	30	23
TOTAL	99	101	100
Political stories as percentage of total	39	39	32

1. Period II only.

Northern Ireland. The proportion was consistently larger than the proportion of stories about British politicians. Except in the case of the *Irish Press* and the *Irish Independent*, it was not as large as the proportion of stories about the various political parties in the north. From these general figures it would appear that the main centre of interest in the *Irish Press* and the *Irish Independent* was in the national politics of Ireland. Interest in the *Irish Times* and RTE's radio news included local provincial politics in the north, as well as the national politics of Ireland and Great Britain.

These generalizations, however, are very dependent on the developments related to Northern Ireland which occurred in each political system during the periods studied. The two elections were held in the north. In Great Britain there was the general election in the first period, but Northern

Ireland policy was not an issue. Nevertheless, the *Irish Times* paid some attention to the activities of the smaller parties and fringe groups on the British mainland who were trying to raise the issue. In both periods there were few developments involving British politicians from the major parties in the problems of Northern Ireland and few statements by them on the issue. The Government of Ireland had also adopted a low profile, apparently to avoid provoking Loyalist fears as their involvement in the Sunningdale Agreement had done. Nevertheless, one member of the cabinet, Dr Conor Cruise O'Brien, was less reticent than his colleagues. In both periods he made comments on the situation in the north, on the first case involuntarily through the leaking of a document he had prepared for a Labour Party policy committee, which provided the basis for long running stories. In the second period O'Brien commented on the results of the Convention Election and also took the opportunity of a visit to the United States to attack those who sympathized with the Provisionals and supplied them with money and arms. Also in the second period the controversial Criminal Law Jurisdiction Bill, itself a legacy of Sunningdale, was passing through the Irish Senate. Relatively speaking, therefore, there was more political activity in Ireland than on the British mainland during the periods studied. It is less surprising that the Irish media should have devoted considerable attention to it than that it attracted so little in the British and provincial media.

Conor Cruise O'Brien dominated political news from the south related to Northern Ireland in a way reminiscent of Enoch Powell's dominance of the British media's reporting of the general election in Northern Ireland. Both men appeared to be skilled in the techniques of news management, releasing statements, giving interviews and, in O'Brien's case, even writing letters to the press to keep themselves at the centre of attention. Both of his major interventions were the result of interviews on RTE's midday radio news programmes, an organization for which O'Brien was responsible in the government as Minister of Posts and Telegraphs. Both men had had extensive and varied careers which gave them complex public persona. Partly as a result of this and partly as a result of stands they had taken on issues in the past, both were known as controversial mavericks within their national political systems.

But the coverage each received was quite different. Whereas much of the reporting of Enoch Powell's activities in the British media was concerned to exploit various aspects of his public persona, little attention was given to O'Brien as a personality in Ireland. Rather it was the fact that he was prepared to take a public position on a series of issues which kept him in the news. The Irish media reported these positions and the ensuing controversies on their own terms, not as indications of O'Brien's potential as a national or party leader. This in spite of the fact that few of O'Brien's activities were concerned with his direct ministerial responsibilities as Minister for Posts and Telegraphs, a source of much irritation to letter writers to the *Irish Times*. These differences can only partly be attributed to a difference of style between the British and Irish press. Enoch Powell was electioneering outside the mainstream of British politics, while O'Brien was a member of the Government of Ireland.

Nevertheless, there does seem to be a real difference in style. This showed itself generally in the greater readiness of the Irish papers to deal with issues rather than personalities.

O'Brien's comments following the Convention Election which were greeted as realistic by Loyalists in the north, provoked anger and dismay among the SDLP. Of all the media included in this study apart from the *Irish News*, those in Ireland were most inclined to take the SDLP seriously. Table 27 shows that in all media in Ireland there were as many or more stories about anti-Unionist as Unionist politicians. These were almost without exception stories about the SDLP or its members. In the second period, while some points from Republican Club speeches were quoted in the *Irish Times*, there were no separate stories about the clubs' campaign in any of the papers. Similarly, there were few reports about the activities of any of the other smaller parties. The Irish papers seemed to have accepted the SDLP as the authentic voice of the minority in the north. As shown in Table 27, this was particularly striking in the results for the *Irish Press* and the *Irish Independent* in the second period in which there were more stories about the SDLP than all the other northern parties combined. The figures for RTE radio news make the political system in the north appear as a two-party system, a result which may be a product of the balance and impartiality characteristic of broadcast news. Nevertheless, the fact that both RTE and the *Irish Times* carried a relatively large proportion of stories about the Unionist Coalition, suggests that while they recognized the SDLP as the voice of the minority, they also realized that power lay with the majority and its representatives.

After the Convention Election all the media noted the sweeping Loyalist victory, but the main issues they took up were concerned with the future role of the SDLP and likely developments in British Government policy. The Irish papers expressed some concern that the meetings of the 'Troops Out Movement', coupled with signs of disunity in the Conservative Party, might indicate growing disillusion among British politicians and herald a greater readiness to consider withdrawal. So far as the future of the SDLP was concerned, the first question was whether the Provisional Sinn Fein boycott had been effective, a topic which seemed taboo in Great Britain and Belfast. Initial reaction that the low poll in some areas simply reflected apathy changed to include the possibility that the boycott and the intimidation which accompanied it had had some effect. This view was supported by statements from SDLP spokesmen. Second, the position adopted by Conor Cruise O'Brien posed a problem for the SDLP as to whether they could still rely on the support of the Irish Government for their two main policies—power sharing and an 'Irish dimension'.

In an interview on the RTE radio news programme *This Week* on 4 May 1975, the Sunday equivalent of the *News at 1.30*, O'Brien took the view that the British and Irish Governments could not bring about power sharing now that it has been rejected at the polls. 'It's not a question of reaching a power sharing executive. It's a question of excluding the emergence of a non-power sharing executive and also the emergence of UDI. . . .' He looked forward to a continuation of direct rule.

Following the interview, the Irish papers took up two related questions—whether his views reflected government policy and their implications for the future of the SDLP. The first was covered by speculative stories about the Taoiseach's views, the probable course of discussions at a meeting of the Irish Cabinet and in reports of a placatory statement put out by the Taoiseach's parliamentary secretary, James Kelly, reaffirming the government's commitment to power sharing and an Irish dimension; the second by accounts of the reactions of anger and dismay which O'Brien's interview had provoked among SDLP leaders as against the approval with which it had been greeted in Loyalist circles. Kelly's reaffirmation of support for the SDLP and its policies brought the two themes together, as encapsulated in the *Irish Press* headline of 6 May—'SDLP Heroes—Kelly'. The lead story that day was on the first meeting of the convention.

That formal event and its implications for future negotiations within the convention itself dominated coverage in the British and Belfast media. The Irish media, however, were more preoccupied with the position of their government and the SDLP, the two political bodies most responsible for providing the minority in the north with some constitutional representation. The concept of a 'minority' in the north had almost disappeared from the British and Northern Ireland media, but was still current among politicians in the SDLP and the Ireland and used in the media in the south. All the media in Great Britain, Northern Ireland and Ireland (Republic) recognized that power sharing was one of the main issues in the election. But there is a considerable difference in the implications of that term depending on the emphasis put on the differences in size and power between the two groups to share power. Without the concept of 'minority', with its overtones of domination and discrimination in the past, arguments over power sharing in the British and Belfast media seemed no more than a constitutional wrangle, designed to frustrate the political will of the majority. Coverage of politics in the Irish media made clear that power sharing involved more than bringing about a coalition government in a multi-party democracy.

Not only did the Irish media differ from those discussed in the previous two sections in their reporting of politics in the north, there were also differences in the style of presentation. The *Irish Times* has more space at its disposal than any other newspaper included in this study and so was inclined to provide its readers with the complete text of speeches and statements which it regarded as important. Among these were transcripts of political interviews conducted the previous day on RTE radio.

The *News at 1.30* and its Sunday equivalent, *This Week*, followed the same format as the BBC Radio 4 news programme, *The World at One* (*The World This Weekend*). After a conventional news bulletin, the programmes carry longer features on particular items. In the study periods many of these were interviews with politicians on the situation in the north. Among these were the two interviews with O'Brien, to which reference has already been made. Other interviews on RTE in both periods shared with the O'Brien interviews the attribute of being newsmaking events in their own right. Interviewees were encouraged to elaborate their position in such a way that the interview itself would become a news story for the future. For example, in the first period RTE interviewed one of the possible republican candidates for Fermanagh and South Tyrone to try to establish why it was taking so long to agree on a candidate; in another programme Enoch Powell was asked to elaborate on his view that Northern Ireland was just another part of the United Kingdom and to spell out the implications of this for the Catholic minority, and on another occasion Roy Bradford, who had been a Unionist member of the ill-fated power-sharing executive under Brian Faulkner, was asked to explain why he had come out openly in support of William Craig, leader of the Vanguard Unionist Party, who opposed power sharing, the Irish dimension and all the initiatives embodied in the executive. The BBC radio news programmes have used this technique of turning an interview into a news story. There was an example of this during the Convention Election campaign, when Brian Faulkner, leader of the UPNI, was interviewed on *The World at One*. Faulkner claimed that another display of Loyalist intransigence at the polls might result in Great Britain adopting a policy of repartition for Northern Ireland, designed to separate the two sections of the community. The *Belfast Telegraph*, reporting the story the same day, pointed out that while the possibility of repartition had been discussed in Great Britain, this was the first time it had been mentioned by a Northern Ireland politician. Next morning the *Irish News* carried a reaction story in which politicians of various persuasions rejected Faulkner's views. The *News Letter* story on UUUC reactions was another which began with the row and the rejection and only reported towards its end what had prompted them.

To describe the medium as using this interview technique to promote reportable news events is to emphasize only one aspect of the process. Clearly in this case, the politician in question had an interest in finding a public forum for his views. In other cases, too, it is a nice question whether the medium was using the politician or vice versa. During the Unionist Workers Council (UWC) strike, Roy Bradford, then Minister of the Environment at Stormont, was interviewed on *The World at One* to make clear that he was sympathetic with the Loyalist case in spite of the fact that he had not yet resigned from the 'power sharing' executive (Fisk, p. 124). By stating his views in public, he helped to undermine the position of Brian Faulkner and the rest of the executive. In the first period of this study, when Bradford announced his complete conversion to the Unionist Coalition cause, he was challenged on RTE to explain his change of mind. The interviewer put it to him that he was making a public statement to try to secure a Unionist coalition nomination for himself in the forthcoming Convention Election. When the confidential Labour Party memorandum, prepared by Dr Conor Cruise O'Brien, was leaked to the press, the RTE interviewer scarcely concealed his suspicion that the minister might have expected a leak even if he had not himself encouraged it. On this occasion the suspicion was that O'Brien wanted to open up a discussion of policy alternatives available to the republic in the event of a 'doomsday situation' arising in the north, in particular to encourage a realistic appraisal of the part the Irish army might play in any such conflict, not that he was pursuing some personal goal.

Nevertheless, both these last examples illustrate another general feature of the Irish media. Compared to the other media in Great Britain and Northern Ireland, the Irish newspapers and Irish radio in its feature coverage were relatively open about the processes of news production which lay behind their coverage. In the cases quoted above, the interviewer was prepared to suggest there might be more to the story than was apparent simply from what the interviewee was saying. RTE also made considerable use of the technique of interviewing newspaper journalists or their own special correspondents to put some new development in perspective. Covering the convention election campaign, BBC Radio Northern Ireland introduced a new programme late at night in which journalists working for Belfast, London and Dublin newspapers reviewed the course of the campaign. Generally, political correspondents working for the northern media seemed more prepared than their colleagues in the south to take the actions and statements of Northern Ireland politicians at face value. As they are themselves participants in the tendentious political system of the north, it is easy to understand why. The papers in Ireland carried political columns which were clearly alive to the ironies of the political machinations occurring in Northern Ireland. The general tone adopted was that of the wordly-wise journalist, wearily cynical about the behaviour of his fellow men. But the newspapers were also prepared to let the readers into their confidence about newsmaking itself. In both election campaigns, stories were published about the actual process of covering an election, discussing the way newspapers were supplied with speeches and press releases, statements and reactions from politicians of all parties.

Conclusion

Coverage of political news in the British media reflected the same journalistic style of simplification and human interest as was apparent in the reporting of violence. In the two periods studied this took the form of an obsessive concentration on Enoch Powell in the first and the routine reporting of the formal details of the convention in the second. The British media, in contrast to the Irish, were little interested in the immediate political issues raised by the Convention Election except in so far as the Conservatives showed signs of breaking away from the bipartisan policy. The Irish, on the other hand, were concerned about the future role of the SDLP in the north.

To some extent this concern was orchestrated by an Irish Cabinet Minister, Dr Conor Cruise O'Brien. At a time when most British and Irish politicians were 'keeping a low profile' on the question of Northern Ireland, O'Brien continually made news, but only in Ireland and the north. The *News Letter* was clearly partisan in its treatment of southern politics, welcoming occasional developments with which it agreed, as in the case of O'Brien's interview in the second period which seemed to accept the impossibility of power sharing, and attacking others by concentrating on Unionist reaction. For example, the leak of O'Brien's doomsday document in the first period was heralded as 'Shock Eire Threat to Convention' and the following day as 'Storm Over O'Brien'. Paisley of the DUP claimed O'Brien stood exposed as an enemy of the Northern Ireland people and Laird of the Official Unionist Party rejected narrow-minded, extremist interference by a hostile republic. The burden of O'Brien's argument had been that, in the event of civil war in the north, the Irish army would be unable to effectively protect the Catholic minority.

The Irish media, particularly the *Irish Times*, were also interested in any sign of political activity on the question of Northern Ireland on the British mainland. This extended beyond the activities of politicians of the main political parties to include various fringe groups and activities which in Great Britain went largely unnoticed except in the pages of the *Morning Star*. The difference between the media coverage in the two countries reflects a difference in the way the story of Northern Ireland was defined, which in turn was dependent on the way the problem was regarded in the political culture of the two societies. In Great Britain, in spite of the fact that the convention was the latest government initiative, the presence of British troops in the province, the low profile adopted by leading politicians and the placing of the conflict outside the arena of party politics, conspired to make both the problem and the news story appear to be mainly one of violence. In Ireland, however, there was much more concern about the political and constitutional future of the province and the relationship between the majority and minority there. In Northern Ireland itself there was the additional local issue of reacquiring some measure of regional political autonomy.

Chapter 4

Other types of news

British media

Other news apart from that which came under the three main headings of violence, law enforcement and politics made up a relatively small proportion of the output of the British news media. So far as these media were concerned, all news related to the affairs of the province was included in the study. The low proportion of 'other news' and within that the low proportion of news not dealing with the troubles underlines the point that, so far as the rest of Great Britain is concerned, it is the troubles which make Northern Ireland news.

There were very few stories in either period in which there were no references to the troubles. Even in those cases where the event had no intrinsic connection with the disturbances there was usually a news point to be made that the event reported was a contrast to the usual run of troubles news. In the first period, for example, both the *Daily Mail* and the *Daily Mirror* ran a picture story about a toy shop party in Belfast intended to promote the toys children and their parents really wanted to play with (not the rocks, bottles, guns and other familiar paraphernalia of the troubles). In the second period, a carnival was planned for Londonderry for the first time since the troubles began and the English soccer team agreed to play in Belfast for the first time for four years. The few stories which included no reference to the troubles were about industrial disputes, industrial prospects, accidental death and murder unrelated to terrorist activities, a court case involving immorality, a new appointment in BBC Northern Ireland, and the illness of the lead singer of a Northern Ireland pop group. Those took up no more than 149.5 column inches in both periods.

Three-quarters of these (115 column inches) appeared in the *Daily Mirror*. On average the *Daily Mirror* carried more Northern Ireland stories in its Irish edition than any other British paper. Among these were big picture stories of girls or children with the implicit or explicit suggestion that there was a more cheerful side to life in Northern Ireland than the troubles. The *Daily Mirror* published pictures of soldiers' pin-ups visiting the province, of beauty contests, of girls winning an art competition with a papier mâché sculpture made, so they said, from old copies of the paper. In some cases, the moral was plainly drawn, as in the headline: 'Bombs and Bullets Out—Beautiful Girls In—Peace in Belfast'. In others, the readers were left to themselves to conclude that life was not so bad after all.

No other British newspaper went so far as the *Daily Mirror* in carrying this message, though they all took advantage of any opportunity to provide a little light relief. In the first period it came to light that one of the historic cannons used in the siege of Londonderry was missing from the city walls, presumably having been removed by souvenir hunters in the British army. This provided the basis for jokey stories in several papers as did a court decision to allow a couple to continue living in their cottage even though the Maze prison had since been built around it. Reference has already been made to the abortive IRA hijack of a light aircraft which received the most attention of any incident in Northern Ireland because of its jokey overtones. In general, the popular press and the *Guardian* seemed most inclined to make what they could of such opportunities for humour. Five per cent of Northern Ireland stories in the popular press and 4 per cent of those in the quality papers dealt with odd or jokey aspects of the troubles. There where no such stories on television reflecting partly a lack of space and partly that, in spite of such traditions as ITN's final story for light relief, television is a news medium which generally takes itself very seriously.

No medium, however, extended its interest to more serious 'good news' about community workers, peace groups and other activities designed to promote peace or better community relations. It so happened that one of the peace groups, the 'People Together' movement, launched a peace petition in the first period which was presented to Merlyn Rees, the Secretary of State for Northern Ireland, in the second. This activity resulted in one story in all the British press. That took up 1.5 column inches in the *Daily Mirror* when the petition was presented. Slightly more attention was paid to statements from members of the Roman Catholic hierarchy, particularly when they condemned violence, however discriminately.

Other statements by religious leaders which received some attention were attacks on internment. This policy continued to be an issue in both periods though by the time of the second it was clearly being phased out by the British Government. Condemnation of it in the first period by the Roman Catholic Bishop of Derry received a passing mention in four papers. When an interdenominational meeting of Irish church leaders, including both Protestants and Catholics, called for its abolition in the second period, it was reported as a story in its own right in *The Times*, the *Guardian* and the *Daily Mirror*. Presumably the extra attention was prompted by the element of surprise that such a statement should come from a mixed body of Protestant and Catholic leaders. Such statements and demonstrations against internment by the Catholic community received little attention from the British media, however, particularly when compared to the publicity given to the releases made in the second period. In all 56 column inches of space were devoted to condemnations of internment as against 121 inches and 20 seconds of national television news time reporting releases.

Closely related to the protests against internment were various protests against prison conditions by those being held under the policy. Because of the significance of various forms of public protest and demonstration in the initial period of the troubles and the potential importance of such acts in reinforcing the solidarity of different sections of the community, a special category of 'protest news' was included in the coding frame. There was little such news, however, in the two periods included in this study and what there was dealt mainly with a series of protests about conditions at the Maze prison and other prison protests and hunger strikes. Overall, this type of news accounted for about 2 per cent of all stories in the British press and there was one story on television about the disturbances at the Maze.

This news was not without interest as both Loyalist and Republican prisoners were held in the jail and both were involved in the protest. The degree to which they were reported as acting together varied from paper to paper. So far as the British papers were concerned, it was clear in some reports that both types of prisoner were involved. Other versions simply used blanket words like prisoners or terrorists, women or wives (one set of disturbances involved visitors). Apart from unnamed 'Republican sources' in one *Daily Telegraph* story, all comments on the disputes came from Loyalist leaders and spokesmen or from the Northern Ireland Office and the prison authorities. The *Daily Mirror* exercised its penchant for not taking life too seriously when it announced one day that the 'Banjo Band' (of Republican prisoners) had been foiled in a raid on the jail tuck shop. The next day, however, it ran an indignant lead story under the headline 'Cave-In', reporting that following a day of disturbances the authorities at the jail had lifted the ban on food parcels and visits. This, the *Daily Mirror* announced, would inevitably bring criticisms that the authorities had caved in in the face of violence, though the paper did not quote any such criticisms and seemed only to be expressing its own frustration at being unable to hold the line.

Northern Ireland media

Understandably, the press in Northern Ireland showed much less of a proprensity to make light of the troubles than their British counterparts. The Belfast media carried stories and features about life in the province which had nothing to do with the troubles and which were not included in this study. Some of this, particularly picture stories in the *Belfast Telegraph* and the *News Letter* featuring happy children, pretty girls, scenes of rural beauty and good weather, provided Northern Ireland readers with the same element of good cheer as readers anywhere are likely to find in their local newspaper. These were rarely presented as a specific contrast to the troubles, as in the British press.

Nor did the Belfast papers follow the British in treating some incidents related to the troubles as an opportunity for jokes and light relief. The disappearance of the Derry cannon and the misfortunes of the couple with the cottage in the grounds of the Maze prison were treated with due gravity, though when a bayonet was found to be missing from a military statue after the cannon incident, the *News Letter* allowed a hint of a smile into its report. Both television stations carried the story of a chimney being demolished by army experts using explosives they had captured from terrorists and both pointed the moral that it was a good use for the explosives. The *Irish News* headlined its report of the publication of some picture postcards showing scenes of the troubles 'Having a Grim Time', but the *News Letter* was not amused. Three days after the other papers reported the publication of the cards, it published a reaction story on its front page in which it reported the protests of leading businessmen and clergy, quoting the Dean of Belfast's view that it was an irresponsible, disgraceful and insidious act and the comments of nameless shoppers that the postcards were 'shameful' and a 'bloody disgrace'.

Far from making light of the troubles the *Belfast Telegraph* and the *News Letter* carried some stories which underlined their effects on the social and economic life of the province. These were mainly about businesses in difficulty or closing down because of the troubles and reports about the probable consequences for young people of living in a situation of continual strife. Some of the latter were the result of conferences called by various groups dealing with different aspects of the situation in Northern Ireland. These attempts to discuss the problems of the province seemed to be of most interest to the *Belfast Telegraph* and the *Irish Times*. Some stories tried to minimize the troubles as, for example, occasional references to the activities of the Northern Ireland Tourist Board trying, in spite of everything, to encourage visitors to Northern Ireland. In the first period a soccer match was organized between the RUC and the Glasgow police. The *Belfast Telegraph* reported an RUC spokesman in Glasgow urging his opposite numbers to come and support their team with the assurance that Northern Ireland was not as bad as people think. The *News Letter* cheerfully proclaimed 'RUC Chief Sells Ulster'.

'Serious good news', in the form of reports of peace group activities and ecumenical meetings, were all reported in a routine way by all three papers and the television programmes. Table 28 shows that there was little difference between the different media in the attention they gave to such activities. Indeed as the *Irish News* has less space for news than the other two papers there is some suggestion that the two sectional papers gave relatively more attention to such activities than the *Belfast Telegraph*. At least it could be argued that they did not play such activities down even though they reached across the sectarian divide. The types of event which received this treatment were major public activities by the peace groups including the launching and presentation of the 'People Together' petition and some smaller reports of fund-raising activities and local meetings.

Another type of activity associated with peace groups and other voluntary workers—community action projects—received very little attention in any medium. Such work is primarily aimed at bringing people together through interpersonal contact, a task for which media publicity has little relevance. Indeed, in the situation of community conflict in Northern Ireland, media publicity may be a positive danger for those seeking to bridge divisions which paramilitary groups have an interest in maintaining. It was widely believed, for example, that 'Nick the Brit', the ex-British soldier who returned to Belfast to become a community worker and who was shot at work on 13 March 1976, paid the price for being too successful in helping the youth in a depressed area of the city. Within the periods covered by this study, the only stories referring to such work were press reports of a speech by the Lord Mayor of Belfast in which he praised the efforts of voluntary workers and a story on *Ulster Reports* about a community festival to be organized in Downpatrick. This was clearly intended to be a public and publicity-seeking event.

Sectionalism between the *News Letter* and the *Irish News* was apparent, however, when comparing the space the different papers gave to reports of meetings and statements which were not ecumenical, but associated with one or the other religion. These results are shown in Table 28. The *Irish News* gave space to Catholic churchmen as against Protestant at a ratio of about 9 : 1. In the *News Letter* the ratio was 7 : 1 in the opposite direction, while each group had nearly the same amount of space in the *Belfast Telegraph*. The tendency to sectionalism in this type of reporting was presumably exaggerated by the fact that the religious leaders were not simply members of the 'other' church, but tended to make statements which were more acceptable to their own side. For example, Catholic leaders were likely to couple condemnations of violence with condemnations of internment, both as a policy contravening social justice and

TABLE 28. Space given to various types of other news in the Northern Ireland media (column inches or seconds)

Type	Belfast Telegraph	News Letter	Irish Times	BBC TV Scene Around Six	UTV Ulster Reports
Peace movement activities and ecumenical meetings	203	290	260.5	809	594
Meetings and statements by Roman Catholic leaders	79.5	23	144.5	122	—
Meetings and statements by Protestant leaders	90	159	15.5	37	205
Civil rights and anti-internment demonstrations and statements	46.5	325	159.5	107	21
Protests at the Maze prison (period I)	216	137	126.5	544	163
Sectional solidarity demonstrations					
Catholic	9.5	6	62.5	—	—
Loyalist	116.5	250	—	75	25

on pragmatic grounds that it provided the IRA with a justified grievance they could exploit to win popular support.

Sectionalism was even more apparent in the reporting of other attacks on internment. The same day (2 October 1974) on which the *Irish News* led on Bishop Daly's condemnation of the policy, its other main front-page story (54 column inches) reported future plans for demonstrations and a general strike to be organized by an association of the Friends and Relatives of the Internees based in Derry. The strike call was noticed by *Scene Around Six* the same day, though the report emphasized that Bishop Daly, whose condemnation of internment had been reported at length in the previous day's programme, was opposed to a strike. Next day, however, all three papers reported the strike was off. The *News Letter* announced this and the Bishop's opposition to the strike in a short story on the front page. A week later when the march was finally held reports of it took up 8 ½ column inches on the front page of the *Irish News*, but only 1 inch and 4 inches on the inside pages of the *News Letter* and the *Belfast Telegraph*. It was also reported in the two television programmes with the news point that the march caused traffic chaos. Once again, however, the visual nature of the event was not an adequate explanation for the attention given to it on television since the only visual presentation used (on *Scene Around Six*) was a reporter-to-camera one in a Derry location.

As well as this march, various other demonstrations and statements against the policy were reported, often as the focus of activities by successors to the original civil-rights associations. Table 28 shows that these were given most space in the *Irish News*. Some such statements reported in the *Irish News* came explicitly from Provisional Sinn Fein sources and it is widely believed that the old civil-rights associations are now controlled by such groups. These figures largely reflect the fact that such sources are acceptable to the *Irish News* but not to the other two papers. In their case the main stories included in the count were reports of a statement from the British NCCL opposing the renewal of anti-terrorist legislation and of the activities of Lord Feather and the Human Rights Commission in Northern Ireland.

In the first period particularly, civil-rights activities were also connected with a series of protests and demonstrations against conditions in the Maze prison. Both Loyalist and Republican prisoners were involved in these protests and a straight column-inch count, shown in Table 28, reveals little sectionalism in the reporting of events. There was a clear difference of interpretation, however, between the *News Letter* and the *Irish News*. Reports in the latter emphasized that both groups were involved and shared the same grievances even though the republicans might have an extra one that the authorities took less notice of representations on their behalf than those from Loyalists. The implication of the *Irish News* style of coverage—that Republican and Loyalists shared common grievances against the British authorities—was made explicit in the paper's lead story of 3 October 1974. The paper reported that the Westminster Parliament would have to re-examine internment because British troops might be unable to contain united rioting by both groups.

It quoted examples of co-operation between the two groups given by Unionist and anti-Unionist politicians. It implied that visiting had been resumed and other facilities restored because of this wider threat which lay behind the rioting. This was the change of policy which the *Daily Mirror* announced as a 'cave in' to violence.

The other two papers did not have any particular explanation for the apparent change of policy by the authorities. The *Belfast Telegraph* quoted a government spokesman as saying the decision followed discussions between the governor and representatives of the prisoners, the *News Letter* reported the resumption of visits very briefly at the end of a front-page story on riots and arson at the Maze. In the story the violent protests were linked with IRA threats to burn the jails while Loyalist leaders were reported to be asking for permission to inspect and meet the authorities. The theme that the Republicans, unlike the Loyalists, were acting violently and outside proper channels was apparent but not consistently developed in other reports of these protests in the *News Letter*. So, too, was the theme that the authorities should have begun to release Loyalist detainees because of the ceasefire declared by the Protestant paramilitary organizations.

Both television programmes had a series of stories on the dispute. *Ulster Reports* was blacked out by a strike on two dates at the end of September and from 2 to 4 October, the crucial times for the resolution of the conflict, so its coverage was less extensive and continuous than that of *Scene Around Six*. In the last days of September, *Scene Around Six* dealt extensively with the different involvement of Loyalist and Republican prisoners. The former were twice reported to have had their privileges restored as they had ended their protests, though they later renewed them. The latter were reported as being supported by Provisional Sinn Fein. The minister responsible, Lord Donaldson, refused to meet representatives of that organization and when Republican groups organized supporting protests outside the jail the Provisional IRA was quoted as threatening to burn the jails down if conditions were not improved. On 1 October both programmes had stories about the trouble caused by a ban on visiting at the prison which centred on would-be visitors waiting to get in and demands by the Loyalist politicians, Paisley and Craig, to be allowed in to see their constituents. The BBC story had apparently contradictory quotes from a minister for Northern Ireland who claimed Paisley was not allowed in because the military had taken over and a spokesman from the Northern Irish office who denied army involvement in spite of Paisley's allegation that he had seen soldiers inside in full riot gear. (These claims and counter claims were also featured in the press.) The next day *Scene Around Six* carried a long visual story of women and children rioting outside the jail which also included the news that the governor had decided to rescind the ban and restrictions on privileges, though visitors and inmates might suffer some inconvenience because of the damage they had caused. This could hardly amounted to an explanation of the decision. The following day, 3 October, *Scene Around Six* carried a story that Loyalist prisoners were still protesting because there had been relatively few releases from their side. By the next day, however, all the trouble seemed to be over and the programme reported briefly that Merlyn Rees had had talks with the governor.

These stories have been illustrated at some length because they provide a good example of the relative breadth of BBC coverage. Its stories carried all the newspoints from the Republican and Loyalist sides except for an explanation of the governor's decision to restore privileges, presumably because there would have been no official confirmation of any explanation. On this occasion, the strike prevented UTV following the events so closely. For the days it was on the air it had similar, though shorter, items than the BBC, including one report in the early days of a foiled escape which the BBC did not carry. The general conclusion is the same as that which was drawn from a comparison of the two stations' political coverage, that the BBC drew a wider sample but from essentially the same universe as UTV. This general point is illustrated in Table 28 which shows that the BBC gave more than one and a half times as much time than UTV to the various types of other news discussed in this chapter.

Apart from the civil rights, anti-internment and prison condition demonstrations, there were also several ceremonies in both periods in which different sections of the community within Northern Ireland affirmed their solidarity and their common beliefs. Among the Catholics there were religious ceremonies and pilgrimages reported most extensively in the *Irish News*, but noticed by the other papers. There were also some Protestant religious ceremonies in memory of significant events in the Protestant past as well as marches and other activities by the Orange Order. These were reported in the *News Letter* and the *Belfast Telegraph* but passed unnoticed by the *Irish News*. Only the largest of all these demonstrations, a march by 30,000 Orangemen in Belfast in the second period to celebrate the opening of a new headquarters, was covered in the television programmes. Table 28 clearly shows the sectionalism one might expect in the reporting of such affirmations of community solidarity.

The Irish media

The Irish media generally carried more stories about the north than their counterparts on the British mainland. In the case of the newspapers, this was reflected in a much more extensive coverage of other news. In the second period the proportion of other stories was lower in the *Irish Press* than the *Irish Times* and the *Irish Independent*. These two papers tended to concentrate on two different types of other news from the north. The *Irish Independent* carried more news about 'ordinary' personal disasters; the *Irish Times*, more on economic and industrial matters. In both cases, this news was reported on its own terms not as a complement, contrast or consequence of the troubles. Similarly, there was no sign in the Irish newspapers of the aggressive cheerfulness of the *Daily Mirror* and the British popular press. There was, however, a sense of weary irony, apparent, for example, in some of the reporting of continuing political machinations or the court case referred to above which carried the message this would be funny if it was not so tragic.

The major public activities of the peace groups, and other ecumenical meetings and activities were all covered as a matter of routine. The presentation of the 'People Together' petition was not covered so extensively as its launch which had taken up 54 column inches in the *Irish Times*. Even so the *Irish Independent* gave the story 21 column inches on its back page. The meeting of Protestant and Catholic leaders at Dundalk in the second period which was noticed by the British and Northern Irish media because of the statement issued against internment, was placed in a wider context by the Irish newspapers. The end of internment was only one of the questions considered by the working party which was billed by the Irish newspapers as a quasi summit conference. Others included such traditional sources of friction between the two sections of the community in the north as the religious barriers to adoption and mixed marriage, the Republic's claim to jurisdiction over the north, the majority's apparent refusal to share power and the way religious differences were made an excuse for sectarian violence. In the second period, too, representatives of the British council of (Protestant) churches met in the north. This was covered in the *Irish Times* and the *Irish Independent*. So, too, were the statements and activities of the Roman Catholic hierarchy including their advice to the Catholic electorate in the north not to observe the boycott of the Convention Election.

There were few protests against prison conditions in the second period. In the first, RTE reported only brief accounts of incidents as they occurred at the Maze, but the *Irish Times* followed developments closely, distinguishing between the different involvement of Loyalist and Republican prisoners at different stages. After the riots on 3 October 1974, the *Irish Times* published a long story discussing the reasons for the governor's change in policy on visits and privileges. To the paper, this appeared to be a climb down and a victory for the Republican prisoners because the authorities were apprehensive there might be a full-scale united riot by both groups. The *Irish Times* also followed the planning and execution of the various sympathy strikes and demonstrations. Other demonstrations by the old civil-rights organizations were briefly noted, but so too were Loyalist demonstrations. The big march to celebrate the opening of a new headquarters for the Orange Order was reported at some length in the *Irish Times* though the main focus of the report in that paper, as it was also in a briefer account in the *Irish Independent*, was on the disturbances the march had caused.

The general conclusion to be drawn from this as from other aspects of the coverage in the Irish newspapers is that Northern Ireland was not a single news story as in the British press which tended to report continued variations on the single theme of 'trouble'. Instead, the north was just another location in which news occurred, albeit a rather special one. This distinction does not apply to RTE's radio bulletins however. They carried a very small proportion of other news, while most of the political, law enforcement and violence news dealt with developments in the troubles.

Conclusion

Other news in the British media illustrated two main features of the way they presented news about Northern Ireland. The first was the tendency to concentrate on aspects of general human interest; the second, the tendency to treat all stories from the north as variations on the single story, 'the troubles'. Both these preoccupations were less apparent in the media from Ireland. There was also a difference of tone between the two which was apparent elsewhere, for example in the political coverage, but most obvious in the treatment of other news. Whereas the British press, led by the *Daily Mirror*, showed a determination to be aggressively cheerful about life in Northern Ireland in spite of everything, the Irish papers adopted a tone of weary cynicism. In Northern Ireland itself, press and television were not prepared to make light of incidents which necessarily had serious implications for some people or embodied sincere attempts to improve life in the province. These latter activities gave rise to a type of 'good news' for which there was little place in the British media, using such canons of news presentation as novelty, importance and human interest, but which was reported regularly in both the local and Irish media.

Chapter 5

Conclusion: reporting social conflict

The previous three chapters have set out in some detail an analysis of the news related to Northern Ireland and the troubles there in two periods in 1974 and 1975. This chapter will be more concerned with the general view of the province and its troubles which appear in the various news media, with the underlying problems these media face in reporting a situation of social conflict on their doorstep, the ways these have been resolved and the consequences for the output. In moving from the particular to the general, it is important to remember that the two periods studied were two moments in a continuing historical process. The situation in the province changed between the two periods. It has changed again since. The level of community murder and assassination has increased; the Provisional IRA has resumed its campaign; the Convention was finally disbanded after failing to reach an agreement acceptable to all parties and the British Government. The arrangements for covering the news have also changed in the course of the troubles, most recently with the decision by police and army sources to withhold the religious affiliations of victims in an attempt to discourage revenge killing.

The most striking change in both the situation, the arrangements for news gathering and the general account of events in the province appears to have occurred at an earlier stage, after August 1969, when the British army went in. So far as the British press was concerned, army involvement made it more of a domestic issue and more like a conventional war story than it had been when the Stormont administration was opposed by its own dissidents. For the Irish, it awoke memories of other occasions when the British army had been involved in Ireland. For all media, it meant that the army became a prominent source of information as well as a party to the conflict. Censorship of Northern Ireland news became an issue in Great Britain after the involvement of the British army. In Ireland it was sparked off by the development of the Provisional IRA campaign. These debates were reviewed in Chapter 1. In both countries, the effects of government intervention were similar. Broadcast news has largely been limited to what could be covered using the 'factual, objective style' of news reporting which concentrates on relaying publicly available information about known events. This style increased the importance of army information officers and official spokesmen generally as sources for broadcast news.

But such sources are themselves participants in the conflict. Their responsibility is less to provide the public with a factual account of events than to further their own ends in the conflict, to fight a propaganda war alongside the war on the streets against those they regard as the enemy.[1] The tactics employed in the propaganda war have changed from period to period. Attempts to blacken the name of the Provisional IRA have been interspersed with others to deny the political, warlike aspects of the conflict altogether, and emphasize its simple criminality. Throughout the aim has been to play down army initiative and action and to emphasize its responsive, peace-keeping role. Also the army has feared becoming involved in a war on two fronts, against members of the Protestant community as well as the Catholics. In propaganda terms this has meant playing down Loyalist violence to such an extent that Protestant extremists themselves have complained about the lack of attention given to their efforts. In both the periods covered by the study a new Loyalist extremist organization emerged and claimed responsibility for a series of murders. Several of these had been wrongly or ambiguously attributed when they had first occurred, apparently as a result of misinformation supplied by the police and the army.

These tactics all had a discernible effect on the account of violence presented in the media, as analysed in Chapter 2.

Stories of actual and potential IRA atrocities were carried in the first period, particularly in the British popular press and the *News Letter*. Several near-misses on children and school buses were reported. In 1973, Simon Hoggart noted that such stories were usually tacked on to the 'rather skeletal description of the day-to-day incidents' provided by the army's 'straightforward information service', as they were 'a fair bet for the first paragraph of a radio bulletin or a newspaper report'.

Throughout the two periods studied, the army appeared as almost above the fray—brave, tormented, but largely inactive except as a rather superior kind of Boy Scout Troop. Simon Hoggart's apocryphal example of a local battalion PRO ringing round to 'sell' a story about his men rescuing a wounded gull from some boys was echoed in several stories of soldiers coming to the aid of the local population on foot, in boats or in helicopters.

In general, the source of violence was portrayed as terrorism, the result of inexplicable, asocial forces.

In so far as it was not terrorism, it was sectarianism, the product of another force, equally inexplicable, but somehow diffused throughout the community.

---

1. Kitson's (1971) manual on low intensity operations refers to this type of warfare as psychological operations. He laments that: 'Although the British seem to persist in thinking of psychological operations as being something from the realms of science fiction, it has for many years been regarded as a necessary and respectable form of war by most of our allies as well as virtually all of our potential enemies' (p. 189), a disclaimer and justification which an Irishman might be forgiven for regarding as 'typically British'.

Or it was feuding. Feuding was irrational because it involved death and injury but more explicable because it occurred among the perpetrators of terrorism and sectarianism who had put themselves outside society and beyond the reach of reason anyway.

These pointers to features of the content discussed in earlier chapters are overgeneralized in the sense that they apply more to the British-oriented media than the Irish-oriented, more to the British popular press, the *News Letter* and broadcasting than to the quality press in Great Britain. Throughout the account in the earlier chapters reference was made to exceptional cases where, for example, a British paper did not opt with the others to attribute a particular incident to the IRA. Individual papers also had their own particular style. The *Daily Express* was most jingoistic in that it apparently wanted its readers to know that a war was going on and their side was winning. The *Daily Mirror* echoed the style it had used in the Second World War, treating the soldiers as good old British tommies and the civilians as people who could be relied upon to keep smiling through. The *Daily Mail* provided remarkably broad coverage of Northern Ireland politics but, like the *Daily Telegraph*, it was concerned to exploit both the politics and the violence in Northern Ireland for party political advantage in Great Britain. In the *Daily Telegraph*, such exploitation had distinctly Powellite overtones. The *Guardian*'s coverage showed breadth in that it took account of Catholic as well as Protestant opinion; *The Times* had in Robert Fisk the only journalist in the periods covered who was able to bring a story to light as a result of his own efforts in seeking out information. His story of Libyan involvement in the arms traffic to Northern Ireland was the only one in the periods studied which broke as a result of journalistic endeavour rather than being triggered off by some public occurrence.

Such pen portraits are a useful corrective to the view that generalization is clear and straightforward. The uniformity of information and interpretation described in the previous chapters is far from complete. In this chapter, however, the aim will be to show that the uniformity (and the variations from it) are partly a product of the information available about events in the province and the control the official sources exercised over it and partly a result of different journalistic styles of relaying, presenting and supplementing such information, as practised in different countries for different audiences.

In making information available, the official sources in the province, the army, the police and the Northern Ireland Office, occupy a strategic position. To quote from Simon Hoggart again:

When the British press prints an account of an incident as if it were established fact and it is clear that the reporter himself was not on the spot, it is a 99 per cent certainty that it is the army's version which is being given.

The evidence for the account given earlier of official tactics used in the presentation of information comes mainly from journalists' accounts, both of general official policy and of particular cases where they have been misled. These accounts, however, have rarely been published in the press or broadcasting news but in books and magazines.[1] This could be taken as an argument for the division of labour among media, except that the audience for the news media, the audience which is presented with the 'established facts', is much larger and less selective than that for the books and journals from which it is possible to find out some of the ways in which those facts were established. Moreover, as the content analysis showed, dealing in 'established facts' is not a necessary feature of journalism. It is a contingent feature of the way journalism is practised in Great Britain. The Irish papers were generally more open about how they had come to know what they reported. The general reasons why British journalism has been particularly concerned to foster the mystique that it deals only in 'established fact' are beyond the scope of this study.

Nevertheless, dealing specifically with Northern Ireland, there are pressing reasons why journalists should continue to take official sources seriously, to regard the information such sources provide as facts, even though they recognize that the sources have an interest in the conflict, may have a policy line to push and have been caught out in the past misleading them or their colleagues. Simon Hoggart's optimistic conclusion that the army PR operation is 'a considerable success', founded on goodwill which 'would be quickly dissipated by an incompetent or else a deliberately misleading operation' is disingenuous to say the least. Hoggart's colleague on the *Guardian*, Simon Winchester, reports several cases in which he was misled by the army and put under pressure by them. Though Winchester's book, *In Holy Terror*, was published after Hoggart's article, the incidents occurred before.

For British journalists there is a predisposition to believe those who in some sense represent the British side. In Northern Ireland, the British have a further advantage in that they can successfully pose as having no side, as being independent champions of law and order:[2]

Our job is to tell the truth at all times and to correct the deliberate misinformation put out by the other side. Occasionally we make mistakes, but we always correct them wherever possible. I have no objection to newspapers printing what the other side says, but I do get angry when they suggest that they are right.

But it may be less a question of what journalists believe than the view they take of their responsibility. This can be interpreted simply as seeing that the British version reaches the British people. This was part of the case Desmond Taylor, Head of News and Current Affairs, BBC, put in an interview in the *Irish Times* (15 November 1975).

I certainly feel that the Army, as the lawful and useful arm of the State, must be given a right to speak its voice and version of things to the people of the State through the public broadcasting system—this has always been my view.

More generally, however, there is simply a tendency to take official sources on trust unless there are good reasons against it. This was poingnantly expressed by Andrew Stephen, Belfast correspondent of the

1. Stephen's article in the *Observer* is a partial exception to this.
2. Fairly senior army PR officer quoted by Hoggart.

Observer, when he wrote: 'The sad experience for most British journalists once they start working in Northern Ireland is that the word of the authorities cannot automatically be relied upon.' This attitude of automatic acceptance is a long way from the position of professional sceptic current in the mythology of journalism and captured by Claud Cockburn with the phrase: 'Don't believe anything until it has been officially denied.' Nevertheless, there are good reasons for it in the contemporary practice of journalism.

The main one paradoxically is competition. In this, as in other spheres, competition tends to produce similarity, not difference. The cautionary tale at the beginning of Andrew Stephen's article was of a bomb explosion in the Catholic Falls Road which, on the face of it, appeared to be the work of Loyalist extremists. The army, however, put about that it was a Provisional IRA bomb intended for elsewhere. 'Before long', Stephen writes, 'a reporter on BBC television's nine o'clock news was informing the nation that it was widely assumed that the Falls Road explosion had been caused by an IRA bomb going off prematurely'. Once such an account is broadcast to the nation, before the morning press has even reached its publishing deadlines, it would be a brave journalist who would report a different version, simply on his own intuition or the word of unofficial sources, and an even braver sub-editor who would let the copy pass.

Foolhardy is perhaps a better adjective than brave to describe such an action. It is not the bravery or integrity of individual journalists, or even particular news desks, that is in question so much as the way their scope for independent action is necessarily circumscribed by the context in which they work. Official sources should be in the best position to know and in any particular case may really have access to information which would authenticate their view and make any deviant interpretation look silly. Stepping out of line may upset the journalist's continuing relationship with such sources—a relationship necessary to produce future stories and information. The British authorities have not resorted to such crude tactics as expelling journalists or preventing their re-entry as the French did in Algeria and the South Vietnamese in Viet-Nam, but there are various sticks and carrots available to encourage journalists to co-operate. These include the quite opposite tactics of preventing the offending journalist from attending regular briefings and so cutting off his easy access to routine information, such as happened to Simon Winchester, or feeding him an exclusive authenticated scoop. Such a scoop will put a different complexion on events from the original, offensive story. It may also win the journalists' co-operation for the future (Hoggart).

If the deviant interpretation were to come from a broadcast journalist then the official sources can do more than make the broadcasting organization look silly. Questions in the House can be orchestrated to inspire ministerial pressure on the broadcasting authorities to remember their responsibilities. This happened in 1971 when the censorship debate was at its height. Through the mechanism of competition, this possibility of influencing broadcast news media is not without its effect on the news carried by the press.

As well as alerting the authorities, deviant interpretations are also liable to be noticed by the reader. British readers may be expected to share with British journalists the same predisposition to believe that their government and their army is on the side of the angels, and to expect very good evidence if it is to be asked to believe otherwise. This is all the more so in a case like Northern Ireland where the issue has been removed from party conflict. Acting in Northern Ireland, the government is able to pose not as a Conservative or a Labour Government but as the British Government. There are few politically partisan differences for the press to exploit on the issue, thus removing one factor which makes for some diversity among the British press on other subjects.

Potentially, therefore, the reporter or editor who sticks his neck out by abandoning the official version has much to lose and little to gain. At the least, there is a risk of losing credibility if the account appears strikingly different from that of the competition. The ubiquity of broadcast news in its various forms and the decline in the practice of reading more than one newspaper have made the broadcast account a more important reference point for press journalists. At the worst, there is a danger of appearing partisan within the terms of the Northern Ireland conflict itself, a position precluded by the behaviour of both sides. To take a view on Northern Ireland now would require so many disclaimers of sympathy, let alone responsibility for the actions of those involved, that it could hardly be fitted into the space generally available in a newspaper, let alone a news programme.[1]

There is no reason to suppose that the journalist consciously calculates these various risks when he writes a story or that he thinks about the accolades he might receive if he went out on a limb against the official interpretation and was proved right. Such accolades are rare and grudgingly bestowed. For every Woodstein able to bask in the glory of media stardom there must be many like Eddie Milne and the journalists who supported him in his campaign against corruption in the Labour Party in the north-east of England. Their triumphs have been conveniently forgotten, not to say wilfully ignored. Journalists' immediate calculations are in terms of what to write about the bomb in the Falls or the Shankhill, faced with the blood and guts of the particular atrocity, conflicting accounts from witnesses who may well be interested parties, an urgent deadline and instructions from the newsroom in London to keep it short because people are not interested in Northern Ireland any more.[2] In the immediate situation the journalist is likely simply to follow working practices as the quickest route to a publishable story. The calculations set out above are to be found embodied in such working practices which are the collective wisdom of how to survive in the craft of journalism.

1. Namely, the space the *Sunday Times* gave to its latest attempt to discuss the question: 'Ulster: What Can We do?', *Sunday Times*, 11 January 1976 and then *The Times* was canvassing alternatives, not taking a particular line.
2. This is a caricatured observation, not a blanket condemnation of all British news editors. For example, towards the end of 1970 Simon Winchester (1975, p. 111) reports receiving instructions from Harry Whewell, Northern News Editor of the *Guardian* as follows: 'I don't care if the readers think it is boring. You report it all, every day, and we'll get through to them in time—it's a duty now. We have to see it through.'

Survival conditions are not the same for all journalists, even for all British journalists working in Northern Ireland. One difference is to be found in the extent to which the individual journalist can control his own copy and see what he wrote, attributed to him in the paper. In general, the quality papers are writers' papers in which a correspondent can expect to see his material in print with only minor amendments. The popular papers are sub-editors' papers. The actual stories which appear in the paper are written in the newsroom from reporters' copy, agency accounts and the sub-editor's feel for the story that is needed on that particular subject, in that particular space, on that particular day, in their paper. A reporter from a popular paper, therefore, has little incentive to provide anything but routine coverage. That is what the sub-editor will probably base the story on anyway. In Belfast, routine coverage can be had by staying in the Europa Hotel, or whatever is currently the journalists' haunt, listening to the local media, attending routine briefings and generally frequenting the bar with the crowd. Correspondents for the quality press and Irish journalists, concerned at the ignorance of Ireland and the Irish apparent in much early British reporting, have come to attribute these deficiencies to this practice of reporting in a herd, a practice from which they disassociate themselves.

Many of the calculations set out above to show how the scales are balanced in favour of official sources are different for an Irish journalist writing for an Irish public. There is no reason why the Irish, journalist or reader, should feel any particular affinity with the British government and the British army, or be prepared to accept their Olympian view of themselves as somehow above and outside the conflict. Nevertheless, even for such journalists the official sources are able to act as powerful gatekeepers controlling the flow of information. In the content analysis several cases were noted where the Irish papers apparently distrusted official accounts, but did not feel able to ignore them until there was clear evidence for an alternative interpretation.

This introduces another feature of information gathering in Northern Ireland, the lack of any credible alternatives to set against the official sources. British journalists like Andrew Stephen, distressed to find they have been led up the garden path by the army, or disturbed at seeing no less a person than the Secretary of State for Northern Ireland apparently taking the House of Commons for a tour of the same cabbage patch, can always console themselves with the thought that 'the word of the terrorist organizations tends to be considerably less reliable still'. Non-official sources may themselves be involved in acts of violence against other citizens if not against the State. In Northern Ireland, it has been relatively easy to meet spokesmen for the different organizations involved, but to get beyond the frontmen may involve clandestine and potentially dangerous meetings with those who at least metaphorically have blood on their hands. Where official sources try to conceal their propaganda intent to maintain their guise of Olympian detachment, non-official sources may make it much more obvious that they are trying to push a line. Of itself this does not make the line less valid, but it is bound to alert the journalist to be more wary.

The content analysis provided several examples of stories in which the non-official version of events turned out to be correct, but where this only came out later because of some other development. Because of the topicality of news 'later' in effect means too late. Few attempts are made to correct the reports of yesterday or the day before once the attention has moved on to today's incidents. The only medium which published an explicit correction of a story published in error was the *Irish Independent*, reinforcing the point that the Irish papers were in general more open about the processes of journalism. Occasionally, non-official sources could authenticate their claims, as, for example, when the Provisional IRA produced the tapes found on the alleged soldier-spy or the Official IRA held a news conference at which small boys testified that they had been paid to spy for the army. Even then these versions did not gain wide credence or coverage.

Of course to say these claims were authenticated begs the question of whether the proof was itself faked. Martin Bell, sometime BBC TV News reporter in Northern Ireland, quotes such a case where it was possible to dismantle an 'atrocity story':

On one occasion during an Army search of the Short Strand area of Belfast, I was assured not once but dozens of times that a priest had been beaten up. It was possible to find the man and to discover that so far from being disturbed by the Army, he had not been aware that the search was going on.

The same point can be made against the authentications provided by official sources. Simon Winchester tells such a cautionary tale in which the army backed up its claims that the searches in the Falls Road on 3 July 1970 had been carried out with a minimum of fuss and interference by pointing out that only fifteen rounds of ammunition had been fired. Later figures were published showing that the correct figure was 1,454 rounds. Winchester (1975, p. 71) comments:

Ever since those later figures were quietly published, many reporters found it terribly hard to accept contemporary accounts of a serious disturbance by the Army's public relations men. Never since then have I found myself able to take the army's explanation about any single incident with any less a pinch of salt than I would take any other explanation.

Ultimately the question of who to believe must be a matter of judgement. There is a tendency in contemporary journalism, however, to abdicate the responsibility for making such a judgement. The tendency is most marked in broadcast news because of the constitutional and organizational circumscriptions within which it operates. The source of an item or an interpretation may become a more important criterion than its truth or falsity. Desmond Taylor, in the statement quoted above, was insisting on the BBC's responsibility to tell the people of the State, the State's version of events. By implication this is a responsibility to be fulfilled regardless of the inherent truth of that version. The story of the disturbances at the Maze prison, noted in the content analysis, provides an example of a case where considerations of the importance of the sources apparently outweighed considerations of who was correct. In that case, in the local BBC TV story, Ian Paisley claimed he had seen troops in riot gear in the prison, while a Minister of State for Northern Ireland denied that troops were involved. Another example of a false assertion passing unchallenged occurred when a spokesman for the Belfast bus crews claimed that there was no sectarianism among the staff. By then it was known that the bus inspector who had been assassinated had been a prominent figure in the UDA.

Martin Bell has provided a succinct account of the reasons for such practices discussing a story where he was faced with two conflicting accounts with no means of choosing between them:

the reporter arrives one dark winter afternoon in a country town with strong Republican traditions. A riot is subsiding, the main street is blocked by a troop of Marines at one end and a burning bus at the other; a 16-year old boy lies dead in the local hospital. The army insist he was armed when they shot him; local people just as positively deny it. There's little the reporter can do but talk to both sides, record their versions of the event, and leave the viewing public to choose between them.

In the previous paragraph of the same article, however, he also set out a case which showed one consequence of the practice. As the reporter

picks his way through the rubble which minutes before was a Belfast pub . . . he finds that the rival sectarian versions of the event are already circulating. A protestant outrage against catholic lives and property? An IRA headquarters where the bomb-makers blew themselves up? Each side in the end will believe what it wants to believe, ascribe the atrocity to the other, and expect the BBC to echo its judgement.

Faced with a bald account of the facts, or rival versions of the facts laid side by side, with no elaboration of the meaning and significance of the incident, how else can the viewing public be excepted to judge than by its pre-conceptions?

Reference was made in the content analysis to several cases in the press as well as in the broadcast bulletins where rival interpretations of an incident were laid side by side. There were also many cases in which the meaning and significance of the incident was not elaborated even to the extent of identifying the victim or attributing the violence. It may be that in any particular case this was simply because the information was not known or was contentious. It is important to note, however, that the most closely controlled medium, RTE, was also the one which provided least details about the incidents reported. In the British broadcast bulletins incident followed incident in a steady stream, with few follow-up or review stories. On RTE it was even more a case of 'one damn thing after another'. The reports were cut to the bare bones of what had happened, where, and who was involved simply in terms of age and sex. This is presumably the bare minimum necessary to fulfil one of the criteria Desmond Fisher set out in the interview quoted above for providing a public service, namely to give 'a straightforward account of what's happening'. For most of the media, reporting Northern Ireland was mainly a process of recording the violence, building on this basic minimum of who, what and where.

Implicitly, however, this minimum already contains a fundamental categorization of the troubles in Northern Ireland. In spite of its simplicity and appearance of raw facticity, it categorizes the incidents as different examples of the general phenomenon, violence against the human race. The general characteristics of age, sex and location are causally unrelated to the incidence of violence, and so descriptive, not explanatory. Their logical extension is to be found in the personal details and accidents of time and space which provide the focus for much of the violence reporting in all media, but particularly in the popular press. They are the stuff of human interest journalism. Another elaborated version is to be found in the comments of community leaders, politicians and public figures that violence is both senseless and horrid. These commentators are licensed to make explicit the values which are already implicit in the style of reporting.

The style of reporting which poses as value free, the simple recording of facts about the world, is thus heavily value laden. Explicitly, pressure and controls are imposed to restrict news to the known facts of the incident. Implicitly, however, this does not just limit the information available. It ensures that the conflict is seen in a particular light because of the nature of the information left. It is a style of journalism which makes violence less rather than more explicable. This is a much more general feature of Northern Ireland reporting and indeed of the reporting of most situations of conflict in the world, than the issues of bias and distortion in the interpretation of particular incidents or the use made of particular sources such as have been discussed so far. It taps a core value in Western liberal democracies, the sanctity of human life; a value which in itself is thoroughly laudable but which when incorporated into a dominant national ideology expressed implicitly and explicitly in news reporting is not without political consequences. The most important of these is to set those who resort to violence outside society.

This is a view which can be sustained politically. After the assassination of the British Ambassador in Dublin in July 1976, the British Prime Minister, James Callaghan, concluded his report to parliament with the lament 'when will this senseless killing stop?' The leader of the opposition, Margaret Thatcher, echoed his sentiments and emphasized that it would not weaken 'our resolve to root out terrorism'. The Ambassador himself was reported as having said that he went to Ireland with no preconceived notions except that he 'just had a hatred of political violence'. But it is a position which has political costs, making some courses of action more difficult to follow. Merlyn Rees or those in his office who had talks with the Provisional IRA had to conceal that they were doing so. They were publicly committed to the position that the IRA were untouchables whom they would not meet, much less treat with.

Similarly, it is a view which can be sustained in journalism, but again not without cost. Repetition of the descriptive labels gunmen, bomber, terrorist, may serve to identify such people as people apart, outside society. The problems arise as their activities continue year after year. Gradually it becomes apparent that the terrorists, to borrow Mao Tse-tung's analogy, are not fish on dry land but fish in the sea.

Second-order explanations are then possible. It can be argued that this only goes to show how unlike other men they are; mad, pathological creatures who have no need of the conventional human comforts. After a series of outrages in England in 1975, Paul Johnson (1975) wrote in the *New Statesman*:

In Britain, as well as in Ulster, we face in the IRA not a nationalist movement, not a league of patriots, not 'guerillas' or 'freedom fighters', or anything which can be dignified with a political name, but an organization of psychopathic murderers who delight in maiming and slaughtering the innocent and whose sole object and satisfaction in life is the destruction of human flesh. The misguided patriots who joined the IRA in the heady days of 1968 and after have melted away and have been replaced by men and women who have far more in common with Ian Brady and Myra Hindley than with old-style terrorists like Michael Collins and De Valera.

This outburst includes attempts to reassign labels and redefine history. These are characteristic ways of isolating the present phenomenon from the past and exposing it to obloquy. They are to be found in the reporting of other types of deviance and other deviant groups (Cohen and Young, 1973). It is also a common feature of war reporting that the other side comes to be portrayed as sub-human barbarians simply because they are the 'other side' (Knightley, 1975).

Another common second-order explanation for the persistence of terrorism is intimidation. In Algeria and Viet-Nam this led to various 'pacification' and 'resettlement' programmes designed to separate the fish from the sea, the terrorists from the local population. Such policies have not been advocated in Northern Ireland, but 'intimidation' is occasionally given as a reason why the British Government and army should adopt a more vigorous security policy. Crudely used 'intimidation' can be made to appear as the single, sufficient cause of Catholic acquiescence in continued violence. To do so, however, is to oversimplify by ignoring other features of the situation.

These may also open up other gaps between the account and the reality. In the content analysis, it was pointed out that while the main preoccupation in the reporting was with terrorist violence, in fact most victims of violence were Catholics. Again second-order explanations can be introduced: this just shows how stupid and senseless the Provisional IRA campaign is when those they are supposed to be protecting or on whose behalf they are supposed to be fighting are the ones who are suffering. Periodically, an incident occurs from which this moral can be clearly drawn. In August 1976, for example, three Catholic children were run down and killed by a car out of control in which terrorists had been trying to escape from the army. Next day the *Daily Telegraph* headline read 'IRA Gunmen's Car Kills Two Children'. Most Catholic victims, however, are not killed and injured unintentionally by the IRA but quite intentionally by Protestant extremists. The style of reporting used in the British-oriented media obscures rather than clarifies this point. Potentially this would provide another explanation for Catholic acquiescence in IRA violence. Unlike 'intimidation', it is essentially a rational explanation, that it is in their interest to acquiesce. An editorial in the *Observer* (15 August 1976), following a week which included the incident in which the three children were killed, provided an unusually complex account of Catholic attitudes.

People in Britain often ask about the real attitude of catholics towards the IRA. It is a naive question. Attitudes are compounded of many strands: certainly an atavistic loyalty to a united Ireland (when in the Republic that aspiration has melted away) but also a fear based on frequent knee-cappings and executions; and another fear: of British ambiguity and lack of persistence, a feeling that troops might be withdrawn, and that if they were the IRA might be the Catholic ghettos' only defence against Protestant extremists. These must all be set against the great longing for peace demonstrated yesterday [by women from Andersonstown at the site where the three children died].

This account is unusual in that it allows the possibility that the behaviour of those linked to the 'other side' may after all be rational. Intrinsically there is no reason why 'our side' should have a monopoly of reason while the behaviour of the 'other side' is irrational or compelled. It is the practice of news reporting which makes it appear that way.

Similarly, although the core value, the sanctity of human life, appears to be universal, its application in the practice of news reporting is partial. Core values are not applied objectively and impartially in the style of journalism which professes those ideals, but in line with the ideology of the state in which the journalism is practised. Audience interest always ensures that death or injury to a national of the State is given more prominence than equivalent or greater sufferings endured by foreigners. It is common in war to find racial overtones in the conflict. Little value is placed on the lives of those on the 'other side', including civilians and non-combatants. Knightley (1975, p. 396), for example, considering the reporting of the Viet Nam war, quotes a British photo-journalist, Philip Jones Griffiths, who explained why he had not taken pictures of Vietnamese women and children being purposively killed by an artillery strike directed at them: 'If I had gone back to Saigon and into one of the agencies and had said "I've got a story about Americans killing Vietnamese civilians", they would have said "So what's new?" It was horrible, but certainly not exceptional, and it just wasn't news.' As Stuart Hall (1972, p. 103) has written: ' "News values" are, at the very least, a man-made system of relevancies ... the idea that such sedimented social knowledge is neutral—a set of technical protocols only is an illusion'.

The conflict in Northern Ireland has not reached anything like the scale of the Viet Nam war. Indeed, many would deny the parallel. The point of the parallel and the denials are usually political, to include or exclude Northern Ireland from the category of colonial or imperialist struggles. That is not the point here. The point is to show that comparable processes are involved in reporting conflict situations with comparable consequences for the version of events carried in the news output. There may be doubts as to whether Northern Ireland should be classed as a war and, if so, what type of war. Nevertheless, the practice of journalism and the values embodied in it interprets the situation there in a way which echoes the reporting of other wars. Because the war is less open, the echoes are more subdued.

In the abstract, the sanctity of human life appears to be a universal value. In practice, incorporated into the ideology of the State, it becomes particular in its application. The value of life on the 'other side' goes down, the value of life on 'our side' up. This is particularly true of those who occupy positions of real or symbolic authority in the State. The death of an ambassador, a judge, a magistrate, is worth more space than that of a 14-year-old mental defective, however heart-rending his story may be in terms of personal human interest. In response to such deaths, society, the social leadership, mobilizes and the media take part in the process of social cauterization described in Chapter 2. Those responsible for law and order in the State move into action and their words and deeds provide plenty of copy for press, television and radio. There were two examples of this in the content analysis. In Northern Ireland itself such cauterization seemed inhibited by the divided nature of the society, but it occurred in subdued form following the killing of the judge and magistrate. In Great Britain the bombing of servicemen and women in the Guildford pubs not only attacked the army, but brought a quasi-foreign war into the heart of England.

Universal respect for the sanctity of human life implies universal condemnation of violence. Again, however, this value is applied selectively to the perpetrators of violence. The scenario of violence in Northern Ireland is complicated by the assassination campaigns of the Loyalist extremist organizations.

Such groups, like the Loyalist extremists, in Northern Ireland, pose special problems for the dominant ideology. Starting from the premise that all violence is bad, all types have to be condemned. But to carry that through beyond a token opposition to 'violence on both sides' or 'wherever it may be found'; to present 'ugly' violence in the same way as 'bad' violence would be to direct the opposition of the State and its people against those whose interests it has decided to protect. Loyalist extremists in Northern Ireland should consider the fate of President Diem and the OAS as a warning that if the 'ugly' violence gets too bad then it simply cannot be coped with on an ideological level. Other action will follow. Indeed, it could be argued that some such action (on a much smaller scale) has already been taken in Northern Ireland with the dissolution of Stormont.

The Algerian and Viet Nam experiences could also be taken as evidence that the dominant ideology can only cope with so much 'good' violence too. In the course of the troubles in Northern Ireland, two incidents stand out as occasions on which it was gradually recognized and accepted that the British forces had overstepped the mark. After Bloody Sunday in Londonderry and after the revelations of the methods of interrogation used on internees at Ballykinler in 1971, the forces of law and order stood charged with using unacceptable violent methods to achieve their end. In both cases, however, the process of securing a conviction was lengthy and tortuous. Faced with revelations in the press, a growing scandal in and out of Parliament, the government of the day 'resorted to widgery' in Robert McKenzie's phrase. It appointed tribunals and commissions of inquiry, staffed by judges and privy counsellors, to sift the evidence and report on the incidents. The events themselves and those involved were then shrouded in the quasi-legal processes of taking and assessing evidence and arriving at carefully considered and scrupulously weighed conclusions. Lengthy reports can be ambiguously interpreted by national media. In the case of the Widgery Report on Bloody Sunday, judicious use of public relations methods ensured that in the British press the army appeared to have been exonerated.[1] These atrocities are then cloaked in an aura of doubt and uncertainty. If they are referred to subsequently, it is likely to be as 'so-called Bloody Sunday' or 'so-called torture', an event which was not quite real.

The interplay of ideology and reality prevents the dominant ideology from becoming a single, monolithic propaganda to which there is no alternative and from which there is no escape. To an extent this interplay is acted out through the news media. In both of the above cases, a newspaper, the *Sunday Times*, played a large part in bringing the issue to light and so prompting the authorities to 'resort to widgery'. An extreme version of the Althusserian argument that the media are to be numbered among the ideological apparatuses of the State, turning out the propaganda of the ruling class to maintain social order can be faulted by such examples. It can also be faulted by journalists, on the simple, pragmatic grounds that news-making does not happen like that. Winchester's (1975, p. 123) defence of an item which appeared in the *Guardian* unambiguously identifying a man who had been shot as a petrol bomber provides a typical example.

We had—at least some unfortunate, hard-pressed London sub-editor had—casually libelled a Belfast worker by the immense pressure of the work so early on that Saturday morning. But we had not libelled him, we had not 'justified his killing' for any reason other than the purely human reasons of tiredness and carelessness. For Bernadette [Devlin] to suggest, as she did by implication both in the Commons and in her subsequent letter to the paper, that the sub-editor, in liaison with the Ministry of Defence, or in deference to a subtle reactionary line on Ulster that she suspected the *Guardian* to have been developing, had concocted the report—this merely displayed the poor girl's naivete, her hysteria and . . . a kind of paranoia.

Such examples of the results and practices of news reporting provide evidence for the 'relative autonomy' which the news media enjoy within the State. Ostensibly the codes and practices of journalism are geared towards the specific ends of those organizations. In practice they also incorporate the goals and values of the State in which they operate. The analysis of the relationship between the news media and official sources of information presented earlier in this chapter shows one of the mechanisms by which the media serve an ideological function within the political system. This is not done under its direction but in pursuit of the subordinate goals of the news organizations themselves, to collect and disseminate 'news' and to attract an audience for it. The same goals underpin

---

1. See Simon Winchester's (1975, p. 21) account of Ministry of Defence leaks to the defence correspondents on the national press prior to the publication of the report.

such standard journalistic practices as paying attention to descriptive accuracy and looking for the human interest in any story. The consequence is the same. The values implicit in these styles of journalism ensure that the reports support the national ideology.

One indicator of autonomy is that different media can be found providing different versions of the same incident or a different general bias in their treatment of the subject. It is these differences which are usually referred to as both the product of and the evidence for a free press. Although the content analysis emphasized broad similarities to be found between national media, and particularly between national media using the same technology and catering for the same market, there was nevertheless plenty of evidence of variety and difference.

Variety in a free press has another advantage. It provides a guarantee of accuracy. The problem of whom to believe, whose version to print has been in the case of Northern Ireland reporting a problem of what meaning and significance to attach to events, not what events have actually happened. The bare minimum of broadcast coverage, as exemplified by RTE's reporting of violent incidents, does ensure that there is public knowledge about what is going on. The fact that Northern Ireland has been a public conflict, in the sense that it has always been relatively easy for reporters to go in and send information out, has prevented disputes arising simply at the level of what has happened. Partisanship between the two Belfast morning papers, for example, seems only rarely to have extended to reports of manufactured incidents and 'atrocities', a phenomenon which has been all too common in other wars. In the content analysis the only story which appeared to cover an incident unreported elsewhere was the *Irish News* story reporting another search by the 'glorious Gloucesters' of the home of a young Catholic mother. There is no way of knowing whether that was a manufactured atrocity or simply an incident which the other news organizations regarded as unimportant in news terms.

The notion of importance in news values is one key to the way in which the news media in different countries come to reflect the ideology of their particular nation. The incident of the army search would have had greater news importance for the Irish-oriented than the British-oriented media. A clearer example from the content analysis was the different importance the British and Irish media attached to the SDLP. For the British press and broadcasting, this party was an also-ran in Northern Ireland politics—'the mainly Catholic SDLP', but, for the Irish, the SDLP were the possible heroes of the piece—the authentic, constitutional representatives of the northern minority. So far as the Irish were concerned, they recognized the Provisional IRA boycott of the Convention Election as a direct threat to that position. The British, on the other hand, simply took it as further evidence that the Provos did not know the rules of the constitutional game and so had wilfully set themselves outside it. There were particular differences of journalistic style between the Irish and British media, as there were also between the various press and broadcasting outlets in each country, but the main difference between them was one of national ideology, based on the different involvement of the two nation-States in the Northern Ireland conflict. There was also a fundamental similarity between them. Both sets of media operate within similar liberal Western democracies. They share similar assumptions about the sanctity of human life and the nature and scope of legitimate political activity.

Such general assumptions and values make for some comparability between specific national ideologies. The ideologies themselves are not simply the mechanical products of apparatuses within a State but sets of beliefs and descriptions with a life of their own. In the course of this chapter, two aspects of this ideological autonomy have been discussed. First, there is the question of how effective the ideology is in provining a comprehensive and satisfying account of events in the world. Second, the problem of maintaining internal consistency. Relatively few gaps have opened up between ideology and reality in the reporting of Northern Ireland. Those discussed above are capable of secondary explanation in the ways illustrated.

Nevertheless, they are apparent to journalists covering the story and though there is little scope to discuss them in the general stream of news reporting, particularly as carried in the British media, feature writers and analysts often take them up. John Cole, for example, writing in the *Observer* of 25 July 1976 pointed to another gap.

The language used in reporting Ulster sometimes obscures the even uglier reality. 'Sectarian murder' serves to convey the horror of parents being shot down before their children, but it implies an irrationality which is too comforting. Often such shootings are the crude discipline of a society which has broken down. A form of capital punishment has been restored in Northern Ireland. It is administered not by the State, at the end of a trial, but by self-appointed judges and executioners on the basis of tittle-tattle. . . . Privately, British officials acknowledge that many of those individually shot—as distinct from people mowed down by sub-machine guns in pubs—are on Army, or police lists. . . . Apart from the sheer personal horror of this, the security and political implications are frightening. Many young men in the Belfast ghettos have concluded that it is safer for them to be in terrorist groups than not.

This gap between public knowledge and reality is another which might have profound political consequences if allowed to continue.

In this case the test of the ideology is whether it is an effective means to reach agreed political goals. John Cole's article, quoted above, starts with a clear statement of these goals:

If evidence were still needed that London, Dublin and Belfast have a common interest in defeating terrorism, last week's assassination in Dublin (of the British Ambassador) proved it.

It ends in the same vein.

Can the two elected governments find means . . . to convince people of their will to win? Or must malevolent events be left to take command as they are increasingly doing? The second process now looks more difficult to arrest than at any time in seven anguished years.

Part of his argument as to why this should be so has been quoted. The real nature of the violence has been obscured and so people remain unaware of its extent and the control which it gives to the para-military organizations over large sections of the population.

Since Cole's article appeared, others have written in the same vein in various quality papers. A new concept has been coined—'the godfathers of the IRA'—and used in both qualities and populars to describe the leaders who exercise this control over their local territories. It seems likely that at least some of the inspiration for this subsequent interest is coming from the Northern Ireland office or British Army PR. At a 1974 conference of journalists and others interested in the reporting of Northern Ireland's troubles, racketeering and extortion in the Loyalist and Republican areas of working-class Belfast was mentioned as one of the great untold stories. This 'news', therefore, is not particularly new, but for some reason, 'now it can be told'.[1]

At the same time, stories have been appearing suggesting a difference of opinion between the army and the politicians on what tactics should be used to deal with an increase in terrorism by the Provisional IRA. Journalists stand to benefit from such differences as both sides may have an interest in flying kites or making information available to influence public or political opinion in their support.

There is no necessary reason, however, why such questions, starting from a gap between ideology and reality, should have to wait for inspiration from a difference of opinion among the authorities themselves, or why, once started, it should stop at the level of means and not embrace ends as well.

At an earlier stage in Northern Ireland, the other two gaps referred to above provided some grounds for doubting whether the basic definition of the conflict as terrorism was correct. John Whale of the *Sunday Times*, looking back on the early days of the crisis in a BBC Radio 3 Programme, the *Communicators*, mentioned that newspapermen

faced the enormous difficulty that the IRA hardly existed at all. It was, at any rate, dormant in 1969, and the principal combatants on that side now, the Provisional IRA, only really had a concrete active existence by the beginning of 1971. Before that time they were to some extent a phantom; indeed, there is a certain amount of evidence for believing that they were turned from a phantom into a fact by the very preparations which were made against them by the forces of order.

The second point about ideology considered as an entity in its own right is its internal consistency. This largely depends on how the values on which it depends are expressed in relation to the particular case to which they are applied. Both the national ideologies discussed in this study, the British and the Irish, share an abhorence of violence and a belief in the

---

1. Even now only part of it is being told. The example current in 1974 was the way the UDA was able to control the distribution of tickets for the England-Northern Ireland football international, held in Belfast.

sanctity of human life. Generally speaking, this value is functional for the authorities in both countries. State violence is delegated to particular functionaries and only excercised under control in extreme circumstances. One reason why public relations men were able to claim that the Widgery Report exonerated the British army's behaviour in Londonderry was because of the conclusion 'there was no general breakdown in discipline'. Violence by anyone else, is however, by definition, unconstitutional. 'Normal processes' are available to discuss legitimate grievances. British politicians have recognized that many of the issues in Northern Ireland are not readily amenable to solution through the normal processes. One response has been simply to blame the belligerence and intransigence of the people of Ireland or Northern Ireland as, for exemple, when William Whitelaw urged the people of Northern Ireland to 'abandon your prejudices and grievances and look simply to the future'.[1] Another has been to try to take the fundamental constitutional issues out of politics as, for example, with the referendum on the border, so that people can then get on with 'the normal things which we argue about here as between parties and at election times'.[2] The most recent was the Convention. These views were both apparent in the reporting of the election for it, discussed in Chapter 3.

But if opposition to violence is generally a mechanism by which deviants can be defined as outsiders and demands supported by violence rejected as unconstitutional, it also poses problems for the ideology if it has to encompass violence used by those it supports. Two different examples of this were cited in the case of Northern Ireland; the problem in the early stages of coping with unnecessary or illegitimate violence used by the forces of the State and more recent difficulties in dealing with violence carried out by those on whose behalf those forces are acting.

The parallels with Viet Nam and other earlier conflicts are particularly instructive, not because the situations or the participants in the conflict are directly comparable, but that such conflicts pose similar problems at an ideological level. The gaps which develop between ideology and reality, and the problems of maintaining the internal consistency of the account, may lead to conflict between the news media and the authorities of the state. The natural reaction of the authorities is to try to force or persuade journalists to 'get on the team', as the American Government put it over Viet Nam. John Whale (1972, p. 4) has made the comparison, writing of the situation in Northern Ireland in the early 1970s:

The United Kingdom authorities put it busily about that for journalists even to report facts, let alone to offer opinions, which reflected on the official line, was plainly treasonous. . . . There was a marked parallel here with the attitude of the United States authorities in the late sixties to public debate about administration policy in Vietnam. The country was at war: there could be no discussion of whether it ought to be fighting the war until the war was won. And if it was never won? Senior officers brought themselves to believe that a chief reason why it was never won was that journalists were allowed even to raise the doubt.

1. Quoted by D. Morley (1976, p. 253).
2. Edward Heath, *Panorama*, BBC TV, 31 July 1972.

Differences may also develop between the various news media or even individual journalists. These differences tend to be seen in general political terms as a difference between left and right, between liberal, progressive media and rightist or conformist media; between liberal, progressive journalists and reactionary, conformist news organizations. Spiro Agnew's attack on the American news media provides another instructive parallel from the Viet Nam war. There is no denying that such differences have some importance, particularly in producing variations in the coverage of particular incidents or ensuring that some news which might otherwise have been suppressed becomes public knowledge after all.

Nevertheless, there is little scope in modern news organizations for personal bias of individual journalists to manifest itself in the news coverage. This individual impotence was nicely captured by Stark in his study of a conservative American newspaper. The progressive, professional journalists working for the paper could only signal their hostility to the paper's policy line by such ploys as picking photographs which showed policy heroes in a bad light. The paper studied by Stark was relatively unusual, at least at the national level in the Western democracies, in being so clearly partisan. To a large extent commercial considerations have ironed out partisan bias among the national news organizations.

The controversies which developed over reporting in Viet Nam and, to a much lesser extent, in Northern Ireland were prompted by the problems of maintaining the internal consistency of the ideology and its relationship to the realities of the conflict, not by the particular bias of individual journalists or the news organizations within which they worked. The hallmark of a free press is not that it should be able to find room for different versions or accounts in its reporting, though that is probably necessary to its achievement. It is that it should be possible to work out in time the internal inconsistencies that develop in the ideology it produces and the gaps which appear between the ideological account and the reality it is reporting. For the sake of the British and the Irish, above all those in the north, it is to be hoped that the journalists and the news media in both countries will recognize such inconsistencies and discrepancies between their accounts and the situation in Northern Ireland, so that their societies may be spared the convulsions which accompanied American withdrawal from Viet Nam and that of the French from Algeria.[1]

The point of these comparisons, and the main aim of this study, has been to show the importance in the long term of journalists telling the truth. This involves rather more than being accurate about facts and quotations, careful about spellings and attributions, necessary though such virtues are. It involves a reflective, critical analysis of routine practices and their consequences through time.

Many journalists immersed in the problems, not to say dangers, of day-to-day reporting find such a request hard to take. There is always another defence. After all, reporters claim, their job is only to pass on what others do and say. This may be a particularly attractive defence

---

1. Again it must be emphasized that these comparisons are not based on any assumption that the ultimate outcome in Northern Ireland will be similar.

when, as John Whale has put it, the combatants, too busy to think themselves, try and prevent journalists from thinking. But Whale (1972, p. 4) goes on to argue that 'journalists are the only people left on the scene who can do that job. No other voice can make itself heard quickly or loudly enough. The notion that there is any part to be played in the affair by reason must be first put forward in newspapers or on the air if at all'. It may be that in the nature of things it is too much to expect these combatants—politicians, public relations experts and participants in a propaganda war—to have much regard for the truth. The least we should expect, however, is that they do not believe their own lies. The journalist's responsibility is to see that does not happen.

Appendix

Abbreviations used in text

Political Parties

NILP	Northern Ireland Labour Party
SDLP	Social Democratic and Labour Party
UPNI	Unionist Party of Northern Ireland
UUUC	United Ulster Unionist Coalition (including OUP (Official Unionist Party); DUP (Democratic Unionist Party); and VUP (Vanguard Unionist Party)).

Republican organizations

IRA	Irish Republican Army
IRSP	Irish Republican Socialist Party

Loyalist paramilitary organisations

PAF	Protestant Action Force
UDA	Ulster Defence Association
UFF	Ulster Freedom Fighters
UVF	Ulster Volunteer Force

Other

NCCL	National Council for Civil Liberties
NICRA	Northern Ireland Civil Rights Association
SAS	Special Air Service

Algeria

FLN	Front de Libération Nationale
OAS	Organisation de l'Armée Secrète

Bibliography

BARRITT, D. F.; CARTER, C. F. 1972. *The Northern Ireland Problems.* 2nd ed. Oxford, Oxford University Press.

BELL, Martin. 1972a. Views. *The Listener*, 6 January.

———. 1972b. Reporting Ulster. *The Listener*, 5 October.

BLUMLER, J. G.; KATZ, E. (eds.). 1974. *The Uses of Mass Communications.* (Sage Annual Review of Communications Research, Vol. III.)

BUTLER, D.; KAVANAGH, I. 1975. *The British General Election of October 1974.* London, Macmillan.

CATHCART, R. 1976. A Definition of Media Responsibility. Paper read to Peace Week Seminar, Dublin.

COCKBURN, Claud. 1971. *I Claud.* Harmondsworth, Penguin.

COHEN, S.; YOUNG, J. 1973. *The Manufacture of News: Deviance, Social Problems and the Mass Media.* London, Constable.

DE PAOR, L. 1970. *Divided Ulster.* Harmondsworth, Penguin.

DEVLIN, Bernadette. 1969. *The Price of My Soul.* London, Deutsch.

DILLON, M.; LEHANE, D. 1973. *Political Murder in Northern Ireland.* Harmondsworth, Penguin.

ELLIOTT, P.; GOLDING, P. 1973. The News Media and Foreign Affairs. In: R. Boardman and A. J. R. Groom (eds.), *The Management of Britain's External Relations.* London, Macmillan.

FIRTH, Gay. 1971. The Polar Press. *Fortnight*, 14 May.

FISK, R. 1975. *The Point of No Return.* London, Andre Deutsch.

FREE COMMUNICATIONS GROUP. *Open Secret*, No. 8.

GARDINER COMMITTEE. 1975. *Measures to Deal with Terrorism in Northern Ireland.* London, HMSO. (Cmnd. 5847.)

GOLDING, P.; ELLIOTT, P.; HALLORAN, J. D.; WELLS, A. In Press. *Making Television News.*

HACKSON, H. 1971. *The Two Irelands: A Dual Study of Intergroup Tensions.* (Minority Rights Group, Report No. 2.)

HALL, S. 1972a. The Limitations of Broadcasting. *Listener*, 16 March.

———. 1972b. External Influences on Broadcasting. In: F. S. Bradley (ed.), *4th Symposium on Broadcasting Policy.* Manchester, University of Manchester. (Mimeo.)

———. 1975. The Structured Communication of Events. *Getting the Message Across*, Paris, Unesco.

HALLORAN, J. D. (ed.). 1970. *The Effects of Television.* London, Panther.

HARBINSON, J. F. 1974. *The Ulster Unionist Party, 1882–1973* (rev. ed.). Belfast, Blackstaff.

HARRIS, R. 1972. *Prejudice and Tolerance in Ulster: A Study of Neighbours and 'Strangers' in a Border Community.* Manchester, Manchester University Press.

HARRISON, M. 1975. On the Air. In: D. Butler and I. Kavanagh (eds.), *The British General Election of October 1974.* London, Macmillan.

HARTMANN, P. 1975–76. Industrial Relations in the News Media. *Industrial Relations Journal*, Vol. 6, No. 4.

HARTMANN P.; HUSBAND, C.; CLARKE, J. 1974. *Race as News*. Paris, Unesco.

HOGGART, Simon. 1973. The Army PR Men of Northern Ireland. *New Society*, 11 October, p. 79–80.

JOHNSON, P. 1975. The Resources of Civilisation. *New Statesman*, 31 October.

KITSON, F. 1971. *Low Intensity Operations*. London, Faber & Faber.

KNIGHTLEY, Phillip. 1975. *The First Casualty*. London, Deutsch.

LIJPHART, A. 1975. The Northern Ireland Problem: Cases, Theories and Solutions. *British Journal of Political Science*, Vol. 5.

McCANN, Eamonn. 1971. *The British Press and Northern Ireland*. Northern Ireland Socialist Research Centre.

MILLIBAND, R. 1972. The Political System and the State. In: R. Blackburn (ed.), *Ideology in Social Science*. Fontana.

MILNE, E. 1976. *No Shining Armour*. London, John Calder.

MORLEY, D. 1976. Industrial Conflict & the Mass Media. *Sociological Review*, Vol. 24, May, p. 245–68.

NELSON, Sarah. 1976. Protestant 'Ideology' Considered: The Case of Discrimination. In: I. Crewe (ed.), *The Politics of Race. British Political Sociology Yearbook*. Vol. 2. Croom Helm.

RED PATRIOT EDITORIAL STAFF. 1974. An Analysis of the Significance of the Ulster Workers' Strike. 14–30 May. Communist Party of Ireland (Marxist-Leninist), Dublin.

ROSE, R. 1971. *Governing without Consensus*, London, Faber.

SCHUTZ, B.; SCOTT, D. 1976. Patterns of Political Change in Fragment Regimes: Northern Ireland and Rhodesia. In: I. Crewe (ed.), *The Politics of Race. British Political Sociology Year Book*. Vol. 2. London, Croom Helm.

SEYMOUR-URE, C. 1975. Fleet Street. In: D. Butler and I. Kavanagh (eds.), *The British General Election of October 1974*. London, Macmillan.

SMITH, A. 1972. Television Coverage of Northern Ireland. *Index*. Summer.

STARK, R. Policy and the Pros: An Organizational Analysis of a Metropolitan Newspaper. *Berkeley Journal of Sociology*, Vol. 7.

STEPHEN, A. 1976. A Reporter's Life in Belfast. *The Observer*, 29 February.

THE SUNDAY TIMES INSIGHT TEAM. 1972. *Ulster*. Harmondsworth, Penguin.

WHALE, J. 1972. *Journalism and Government*. London, Macmillan.

WINCHESTER, Simon. 1975. *In Holy Terror*. London, Faber.

WINDLESHAM, D. 1975. *Politics in Practice*. London, Cape.